◯ SIGNET (0451)

FOR THE SPORTS FAN . . .

- ☐ **THE COMPLETE HANDBOOK OF PRO BASKETBALL: 1990 EDITION edited by Zander Hollander.** The most comprehensive handbook available from opening tap to championship buzzer, it's like having 27 team yearbooks in one, plus a complete TV viewer's guide. Bird, Jordan, Magic, Wilkins, Stockton, Dumars, they're all here—with 300 profiles, 300 photos, schedules, rosters, scouting reports and career records. (162838—$5.95)

- ☐ **THE COMPLETE HANDBOOK OF BASEBALL: 1990 EDITION edited by Zander Hollander.** The essential book for every baseball fan. Twenty-six team yearbooks in one, with nearly 300 player and manager profiles, year-by-year stats, all time records and award winners, and hundreds of photos. (164490—$5.95)

- ☐ **EVERYTHING YOU ALWAYS WANTED TO KNOW ABOUT SPORTS and Didn't Know Where to Ask by Mickey Herskowitz and Steve Perkins.** Here is the book that answers every question a sports fan ever had in the back of his mind and tells the truth about all the whispered rumors of the sports world. (124715—$2.75)

- ☐ **GREAT BASEBALL FEATS, FACTS & FIRSTS by David Nemec.** Thousands of scores, stats and stories in one amazingly complete volume! Discover the unconventional records, the offbeat feats, the historic scores and the one-of-a-kind characters that keep baseball flying—in this comprehensive up-to-the-minute encyclopedia. (161246—$4.95)

- ☐ **TENNIS, ANYONE? by Dick Gould, famed tennis coach.** Superb instructional photographs and diagrams of strokes and strategy ... "A magnificent job ... this book is a must!"—Pancho Segura, all-time great player and coach to Jimmy Connors (159284—$4.95)

- ☐ **THE GOLFER'S STROKE SAVING HANDBOOK by Craig Shankland, Dale Shankland, Dom Lupo and Roy Benjamin.** For the amateur and the weekend golfer, the closest thing to a series of playing lessons from a pro. How to hit the best possible shot in any kind of situation, plus vital tips for all the strokes with advice relating to both technique and terrain. All tested and proven. (155378—$4.50)

Prices slightly higher in Canada

Buy them at your local bookstore or use this convenient coupon for ordering.

NEW AMERICAN LIBRARY
P.O. Box 999, Bergenfield, New Jersey 07621

Please send me the books I have checked above. I am enclosing $_____
(please add $1.00 to this order to cover postage and handling). Send check or money order—no cash or C.O.D.'s. Prices and numbers are subject to change without notice.

Name_____

Address_____

City _____ State _____ Zip Code _____

Allow 4-6 weeks for delivery.
This offer, prices and numbers are subject to change without notice.

1990
16th EDITION
THE COMPLETE HANDBOOK OF
PRO FOOTBALL

EDITED BY ZANDER HOLLANDER

AN ASSOCIATED FEATURES BOOK

A SIGNET BOOK

ACKNOWLEDGMENTS

We thank all who helped make possible the 16th edition of *The Complete Handbook of Pro Football*: contributing editor Eric Compton, the writers and Rich Rossiter, Kevin Mulroy, Linda Spain, Dot Gordineer, Westchester Book Composition/Rainsford Type, Elias Sports Bureau, Pete Abitante, Dick Maxwell, Joe Browne, Jim Heffernan, Leslie Hammond, Vin Marino and the NFL team publicists.

Zander Hollander

PHOTO CREDITS: Cover—Mitch Reibel; back cover—Jon Kirn. Inside photos—Malcolm Emmons, George Gojkovich, Ira Golden, Pete Groh, Vic Milton, Mitch Reibel, UPI, Wide World, Capitol Cities/ABC, NFL and college team photographers. Cartoon on page 6 by Ed Murawinski.

SIGNET
Published by the Penguin Group
Penguin Books USA Inc., 375 Hudson Street, New York,
New York 10014, U.S.A.
Penguin Books Ltd, 27 Wrights Lane, London W8 5TZ, England
Penguin Books Australia Ltd, Ringwood, Victoria, Australia
Penguin Books Canada Ltd, 2801 John Street, Markham, Ontario,
Canada L3R 1B4
Penguin Books (N.Z.) Ltd, 182-190 Wairau Road, Auckland 10,
New Zealand

Penguin Books Ltd, Registered Offices:
Harmondsworth, Middlesex, England

First Published by Signet, an imprint of New American Library,
a division of Penguin Books USA Inc.

First Signet Printing, August, 1990
10 9 8 7 6 5 4 3 2 1

Copyright © Associated Features, Inc., 1990
All rights reserved

 REGISTERED TRADEMARK—MARCA REGISTRADA

Printed in the United States of America

Without limiting the rights under copyright reserved above, no part of this publication may be reproduced, stored in or introduced into a retrieval system, or transmitted, in any form, or by any means (electronic, mechanical, photocopying, recording, or otherwise), without the prior written permission of both the copyright owner and the above publisher of this book.

CONTENTS

Super Showdown!
  1989 Niners vs. 1979 Steelers ....By Joe Gergen 6

Jim Everett:
  Quarterback of the '90s .... By Chris Dufresne 20

The Miracles & Mastery
  of Al Michaels .... By John Freeman 28

The Quiet Roar
  of the Lions' Barry Sanders .... By Mitch Albom 36

Inside the NFC .... By Jon Gelberg 44

  Atlanta Falcons.............46   New Orleans Saints 112
  Chicago Bears 56   New York Giants 121
  Dallas Cowboys 65   Philadelphia Eagles........130
  Detroit Lions...............75   Phoenix Cardinals..........139
  Green Bay Packers...........84   San Francisco 49ers........148
  Los Angeles Rams............93   Tampa Bay Buccaneers 158
  Minnesota Vikings 103   Washington Redskins........167

Inside the AFC .... By Brian White 176

  Buffalo Bills 178   Los Angeles Raiders 241
  Cincinnati Bengals 187   Miami Dolphins 250
  Cleveland Browns 196   New England Patriots.......260
  Denver Broncos 205   New York Jets 269
  Houston Oilers 214   Pittsburgh Steelers........278
  Indianapolis Colts.........223   San Diego Chargers 287
  Kansas City Chiefs 232   Seattle Seahawks 296

NFL Statistics 304
NFL Standings: 1921-1989 324
NFL Draft 346
NFL Schedule 362
NFL TV Schedule 366

Editor's Note: The material herein includes trades and rosters up to the final printing deadline.

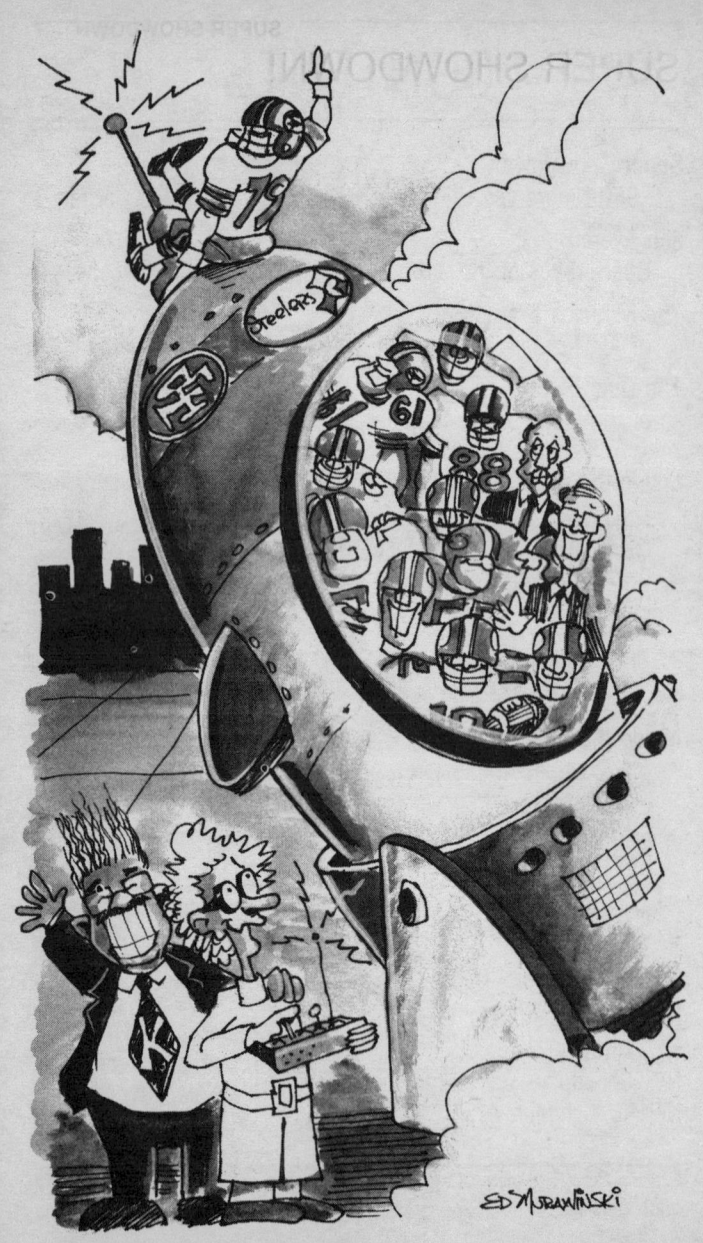

SUPER SHOWDOWN!

1989 NINERS
VS.
1979 STEELERS

By JOE GERGEN

They were a strange sight, a team of professional football players, in full pads and uniforms, standing in the parking lot of an otherwise deserted shopping mall in the wee small hours of the morning. Then again, this was no ordinary trip on which they were about to embark. It was a journey into the past.

Having dominated their era in the National Football League, the San Francisco 49ers were prepared to travel back to the future in search of meaningful competition. Edward DeBartolo Jr., the owner and president who had spared no expense in building the organization into the foremost football franchise of the 1980s, was putting some of his considerable fortune on the line to prove beyond doubt the 49ers were the best team ever. He was going to challenge the Pittsburgh Steelers of the 1970s in their time and place.

It was a brilliant idea whose execution was greatly enhanced by the fact that the very shopping center where Dr. Emmett Brown had carried out his experiments in time travel for the motion picture was owned by the DeBartolo Company. That should have come as no great surprise since the company built by Edward DeBartolo Sr. was the nation's largest developer and manager of shopping malls. Still, there remained the matter of financing a vehicle large enough to transport an entire team, coaching staff, support crew

---

Joe Gergen, columnist for Newsday *and* The Sporting News, *pilots his own dream machine in his account of* The Game for All Ages.

Joe Montana wants to settle it once and for all.

and a large media contingent into the previous decade. One DeLorean simply wouldn't do.

Part of the cost for the project was underwritten by a consortium of promoters, which included the unlikely trio of Don King, Bob Arum and Donald Trump. They, in turn, expected to offset the $50 million site fee with revenue from a pay-per-view arrangement that had been authorized by first-year NFL commissioner Paul Tagliabue specifically for what was being billed as The Game for the Ages. It was an unusual situation, to say the least.

To the fans attending the contest in 1980, of course, this would be nothing more than an exhibition game for the Steelers, who had just annexed their fourth Super Bowl championship in a span of six seasons. They would have no knowledge that the 49ers were about to raise comparison with the Steelers by winning four NFL titles in the following 10-year period. But the vast television audience watching the game in arenas, bars and their own living rooms via the technology of 1990 would be aware that this was the most momentous confrontation in league history. And, yes,

SUPER SHOWDOWN 9

Mean Joe Greene can't wait to stuff Montana.

the use of instant replay was approved by both sides, with an explanation to the crowd that this was a one-game experiment.

"Only in America," King thundered, his voice ricocheting off the walls of the empty stores at the Twin Pines Mall, at 1:15 in the morning as the principals waited for the takeoff. The parking lot was bright as the sun, thanks to the presence of artificial lighting needed for the live television broadcast. King and Arum were separated by Tagliabue and former commissioner Pete Rozelle while Trump stood alone. He was traveling in a separate vehicle, which he was calling a Trumpmobile, built to his specifications by Brown. Unlike the others, the man had his own plutonium source.

Within minutes, the two machines were wheeled into the parking lot. The Trump version appeared to be a souped-up Rolls Royce, complete with uniformed chauffeur. The inventor himself was at the helm of the primary vehicle, which looked like a cross between a mammoth bus and a battleship. "Climb aboard," the scientist with the manic white hair called out as he lowered two gangplanks to the ground with the flick of a switch.

The seating was relatively tight inside but then the trip would take no more than a split second once the machine reached the speed of 88 miles per hour. "Just imagine," Ronnie Lott said, "here they've been tearing down the Berlin Wall and we're going to find the Steel Curtain."

"Hey, Joe," Jerry Rice called out to his quarterback, "how does it feel to be playing against your idols?" Montana had grown up in Monongahela, Pa., in the Beaver Valley northwest of Pittsburgh where so many outstanding quarterbacks had been raised. He was still in high school when the Steelers won their first NFL championship. In his first pro season, 1979, Pittsburgh concluded the decade with its fourth title.

Montana reached into his equipment bag and fished out a tattered piece of cloth. He tossed it toward Rice, who plucked it out of the air one-handed, as if it were a football. "What's this?" the all-pro receiver asked. "Your dirty laundry?"

"That," Montana said, "is a genuine 'Terrible Towel.' You can expect to see a lot of these. The Steelers' fans used to wave them before every game."

"I remember that from television," Rice said. "Do you think we'll see that guy in the gorilla suit, too?"

Matt Millen pounded the back of the seat in front of him, jarring the Walkman from the ears of fellow linebacker Charles Haley. "No such luck," said Millen, a Pennsylvania native.

"[Roy] Gerela lost his job in '79. And I wanted to take a shot at that guy in the suit, too."

The conversation was interrupted by a voice over the intercom system. "This is your captain speaking," Dr. Brown said. "Please fasten your seat belts and no smoking. Sorry we won't have time to serve you any meals. Our estimated time of arrival is 10 A.M., Aug. 31, 1980. We'll be there in a blink."

One minute, the 49ers were peering into the darkness outside Hill Valley. In the next breath, they were staring at the outlines of Ohio Stadium in Columbus. They had zoomed directly into the mostly-empty parking lot of the celebrated college stadium whose regular clientele was still getting used to life without Woody Hayes. The legendary coach had been victimized by his own temper at the conclusion of the 1978 season, attacking a Clemson linebacker along the sidelines following an interception.

Ohio Stadium was an ideal choice for the game for reasons that included a seating capacity in excess of 80,000. It also was located within driving distance of Pittsburgh and the headquarters of the DeBartolo Corporation in Youngstown, Ohio. It also wasn't

SUPER SHOWDOWN 11

Starting lineups for The Game of All Ages:

1979 STEELERS **1989 49ERS**

OFFENSE

82 John Stallworth	WR	82 John Taylor
55 John Kolb	LT	77 Bubba Paris
57 Sam Davis	LG	62 Guy McIntyre
52 Mike Webster	C	61 Jesse Sapolu
72 Gerry Mullins	RG	69 Bruce Collie
79 Larry Brown	RT	79 Harris Barton
89 Bennie Cunningham	TE	84 Brent Jones
88 Lynn Swann	WR	80 Jerry Rice
12 Terry Bradshaw	QB	16 Joe Montana
32 Franco Harris	RB	33 Roger Craig
20 Rocky Bleier	RB	44 Tom Rathman

DEFENSE

68 L.C. Greenwood	LB	78 Pierce Holt
75 Joe Greene	LT-NT	95 Michael Carter
67 Gary Dunn	RT-RILB	99 Mike Walter
76 John Banaszak	RE	75 Kevin Fagan
53 Dennis Winston	LOLB	94 Charles Haley
58 Jack Lambert	MLB-LILB	54 Matt Millen
56 Robin Cole	ROLB	58 Keena Turner
29 Ron Johnson	LCB	26 Darryl Pollard
47 Mel Blount	RCB	29 Don Griffin
31 Donnie Shell	SS	31 Chet Brooks
24 J.T. Thomas	FS	42 Ronnie Lott

Terry Bradshaw has proved he can spell victory.

SUPER SHOWDOWN 13

far from King's farm in the northern part of the state.

King, of course, had an ulterior motive. "So this is where Buster Douglas wanted to stage his defense," he said, emerging into 1980. "How long before the start of the game?" he asked DeBartolo.

"About three hours," the Niners' owner replied.

"I think," King said, "I'll go look up Douglas and see what kind of prospect the young man was. Maybe I'll even sign him to a long-term contract."

The sight of King striding away set off alarms with Arum. "I'll bet I know where he's going," the rival promoter said to Tagliabue. "It would be just like King to fix a fight 10 years before it was held." Before the commissioner could say anything, Arum began racing toward the street, yelling "Taxi."

While the Niners filed into their dressing room for the long wait, the cameramen fanned out around the stadium and the broadcasting crew adjourned to the press box. Among the analysts was Bill Walsh, who had created the 49er dynasty but retired from coaching the previous year. Walsh had wanted to coach in this game but it was decided, in all fairness, that the last of the four San Francisco champions would meet the last of the four Pittsburgh champions, with no alterations in their casts. So George Seifert, the brilliant defensive strategist who did such a remarkable job after replacing Walsh on the sidelines, would be matched against Chuck Noll.

It was a treat for the Niners' executives to visit before the game with Art Rooney, the patriarch of the Steelers and the entire NFL. Up in the press box, everyone gathered around the old man to say hello. "I like that young quarterback from Notre Dame," Rooney told John McVay. "Is he going to start today?"

"I think it's safe to say that Montana will be starting for this team for a long time to come," replied McVay with a conviction reinforced by a knowledge of the future.

Finally, it was time. The captains assembled in the middle of the field for the coin toss, surrounding Rozelle, the former commissioner whose long reign spanned both dynasties. Jack Lambert called heads and heads it was. The Steelers, wearing black jerseys, chose to receive and Larry Anderson returned Paul Cofer's kick to the Pittsburgh 27. Terry Bradshaw led the Steelers' offense onto the field.

As recently as 19 months earlier, Bradshaw had been the object of ridicule despite two championship rings to his credit. He was a prematurely balding veteran with a downtown arm and a down-home philosophy that sometimes resulted in the misconception he

14 THE COMPLETE HANDBOOK OF PRO FOOTBALL

was the Ozark Ike of football. In the week before Super Bowl XIII against the Cowboys, Dallas linebacker Thomas Henderson again raised the issue in colorful fashion.

Henderson, who answered to the nickname of Hollywood and liked to hear himself speak, claimed that Bradshaw couldn't spell cat "if you spotted him the 'c' and the 'a.' " The quarterback laughed it off at the time but he was not amused. And he took out his annoyance on the Cowboys, riddling them for 318 yards and four touchdowns in a 35-31 victory that wasn't as close as the score indicated.

For his efforts, he was acclaimed as the game's Most Valuable Player. A year later, after rallying the Steelers from a fourth-quarter deficit to a 31-19 triumph over the Los Angeles Rams in Super Bowl XIV, he was similarly honored again. He shared the record of being named MVP twice with Bart Starr of the Green Bay Packers until Montana won a third Super Bowl MVP trophy a decade later in the rout of the Broncos.

Bradshaw was not ignored at Super Bowl XXIV, either, even though he had retired many years earlier. He was on hand, as an analyst for CBS and to participate in the coin-toss ceremony, and he used the occasion to speak his mind on the subject of Denver quarterback John Elway, whom he disparaged, and the Broncos, to whom he gave two chances: slim and none. "This sucker could be as bad as 55-3," he said. "Believe me!"

Those who did were well-advised. As it developed, the Niners were credited with a 55-10 conquest, and the Broncos' only touchdown followed a questionable pass-interference penalty. Additionally, Elway had a dreadful evening, throwing two interceptions and gaining a measly 108 yards through the air.

The television viewers in 1990 were mindful of all that business as Bradshaw approached the line of scrimmage. In the course of their dynasty, the Steelers had evolved from a team founded on a strong ground game to one increasingly reliant on the quarterback and his dazzling wide receivers, Lynn Swann and John Stallworth. And Bradshaw wanted to make certain the Niners were conscious of the pair's potential. On first down, he threw down the middle for Stallworth, running a hook-and-go from slot formation. The pass was slightly overthrown but the message had been delivered.

A pitch to Franco Harris resulted in a seven-yard gain on second down and Rocky Bleier ran for the game's initial first down on a classic trap play. But the Steelers stalled at midfield and punted. San Francisco began its first possession from its own 22. Montana's first play also was a familiar one, the quick slant to John Taylor on the left side. Only an ankle tackle by safety Donnie

Shell prevented the man from splitting the defense, as he would do so often in 1989.

Fullback Tom Rathman banged for three yards and the Niners were on the move. Rathman caught a swing pass for another first down and Roger Craig high-stepped for 12 yards to push into Pittsburgh territory. The Iron Curtain finally stiffened when, on third-and-five from the Steelers' 30, the big Pittsburgh cornerbacks bumped the San Francisco receivers out of their patterns and Montana had to wait longer than he intended for them to break free. That gave Mean Joe Greene time to wrap his huge arms around the quarterback for a 10-yard sack. The Niners had to punt.

Starting from their own 20, the Steelers marched smartly to midfield, the key play a 16-yard strike to Swann. On second-and-three, Bradshaw faked Bleier into the line and dropped back. Eluding a big rush from Charles Haley and Kevin Fagan, he hit Stallworth on the fingertips and the receiver pranced into the end zone for the game's first score.

That didn't faze the Niners but the next sequence did. After advancing across the 50, Montana was chased around his own backfield by Greene and L.C. Greenwood as he looked for Rathman. He threw off-balance down the middle, only to have the ball tipped into the air and recovered by Jack Lambert. It took four Niners to subdue the fierce middle linebacker.

Montana, who hadn't thrown a single interception in four Super Bowls, was disgusted with himself when he came off the field. "Don't worry, Joe," Seifert said. "That man's a Hall of Famer."

"Hell," the quarterback said, "they're all Hall of Famers. But it shouldn't have happened. We've got to do a better job of neutralizing Greene."

Bradshaw, meanwhile, was taking advantage of the turnover. He passed to Harris for 12 yards, tight end Bennie Cunningham for 11 and, after a first down on the ground, he threw high for Swann. The acrobatic receiver made a remarkable tumbling catch at the goal line and landed in the end zone: Pittsburgh 14, San Francisco 0.

This time, the Niners would not be kept off the scoreboard. They drove 55 yards in all, but had to settle for a Mike Cofer field goal when Lambert met Rathman helmet to helmet at the line of scrimmage on third-and-two, both men wobbling off the field. And that's the way the first half ended, with the Steelers holding a 14-3 lead.

While offensive coordinator Mike Holmgren tinkered with the Niners' high-tech offense, the Ohio State marching band prepped for its Big Ten season with an early rendition of its famous "Script

16 THE COMPLETE HANDBOOK OF PRO FOOTBALL

Lynn Swann breaks the ice on a pass from Bradshaw.

SUPER SHOWDOWN 17

Ohio." The band director rejected the suggestion of King, who had brought along 17-year-old Douglas as his guest. King wanted the youngster, whom he identified as the future heavyweight champion of the world, to dot the "i" but the man was skeptical. Besides, Trump already had paid for the privilege.

San Francisco received the second-half kickoff and disaster struck immediately. Terrence Flagler was turned upside down on the return and fumbled. The Steelers couldn't manage a first down but Matt Bahr's field goal pushed the lead back to two touchdowns, at 17-3. "Just give me some time," Montana asked his offensive linemen.

The big guys up front, underrated throughout the team's decade at the top, began controlling the line of scrimmage. Rathman continued to punch holes up the middle when he wasn't swinging out of the backfield for passes. When Montana thought he had set up the Steelers, he threw the quick slant for Jerry Rice, who snatched the ball out of the air and displayed surprising quickness in beating the safeties to the middle of the field. The play covered 55 yards and San Francisco was back in the game.

But Bradshaw wasn't finished, either. He and Swann hooked up on two hitch patterns and a strike to Stallworth positioned the Steelers for another Bahr field goal. The 10-point margin loomed large as the third quarter ended.

Taylor caught two passes on the next drive and Craig galloped for a 12-yard gain. Then Rathman plowed over Lambert for another first down. With no room for error, Montana feathered a pass for Rice in the right corner of the end zone and the receiver caught the ball while falling on his back. Cofer's extra point sliced the Pittsburgh lead to 20-17.

The Steelers ground out two first downs but, on third-and-six, Bradshaw was confused by the San Francisco defense and threw into the arms of linebacker Mike Walter. San Francisco had the ball near midfield but Lambert's brilliant play stopped the Niners cold. They had to punt, hoping their defense could give them one more chance.

Pittsburgh advanced the ball only 15 yards before punting. As the result of a clipping penalty, San Francisco started at its own 13. There were two minutes left, a familiar position for Montana, who completed his first four passes of the drive before using the second of his three timeouts. The Niners were in Pittsburgh territory when the quarterback handed off twice, to Rathman and Craig, for a total of 14 yards. Montana killed the clock at 0:34, by firing a pass into the ground.

On the sidelines, Seifert suggested two safe plays. The Niners

18 THE COMPLETE HANDBOOK OF PRO FOOTBALL

Jerry Rice celebrates another Niner crowning.

needed one first down to make the field-goal attempt virtually automatic. Montana nodded and went back to the huddle. "I'll make the call at the line when I see the defense," he told his teammates.

Craig swept tight on first down and squirmed out of bounds after a gain of three. But a swing pass to Rathman on second down was well-covered and Montana deliberately threw it well over Rathman's head and beyond the sidelines. Twenty seconds remained, time for one last play before the Niners went for the tie.

As he had in the famous play that capped the first great drive of the team's championship era, the pass to Dwight Clark that beat the Cowboys in 1981, Montana rolled right to buy some time. Rice ran a post pattern, then cut right and slid along the back of the end zone, facing Montana. The quarterback released the pass just before Greene landed atop him. He didn't even see Rice's hands rise above those of two defenders and grasp the ball out of the air.

The Catch II lifted San Francisco to a stunning 24-20 triumph. The future had triumphed over the past, barely. "I wouldn't want to face those guys every year," decided Bubba Paris.

As the Niners departed on their mysterious vehicle after dark, Montana said aloud, "Goodbye, Columbus." And DeBartolo had a message for his team as they zoomed back to 1990 to face another challenge from the present.

"If you guys win another Super Bowl this year," the owner said, "we're going to challenge the Packers."

"You really think they'll win the Central Division?" cornerback Tim McKyer said.

"Not these Packers," DeBartolo corrected. "Lombardi's Packers. I think it's time Joe got to meet Bart Starr."

20 THE COMPLETE HANDBOOK OF PRO FOOTBALL

For Jim Everett, the only unconquered mountain is Montana.

JIM EVERETT: QUARTERBACK OF THE '90s

By CHRIS DUFRESNE

The quarterback of the Los Angeles Rams, maybe the city's best ever after just four seasons, has failed as of this writing to audition for any movie parts that might involve, say, kissing Kim Basinger on the lips; or introducing his own line of men's cologne. So what's wrong with the sap? Everything, if you were expecting someone wrapped in Hollywood and Vines. This quarterback drives a Jeep, not a Mercedes, and still doesn't get recognized as often as he should in the check-out stands at Yorba Linda, Cal.

Jim Everett set five team passing records in 1989 for the Rams, led the NFL in touchdown passes for the second consecutive season, took his team to the NFC's conference title game; yet still prefers to do his own laundry. He's 27, single, and very rich, but not as very rich as he might have been.

In a sporting age where franchise loyalties are more often set aside for self-interests and personal greed, Everett stands alone in the pocket. On Jan. 22, nine days before he would have become a free agent, Everett re-signed with the Rams for $14 million over six years.

A free enterprise system clutched its heart.

Everett set the American business ethic back 50 years. You say $14 million's not bad; that he'll never eat TV dinners again.

Okay, but what if he could have held out for a TV station?

Everett, willfully and of his own volition, committed two ne-

---

Chris Dufresne has covered the Rams for the Los Angeles Times *since 1986, the year Jim Everett arrived. Coincidentally, Dufresne also recently signed a six-year, $14-million deal to remain with his newspaper, declining the chance to become a free agent on Feb. 1.*

gotiating acts of hari-kari: he signed for too many years and not enough money. In fact, as Everett was crossing the Ts on his contract, which works out to about $2.3 million per season, the 49ers were already talking to Joe Montana about a contract extention worth $3 million per season.

So, let's see, if Everett's contract was outdated before the ink dried, what's it going to be worth in two years? Six years? Everett had the best of both worlds and ended up on another planet. He could have commanded at least $3 million per season from the highest bidder on the open market, forcing the Rams to match a team's best offer to keep him in Orange County, which the Rams would have done or risked having their offices pelted with cheese and wine trays.

Everett had a franchise on its knees—the stuff of a superstar's wildest dreams—and let it off the hook for no other reason than he didn't feel right taking advantage of a situation.

Don't think for a second that Everett was duped by management. He was represented by superagent Marvin Demoff and advised by his parents, both educators. Everett was an honor student in college, too, so this wasn't a case of someone carving an "X" onto his contract with a penknife.

Turns out Everett only pleads guilty to having a conscience.

"I like being a Ram," Everett explains, "I didn't want to go anywhere else. I wanted to play for the L.A. Rams, for one of the best coaches [John Robinson], for one of the best offensive coordinators [Ernie Zampese], on a team with the best young talent. There was no need [to shop around]. I didn't think a couple extra dollars here and there were important. The Rams made a commitment to me when they took me from Houston. I'm still in debt to them." Still in debt to them? No, this isn't any ordinary Jim.

And what about other quarterbacks and their tax brackets? "What those guys make in their places is perfectly fine," he says. "The question is: Is Jim Everett happy? And I can honestly say yes. I can't say that I would never be a free agent. But other things are much more valuable."

For instance: playing in Orange County vs. Houston. Everett was the Oilers' first-round pick in 1986 after his career at Purdue, the same university, by the way, that suggested to Everett as a freshman that his career might be at tight end, not quarterback. Good thing Everett wasn't listening.

With Warren Moon entrenched in Houston, Everett told the Oilers not to bother with their draft pick. They did nevertheless, forcing Everett to make it clear he wouldn't be reporting. Houston,

Everett dons a bobby's hat before London exhibition game.

in turn, shipped Everett to the Rams in September 1986, for two-first round picks, a fifth-rounder, All-Pro guard Kent Hill and defensive end William Fuller. Everett was a starter by midseason, one reason to be forever indebted. At last look, Moon was still slinging it pretty well in the Astrodome.

Also, Everett had no interest in being trapped in a provincial football market and becoming another one of football's Boys in the Bubble, such as John Elway in Denver.

For continuity purposes only, the Rams left "Los Angeles" on their letterhead when they bolted to Anaheim a decade ago. But make no mistake, they're a team of the suburbs now, complete with their own fan base and texture.

How to explain? Orange County is well, Orange County: sunshine, trees, beaches, shopping malls, attitudes, Nazi surf punks, oil spills, track homes—everything but oranges. A place where a quarterback can still stretch his legs a bit and not worry about ending up on the evening news. And while football is marginally important there, it takes a back seat to the daily events of a sprawling metropolis.

24 THE COMPLETE HANDBOOK OF PRO FOOTBALL

So when someone suggests to Everett that he might have profitted more by playing elsewhere, he wants to know at what cost? He has visions of Elway fending off the hordes in Denver, where the media tracks a quarterback's every move, even stooping to the depths of sorting out the Elways' Halloween candy and then reporting dutifully to an awaiting public.

Everett doesn't need to be *that* famous. "I've never been that way about stardom," he said. "I always had my favorites as a kid, but it wasn't the fact they were stars. It was the fact they were good, and they were good people."

So while Elway suffocates in the shade of the Rockies, Everett suns himself at Newport Beach whenever he pleases—(Look, ma, no police escorts!). Rarely is he bothered to the point of harassment. With his Jeep top down, and his face open to the wind, Everett can go some days without being recognized in Orange County, although he admits anonymity isn't what it used to be.

"The attention is on the rise," he said, "which I think is normal. But other than that, my day-to-day life is taken in stride, like anyone else's. There are no restrictions, and that's the one thing I like about Orange County. People are laid back. I'm not that big of deal."

Last offseason, Everett and some friends made their way to a local theme restaurant where customers dress in medieval costumes and gnaw on leg of oxen while watching simulated jousting contests. Aren't there places like this everywhere?

"I put on a damn crown and rooted for the blue section [of jouster rooters] and no one even came up to me for an autograph," Everett remembers.

Everett isn't too good to be true; it only seems that way. He can be raunchy around the boys and isn't afraid of a six-pack or a few four-letter words; yet he protects his public image like a mother hen. Basically, though, Everett is what he is: a star quarterback, somewhat calculated and goal-oriented, with a strong family foundation on which to rely; a young man who also happens to be having the time of his life.

Everett recently purchased a ranch home in Orange Park, a rural suburb of what used to be a rural suburb, Anaheim. He spent the offseason remodeling the place to his tastes. When reached for this story, he was teaching his golden retriever, Gunner, to, well, retrieve. Everett has a basketball hoop nailed up in his front driveway.

Refreshingly, Everett's only vice is golf (not drugs), although a back injury suffered late in the season kept him off the links until March, a fate almost worse than death. He reluctantly declined celebrity/player invitations to the Bob Hope Desert Classic and Los Angeles Open. Everett has his own annual charity tournament, held in April at the PGA West course in La Quinta, Cal. Everett says he's about a 12-handicapper and his fondest golfing memory remains shooting par at the New Mexico state championships when he was a senior at Albuquerque's Eldorado High School.

Ever the competitor, Everett admits he's not as good a golfer as Miami quarterback Dan Marino, who also hosts his own tournament. "He would have to give me a stroke on each side," Everett claims.

Everett is about as Albuquerque as a fella can get, really. His best friends remain old high school buddies. He prefers boots over topsiders; jeans over slacks. His loyalties are strongest in family: his sister Jackie, a year older than Jim, and his parents, Bonnie and James Sr.

Everett leads his public life like someone out to please his parents. If Everett seems driven and competitive, it was a spark nurtured from his goal-oriented, no-nonsense upbringing. The Everetts moved from Kansas to New Mexico in 1970. Jim's dad is a professor of special education at the University of New Mexico. His mother teaches special education in the local school district.

Everett says he dared not ever come home with a bad report card. He had his career goals mapped out at an early age. The Everetts used to analyze problems at scheduled family meetings.

Since becoming a Ram in 1986, in fact, Everett's path has been slowed only by one perennial nemesis, San Francisco quarterback Joe Montana, who has successfully squashed all Ram dreams—the past two seasons, in particular.

As long as Montana remains in the game, it seems Everett will never rise to his rightful level. For instance, did you know that no NFL quarterback the past two seasons has thrown for more yardage and touchdown passes than Jim Everett? Because of Montana, probably not. Everett's averaged 4,137 yards passing and 30 touchdowns per season in that span. Yet, it's Montana's 49ers who keep winning championships and denying Rams at every turn.

In 1989, Everett finished second in the NFC with a glowing 90.6% efficiency rating. Not as glowing when compared to Montana, who finished first with the highest rating of all time, 112.4.

The Rams have finished second to the 49ers the last two seasons in the NFC West. The 49ers have won 24 of their last 27 games. Two of the losses have come to the Rams. In fact, the Rams could have swept this year's regular-season series had they managed to hold a 17-point fourth-quarter lead at Anaheim Stadium on

Dec. 11.

Everett, dogged for not possessing Montana's magical comeback abilities before 1989, spurned his critics last season by leading the Rams to a 6-3 record in games decided in the last two minutes. Seven games were decided in the last 16 seconds or less, five as time expired.

In an 20-17 overtime win over the New Orleans Saints on Nov. 26 at the Superdome, Everett threw for a career-high 454 yards, 336 of those going to Flipper Anderson, who set the league's single-game record with his performance.

But whatever strides the Rams have made, the lasting images will be of last January's dismal 30-3 loss to the 49ers at Candlestick in the NFC title game. Turns out, the Rams played the 49ers tougher than either Minnesota in the first round or Denver in the Super Bowl, but it was of little consolation to the one team convinced it should have ended the 49ers' domination.

Everett, in turn, suffered through his worst day as a professional—before a national audience and intense scrutiny, no less—completing just 16 of 36 passes for 141 yards and three interceptions. In the second half, touched by no defender, Everett sacked himself in an embarrassing moment that pretty much summed up his day.

"It was a devastating loss for us," Everett reflected. "I thought we were a lot better than we were on that Sunday. We've got to live with that all year. We got beat by a great football team. It shows us where we need to go. They're right there in our own backyard."

There's nothing wrong with the picture of Everett's life that couldn't be remedied with a Montana retirement party. Some players might request counselling knowing that perhaps the greatest quarterback ever looms not only in your division, but also in your own state. Soon after his fourth Super Bowl win, Montana zoomed into Los Angeles for the day to announce a multimillion dollar endorsement deal with L.A. Gear, a sports apparel manufacturer. Right there on Everett's home turf! The nerve! Everett's only national television endorsement to date has been a bit part in Bo Jackson's Nike commercial ("Bo knows football," he says), a cameo arranged by agent Demoff.

In truth, Everett says he's thoroughly invigorated by Montana's presence in his football life, however frustrating it might seem at the moment.

"I see it as the ultimate challenge," Everett says of his divisional foe. "Why not have a chance to play the best two times a year? That's what you're looking for in competition. It's fun to

JIM EVERETT

Everett and Ronnie Lott (3 int.) after NFC title game.

win, but it's great when you beat the best.''

Everett says the turning point of his career came last Oct. 1 when he drove the Rams 72 yards in the final two minutes to beat the 49ers, 13-12, as time expired at Candlestick.

"If we had to play them every week, I'd like that," Everett says. "We'd get better. Anyway, he's [Montana] not going anywhere. Eddie [owner DeBartalo Jr.] is paying him too much money. You have to face that fact that Joe is around and deal with it. You improve yourself, and find a way to beat him."

For Everett, Montana is the only mountain left to conquer. In less than four years, he's already rewritten much of a Ram record book that already includes such quarterback greats as Bob Waterfield, Norm Van Brocklin and Roman Gabriel. Everett became the first Ram to ever pass for more than 4,000 yards in a season in 1989, throwing for 4,310. He also set franchise records for pass attempts in a season (518) and holds the team's all-time mark for completion percentage at 57 percent.

Maybe some day Everett even makes the Pro Bowl.

Miracles & Mastery of Al Michaels

The MNF team: Dan Dierdorf, Frank Gifford, Al Michaels.

By JOHN FREEMAN

The date was Oct. 17, 1989. The time was 5:04 P.M. The place was San Francisco's Candlestick Park. It was minutes away from the scheduled start of Game 3 of the World Series.

ABC's Tim McCarver was voicing over video action from Game 2 when he was interrupted by partner Al Michaels, who blurted out: "I'll tell you what! We're having an earth..."

Michaels was cut off in mid-word, so it wasn't immediately clear what had happened. For the moment, the screen went blank, replaced by a graphic that said we were watching the World Series on ABC. We weren't.

A minute or so passed before Michaels came back on the air. With a hint of jauntiness in his voice, he said over a din of confusion: "I don't know if we're on the air or not, and I'm not sure if I *care* at this particular moment, but folks, that's the greatest opening in the history of television, bar none."

Fate had dealt Michaels' favorite city a damaging blow and it was his own fate to be thrust into a different role, that of a hard-news reporter. For the next several hours, Michaels did play-by-play of an earthquake's aftermath. He was calm and dispassionate when he needed to be, and brimming with emotion when he couldn't help himself, as minute by minute he fit the pieces together for ABC's Ted Koppel. It was riveting cinema verite, tube-style.

A former Bay Area resident and a one-time voice of the Giants, Michaels knew the territory. He also knew the psychological effect as he conveyed a sense of drama as it shocked him—and everyone—in human terms, not just in the collapse of a Bay Bridge section and the rubble of fallen neighborhoods and the billowing smoke.

And so, following ABC's marathon coverage of the quake, it was sunrise when Michaels finally reached his San Francisco hotel room. As morning dawned, he and his wife, Linda, had to walk up 13 floors to reach their room because the elevator was out.

"Then," he later recalled, "I sat down and cried. My heart was broken."

As Geoffrey Mason, ABC Sports executive producer, said of Michaels' reporting: "There aren't very many people who have the depth of understanding about what the quake meant to Al. And we all knew, working with him that night, that underneath his professional exterior beat a tummy that was just dying to cry."

Mason has since compared Michaels' work to that of Jim McKay in the 1972 Olympic Games in Munich when Arab terrorists kidnapped and assassinated Israeli athletes as the world watched in horror.

John Freeman, a native San Diegan who is TV-radio sports columnist for the San Diego Tribune, *previously worked in New York for the National Basketball Association and the Yankees. He left George Steinbrenner and the Bronx Zoo of his own volition.*

30   THE COMPLETE HANDBOOK OF PRO FOOTBALL

"They both did everything asked of them and both excelled at the highest level in a time of crisis," said Mason, who covered both events for ABC. "What more could you ask?"

Just as no one who listened to Michaels' descriptions of the Quake of '89 will forget that evening, few have forgotten the "Miracle on Ice" of 1980, when the underdog U.S. hockey team upset the USSR in the Olympic semifinals.

As the final pulsating seconds ticked off, Michaels shouted amid the din: "Do you believe in miracles! Yes!!!"

It was far from being a premeditated call. As he says now, "I just wanted to make sure I was accurate, and had the right guy with the puck when it ended.... I didn't even know what I had said. I was just lucky. The word 'miraculous' came into my mind, and the others just followed."

It was sheer Al Michaels: as intense as it was unimprovised, as celebratory as it was accurate. It was damned perfect, is what it was, and it is likely to remain his signature call forever.

But Michaels, 45, should be duly credited with far more on-air triumphs.

So let's say it flat out: he ranks at the top of his field in whatever sport he does—football, baseball, hockey, figure-skating or horse-racing, which remains his consuming passion as a sometime handicapper and recent owner of a half-interest in a thoroughbred ("I don't know which half yet but we'll find out soon enough," he says).

More to the point, his play-by-play work on "Monday Night Football" is nothing less than superb. He ranks with CBS' Pat Summerall and NBC's Dick Enberg among the best network voices doing NFL football, perhaps the best, though Michaels modestly insists it's not his aim to be recognized as the best. He wants to be regarded as "the consummate professional," no matter the sport.

"I hate to sound like George Allen because it's such a cliche, but I've always put 110 percent into my work, whatever I've done," says Michaels. "I don't leave anything to chance. That's the only way I know to work. I do my job and let others worry about who's the best."

He remains endlessly flattered when fans approach him at airports—even today, 10 years later—and ask him as their chummy way of saying hello, "Hey, Al, do you believe in miracles?" But there's clearly more to Al Michaels than those bookends of the '80s—one hockey game and one earthquake.

"To me, it's an incredible irony that everything I've done in my career is spun off of baseball, but what I'm known for is

Michaels (c.) at Quake Series with McCarver, Palmer.

hockey and an earthquake," says Michaels. "It's been a wild decade, that's for sure."

"Monday Night Football" has survived many personnel changes during its two decades—Michaels has been the lead voice since 1986—and it may never again attain its manic levels of the early '70s.

And what a blessing.

With Michaels calling the play-by-play, phony glitz and shameless hype have been replaced by Michaels' professionalism, laced with good-natured humor and insights from partners Dan Dierdorf and—less so—Frank Gifford. MFN is more watchable than ever because they play it straight.

"We're not doing comedy here," says Michaels, "we're doing a football game. I suppose we can be as off-the-wall as anyone from time to time. But you don't want to go too far."

Not that Michaels and Dierdorf don't share some laughs on and off the air. They do.

"We crack each other up all the time," says Dierdorf, whose caustic sense of humor matches that of Michaels'. "I'm always

32 THE COMPLETE HANDBOOK OF PRO FOOTBALL

trying to get his goat. We have a lot of belly laughs together."

Given a choice, however, between doing straight play-by-play or yukking it up with his buddies, Michaels usually plays it straight, never forcing humor into situations where it doesn't belong.

"What I want the fan to say to himself when I'm announcing a game is, 'If Michaels said it, I believe it,' " he said. "That's what matters most to me."

Michaels has always been goal-oriented, almost to a fault. Brooklyn-born and raised on Long Island, N.Y. (his family moved to Southern California when he was in high school), he's always pushed himself to greater heights. He's always sought more, more, more.

At age 22, fresh out of Arizona State, Michaels sent an audition tape that landed him a job as Chick Hearn's sidekick with the NBA's Los Angeles Lakers. It didn't take long before Michaels realized that Chick didn't want or need a sidekick and resented having some kid—especially someone as feisty as Michaels—working with him.

After a month or so, Michaels was told (not by Hearn, but by a team official) that he had been fired. He was crushed ("It broke my spirit"), but it wasn't long before he found another job, doing baseball for the minor-league Hawaii Islanders.

Three years later, he moved up, to the Cincinnati Reds.

That was fine—he was only 25—but it wasn't enough. Even doing a World Series on network TV at age 27 wasn't enough. Jumping to the San Francisco Giants for a six-figure salary wasn't enough. He wanted more, and when ABC Sports signed him in 1976, he was satisfied, but only for a short while.

Four years later came the "Miracle on Ice." It wasn't enough.

He wanted to work baseball as ABC's top guy. He made that demand of Roone Arledge, and got his wish, replacing Keith Jackson and teaming up with Tim McCarver and Jim Palmer—an inspired team that arguably was baseball's best-ever.

Later, when Dennis Swanson took over ABC's reigns in 1986, Michaels was named to replace Gifford on MNF's play-by-play. Howard Cosell was dropped, Dierdorf was added, and MNF entered a new era.

"The series has held up remarkably well," says Michaels of "Monday Night Football," now in its 21st season. "It's higher rated now than it was in the so-called halcyon days."

Michaels insists that criticism of his play-by-play skills does not bother him as much as it once did. But not so long ago, he was known to take the slightest ounce of criticism and scratch back angrily.

During the '87 World Series, for example, Michaels became involved in an ugly snit with a Minneapolis TV critic. What started the feud was Michaels' off-air remarks, complaining about the second-rate hotel where he was staying, the dullness of the game and how he preferred doing MNF to baseball.

The remarks were made during ABC's commercial breaks, but the critic—and other satellite viewers around the country—heard every word on the pickup.

The critic, Bob Lundegaard, quoted Michaels' word for word, a move Michaels felt was "morally unfair"—not because he was misquoted but because he regarded his off-air comments to be off-limits.

"He wrote it as if I was caught with my pants down," said Michaels. "I wasn't. I had begun my broadcast saying, 'Okay, dish freaks, here we go.'"

The next night, after Lundegaard's column appeared in print, Michaels was ready for a direct assault. He got personal, viciously so.

According to a *Sports Illustrated* account, Michaels began by saying: "Folks, those of you looking in on Telstar, there's a scum bag out there by the name of Bob Lundegaard . . ." A few innings later, Michaels started again: "Let me go through Lundegaard's trash for syringes. Nobody straight could do that."

ABC technicians cut off the audio feed, but the damage had been done—especially to Michaels' reputation. Three years have passed, and Michaels regrets the incident. But he still maintains that what Lundegaard did was wrong.

"All I know is, the guy was lazy," he said. "It was a corollary to my being very precise. Do I deserve to get ripped from time to time? Of course. All I'm saying to those critics who write about me, is, 'Hey, guys, work at your job, be right, get all your facts together. Be right.' If you're gonna blast me, that's okay. Just make it honest and fair."

Wherever Michaels goes these days, he's forever being asked about what exactly happened between him and Cosell. Michaels talks about Cosell with some reluctance, because the two were once friendly, or as friendly as anyone could be with Cosell.

"I had a very complex relationship with him," says Michaels. "It was very good for a number of years. Then it disintegrated and fell apart in 1984 and '85 when Howard got tired, crotchety and bored. He was difficult to work with. He reached a point where whenever we'd come to a game, it was obvious he didn't want to be there."

34 THE COMPLETE HANDBOOK OF PRO FOOTBALL

The publication in late 1986 of Cosell's book, *I Never Played the Game*, contained several unflattering comments about Michaels and many more about nearly everyone with whom Cosell had shared an ABC microphone over the years.

At Michaels' urging, Roone Arledge, then ABC Sports' president, hastened Cosell's retirement just prior to ABC's telecast of the '86 World Series. Tim McCarver took Cosell's place in the booth, a move that Michaels refers to today as "the greatest trade in the history of broadcasting."

Despite Al's pleadings that he's not over-sensitive to the views of critics, his younger brother, 39-year-old David, knows better. Now an NFL producer at CBS Sports, David is not afraid to tweak Al's pursuit of perfection.

"He *is* difficult to deal with," says David, "simply because he expects everyone to adhere to the same high standards he believes in. He can be a pain sometimes."

When the two brothers were growing up on Long Island, they shared a bedroom and nearly every night, when Al was about 14 and David was 9, they would pretend to telecast horse races and auto races from the family's den. Their father was the public address announcer at an auto track in nearby Freeport, N.Y.

"Al would presume that nobody in the family knew who won and then do the race," says David. "He was great, just like he is now. But he took it real seriously. And he didn't want anybody messin' with his stat sheets, ever. If I ever touched one of his souvenir programs, he'd go *crazy!* It was like, 'Keep your hands off my property!' "

What most impressed David about his big brother was Al's command of all those statistics, especially those on baseball cards. "He'd have every single player's stats memorized; it used to drive me nuts," says David.

Did David ever catch Al making a statistical error?

"Not ever," he says, "and that amazed me, especially since he got horrible grades in school. He might have been lucky to have a 'C' average in high school. He always refused to play 'the game' for grades, just like now. He plays his own game; he's his own man."

Michaels has been known to vent his emotions within network corridors, insisting that ABC do things his way or else. Earlier this year, he got his wrist slapped and was briefly suspended by ABC Sports boss Dennis Swanson for violating a network taboo against nepotism.

Michaels hired his teen-age daughter to work as a runner at a figure-skating event that ABC carried in March. Neither Swanson nor Michaels issued any public statements on the matter, but Michaels is known to have been incensed. Indeed, it's not unlikely that Michaels would attempt to jump to another network after the $1.5 million-per-year contract at ABC expires in two years. Or perhaps before—in view of Michaels' displeasure and Brent Musburger's signing with ABC.

It's also conceivable that Michaels could leave sports altogether and pursue a role as host of ABC's "Good Morning America" or NBC's "Today" or CBS' "CBS Morning News." He has had successful guest-host stints on "Good Morning America" and hopes to do more, but strictly as a sidelight to sports.

"All I can say is, I don't want to leave sports right now," says the two-time Emmy Award-winning sportscaster. "As for the future, I don't know what I'll be doing and I don't know what I'll want to be doing in a few years. In my next life, if God gets even with me, I'll probably be a cockroach in the Sudan or somewhere, who knows?"

As intensely competitive as Michaels was early in his career, fighting for every inch of his success, he has gained a different perspective in recent years.

"I'll admit there was a time when I was worried about where my career was going," he says. "I don't want to do that anymore because all of a sudden, you look back and say, 'Where the hell did it go?'"

And so, Al Michaels, who for so many years was never quite satisfied with his career, finds himself himself counting his blessings—his wife of 24 years, Linda, and the couple's two children, Steven, 22, a student at San Diego State, and Jennifer, 18, a high school student. The family lives in a stately colonial-styled home in Brentwood, Cal., a fashionable West Los Angeles neighborhood near UCLA.

"I wouldn't want people to have the misperception that the only thing I care about is my job, because it isn't," he says.

"What's paramount to me is my family. I know this much: "I've been a damn good husband and damn good father. My kids are happy and well-adjusted and when you look at the demands of this business, crazy as it is, it's difficult to keep a family together. Linda and I have done that and that's the most important thing in the world to me."

Barry Sanders ran off with Rookie-of-the-Year honors.

THE QUIET ROAR OF THE LIONS' BARRY SANDERS

By MITCH ALBOM

First of all, Barry Sanders doesn't mind dancing. As long as someone else is doing it. Sure, when he scores a touchdown, he hands the ball to the referee like a mailman delivering a phone bill. But he isn't bothered by those who prefer a wiggle or a shake.

"Hey, I used to love Billy [White Shoes] Johnson and the Washington Smurfs and all," he says, looking down at his hands. "It's just... not me."

Nor does he have a problem with fame. Oh, it's true he asked if he could skip his own Heisman award ceremony and he passed up an invite to the White House because he had to study. But he doesn't condemn players who search for the spotlight. "It's just," he says, "not me."

What just *is* Barry Sanders? Nobody seems to know. Everybody wants to. Three months after slipping on a Lions uniform, Sanders was the most compelling figure on the Detroit sports pages. Isiah Thomas might be throwing in baskets and Steve Yzerman might be skating circles around defensemen, but, let's be honest, we have seen the magic. This is new. This is thrilling.

This is a man who takes a football, flips on his engine and leaves defenders frozen like tanks. Here comes Barry. There goes Barry. In 1989 he was the best rookie in the NFL and one of the top running backs in the game. Already? Already. Walter Payton, after watching Sanders' first 10 Sundays, announced that "Barry is better than I was."

Better than Payton? Who is this guy? What makes him tick?

Mitch Albom of the Detroit Free Press *won the Associated Press sports editors' award as the nation's best sports columnist in 1987, 1988 and 1989. This article has been reprinted with permission.* © 1989 Detroit Free Press.

Why is that important? Sanders wonders. *Isn't it enough that I run? Don't they know what I know?*

A humble man can do anything without a lot of noise.

When Barry was a child in Kansas, he used to pretend he was a super hero. He would enter the house and jump for the ceiling, his fingers straining for a touch, higher, higher.

"Cut it out, damn it!" his father would yell. "Before I smack you!"

So he learned to fly quietly.

He has been doing it ever since.

"People write that I'm this nice, shy choir boy," says Sanders, sitting by his locker at the Silverdome, a towel draped over his bare shoulders. "But that's not really true. That's just an image. They have to come up with some image for me because plain people don't sell newspapers.

"I like to talk. I have friends. But it's hard to find someone who doesn't want to talk football these days. And football is *not* the most important thing in my life. Religion, my family, being at peace with myself . . . and then maybe football. I wonder all the time what I might be doing if not playing this game."

It's hard to imagine; his body almost screams athletics. Look at those thighs, so massive, so hard. Look at those arms, like steel cables. It is as if someone poured concrete into a 5-foot-8 flesh mold. His close-cropped hair frames a smooth face that, believe it or not, is often smiling. Really.

"Are you embarrassed by fame?" he is asked.

"No."

"Are you embarrassed by wealth?"

"No."

"What embarrasses you?"

He rubs his ear. "I guess walking in the middle of a crowd and slipping and falling on my behind. That would embarrass me."

See? A joke. Barry Sanders laughs in a gushing giggle, like he did when he was a kid back in Kansas. It was there, in that three-bedroom house in the poorer section of Wichita, where he jumped for the ceiling and felt the wrath of his father. It was there where he met rich kids who would tease him about all those people living in one house. It was there where he would walk with a hatpin in his teeth, like a toothpick. It looked cool, until one day he accidentally swallowed it, and from then on, never needed a prop for his ego.

It was there where he watched his mother and listened to her sighs and heard his own voice. To understand Barry Sanders, you

BARRY SANDERS 39

Coach Wayne Fontes and Sanders view promising future.

must recognize his childhood. At age 22, he is still, in a way, going through it.

There were only two rules in the Sanders' home. Rule No. 1: Never disobey Dad. Rule No. 2: Never forget Rule No. 1.

William Sanders is a disciplined, headstrong man, father of 11, who used to race his sons backwards to prove he was fast. Before Barry was born, he worked in a meat scrap company, dumping the bones of dead animals.

"One day I went for a drink of water," he said, "and I turned around and the boss was right there staring at me. I said, 'Hey, why don't you get off my back?' And he said, 'Hit the road.' He fired me.

"I went to the union, filed for arbitration and won. They said I could have my job back. I said, 'Give me my money. I'm not working here.'"

He turned to roofing, carpentry, home repairs. When he needed assistance, he took his three sons, William Jr., Byron and Barry, the baby. All day they would labor, with the hammers, the tar, sweating in the hot summer sun. You did not complain in the

Sanders family. Not unless you wanted a good whupping. Dad said, "Get in the car." You got in the car. Dad said, "Get off that telephone and stop talking to girls." You got off the telephone and stopped talking to girls.

Money? Barry was amazed that kids in school actually got an allowance "just for being alive." There were no allowances in the Sanders family. "Your pay is having a roof over your head and food to eat," said Mr. Sanders.

Although he had eight daughters, William preferred sons. "Boys grow up to be football players," he said, as if it were their destiny. Of course, with 10 siblings, it's hard to tell if that was destiny pushing you or just someone's elbow at the dinner table. In the fourth grade, Barry's sister bought him an electric football set for Christmas. He spun the little men and watched them rumble along the metal field. "I identified," he admits, "with the running back."

So it begins. That same year, he signed up for football with the Beech Red Barons, a local youth team. No one figured Barry for an athlete. He was puny. On the day of Barry's first game, William Sanders went instead to watch Byron. Byron was big. Byron was strong. Byron had a chance of growing into an NFL player, who might make some big money "and get me off the damn rooftops," said Mr. Sanders. Go, Byron! During the game, a friend came running over, out of breath.

"Hey, Bill. You ought to see what Barry's doing down on the other field!"

"What are you talking about?"

"He's scored three touchdowns already. He's running past everybody."

"Barry?" said the father. "Barry can't even play football."

Well, he said Barry couldn't fly either.

"I take after my mother," Barry says. "The only way I take after my father is that he was a great athlete. But my mother is the type who doesn't talk to hear herself talk. She would rather see other people happy than herself. I've never heard her curse. I've never seen her take a drink. She's a Christian woman. A real one."

"Do you try to live up to her standards?" he is asked.

"Yes."

"Do you fall short?"

He smiles. "Most people do."

Shirley Sanders spent nearly half her adult life pregnant or giving birth. Eleven children. She bathed them. Fed them. Took them to church. Young Barry adored her, she seemed so smart, so disciplined. But he would watch when she and her husband argued and saw how she always backed down, even when she was right.

"My father is a male chauvinist," Barry says, matter-of-factly. "He always had to be right because he was the man."

Absorb and endure. That is what his mother did. And when it came time to choose between role models, Barry chose her. Thus, when the high school coach failed to start him as tailback because he claimed Barry was "afraid of contact," Sanders did not argue, the way his father might. He kept his anger to himself.

Absorb and endure. When he finally got to start (not until his senior year) he rushed for 274 yards and scored four touchdowns in his first game. He slipped tackles so easily, the referees checked his uniform for vaseline.

Absorb and endure. In college, at Oklahoma State, he was given a summer job packing groceries at a supermarket. It paid $3.35 an hour. Other players on the team were given jobs paying three times that much. He knew it. He kept it inside. Four months later, he crushed the NCAA record for yards rushing in a single season (2,628, an average of 238.9 a game). He won the Heisman. He would never need a grocery store job again.

Absorb and endure. During contract talks with the Lions, William Sanders seemed to run the show. He spoke bluntly; he called the offers insulting. As the holdout grew, he gave the impression that Barry was only interested in money. It wasn't true. Barry knew it. "People would tease me, saying, 'Your father's doing all your talking for you.'"

But like his mother, he would never tell his father to be quiet. Absorb and endure.

And be humble. Even now, with the money he earns (a five-year, $5.9-million contract) he does not drive a Mercedes or a Porsche. His clothes are simple. There are no gold chains. Although his father nearly dragged him out of college one year early—"You go out for spring football, I'll break your legs myself," he once said—life in Wichita hasn't changed much. Barry has offered his parents whatever they want. Money is in the bank. "We're on Easy Street now," says William Sanders. "But we still live in the same house."

A good metaphor. Is it possible to be Big Time and Small Time at the Same Time? Apparently so. Sanders once told a TV reporter he hoped Rodney Peete would win the Heisman instead of him. Huh? The day he announced his NFL eligibility, he missed a plane because the clutch blew out on his rickety old car. *Is he for real?* People wonder.

42 THE COMPLETE HANDBOOK OF PRO FOOTBALL

No-dance Sanders does simple handoff after his TDs.

He is for real. Give him a roof, a bed, some food and a bible and he will want for nothing. "My mother wouldn't," he says simply.

This is a guy who can count on one hand the number of parties he's been to in his life. In high school, he was nominated for Homecoming King. Much to his dismay, he won.

"There's a picture I have of him and the Homecoming Queen that night," says Mark McCormick, his lifelong friend, a journalism student at Kansas. "You should see it. She looks so happy, all smiles—and Barry looks like he's constipated."

Well, since when is it a crime not to like the spotlight? Sanders, who says that trusting people is "harder than ever," still treats his old friends royally. Three years ago, McCormick was struggling to get by at college. Sanders took half the money he was getting on scholarship and immediately offered it to his friend. No questions asked.

When Barry signed his huge contract with the Lions, he promptly gave one-tenth of his $2.1-million signing bonus to his church back in Kansas. A tenth? "Tithing, it's in the bible," he says.

He gave his Heisman Trophy to the family's favorite restaurant. He gladly signs autographs for children but is wary of adults. A woman once invited him to a party. "What will we do there?" he asked.

"We'll get high, have some drinks."

"No, thanks," he said. He went back to his room and watched TV.

And now everybody is watching him. Usually from behind. His stop-start, dip-and-spin running makes you dizzy with excitement. The yardage meter rolls like a pinball machine.

"I *looove* blocking for that guy," says Lomas Brown, the offensive tackle. Was that a Lion talking? You bet. Sanders has helped rinse this team of a losing attitude and dipped it into the world of the possible. Hey! We can win! We've got a superstar here!

Now all they have to do is get used to that humility. In the locker room, his teammates razz him, but he often ignores their teasing and they find themselves awkwardly walking away. "Yo, man, just kidding," they'll say.

Yes, he is for real, a white-hot talent in burlap wrapping. So he doesn't mind dancing—as long as *you* do it. And talk shows are fine—but why don't *you* take the microphone? Okay? "People shouldn't think because I'm quiet I don't make my own decisions," he says. "I just prefer to watch people at first, to see if their walk is as big as their talk."

His is. He stretches the towel behind his neck and every muscle in his shoulders and arms seems to pop out through the skin. Yes, it is true, he may have the world at his feet. But he will probably step over it.

The question seems to be: When will Barry Sanders change? The answer seems to be: What for?

INSIDE THE NFC

By JON GELBERG

PREDICTED ORDER OF FINISH

EAST	CENTRAL	WEST
N.Y. Giants	Minnesota	San Francisco
Washington	Detroit	L.A. Rams
Philadelphia	Chicago	New Orleans
Dallas	Green Bay	Atlanta
Phoenix	Tampa Bay	

NFC Champion: San Francisco

The San Francisco 49ers survived a coaching change, a brutal schedule and even an earthquake to repeat as the Super Bowl champions last year. This year, the only thing standing between them and a third straight championship is complacency.

With Joe Montana orchestrating again, the 49ers remain the class of the Western Conference. Several key Plan-B acquisitions and solid draft choices will make them even better in 1990.

The Rams have a great offensive team led by Jim Everett, but the defense isn't anywhere near good enough to put them on a level with the 49ers.

The Saints wish that the NFL powers-that-be would take a Southeastern team out of the Western Division and put it somewhere where they might have a chance at making the playoffs. That's not happening, so this talented team goes home to yet another early vacation.

The Atlanta Falcons, under ex-Oiler coach Jerry Granville, are

---

Jon Gelberg, lawyer-turned-sportswriter, covers the New York Giants for the Asbury Park Press.

likely to be the most improved team in football. This year, they will be a nuisance. Next year, a factor.

If Herschel Walker can play like the Walker of old, the Vikings win the Central Division handily. If not, then the Lions and Bears will each have a shot.

The Lions, who finished the 1989 season as one of the hottest teams in football, will be even better this time with the addition of quarterback Andre Ware.

The Bears will be rejuvenated with a huge infusion of new blood. As with any young club, there will be a period of adjustment. That period will probably be just long enough to kill their chances for a division title.

The Green Bay Packers enjoyed a wonderful renaissance in 1989, as Don Majkowski blossomed at quarterback. But 1990 will send the Pack back to the pack. The offense has plenty of weapons, but the defense is second-tier at best.

The best thing you can say about Tampa Bay is that they will be hosting the Super Bowl this year. Don't worry about any home-field advantage.

In typical Eastern Division fashion, the Giants, Eagles and Redskins will battle down to the final weeks before a champion is crowned.

Like last year, the Giants will emerge on top. Rodney Hampton gives New York a dangerous running game that will make Phil Simms twice as effective. Defensively, a restocked defensive line will give Lawrence Taylor and Carl Banks more freedom to wreak havoc.

The Eagles had a chance to grab hold of the division, but they failed to take a running back early in the draft. Left with an unbalanced offense, the Eagles will be bridesmaids at best.

The Redskins came on strong at the end of last year and have enough excellent young players to make a run at the title.

The Cowboys will be much improved in all areas. That doesn't mean they'll contend, but it should be enough to get them out of the cellar.

The Cardinals, under new coach Joe Bugel, are rebuilding, but the foundation isn't even in place yet.

This year's playoffs will look remarkably like last year's. The Rams will emerge from the wild-card pack. The Giants get their revenge on the Rams, stomping them in a conference semifinal, while the 49ers squeak by the Vikings in the other.

Once again, the 49ers turn up the heat in the NFC championship game, sending the Giants back home.

Who do the 49ers face in Super Bowl XXV? It doesn't matter.

ATLANTA FALCONS

TEAM DIRECTORY: Chairman: Rankin Smith Sr.; Pres.; Rankin Smith Jr.; VP: Taylor Smith; VP-Player Personnel: Ken Herock; Dir. Pub. Rel.; Charlie Taylor; Head Coach: Jerry Glanville. Home field: Atlanta Stadium (59,643). Colors: Red, black, silver and white.

SCOUTING REPORT

OFFENSE: There's too much talent here for the Falcons to have finished the 1989 season with the league's 24th-ranked offense.

The passing game has the potential to be one of the best in the league. Chris Miller (280-of-526, 3,459 yards, 16 TDs) is an excellent quarterback and he has several quality targets. Shawn Collins more than lived up to his surprise first-round selection, leading all rookies in receptions (58). Newly acquired Andre Rison led all AFC rookie receivers with 52 catches at Indianapolis last year.

Since the Falcons ranked 28th in the league in rushing, the only way to go is up. Rookie running back Steve Broussard gives the Falcons instant offense. John Settle is capable of bigger things than the 689 yards he produced last year, while Keith Jones should be given a serious look as a ball-carrier.

The offensive line will be dangerous with the addition of the Colts' Pro Bowl tackle Chris Hinton. Pity the defensive lineman who has to look at Hinton and Bill Fralic side by side. The Falcons also picked three Plan-B linemen in hopes of giving Miller the protection he needs.

DEFENSE: If Falcons' fans are looking for encouragement, the defense is the right place to start. New coach Jerry Glanville has an excellent defensive mind, and he's got the young bodies to execute his game plan.

The linebacking corps could become the best in the league. Aundray Bruce, Marcus Cotton, rookie Darion Connor and Jessie Tuggle have youth (none over 25), talent, and now have the teacher they need to be even better.

The defensive line is anchored by Tony Casillas, but there's not much more to choose from. Mike Gann and Ben Thomas are adequate at best. Glanville has high hopes for third-round tackle Oliver Barnett.

The defensive backfield was greatly improved with the addition of Neon Deion Sanders. He is nearly as good as he thinks he is.

ATLANTA FALCONS 47

Chris Miller: Lowest interception pct. in NFL (1.9).

Safeties Evan Cooper and Tim Gordon combined for eight interceptions.

KICKING GAME: A healthy Paul McFadden would be welcome; otherwise there's a huge hole. Scott Fulhage ranked eighth in the NFL in punting with a 41.3 average.

The return game improved with the addition of Sanders, a threat to return any kick or punt for a touchdown. The kick-coverage unit was solid, giving up 19.8 yards per return, but the punt coverage (10.7 yards per return) must improve.

FALCONS VETERAN ROSTER

HEAD COACH—Jerry Glanville. Assistant Coaches—Jimmy Carr, Bill Kollar, Wayne McDuffie, Jimmy Robinson, Tom Rossley, Keith Rowen, Ray Sherman, Doug Shively.

No.	Name	Pos.	Ht.	Wt.	NFL Exp.	College
82	Balley, Stacey	WR	6-1	163	9	San Jose State
62	Barrows, Scott	G-C	6-3	280	5	West Virginia
65	Bingham, Guy	C-G	6-3	260	11	Montana
70	Bowick, Tony	NT	6-2	265	2	Tenn.-Chattanooga
94	Brinson, Dana	WR	5-9	167	2	Nebraska
93	Bruce, Aundray	LB	6-5	245	3	Auburn
77	Bryan, Rick	DE	6-4	265	7	Oklahoma
23	Butler, Bobby	CB	5-11	175	10	Florida State
10	Campbell, Scott	QB	6-0	195	5	Purdue
25	Case, Scott	CB	6-0	178	7	Oklahoma
75	Casillas, Tony	NT	6-3	280	5	Oklahoma
74	Clayton, Stan	G	6-3	265	3	Penn State
96	Cline, Jackie	DE-NT	6-5	280	4	Alabama
85	Collins, Shawn	WR	6-2	207	2	Northern Arizona
51	Cotton, Marcus	LB	6-3	225	3	Southern California
5	Davis, Greg	K	5-11	197	4	Citadel
22	Dimry, Charles	CB	6-0	175	3	Nevada-Las Vegas
86	Dixon, Floyd	WR	5-9	170	5	Stephen F. Austin
90	Dixon, Titus	WR	5-6	152	2	Troy State
64	Dukes, Jamie	G	6-1	285	5	Florida State
86	Floyd, Victor	RB	6-1	201	2	Florida State
79	Fralic, Bill	G	6-5	280	6	Pittsburgh
17	Fulhage, Scott	P	5-10	193	4	Kansas State
76	Gann, Mike	DE	6-5	270	6	Notre Dame
41	Gordon, Tim	S	6-0	188	4	Tulsa
99	Green, Tim	LB	6-2	245	5	Syracuse
81	Haynes, Michael	WR	6-0	180	2	Northern Arizona
91	Hinnant, Michael	TE	6-3	258	3	Temple
75	Hinton, Chris	T-G	6-4	300	8	Northwestern
69	Hoover, Houston	T-G	6-2	290	3	Jackson State
68	Hunter, John	T	6-8	296	2	Brigham Young
43	Johnson, Tracy	RB	6-0	280	4	Alabama
28	Johnson, Undra	RB	5-9	199	2	West Virginia
38	Jones, Keith	RB	6-1	210	2	Illinois
40	Jordan, Brian	S	5-11	202	2	Richmond
78	Kenn, Mike	T	6-7	277	13	Michigan
33	Lang, Gene	RB	5-10	206	7	Louisiana State
	Lee, Gary	WR	6-1	201	4	Georgia Tech
63	Lee, Ronnie	T	6-3	277	12	Baylor
6	McFadden, Paul	K	5-11	166	7	Youngstown State
7	Millen, Hugh	QB	6-5	216	4	Washington
12	Miller, Chris	QB	6-2	195	4	Oregon
84	Milling, James	WR	5-9	156	2	Maryland
39	Mitchell, Roland	CB	5-11	180	3	Texas Tech
36	Paterra, Greg	RB	5-11	211	2	Slippery Rock
49	Primus, James	RB	5-11	196	3	UCLA
59	Rade, John	LB	6-1	240	8	Boise State
95	Reid, Michael	LB	6-2	235	4	Wisconsin
85	Rison, Andre	WR	6-0	191	2	Michigan State
56	Ruether, Mike	C	6-4	275	7	Texas
21	Sanders, Deion	CB	6-0	187	2	Florida State
44	Settle, John	RB	5-9	205	4	Appalachian
37	Shelley, Elbert	S	5-11	180	4	Arkansas State
67	Taylor, Malcolm	DE	6-6	280	7	Tennessee State
53	Thaxton, Galand	LB	6-1	242	2	Wyoming
72	Thomas, Ben	DE	6-3	275	5	Auburn
89	Thomas, George	WR	5-9	169	2	Nevada-Las Vegas
58	Tuggle, Jessie	LB	5-11	230	4	Valdosta State
66	Utt, Ben	G	6-6	293	9	Georgia Tech
	Watts, Randy	DE-NT	6-6	279	2	Catawba
87	Wilkins, Gary	TE	6-2	235	3	Georgia Tech

TOP DRAFT CHOICES

Rd.	Name	Sel. No.	Pos.	Ht.	Wt.	College
1	Broussard, Steve	20	RB	5-6	201	Washington State
2	Conner, Darion	27	LB	6-2	256	Jackson State
3	Barnett, Oliver	55	DE	6-3	285	Kentucky
5	Redding, Reggie	121	TE	6-4	276	Cal-Fullerton
6	Pringle, Mike	139	RB	5-8	186	Cal-Fullerton

ATLANTA FALCONS 49

THE ROOKIES: The Falcons had a great draft before ever selecting a player. They gave up the rights to No. 1 (Indy got Jeff George) and got the equivalent of two No. 1's in Rison and Hinton. Washington State's Broussard will step in as the No. 1 halfback. Jackson State's Conner may start at linebacker and Kentucky's Barnett has an outside shot at defensive tackle.

OUTLOOK: Much better than last year's 3-13, but as long as the 49ers, Rams and Saints are the only other tenants in this upscale division, it will be impossible to escape the basement. Don't look for miracles, but anticipate at least a couple of upsets.

FALCON PROFILES

CHRIS MILLER 25 6-2 195   Quarterback

Enjoyed one of best seasons by a quarterback in the history of the franchise... Completed 280 of 526 passes for 3,459 yards... Threw 16 touchdowns and only 10 interceptions, an exceptional ratio when you consider how often he was forced to throw while Falcons trailed ... Broke team records with 66 passes and 37 completions against the Lions... Reached the 6,000-yard mark last season; only four quarterbacks in the history of the league reached that plateau at an earlier age... Went 185 passes without an interception... Even kicked a 25-yard field goal ... An excellent shortstop, Miller was drafted by the Blue Jays and the Mariners... Rewrote all the passing records at Oregon ... Thirteenth selection in 1987 draft... Born Aug. 9, 1965, in Pomona, Cal.... Earned $450,000 last year.

DEION SANDERS 23 6-0 187   Cornerback

Led team in interceptions (5), punt returns (11.0) and kickoff returns (20.7)... Fifth pick in '89 draft returned a punt 68 yards for a touchdown against the Rams on opening day... Excellent baseball prospect as well in Yankee organization... An outfielder, he batted .212 in brief major-league stint last year... His 1,086 total yards led Falcons... One of the brashest, cockiest players to come into the league in a long time

... Nicknamed "Neon Deion," "Money" and "Prime Time"... All-America at Florida State... Showed up for his final college home game wearing a tuxedo and riding in a chauffeured limousine... Born Aug. 9, 1967, in Ft. Myers, Fla... In second year of four-year contract paying $4.4 million.

BILL FRALIC 27 6-5 280 Guard

One of the top guards in the NFL... Just missed fourth consecutive trip to the Pro Bowl... Snubbed by his peers, but won first team All-Pro honors from UPI... Training camp holdout in '89 signed a three-year deal on Sept. 5... Activated for second game and started the final 15... Selected as *Sports Illustrated's* Rookie of the Year in 1985... Made a starter on his first day of practice... Participated in Wrestlemania II in April 1986... Second player taken in the 1985 draft after a stellar career at Pittsburgh... Born on Halloween, Oct. 31, 1962, in Pittsburgh... Earned $650,000 last year.

SHAWN COLLINS 23 6-2 207 Wide Receiver

Led all rookie receivers with 58 catches (no fumbles) and 862 yards... First team All-Rookie honors... Started in all 16 games... A big-play receiver, Collins had 16 catches over 20 yards... His 58 receptions tied Art Monk for the highest total by a first-round draftee in the 1980s... Monk also happens to be Collins' idol... Is an excellent blocker and played some tight end at Northern Arizona... Was 27th player taken in the 1989 draft... Northern Arizona was the only college to offer him a scholarship... Born Feb. 20, 1967, in San Diego... Signed a four-year, $1.771-million contract last year.

ANDRE RISON 23 6-0 191 Wide Receiver

Showed several flashes of greatness in rookie season with the Colts and now he's a Falcon via the deal that brought him and two draft picks for the rights to the No. 1 draft pick (QB Jeff George)... Caught 52 passes for 820 yards and four TDs while making 13 starts... First Colts' rookie to record more than 50 receptions since Randy McMillan in 1981... Had three

ATLANTA FALCONS 51

100-yard receiving games... He and Albert Bentley were only Colts to catch a pass in each game... Provided highlight-film material with TD at Miami on which he dodged six defenders inside the five... First-round pick out of Michigan State... Didn't play in strong passing attack in college, so some questioned his ability... Broke school receiving record of 2,347 yards set by baseball star Kirk Gibson... Was all-state basketball selection in high school while playing on same team as Glen Rice of the Miami Heat... 1989 salary: $175,000 with $85,000 in bonuses. 1990 salary: $275,000... Born March 18, 1967, in Muncie, Ind.

KEITH JONES 24 6-1 210   Running Back

A third-round draft pick in '89 who proved he had the right stuff... Ran 52 times for 202 yards and led the Falcons with six touchdowns... Caught 41 passes for 396 yards... Returned 23 kicks for 440 yards... Ranked second on the team in rushing and in receptions... Started nine games... Missed two with injuries... Though he handled the ball 116 times, he never fumbled... Threw four touchdown passes off the halfback option in college... Born March 20, 1966, in Rock Hills, Mo.

JOHN SETTLE 25 5-9 207   Running Back

Led the Falcons in rushing with 689 yards on 179 carries, but this was a letdown after spectacular 1988 season... Caught 39 passes for 316 yards... Scored five touchdowns (three rushing, two TD catches)... Had 1,594 total yards in his 1988 Pro Bowl campaign... Was the first free agent since the 1970 merger to rush for over 1,000 yards... Best game came against the Cardinals (87 yards rushing, 46 yards receiving)... Four-year starter at Appalachian State... Ignored in the draft despite rushing for 4,409 yards in his career... He had a terrible performance at the scouting combines due to flu and a 101 temperature... Set numerous school and conference records... Born June 2, 1965, in Ruffin, Ga.... Earned $125,000 last year.

JESSIE TUGGLE 25 5-11 230 Linebacker

In his first year as a full-time starter, Tuggle led Falcons in tackles with 183... Had three 16-tackle games... Only one sack... Recorded 103 tackles in 1988 despite starting only eight games... One of the Falcons' best special-teams tacklers... A virtual unknown out of Valdosta State, where he had 340 tackles, he was completely passed over in 1987 draft ... With his lack of size, few NFL scouts thought he had a chance to make it in the pros... One of very few players to play their high school, college and professional football in Georgia... Born Feb. 14, 1965, in Spalding, Ga.

TONY CASILLAS 26 6-3 280 Nose Tackle

Continues to be one of the best defensive tackles in the league... Finished second on the team with 152 tackles... Forced two fumbles and recovered three... Tied for second on the team with 16 quarterback hurries... Recorded two sacks... Second-team UPI All-Pro... Pro Bowl alternate in 1988 and 1987... Earned All-Rookie honors in 1986 after recording 111 tackles... Had a three-week leave of absence from the Falcons' 1988 training camp when he underwent therapy for a stress disorder at Emory University... Second player taken in the 1986 draft after winning the Lombardi Trophy as the best lineman in the country... Two time All-American at Oklahoma... Born Oct. 26, 1963, in Tulsa, Okla... Earned $300,000 last year.

CHRIS HINTON 29 6-4 300 Tackle

Six Pro Bowls in seven seasons says it all for the steady veteran who came from the Colts with Andre Rison and two draft picks for the rights to the 1989 No. 1 draft pick (QB Jeff George)... Hinton missed two games in '89 because of a hamstring injury... Limited Bills' Bruce Smith to no tackles and one quarterback pressure on Oct. 8... Has been to Pro Bowl as guard and tackle... First rookie offensive lineman in history to make Pro Bowl... Was All-Big Ten tackle at Northwestern in first season at the position... Played linebacker and tight end previously... Fourth pick in '83 draft... 1989 salary: $550,000 ... Born July 31, 1961, in Chicago.

ATLANTA FALCONS 53

MARCUS COTTON 24 6-3 225 Linebacker

Emerging as one of the top pass-rushing linebackers in the game... Used excellent speed to lead the team with nine sacks despite playing primarily on obvious passing downs... The quarterbacks he has sacked join what Marcus calls "The Cotton Club"... Started only one game, but has an excellent chance of breaking into the starting lineup this year... Suffered through an injury-plagued rookie season... Recorded five sacks as a rookie... Second-round pick in 1988 out of USC... Played two years of basketball at USC... Big on cars and motorbikes... His Mercedes convertible has two telephones... Born Aug. 11, 1966, in Los Angeles... Earned $200,000 last year.

AUNDRAY BRUCE 24 6-5 245 Linebacker

Suffered through a frustrating sophomore season after winning All-Rookie honors in 1988... Spent the season in battle with then-head coach Marion Campbell... Ejected from Cardinals' game for fighting and was benched for a game for his poor attitude... Probably the happiest man in America when Jerry Glanville replaced Marion Campbell... Started 13 games at left outside linebacker... Finished 10th on the team with 66 tackles... Second in sacks (6) and quarterback hurries (12)... First player taken in the 1988 draft after a brilliant career at Auburn... Is the 13th of a family of 14 children... Born April 30, 1966, in Montgomery, Ala... Earned $400,000 last year.

COACH JERRY GLANVILLE:
Head coaching job in Atlanta is a homecoming for this former Falcon assistant... Comes to the Falcons with one of the most bizarre reputations in football... Has a knack for building teams with nasty dispositions and dirty tactics... Often wears a bullet-proof vest when he's on the road... Is also known as one of the great squanderers of talent... Lost last year's AFC wild-card game to the Steelers... Must have done something right, though, since he led the Oilers to the playoffs in three of his

54 THE COMPLETE HANDBOOK OF PRO FOOTBALL

four years as head coach... Though he dresses exclusively in black, he's one of the most colorful men in the business... Known for leaving tickets to such luminaries as Elvis Presley and others both real and fictional... Joined the Oilers in 1984 as a defensive coordinator, became head coach for the final two games of the 1985 season before taking over the job full time... Served as an assistant with the Bills, Lions and Falcons ... Regular-season record as head coach is 33-32... Played linebacker at Northern Michigan... Born Oct. 14, 1941, in Detroit.

LONGEST PASS PLAY

BOB BERRY TO HARMON WAGES

Halfback Harmon Wages was never a contender for the Hall of Fame. He began his career as a free agent out of the University of Florida and hooked on with the Falcons in 1968.

His most memorable game came on Dec. 7, 1969, against the Saints in Atlanta. Wages led the way to one of the few laughers in Falcon history, a 45-17 romp. The highlight was Wages' 88-yard touchdown reception from Bob Berry. But Wages also had a 66-yard touchdown run and he even threw a 16-yard TD pass to Paul Flatley on a halfback option.

Both the catch and the run still stand as team records.

INDIVIDUAL FALCON RECORDS

Rushing

Most Yards Game:	202	Gerald Riggs, vs New Orleans, 1984
Season:	1,719	Gerald Riggs, 1985
Career:	6,631	Gerald Riggs, 1982-88

Passing

Most TD Passes Game:	4	Randy Johnson, vs Chicago, 1969
	4	Steve Bartkowski, vs New Orleans, 1980
	4	Steve Bartkowski, vs St. Louis, 1981
Season:	31	Steve Bartkowski, 1980
Career:	149	Steve Bartkowski, 1975-85

ATLANTA FALCONS

Receiving

Most TD Passes Game:	3	Lynn Cain, vs Oakland, 1979
	3	Alfred Jenkins, vs New Orleans, 1981
	3	William Andrews, vs Denver, 1982
	3	William Andrews, vs Green Bay, 1983
	3	Lynn Cain, vs L.A. Rams, 1984
	3	Gerald Riggs, vs L.A. Rams, 1985
Season:	13	Alfred Jenkins, 1981
Career:	40	Alfred Jenkins, 1975-83

Scoring

Most Points Game:	18	Lynn Cain, vs Oakland, 1979
	18	Alfred Jenkins, vs New Orleans, 1981
	18	William Andrews, vs Denver, 1982
	18	William Andrews, vs Green Bay, 1983
	18	Lynn Cain, vs L.A. Rams, 1984
	18	Gerald Riggs, vs L.A. Rams, 1985
Season:	114	Mick Luckhurst, 1981
Career:	558	Mick Luckhurst, 1981-87
Most TDs Game:	3	Shared by Lynn Cain, Alfred Jenkins, William Andrews and Gerald Riggs
Season:	13	Alfred Jenkins, 1981
	13	Gerald Riggs, 1984
Career:	48	Gerald Riggs, 1982-88

CHICAGO BEARS

TEAM DIRECTORY: Chairman: Edward B. McCaskey; Pres.: Michael B. McCaskey; VP-Player Personnel: Bill Tobin; Dir. Adm.: Tim LeFevour; Dir. Finance: Ted Phillips; Dir. Marketing and Communications: Ken Valdiserri; Pub. Rel. Dir.: Bryan Harlan; Head Coach: Mike Ditka. Home field: Soldier Field (66,946). Colors: Orange, navy blue and white.

SCOUTING REPORT

OFFENSE: The Bears needed to settle the quarterback issue as early in training camp as they could. Mike Tomczak (156-306, 2,058 yards, 16TDs, 16 int.) wasn't nearly as good as a full-time starter as he had been as Jim McMahon's reliever. Jim Harbaugh (111-178, 1,204 yards, 5 TDs, 9 int.) showed signs of brilliance, but wasn't given enough time to develop.

Whoever gets the nod as the starting quarterback will have to find a way to get the ball to Wendell Davis. The already weak receiving game will find it hard to compensate for the Plan-B loss of Dennis McKinnon.

The running game is set with the impressive duo of Neal Anderson (1,275 yards, 4.7 avg.) and Brad Muster (327, 4.0). Hopefully, an aging offensive line can continue to open the gaping holes that have been there for so long.

DEFENSE: The Bears ranked second in the NFL in defense in 1988 and 25th last year. The primary reason for the decline was a spate of injuries. Only Steve McMichael and Mike Singletary played every game. The crippling loss of Dan Hampton enabled opponents to double-team Richard Dent.

Things should improve considerably this year. Three rookie starters from 1989, Donnell Woolford, John Roper and Trace Armstrong, should be more comfortable with a full season under their belts. And now there is rookie safety Mark Carrier.

KICKING GAME: No real problems. Kevin Butler (15-of-19 FG attempts) is among the league's best kickers, while Maury Buford (39.5 avg.) was adequate handling the punting duties.

The Bears' return game had only mixed results. Led by Dennis Gentry, the Bears ranked third in the conference in kick returns (21.1 yards per return), but they ranked a pitiful 13th in the NFC in punt returns (6.9 yards per return).

CHICAGO BEARS 57

Pro Bowler Neal Anderson was fourth in NFL rushing.

THE ROOKIES: The Bears raised a few eyebrows when they passed over Andre Ware and invested the sixth pick in the draft on USC's Carrier. They waited until the second round to take care of a more pressing need, the defensive line, when they chose TCU's Fred Washington. Their next pick, Fresno State linebacker Ron Cox, led the nation in sacks.

BEARS VETERAN ROSTER

HEAD COACH—Mike Ditka. Assistant Coaches—Steve Kazor, Greg Landry, Jim LaRue, John Levra, Dave McGinnis, Vic Rapp, Johnny Roland, Dick Stanfel, Vince Tobin, Zaven Yaralian

No.	Name	Pos.	Ht.	Wt.	NFL Exp.	College
35	Anderson, Neal	RB	5-11	210	5	Florida
93	Armstrong, Trace	DE	6-4	259	2	Florida
78	Becker, Kurt	G-T	6-5	280	9	Michigan
62	Bortz, Mark	G	6-6	272	8	Iowa
86	Boso, Cap	TE	6-3	240	4	Illinois
8	Buford, Maury	P	6-0	198	9	Texas Tech
6	Butler, Kevin	K	6-1	195	6	Georgia
94	Chapura, Dick	DT	6-3	275	3	Missouri
74	Covert, Jim	T	6-4	278	8	Pittsburgh
82	Davis, Wendell	WR	5-11	188	3	Louisiana State
95	Dent, Richard	DE	6-5	260	8	Tennessee State
37	Douglass, Maurice	CB-S	5-11	200	5	Kentucky
22	Duerson, Dave	S	6-1	212	8	Notre Dame
68	Dyko, Chis	T	6-6	295	2	Washington State
67	Fontenot, Jerry	C-G	6-3	272	2	Texas A&M
23	Gayle, Shaun	S	5-11	194	7	Ohio State
29	Gentry, Dennis	WR	5-8	180	9	Baylor
31	Green, Mark	RB	5-11	184	2	Notre Dame
99	Hampton, Don	DT	6-5	274	12	Arkansas
4	Harbaugh, Jim	QB	6-3	205	4	Michigan
63	Hilgenberg, Jay	C	6-3	265	10	Iowa
24	Jackson, Vestee	CB-S	6-0	186	5	Washington
92	Johnson, Troy	LB	6-0	236	3	Oklahoma
53	Jones, Dante	LB	6-1	236	3	Oklahoma
88	Kozlowski, Glen	WR	6-1	205	4	Brigham Young
76	McMichael, Steve	DT	6-2	260	11	Texas
84	Morris, Ron	WR	6-1	195	4	Southern Methodist
51	Morrissey, Jim	LB	6-3	227	6	Michigan State
25	Muster, Brad	RB	6-4	232	3	Stanford
36	Paul, Markus	S	6-2	199	2	Syracuse
72	Perry, William	DT	6-2	330	6	Clemson
52	Pruitt, Mickey	LB	6-1	215	3	Colorado
59	Rivera, Ron	LB	6-3	240	7	California
55	Roper, John	LB	6-1	228	2	Texas A&M
50	Singletary, Mike	LB	6-0	228	10	Baylor
32	Stinson, Lemuel	CB-S	5-9	159	3	Texas Tech
49	Tate, David	S	6-0	177	3	Colorado
57	Thayer, Tom	G	6-4	270	6	Notre Dame
80	Thornton, Jim	TE	6-2	242	3	Cal-Fullerton
18	Tomczak, Mike	QB	6-1	195	6	Ohio State
78	Van Horne, Keith	T	6-6	283	10	Southern California
73	Wojciechowski, John	G-T	6-4	270	4	Michigan State
21	Woolford, Donnell	CB-S	5-9	188	2	Clemson

TOP DRAFT CHOICES

Rd.	Name	Sel. No.	Pos.	Ht.	Wt.	College
1	Carrier, Mark	6	DB	6-1	180	USC
2	Washington, Fred	32	DT	6-2	277	Texas Christian
2	Cox, Ron	33	LB	6-2	242	Fresno State
3	Ryan, Tim	61	DT	6-3	268	USC
3	Willis, Peter Tom	63	QB	6-2	188	Florida State

CHICAGO BEARS 59

OUTLOOK: After an awful finish in a 6-10 season, everything is looking up again. With a roster suddenly filled with young, talented players, Mike Ditka's Bears should be on the way to rejoining the league's elite, but not immediately. It's tough to figure how any team will finish in the tight Central Division, but you can count the Bears out of a division championship this year.

BEAR PROFILES

NEAL ANDERSON 26 5-11 210   Running Back

After two straight Pro Bowl invitations, Anderson's finally out of Walter Payton's shadow ... Rushed for 1,275 yards on 275 carries, averaging 4.7 yards per carry ... Became only the second Bear to rush for over 1,000 yards in consecutive seasons ... Ranked fourth in the NFL in rushing ... Had a total of 15 touchdowns (11 rushing, 4 receiving) ... Caught 50 passes for 434 yards ... Led the Bears in rushing for the third straight year ... Led in receptions for the second time in three years ... Rushed for 1,106 yards in 1988 ... Top rusher in 1988 Pro Bowl (85 yards) ... First-round pick in 1986 out of Florida ... Finished as Florida's all-time leading rusher ... Born Aug. 14, 1964, in Graceville, Fla. ... Earned $290,000 last year.

JAY HILGENBERG 30 6-3 265   Center

Capped off excellent season when he was named a Pro Bowl starter ... This isn't exactly news for a guy who has held that spot for the last five years ... One of the main reasons why the Bears have had a 1,000-yard rusher in every non-strike year that he's been playing ... Has now started in 100 straight games, especially significant considering that he's played with a broken hand, dislocated elbow and torn rotator cuff in that span ... Became a starter midway through the 1983 season ... Though he was All-Big 10 at Iowa for two years, Hilgenberg was ignored in the draft ... Signed as a free agent two weeks after the '81 draft ... Born March 21, 1960, in Iowa City, Iowa ... Earned $510,000 last year.

RICHARD DENT 29 6-5 260　　　　　　　　Defensive End

Recovered from a 1988 broken leg to lead the Bears with nine sacks... Sack total was Dent's lowest since his rookie year... Has 79 sacks over the last six seasons... Last season was the first time in six years that he failed to record double-digit sacks... Led the NFL in sacks in 1985 with 17... MVP of Super Bowl XX, a rare achievement for a defensive player... Two-time Pro Bowler... As a Tennessee State senior, he was underweight and unappealing to the pro scouts at draft time in 1983, but the Bears liked him as a pass-rusher and took him on the eighth round (203rd player)... They bulked him up and he produced... Born Dec. 13, 1960, in Atlanta... Earned $900,000 last year.

KEVIN BUTLER 28 6-1 195　　　　　　　　Kicker

Another solid season... Connected on 15 of 19 field-goal attempts for the second straight season... Set an NFL record for most consecutive field goals (24), not missing between 10/16/88 and 12/3/89... His accuracy is remarkable when you consider that he does half of his kicking in the wind and cold of Chicago... Finished with 88 points... Missed two extra points, only the fifth and sixth misses of his career... Set a rookie scoring record in 1985 with 144 points as he hit on 31 of 38 field goals and was 51-for-51 in extra points... Has averaged 104 points for five years... Was a fourth-round pick out of Georgia... Born July 24, 1962, in Savannah, Ga.... Earned $300,000 last year.

STEVE McMICHAEL 32 6-2 260　　　　　　　Defensive Tackle

Easily the MVP of the Bears' defensive unit... Gave the team a strong inside pass rush... One of two Bears to start every game on defense... Has now started in 101 straight games, most on the team... Finished the season ranked second in sacks (7½) and tackles (108)... Led the Bears in sacks in 1988 with a career-high 11½... Career got off to a shaky start after he was cut by the Patriots in his first training camp... Third-round pick in 1980 out of Texas... Signed with the Bears as a free agent in

1981 . . . Born Oct. 17, 1957, in Houston . . . Earned $500,000 last year . . . Hunts rattlesnakes in offseason, quarterbacks in season.

MIKE SINGLETARY 31 6-0 228 — Linebacker

Another year, another Pro Bowl start (his seventh) . . . Only Walter Payton has been to more Pro Bowls in Bear history . . . Started all 16 games and led the Bears with 151 tackles . . . Has ranked first or second on the team in tackles in each of the last eight seasons . . . Tied for the team lead in fumbles forced (2) . . . Remains a favorite target for TV cameras with his icy, intense glare . . . Two-time NFL Defensive Player of the Year (1985 and 1988) . . . Though he was twice named SWC Player of the Year at Baylor, he lasted until the second round of the draft due to his relative lack of size . . . Bears got him with 49ers' pick in second round, giving up their second- and fifth-round picks . . . Born Oct. 9, 1958, in Houston . . . Earned $725,000 last year.

MIKE TOMCZAK 27 6-1 195 — Quarterback

With the trade of Jim McMahon, Tomczak finally got to be the starter, but failed to take advantage . . . Started 11 games, but couldn't win the job outright from Jim Harbaugh . . . Completed 156 of 306 passes for 2,058 yards with 16 TDs and 16 interceptions . . . Earned NFC Offensive Player of the Week for performance against the Eagles on Oct. 2 (24 of 38 for 266 yards and three touchdowns) . . . Had a remarkable effort against Tampa, coming in with just 2:57 remaining in the fourth quarter and throwing three touchdown passes . . . Backed up McMahon for his first four seasons . . . Three-year starter at Ohio State, but was ignored in the 1985 draft . . . Signed as a free agent . . . Born Oct. 23, 1962, in Chicago.

JIM HARBAUGH 26 6-3 205 — Quarterback

Expected to again battle with Mike Tomczak for the starting job . . . Started five games, completing 111 of 178 passes for 1,204 yards with five touchdowns and nine interceptions . . . His completion percentage (62.4 percent) established a Bears' record . . . His career completion percentage (58 percent) is also a team record . . . Proved himself an able runner, going

276 yards on 45 carries, while scoring three touchdowns... Started two games in 1988, losing to the Rams and beating the Lions... Third-string quarterback as a rookie in 1987... First-round pick out of Michigan, where he was the first in school history to pass for over 2,000 yards... Born Dec. 23, 1963, in Ann Arbor, Mich.... Earned $255,000 last year.

DONNELL WOOLFORD 24 5-9 188   Cornerback

It was trial by fire for this talented but beleagured rookie... Forced to cover the top receiver on virtually every team, Woolford was burned enough to have his coach declare "this guy can't cover anybody"... Still managed to snag three interceptions... Frustrations were compounded by injuries to his shoulder, eye and hand that forced him to miss five games ... Started all 11 games he played in... Earned All-American honors as a junior and senior at Clemson... Did not allow a touchdown pass in his senior season... Taken with the 11th pick of the first round... Choice obtained in deal that sent Willie Gault to the Raiders... Born Jan. 6, 1966, in Fayetteville, N.C.

BRAD MUSTER 25 6-4 232   Fullback

Perfect complement to Neal Anderson in the backfield... Started all 16 games and proved himself as a blocker, runner and receiver... Ranked second on the team in rushing with 327 yards on 82 carries (4.0 average)... Caught 32 passes for 259 yards... Excellent nose for the end zone, rushing for five touchdowns and catching three touchdown passes (the eight TDs were second to Anderson's 15)... Scored two touchdowns against both the Lions and Packers... Endured a frustrating rookie season after coming to the Bears as their first-round pick out of Stanford ... Didn't start as a rookie and rushed for only 197 yards in 1988 ... An excellent student, Muster mustered a 3.07 GPA as an economics major... Born April 11, 1965, in San Marin, Cal... Earned $225,000 last year.

CHICAGO BEARS 63

COACH MIKE DITKA: Had trouble coaching a young and injured team... Gave up on the team early... When the Bears were 6-4, Ditka said they wouldn't win another game... And they didn't... Viciously attacked some of the younger players, giving Donnell Woolford an especially hard time... Suffered through only his second losing season... Career regular-season coaching record dipped to 79-41... Survived a 1988 heart attack, returning before the end of the season... Coached the Bears to their only Super Bowl title in 1985, when team won 18 of 19 games... Ditka is the only Bears' coach to take the team to the playoffs in five consecutive seasons (1984-88)... Served nine years as an assistant with the Cowboys before taking Bears' job in 1982... Enjoyed a Hall of Fame career with the Bears, Eagles and Cowboys... Went to the Pro Bowl five times... A great tight end, he had 427 career receptions for 5,812 yards and 43 touchdowns, and was inducted into the Pro Football Hall of Fame in 1988... All-American at Pitt... Born Oct. 13, 1939, in Carnegie, Pa.

LONGEST PASS PLAY

BILLY WADE TO JOHN FARRINGTON

In his first seven years in the NFL (1954-60), Billy Wade had the misfortune of playing for L.A. Ram teams that offered shoddy pass protection.

But things turned around for the Vanderbilt grad when he became the Bears' quarterback in 1961. This was the time of such quarterbacks as Bart Starr, Johnny Unitas and Y.A. Tittle.

Of his 17 TD strikes in '61, the most dramatic came on Oct. 8 against the Lions in Chicago. The Bears were down, 10-0, when Wade connected on a 98-yard bomb to John Farrington. The Bears wound up winning, 31-17.

In that same season, a tight end named Mike Ditka was named Rookie of the Year.

INDIVIDUAL BEAR RECORDS

Rushing

Most Yards Game:	275	Walter Payton, vs Minnesota, 1977
Season:	1,852	Walter Payton, 1977
Career:	16,726	Walter Payton, 1975-87

Passing:

Most TD Passes Game:	7	Sid Luckman, vs N.Y. Giants, 1943
Season:	28	Sid Luckman, 1943
Career:	137	Sid Luckman, 1939-50

Receiving

Most TD Passes Game:	4	Harlon Hill, vs San Francisco, 1954
	4	Mike Ditka, vs Los Angeles, 1963
Season:	13	Dick Gordon, 1970
	13	Ken Kavanaugh, 1947
Career:	50	Ken Kavanaugh, 1940-41, 1945-50

Scoring

Most Points Game:	36	Gale Sayers, vs San Francisco, 1965
Season:	144	Kevin Butler, 1985
Career:	750	Walter Payton, 1975-87
Most TDs Game:	6	Gale Sayers, vs San Francisco, 1965
Season:	22	Gale Sayers, 1965
Career:	125	Walter Payton, 1975-87

DALLAS COWBOYS

TEAM DIRECTORY: Owner/Pres./GM: Jerry Jones; VP-Pro Personnel: Bob Ackles; Pub. Rel. Dir.: Greg Aiello. Head Coach: Jimmy Johnson. Home field: Texas Stadium (65,024). Colors: Royal blue, metallic blue and white.

SCOUTING REPORT

OFFENSE: Welcome to the 1990s and the Age of Aikman.

Forget the glory days of the not-so-recent past. The Cowboys' fortunes now ride on Troy Aikman's multimillion-dollar arm. Aikman's legit, despite his poor numbers as a rookie (155-of-293, 1,749 yards, 9 TDs, 18 int.). His biggest problem is finding somebody to throw to.

Linebacker Eugene Lockhart topped the NFL in tackles.

Michael Irvin's health is questionable, as are James Dixon's hands. Ex-Bear Dennis McKinnon should provide some stability. Tight end Jay Novacek figures as a good Plan-B acquisition. Add rookie wide receiver Alex Wright.

Who will be carrying the load for the Cowboys' running game? The Cowboys hope it will be rookie running back Emmitt Smith. Daryl Johnston is a solid blocker and hard-nosed runner, but not the one to build the running attack around. Keith Jones and Tommy Agee are two more Plan-Bs.

The offensive line is steady, if unspectacular. Mark Stepnowski is solid and ex-Ram Tony Slaton should be a big help.

DEFENSE: The unit got better and better as the year went on. After giving up 29 points a game through the first half of the season, the Cowboys gave up an average of 20 points in the second half.

Jim Jeffcoat was the best of an otherwise inferior defensive line. The inability of the line to stop the run was one of the reasons why linebacker Eugene Lockhart ended up leading the NFL in tackles (222). As a group, the Cowboy linebackers were excellent at stopping the run, but were extremely vulnerable to short passes.

Jimmy Johnson will have to build his secondary from scratch. There were no guaranteed jobs going into training camp.

KICKING GAME: Mike Saxon is a decent punter, but the kicking game is in shambles. Luis Zendejas was 14-for-24 with the Eagles and Cowboys and may find himself out of a job. The return game featured Dixon, who averaged 25.1 per kick return. The punt-return team wasn't quite as successful.

THE ROOKIES: Herschel Walker won't be missed when Florida State's Smith, the Cowboys' first pick, a junior, takes the field. Auburn's Wright, an Al Toon clone, will make Aikman a very happy quarterback. Jimmy Jones, who played for Jimmy Johnson at Miami, could step into the starting lineup at defensive tackle.

OUTLOOK: There's reason to be encouraged, but the prospects for 1990 would have been a whole lot better if the Cowboys (1-15 last year) hadn't squandered the first selection in this year's draft for Steve Walsh.

Face it, Dallas isn't going to the playoffs this year or next, but a leap out of the cellar isn't an unrealistic goal for Johnson.

COWBOYS VETERAN ROSTER

HEAD COACH—Jimmy Johnson. Assistant Coaches—Hubbard Alexander, Joe Brodsky, Dave Campo, Butch Davis, Steve Hoffman, Alan Lowry, Dick Nolan, Jerry Rhome, Dave Shula, Dave Wannstedt, Tony Wise.

No.	Name	Pos.	Ht.	Wt.	NFL Exp.	College
32	Agee, Tommie	RB	6-0	218	3	Auburn
8	Aikman, Troy	QB	6-3	220	2	UCLA
36	Albritton, Vince	S	6-2	214	7	Washington
31	Ankrom, Scott	S	6-1	194	2	Texas Christian
40	Bates, Bill	S	6-1	199	8	Tennessee
79	Broughton, Willie	DT	6-5	275	4	Miami
75	Carter, Jon	DT	6-4	273	2	Pittsburgh
	Cheek, Louis	T	6-6	295	3	Texas A&M
58	Cooks, Terrence	LB	6-0	230	2	Nicholls State
55	Del Rio, Jack	LB	6-4	236	6	Southern California
86	Dixon, James	WR	5-10	181	2	Houston
85	Folsom, Steve	TE	6-5	240	5	Utah
38	Francis, Ron	CB	5-9	186	4	Baylor
	Gibson, Antonio	S	6-3	204	5	Cincinnati
66	Gogan, Kevin	T	6-7	309	4	Washington
60	Hamel, Dean	DT	6-3	276	6	Tulsa
	Harris, Rod	WR	5-10	183	2	Texas A&M
45	Hendrix, Nanny	CB	5-10	186	5	Utah
30	Holt, Issiac	CB	6-2	202	6	Alcorn State
20	Horton, Ray	S	5-11	190	8	Washington
99	Howard, David	LB	6-2	230	6	Long Beach State
88	Irvin, Michael	WR	6-2	202	3	Miami
77	Jeffcoat, Jim	DE	6-5	253	8	Arizona State
84	Jennings, Keith	TE	6-4	251	2	Clemson
	Johnson, Greg	G	6-4	295	2	Oklahoma
	Johnson, Steve	TE	6-6	245	2	Virginia Tech
91	Johnson, Walter	LB	6-0	240	4	Louisiana Tech
48	Johnson, Daryl	RB	6-2	237	2	Syracuse
72	Jones, Ed	DE	6-9	270	16	Tennessee State
	Jones, Keith	RB	5-10	182	2	Nebraska
68	Ker, Crawford	G	6-3	286	6	Florida
15	Laufenberg, Babe	QB	6-3	203	5	Indiana
	Lee, Greg	CB-S	6-2	204	2	Arkansas State
56	Lockhart, Eugene	LB	6-3	230	7	Houston
83	Martin, Kelvin	WR	5-9	163	4	Boston College
81	McKinnon, Dennis	WR	6-1	185	7	Florida State
61	Newton, Nate	G	6-3	318	5	Florida A&M
73	Noonan, Danny	DT	6-4	270	4	Nebraska
51	Norton, Ken	LB	6-2	234	3	UCLA
89	Novacek, Jay	TE	6-4	235	6	Wyoming
64	Rafferty, Tom	C	6-3	265	15	Penn State
	Robinson, Lybrant	DE	6-5	250	2	Delaware State
39	Sargent, Broderick	RB	5-11	220	4	Baylor
4	Saxon, Mike	P	6-3	196	6	San Diego State
35	Scott, Kevin	RB	5-9	177	3	Stanford
94	Shannon, Randy	LB	6-1	221	2	Miami
87	Shepard, Derrick	WR	5-10	187	3	Oklahoma
65	Slaton, Tony	C-G	6-3	280	7	Southern California
	Smith, Tim	RB	5-11	222	3	Texas Tech
57	Smith, Vinson	LB	6-2	230	2	East Carolina
54	Solomon, Jesse	LB	6-0	235	5	Florida State
70	Stepnoski, Mark	C-G	6-2	269	2	Pittsburgh
25	Tautalatasi, Junior	RB	5-11	208	5	Washington State
92	Tolbert, Tony	DE	6-6	241	2	Texas-El Paso
71	Tuinei, Mark	T	6-5	286	8	Hawaii
95	Walen, Mark	DT	6-5	267	3	UCLA
3	Walsh, Steve	QB	6-3	195	2	Miami
	Washington, James	S	6-1	196	3	UCLA
78	Widell, Dave	T	6-6	292	3	Boston College
23	Williams, Robert	CB	5-10	184	4	Baylor
96	Willis, Mitch	DT	6-8	285	5	Southern Methodist
6	Zendejas, Luis	D	5-9	179	4	Arizona State
76	Zimmerman, Jeff	G	6-3	313	3	Florida

TOP DRAFT CHOICES

Rd.	Name	Sel. No.	Pos.	Ht.	Wt.	College
1	Smith, Emmitt	17	RB	5-10	201	Florida
2	Wright, Alexander	26	WR	5-11	184	Auburn
3	Jones, Jimmie	64	DT	6-6	261	Miami
5	*Smagala, Stan	123	DB	5-9	189	Notre Dame
9	Gant, Kenneth	221	DB	5-11	178	Albany (Ga.) State
11	Harper, Dave	277	LB	6-1	220	Humboldt State

*Drafted by Raiders, traded to Cowboys

COWBOY PROFILES

JIM JEFFCOAT 29 6-5 263 — Defensive End

Had one of the best years of his career... Recorded 11½ sacks after getting just 1½ in first seven weeks... Returned a fumble 77 yards for a touchdown against the Redskins... The opportunistic Jeffcoat now has four touchdowns in his career... Two of his interceptions/touchdowns have come against Phil Simms following tips by Ed "Too Tall" Jones... Has 60½ sacks in the last six seasons, the most on the Cowboys... Outstanding in Arizona State's 1983 Fiesta Bowl victory over Oklahoma, recording 16 tackles, causing a fumble and getting a sack... Cowboys' first-round pick in 1983... Born April 1, 1961, in Cliffwood, N.J.... Earned $340,000 last year.

EUGENE LOCKHART 29 6-2 230 — Linebacker

All-Pro honors from Associated Press after leading the NFL with 222 tackles... His tackle total established a team record... Had at least 10 tackles in every game... Added two sacks, two interceptions and eight passes defensed... Recovered a fumble against the Packers and returned it 40 yards for a touchdown... Recorded 19 tackles against the Cards... In his six years in the league, Lockhart has 758 tackles... Sixth-round pick out of Houston in 1984... Started at middle linebacker as a rookie... Born March 8, 1961, in Crockett, Tex... Earned $350,000 last year.

TROY AIKMAN 23 6-3 220 — Quarterback

Earned only mixed reviews after an inconclusive rookie season... Missed five weeks with broken left index finger... Set NFL rookie single-game passing record with 379 yards against the Cards... Threw four touchdown passes against the Rams... Effective scrambler, was 11 for 14 running for first downs on third-down plays... Completed 155 of 293

DALLAS COWBOYS 69

passes for 1,749 yards... Horrendous interception (18) vs. touchdown (9) ratio... Quarterback rating of 55.7 was less than half of league leader Joe Montana's 112.4... Ranked second on the team in rushing with 302 yards on 38 carries... First player selected in the 1989 draft, out of UCLA... Ranks third on all-time NCAA passing list... Began his college career at Oklahoma, but transferred after two years... Born Nov. 21, 1966, in Cerritos, Cal.... Signed a six-year deal worth $11.037 million.

JAMES DIXON 23 5-10 181   Wide Receiver

Enjoyed an excellent rookie season... Took advantage of opportunity created by injuries to catch 24 passes for 477 yards... Averaged 19.9 yards per reception... Second in the NFC in kick returns, averaging 25.1 yards... Returned a kickoff 97 yards for a touchdown against the Chiefs... Had six catches for 203 yards against the Cardinals... Ignored in the draft despite putting up large numbers as part of the University of Houston's run-and-shoot offense... Finished second in the country (behind teammate Jason Phillips) in receiving as a senior in 1988, with 102 catches for 1,103 yards and 11 TDs... Picked up by the Cowboys as a free agent... Born Feb. 2, 1967, in Vernon, Tex.

MARK STEPNOWSKI 23 6-2 269   Center

Look for Stepnowski as a mainstay on the Cowboys' offensive line for years to come... Earned starting job as rookie last year, starting final four games... Excellent career at Pitt, where he was a starter as a freshman... Was two-time academic All-American as well as AP All-American... Outland Award finalist... His father Marty was a teammate of former Raiders' wide receiver Fred Biletnikoff at Erie Tech High in 1960 ... Born Jan. 20, 1967, in Erie, Pa.

DARYL JOHNSTON 24 6-2 237　　　　　　　　Fullback

The Cowboys are hoping that Johnston will be a fixture in their backfield... Excellent pass-blocker... Ran the ball only 67 times for 212 yards as a rookie... Caught 16 passes for 133 yards and three TDs... Was overshadowed at Syracuse, where QB Don McPherson got most of the attention... Also serves as the Cowboys' backup punter... Had a 71-yard punt at Syracuse... His mother had to hide the kitchen chairs when he was five, so he wouldn't throw them... Second-round pick of the Cowboys in 1989... Class valedictorian in high school (4.0 GPA)... Born Feb. 10, 1966, in Youngstown, N.Y.

DENNIS McKINNON 29 6-1 185　　　　　Wide Receiver

Arrived as a Plan-B free agent from the Chicago Bears... Caught 28 passes for the Bears last year for 418 yards and three touchdowns... Lost his starting job midway through the season after leading the Bears in 1988 with 45 receptions for 704 yards... Returned two punts for touchdowns in 1987, one for 94 yards against the Giants and one for 65 yards against the Bucs... Missed the entire 1986 season after knee surgery... Caught TD passes in each of the first five games of the 1985 season... Made the Bears in 1983 as a free-agent special-teams specialist... Played at Florida State... Born Aug. 12, 1961, in Quitman, Ga.

RAY HORTON 30 5-11 190　　　　　　　　Free Safety

The best of the Cowboys' 1989 Plan-B acquisitions, he was signed as an unprotected free agent after six seasons with the Bengals... Finished second on the Cowboys in tackles with 117... Led all defensive backs in tackles... Started 14 games... Second-round pick by the Bengals in 1983 out of Washington... Earned All-American honors... Had a career-high five

DALLAS COWBOYS 71

interceptions as a rookie, including a 55-yarder for a touchdown
... Played in 1988 Super Bowl as a nickel back... Twice passed
his fire-fighters' exam... Climbed the famous K-2 Mountain in
China... Born April 12, 1960, in Tacoma, Wash.... Earned
$360,000 last year.

STEVE WALSH 23 6-3 195   Quarterback

Cowboys gave up what proved to be the first pick of the 1990 draft when they selected Walsh in the supplemental draft... He was shopped around, but the Cowboys couldn't get the price they wanted... Clause in his contract allowed him to veto deal to the Vikings... One of five players on the squad who played for Jimmy Johnson at the University of Miami... Started five games after Troy Aikman broke his finger... Completed 110 of 219 passes for 1,371 yards... Threw five touchdown passes, but was intercepted nine times.... Had 23-1 record as a starter at Miami... Led the Hurricanes from a 30-14 deficit to 31-30 victory against Michigan... Needed only two starts as a pro to have more losses than he did in entire college career... Born Dec. 1, 1966, in St. Paul, Minn.... Earned $1.65 million last year.

TONY SLATON 29 6-3 280   Center/Guard

Buried behind All-Pro center Doug Smith with the Rams, Slaton is hoping for a chance to start with the Cowboys... Signed as a Plan-B free agent in March... Has played at both guard and center... Excellent run-blocker... Started five games in 1985 at center when Smith went down... Drafted in the sixth round of the 1984 draft by the Bills... Failed to survive his initial training camp, but was immediately signed by the Rams ... Was an All-American at USC... Blocked for Marcus Allen during his Heisman season... Raises tropical fish in his spare time... Born April 12, 1961, in Merced, Cal.

KELVIN MARTIN 25 5-9 163   Wide Receiver

Led the Cowboys with 46 receptions for 644 yards... Missed the final five games of the year after injuring his knee... Began his career as a punt-returner, but has emerged as the Cowboys' top receiver... Returned four punts for an 8.0 average... Returned 66 punts for 8.7-yard average in first two seasons... Caught 49 passes for 622 yards in 1988... Fourth-round draft pick in 1987... Finished in the top 10 in the country in punt returns in each of his last three years at Boston College... Led the nation with 19.6 yards per catch in 1985... Born May 14, 1965, in Jacksonville, Fla.... Earned $115,000 last year.

COACH JIMMY JOHNSON:

Suffered through a difficult rookie season, winning only once in 16 games... Sacrificed a shot at more victories in 1989 by going with younger players and by trading away Herschel Walker... Good friend, former college teammate and roommate of team owner Jerry Jones... Lost more games with the Cowboys last year than he had in entire five-year career at the University of Miami... Compiled a 52-9 record at Miami, winning the national championship in 1987... Has long been surrounded by controversy... His Miami teams were accused of being among the dirtiest in college football... He began a feud with Buddy Ryan last year, accusing the Eagles' coach of offering bounties on his players... Played defensive tackle on Arkansas' 1964 national championship team... Was a head coach at Oklahoma State, where he compiled a 29-25-3 record in five seasons... Only the second head coach in Cowboys' history... Born July 16, 1942, in Port Arthur, Tex.

LONGEST PASS PLAY

DON MEREDITH TO BOB HAYES

They were a supercharged battery—the Cowboys' Don Meredith and Bob Hayes—on Nov. 13, 1966, in Washington. With Meredith pitching and Hayes catching nine passes, they teamed for 246 yards, the big one coming in the third quarter with the Cowboys on their own five-yard line.

"Okay," Meredith said in the huddle, "this one goes for 95."

Meredith backed up into his end zone, waited for Hayes to get past Redskin cornerback Lonnie Sanders and threw it. Hayes caught the ball on the Skins' 35 and was gone.

"I didn't fake nobody," Hayes said. "I was just out of the blocks and flew as fast as I could."

On a day when Meredith connected on 21 of 29 passes for 406 yards, Dallas edged the Redskins, 31-30, on the way to the NFL title game. They'd lose that one, 34-27, to Green Bay, which went on to win Super Bowl I over Kansas City, 35-10.

INDIVIDUAL COWBOY RECORDS

Rushing

Most Yards Game:	206	Tony Dorsett, vs Philadelphia, 1978
Season:	1,646	Tony Dorsett, 1981
Career:	12,036	Tony Dorsett, 1977-87

Passing

Most TD Passes Game:	5	Eddie LeBaron, vs Pittsburgh, 1962
	5	Don Meredith, vs N.Y. Giants, 1966
	5	Don Meredith, vs Philadelphia, 1966
	5	Don Meredith, vs Philadelphia, 1968
	5	Craig Morton, vs Philadelphia, 1969
	5	Craig Morton, vs Houston, 1970
	5	Danny White, vs N.Y. Giants, 1983
Season:	29	Danny White, 1983
Career:	154	Danny White, 1976-87

Receiving

Most TD Passes Game:	4	Boy Hayes, vs Houston, 1970
Season:	14	Frank Clarke, 1962
Career:	71	Bob Hayes, 1965-74

Scoring

Most Points Game:	24	Dan Reeves, vs Atlanta, 1967
	24	Bob Hayes, vs Houston, 1970
	24	Calvin Hill, vs Buffalo, 1971
	24	Duane Thomas, vs St. Louis, 1971
Season:	123	Rafael Septien, 1983
Career:	874	Rafael Septien, 1978-86
Most TDs Game:	4	Dan Reeves, vs Atlanta, 1967
	4	Bob Hayes, vs Houston, 1970
	4	Calvin Hill, vs Buffalo, 1971
	4	Duane Thomas, vs St. Louis, 1971
Season:	16	Dan Reeves, 1966
Career:	86	Tony Dorsett, 1977-87

DETROIT LIONS

TEAM DIRECTORY: Pres.: William Clay Ford; Exec. VP/Chief Exec. Off.: Charles Schmidt; VP-Player Personnel: Jerry Vainisi; Dir. Pub. Rel.: Bill Keenist; Head Coach: Wayne Fontes. Home field: Pontiac Silverdome (80,500). Colors: Honolulu blue and silver.

SCOUTING REPORT

OFFENSE: Thanks to Barry Sanders and the jelling of the run-and-shoot offense, the 7-9 Lions won their final five games of 1989. The same offense that struggled through the first half of the year, averaged 28 points a game in the final month.

LB Chris Spielman made Pro Bowl in his second year.

76 THE COMPLETE HANDBOOK OF PRO FOOTBALL

Now that Andre Ware is on the scene, the run-and-shoot should fire on all cylinders. The 1989 Heisman Trophy winner, a junior out of Houston, is regarded as the most prolific run-and-shoot quarterback since Neil Lomax at Portland State. He has the physical tools to make the transition to the pro game. Since there are no guarantees, Rodney Peete remains as QB insurance.

The running game is no problem. Rookie of the Year Sanders (with an NFC-leading 1,470 yards, 5.3 avg.) is a natural and perfectly suited to the wide-open game.

Richard Johnson was the top receiver with 70 catches, but the Lions need another top-flight speedster. Plan-B acquisition Terry Greer, who was buried with the 49ers, will get his chance.

The offensive line is adequate, but outside of Lomas Brown, there are no standouts.

DEFENSE: Very good and getting better. There's talent everywhere. The defensive line is in excellent shape with All-Pro nose tackle Jerry Ball leading the way.

The linebacking corps is talented and deep. There's balance with All-Pro Chris Spielman on the inside and Mike Cofer and Jimmy Williams on the outside.

The secondary is led by Bennie Blades, a punishing tackler, and Terry Taylor, a top-flight cover man.

KICKING GAME: The Lions have been able to boast of exceptional special teams led by punt-returner Walter Stanley, kickoff-returner Mel Gray, kicker Eddie Murray and punter Jim Arnold. But they've lost Stanley to the Redskins via Plan B.

The kick coverage is also excellent, limiting the opposition to 8.1 yards per punt return and 16 yards per kick return.

THE ROOKIES: Ware is going to make things interesting and exciting. You can't ask for a better gun at the helm. The Lions also got some help on the defensive line, grabbing USC's Dan Owens and Pittsburgh's Mark Spindler, a junior. If Spindler's knee holds up, the Lions may have solved most of the defensive line problems.

OUTLOOK: Look for Wayne Fontes' Lions to bring even greater parity to the Central Division. Can this team win the title? It's possible. Could they finish as low as fourth? Equally possible. One thing is certain: the Lions will be one of the most exciting teams in the league.

LIONS VETERAN ROSTER

HEAD COACH—Wayne Fontes. Assistant Coaches—Don Clemons, Darrel Davis, Len Fontes, Frank Gansz, Bert Hill, June Jones, Dave Levy, Billie Matthews, Lamar Leachman, Herb Paterra, Charlie Sanders, Jerry Wampfler, Woody Widenhofer.

No.	Name	Pos.	Ht.	Wt.	NFL Exp.	College
32	Alexander, Bruce	CB	5-9	169	2	Stephen F. Austin
65	Andolsek, Eric	G	6-2	286	3	Louisiana State
6	Arnold, Jim	P	6-3	211	8	Vanderbilt
93	Ball, Jerry	NT	6-1	292	4	Southern Methodist
36	Blades, Bennie	S	6-1	221	3	Miami
97	Brooks, Kevin	DE-NT	6-6	278	6	Mighigan
75	Brown, Lomas	T	6-4	275	6	Florida
95	Brown, Mark	LB	6-2	240	8	Purdue
50	Caston, Toby	LB	6-1	243	4	Louisiana State
82	Clark, Robert	WR	5-11	173	3	North Carolina
30	Cocroft, Sherman	S	6-1	190	5	San Jose State
55	Cofer, Michael	LB	6-5	245	8	Tennessee
39	Crockett, Ray	CB	5-9	181	2	Baylor
67	Dallafior, Ken	G-C	6-4	279	6	Minnesota
79	Duckens, Mark	DE	6-4	270	2	Arizona State
77	Ferguson, Keith	DE	6-5	276	10	Ohio State
80	Ford, John	WR	6-2	204	2	Virginia
14	Gagliano, Bob	QB	6-3	196	6	Utah State
98	Gibson, Dennis	LB	6-2	243	4	Iowa State
53	Glover, Kevin	C-G	6-2	282	6	Maryland
23	Gray, Mel	WR-KR	5-9	166	5	Purdue
62	Green, Curtis	DE-NT	6-3	273	10	Alabama State
89	Greer, Terry	WR	6-1	192	5	Alabama State
58	Jamison, George	LB	6-1	228	4	Cincinnati
84	Johnson, Richard	WR	5-6	185	2	Colorado
57	Jones, Victor	LB	6-2	240	3	Virginia Tech
49	Judson, William	CB	6-1	192	9	South Carolina State
90	Karpinski, Keith	LB	6-3	225	2	Penn State
16	Long, Chuck	QB	6-4	221	5	Iowa
83	Matthews, Aubrey	WR	5-7	165	5	Delta State
29	McNorton, Bruce	CB	5-10	175	9	Georgetown (Ky.)
25	Miller, Chuck	CB-S	5-10	180	2	UCLA
44	Miller, John	S	6-1	195	2	Michigan State
3	Murray, Eddie	K	5-10	175	11	Tulane
51	Noga, Niko	LB	6-1	235	7	Hawaii
26	Painter, Carl	RB	5-9	188	3	Hampton Institute
9	Peete, Rodney	QB	6-0	195	2	Southern California
96	Pete, Lawrence	NT	6-0	282	2	Nebraska
24	Phillips, Jason	WR	5-7	168	2	Houston
31	Richard, Gary	CB	5-10	176	2	Missouri
73	Salem, Harvey	T-G	6-6	289	8	California
20	Sanders, Barry	RB	5-8	203	2	Oklahoma State
64	Sanders, Eric	T-G	6-7	286	10	Nevada-Reno
54	Spielman, Chris	LB	6-1	247	3	Ohio State
21	Taylor, Terry	CB	5-10	191	7	Southern Illinois
60	Utley, Mike	G-T	6-6	279	2	Washington State
28	Welch, Herb	S	5-11	180	6	UCLA
35	White, William	CB-S	5-10	191	3	Ohio State
4	William, Byron	WR	6-2	185	3	Texas-Arlington
76	Williams, Eric	DE	6-4	286	7	Washington State
59	Williams, Jimmy	LB	6-3	225	9	Nebraska

TOP DRAFT CHOICES

Rd.	Name	Sel. No.	Pos.	Ht.	Wt.	College
1	Ware, Andre	7	QB	6-2	205	Houston
2	Owens, Dan	35	DE	6-3	268	USC
3	Spindler, Marc	62	DE	6-5	277	Pittsburgh
4	Hinckley, Rob	90	LB	6-5	246	Stanford
4	Oldham, Chris	105	DB	5-9	183	Oregon

LION PROFILES

BARRY SANDERS 22 5-8 203 — Running Back

By the time his first NFL game was over, any doubts that Sanders would become one of the great stars in the league were erased... Honors included NFC Rookie of the Year, All-Pro and Pro Bowl selection... Though he missed all of training camp and didn't play until midway through Week Two, he led the NFC with 1,470 yards on 280 carries... Broke Billy Sims' team record of 1,437 yards... Added 24 receptions for 282 yards... Explosively fast with excellent moves... His game is perfect for the Lions' run-and-shoot offense... Third player taken in the draft after Heisman Trophy year for Oklahoma State... Set 13 NCAA single-season records, including touchdowns (39), rushing yards (2,628) and all-purpose yards (3,249)... Played much of his college career in the shadow of Thurmon Thomas... Born July 16, 1968, in Wichita, Kan.... Signed a five-year, $6.1-million contract prior to rookie season.

RODNEY PEETE 24 6-0 195 — Quarterback

Suffered through an injury-riddled rookie season... Peete was slated to start in the season-opener, but in the Lions' final preseason game, he sprained his left knee... Got first start in Week Six against Tampa Bay and earned NFC Offensive Player of the Week honors, completing 17 of 31 passes for 268 yards and rushing for 78 yards and one touchdown... Reinjured the knee in Week 11, returned in Week 13, but was injured again... Completed 103 of 195 passes for 1,479 yards, with five touchdowns and nine interceptions... Rushed for 148 yards on 33 carries... Though he finished second in the Heisman Trophy balloting to Barry Sanders, Peete wasn't selected until the sixth round... A first-team All-American at USC... Broke virtually every Trojan passing record... His father is an assistant coach with the Packers... Born March 16, 1966, in Tuscon, Ariz.

DETROIT LIONS 79

MEL GRAY 29 5-9 166 — Wide Receiver/KR

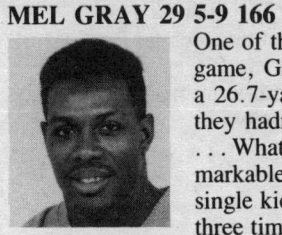

One of the most electrifying return men in the game, Gray led the NFC in kick returns with a 26.7-yard average... Made the Saints wish they hadn't let him go as a Plan-B free agent ... What makes the average even more remarkable is that he did it without returning a single kick over 57 yards... Ran the ball only three times for 22 yards... Had a solid season for New Orleans in 1988... Finished fifth in the NFC in kick returns (20.9 average) and second in the NFL in punt returns (12.2 average)... Led the NFL in punt returns in 1987... Began his career with the USFL's Los Angeles Express... Led Purdue in rushing in his two years there... Born March 16, 1961, in Williamsburg, Va.... Earned $400,000 last year.

EDDIE MURRAY 34 5-10 175 — Kicker

Earned Pro Bowl and All-Pro honors by missing only one field-goal attempt all season... What made his achievement so remarkable was that this was his second straight season in which he connected on 20 of 21 field-goal attempts... The only other kicker in league history to miss only a single attempt in a full season was Mark Moseley of the Washington Redskins... Stands in fourth place on the NFL's all-time field-goal kickers' list with a .763 percentage... First in the NFC among active scorers with 943 points... Was the Pro Bowl MVP as a rookie in 1980... Set an NFL playoff record with a 54-yard field goal against the 49ers in 1983... Seventh-round draft pick in 1980 out of Minnesota... Born Aug. 28, 1956, in Halifax, Nova Scotia ... Earned $350,000 last year.

RICHARD JOHNSON 28 5-6 185 — Wide Receiver

After bouncing around several NFL camps, found a home in Detroit... Thrived in the Lions' wide-open offense... Signed as a free agent on March 15, 1989... Led the Lions in receptions (70), receiving yards (1,091) and touchdown catches (8)... Averaged 15.6 yards per catch... Ran 12 times for 38 yards... His 70 catches was the second-highest total in

Lions' history behind James Jones (77 catches in 1984)... His 1,091 yards was also the second-highest total behind Pat Studstill (1,266 yards in 1966)... NFL's Offensive Player of the Week in Week 13 after an eight-catch, 248-yard performance against the Saints... Played his college ball at Colorado... Born Oct. 19, 1961, in San Pedro, Cal.

CHRIS SPIELMAN 24 6-1 247   Linebacker

One of the best linebackers in the game and getting better all the time... Earned a starting job in the Pro Bowl in only his second year in the league... Led the Lions with 125 tackles... Recorded 4½ sacks and forced one fumble... Broke a team record with 153 tackles as a rookie... Has started all 32 games in his career... Was the Lombardi Award winner after his senior season at Ohio State... The Buckeyes' all-time leading tackler, Spielman averaged over 10 tackles a game for his college career... This potential Hall of Famer grew up, appropriately enough, in Canton, Ohio, where he was born on Oct. 11, 1965... Earned $190,000 last year.

MICHAEL COFER 30 6-5 245   Linebacker

After going to the Pro Bowl in 1988, 1989 was a year filled with injuries and frustration... Cofer missed nine starts as he was plagued by injuries to his knee, shoulder and arch... Despite his limited playing time, Cofer still managed to tie for the team lead with 9½ sacks... Finished 13th on the team with only 34 tackles... Enjoyed his best season in 1988, when he had 12 sacks and 75 tackles... Relies mostly on his excellent speed and quickness to get to opposing quarterbacks... Third-round draft choice in 1985 out of Tennessee... Born April 7, 1960, in Knoxville, Tenn.... Earned $700,000 last year.

DETROIT LIONS 81

JERRY BALL 25 6-1 292 — Nose Tackle

After three excellent seasons, Ball finally made it to the Pro Bowl... Named the team's defensive MVP by his teammates... Recorded 73 tackles and nine sacks... Recorded two sacks against the Vikings and Packers... Recovered three fumbles... Ball's statistics do not reveal the way he was able to collapse opponents' pass-blocking, forcing quarterbacks out of the pocket and allowing his teammates to collect easy sacks... Named as a Pro Bowl alternate in 1988... In his three seasons, he has started every non-strike game and carries a 44-game starting streak into the 1990 season... Earned All-American honors at SMU... Was an all-state fullback in high school and had the second-longest high-school shotput in 1982... Born Dec. 15, 1964, in Beaumont, Tex.... Earned $525,000 last year.

LOMAS BROWN 27 6-4 275 — Tackle

Must be feeling jinxed after yet another Pro Bowl snub... Had another excellent year despite playing most of the season on a gimpy left knee... Must be given much of the credit for Barry Sanders' running spree... Pro Bowl alternate after the 1987 and 1988 seasons... Started all 16 games and has now missed only one start in his five-year career... Two-time All-American at Florida... Played inside linebacker in high school, where he earned all-state honors... First-round draft choice in 1985... Born March 30, 1963, in Miami, Fla.... Earned $425,000 last year.

JIM ARNOLD 29 6-3 211 — Punter

Missed a trip to the Pro Bowl after two consecutive starts... Averaged 43.1 yards per punt... In 1988, led the NFC in punting average (42.4 yards) and net average (35.9 yards)... Signed with the Lions as a free agent in 1986... Set an NFL record in 1987 with a net average of 39.6 yards... Set a Pro Bowl record after the 1987 season, averaging 49.6 yards per kick... Drafted by the Chiefs in the fifth round in 1983... Led the NFL in punting in 1984 (44.9-yard avg.)... Slumped in 1985, averaging only 41.2 yards per kick, and was waived by the Chiefs... Has performed as a standup comic at Mark Ridley's

82   THE COMPLETE HANDBOOK OF PRO FOOTBALL

Comedy Castle... Led the nation in punting in his senior year at Vanderbilt (45.8-yard avg.)... Born Jan. 31, 1961, in Dalton, Ga.... Earned $250,000 last year.

COACH WAYNE FONTES: A season that began with the frustration of a 0-5 start finished with the Lions winning seven of their final nine games ... Fontes has to be given credit for keeping his team from falling apart... Rather than give up on the Lions' controversial Silver Stretch offense, Fontes embraced it and it paid off at the end of the season... Basically a defense-oriented coach, Fontes is building one of the top units in the game... Last year was Fontes' first as a full-time head coach... He became the interim head coach following the firing of Darryl Rogers in the middle of the 1988 season... Served four years as the Lions' defensive coordinator after spending nine years with the Tampa Bay Bucs... Played defensive back with the Jets in 1963 and 1964... Still holds the Jets' record for longest interception return... Did his college coaching at Dayton, Iowa and USC... Played his college ball at Michigan State... Born Feb. 2, 1940, in Canton, Ohio.

LONGEST PASS PLAY

KARL SWEETAN TO PAT STUDSTILL

Behind four Johnny Unitas TD passes, the Colts were leading the Lions, 38-7, in the fourth quarter on Oct. 16, 1966, at Baltimore.

Lion quarterback Milt Plum, suffering from a sprained knee and a bruised ego, was benched in favor of rookie Karl Sweetan. With the ball on the Lion one-yard-line, Sweetan threw a dart to Studstill on the Detroit 40. Studstill outran Colt safety Bob Boyd for the remaining 60 yards and the Sweetan-Studstill duo had a 99-yarder that set the Detroit record and tied the NFL mark.

Of course, Baltimore won the game, 45-14.

INDIVIDUAL LION RECORDS

Rushing

Most Yards Game:	198	Bob Hoernschemeyer, vs N.Y. Yanks, 1950
Season:	1,470	Barry Sanders, 1989
Career:	5,106	Billy Sims, 1980-84

Passing

Most TD Passes Game:	5	Gary Danielson, vs Minnesota, 1978
Season:	26	Bobby Layne, 1951
Career:	118	Bobby Layne, 1950-58

Receiving

Most TD Passes Game:	4	Cloyce Box, vs Baltimore, 1950
Season:	15	Cloyce Box, 1952
Career:	35	Terry Barr, 1957-65

Scoring

Most Points Game:	24	Cloyce Box, vs Baltimore, 1950
Season:	128	Doak Walker, 1950
Career:	943	Eddie Murray, 1980-89
Most TDs Game:	4	Cloyce Box, vs Baltimore, 1950
Season:	16	Billy Sims, 1980
Career:	47	Billy Sims, 1980-84

GREEN BAY PACKERS

TEAM DIRECTORY: Chairman: Judge Robert J. Parins; Pres.: Bob Harlan; Sec.: Peter Platten III; Exec. VP-Football Operations: Tom Braatz; Exec. Dir. Pub. Rel.: Lee Remmel; Head Coach: Lindy Infante. Home fields: Lambeau Field (59,543) and County Stadium, Milwaukee (56,051). Colors: Green and gold.

SCOUTING REPORT

OFFENSE: If the Packers had nothing more to offer than Don Majkowski throwing to Sterling Sharpe, they would still have one of the more dangerous offenses in the league. But there's more ...plenty more.

The running game came alive last year. Brent Fullwood and Keith Woodside, an impressive young tandem, combined for 1,094 yards on the ground and 78 receptions for 741 more yards. And they'll be joined by rookie running back Darnell Thompson.

Majkowski had more attempts than anyone in the league (599), completing 353 for 4,318 yards and 27 TDs. Sharpe was the NFL's leading pass receiver with 90 for 1,423 yards and 12 TDs. The Packers' other principal receivers include Perry Kemp and Herman Fontenot.

The offensive line is solid and should be better, assuming the emergence of Tony Mandarich.

DEFENSE: The Packers have a franchise defensive star in Tim Harris, but the rest of the unit isn't even close. The defensive line was inadequate, filled with players who would be backups anywhere else. The linebackers, outside of Harris, are mediocre. Hence the drafting of Tony Bennett.

The secondary has more talent than the rest of the defense, but this overaged bunch may start to spoil soon. The Plan-B acquisition of Jerry Holmes is a plus.

KICKING GAME: The only bright spot is Chris Jacke, who scored 108 points as a rookie. He was 42-for-42 on PATs and 22-for-28 on field goals. Punter Dale Hatcher, a Plan-B man from the Rams, will vie with incumbent Don Bracken.

The Packers' return game was awful. They averaged 18 yards per kick return (12th in the NFC) and 8.3 yards per punt return (11th in the NFC).

Their coverage teams were even worse. The Packers ranked

GREEN BAY PACKERS 85

Don Majkowski passed his way to first Pro Bowl berth.

last in the league in kick coverage (22.0 yards per return) and punt coverage (13.9 yards per return).

THE ROOKIES: The Packers had two first-round picks and both were widely second-guessed. Green Bay passed over a number of higher-rated linebackers and took Mississipi's Bennett. With their second first-round, they went for Minnesota's Thompson. Florida State's LeRoy Butler should help in the secondary.

PACKERS VETERAN ROSTER

HEAD COACH—Lindy Infante. Assistant Coaches—Greg Blanche, Hank Bullough, Joe Clark, Charlie Davis, Buddy Geis, Dick Jauron, Virgil Knight, Dick Moseley, Willie Peete, Howard Tippett.

No.	Name	Pos.	Ht.	Wt.	NFL Exp.	College
67	Ard, Billy	G	6-3	270	10	Wake Forest
76	Arley, Mike	T	6-5	285	2	San Diego State
83	Bland, Carl	WR	5-11	182	7	Virginia Union
61	Boyarsky, Jerry	NT	6-3	290	10	Pittsburgh
17	Bracken, Don	P	6-1	211	6	Michigan
62	Brock, Matt	DE	6-4	267	2	Oregon
32	Brown, Dave	CB-S	6-1	197	16	Michigan
93	Brown, Robert	DE	6-2	267	9	Virginia Tech
51	Bush, Blair	C	6-3	272	13	Washington
63	Campen, James	C-G	6-3	270	4	Tulane
26	Cecil, Chuck	S	6-0	184	3	Arizona
55	Clark, Greg	LB	6-1	234	3	Arizona State
92	Cribbs, James	DE	6-3	269	2	Memphis State
60	Croston, David	T	6-5	280	2	Iowa
49	Dee, Donnie	TE	6-4	252	3	Tulsa
56	Dent, Burnell	LB	6-1	236	5	Tulane
80	Didier, Clint	TE	6-5	240	9	Portland State
8	Dilweg, Anthony	QB	6-3	215	2	Duke
99	Dorsey, John	LB	6-2	243	6	Connecticut
94	Fears, Willie	DE-NT	6-5	285	2	Arkansas-Pine Bluff
27	Fontenot, Herman	RB	6-0	206	6	Louisiana State
30	Frazier, Paul	RB	5-8	196	2	NW Louisiana
21	Fullwood, Brent	RB	5-11	209	4	Auburn
23	Greene, Tiger	S	6-0	194	6	Western Carolina
35	Haddix, Michael	RB	6-2	227	8	Mississippi State
72	Hall, Mark	DE	6-4	285	2	SW Louisiana
65	Hallstrom, Ron	G	6-6	290	9	Iowa
97	Harris, Tim	LB	6-6	245	5	Memphis State
48	Harris, William	TE	6-5	254	3	Bishop (Tex.)
5	Hatcher, Dale	P	6-3	240	6	Clemson
50	Holland, Johnny	LB	6-2	221	4	Texas A&M
44	Holmes, Jerry	CB	6-2	175	9	West Virginia
13	Jacke, Chris	K	5-11	197	2	Texas-El Paso
24	Jakes, Van	CB	6-0	190	7	Kent State
88	Johnson, Flip	WR	5-10	183	3	McNeese State
53	Johnson, M.L.	LB	6-3	229	4	Hawaii
81	Kemp, Perry	WR	5-11	170	4	California State (Pa.)
10	Kiel, Blair	QB	6-0	214	6	Notre Dame
22	Lee, Mark	CB	5-11	189	11	Washington
7	Malkowski, Don	QB	6-2	207	4	Virginia
77	Mandarich, Tony	T	6-5	315	2	Michigan State
47	Martin, Tracy	WR	6-2	205	2	North Dakota
96	Miller, Shawn	DE	6-4	255	7	Utah State
57	Moran, Rich	G	6-2	275	6	San Diego State
37	Murphy, Mark	S	6-2	201	9	West Liberty
79	Nelson, Bob	NT	6-4	275	4	Miami
91	Noble, Brian	LB	6-3	252	6	Arizona State
6	Norseth, Mike	QB	6-2	205	3	Kansas
96	Patterson, Shawn	DE	6-5	261	3	Arizona State
28	Pitts, Ron	CB	5-10	175	5	UCLA
85	Query, Jeff	WR-KR	5-11	165	2	Millikin
75	Ruettgers, Ken	T	6-5	280	6	Southern California
84	Sharpe, Sterling	WR	5-11	202	3	South Carolina
89	Spagnola, John	TE	6-4	242	11	Yale
54	Stephen, Scott	LB	6-2	232	4	Arizona State
70	Uecker, Keith	G-T	6-5	284	7	Auburn
73	Veingrad, Alan	T	6-5	277	4	East Texas State
87	Weathers, Clarence	WR	5-9	180	8	Delaware State
52	Weddington, Mike	LB	6-4	245	5	Oklahoma
86	West, Ed	TE	6-1	243	7	Auburn
68	Winter, Blaise	DE-NT	6-3	275	6	Syracuse
33	Woodside, Keith	RB	5-11	213	3	Texas A&M
46	Workman, Vince	RB	5-10	193	2	Ohio State
64	Yarno, George	C-G	6-2	270	10	Washington State

TOP DRAFT CHOICES

Rd.	Name	Sel. No.	Pos.	Ht.	Wt.	College
1	Bennett, Tony	17	LB	6-1	234	Mississippi
1	Thompson, Darrell	19	RB	6-0	219	Minnesota
2	Butler, LeRoy	48	DB	5-11	193	Florida State
3	Houston, Bobby	75	LB	6-1	223	NC State
4	Harris, Jackie	102	TE	6-3	230	NE Louisiana

GREEN BAY PACKERS

OUTLOOK: The Packers' 10-6 record in Lindy Infante's third season was a deceptive one. They won four games by a single point and seven by four or fewer. Remember, also, that the Packers played the easiest schedule in the league. With the improvement in Detroit and a likely turnaround for the Bears, look for Green Bay to return to familiar territory, below the .500 mark.

PACKER PROFILES

DON MAJKOWSKI 26 6-2 207 — Quarterback

Emerged in 1989 as one of the league's top young quarterbacks, earning his first trip to the Pro Bowl in his first full season as a starter... Completed 353 of 599 passes for 4,381 yards ...His yardage led the NFL...Threw 27 touchdown passes (third in the league) but gave away 20 interceptions. Only Vinny Testaverde and Dan Marino threw more... Excellent runner, carried 75 times for 358 yards and five touchdowns... Split time with Randy Wright in 1988... Nicknamed "Magic" because his last name was so difficult to pronounce (Mah-cow-skee)... He was a longshot to make the team as a 10th-round pick out of Virginia... All-time Cavalier leading passer and leader in total offense... Born Feb. 25, 1964, in Depew, N.Y.... Earned $250,000 last year.

STERLING SHARPE 25 5-11 202 — Wide Receiver

Solidified his position among the league's elite receivers... Led the NFL with 90 receptions while ranking second only to Jerry Rice in receiving yards with 1,423... Pro Bowl starter ... First Packer to lead the NFL in receptions since Don Hutson did it in 1945... Also ranked second to Rice with 12 touchdown receptions, most by a Packer since 1956... Caught 55 passes as a rookie in 1988 for 791 yards and one touchdown... First-round pick out of South Carolina in 1988, where he set school records for receptions (163), receiving yards (2,444) and touchdowns (25)... Born April 6, 1965, in Glenville, Ga.... Earned $300,000 last year.

88 THE COMPLETE HANDBOOK OF PRO FOOTBALL

TIM HARRIS 25 6-6 245 — Linebacker

One of the biggest talents and biggest mouths in the game... Fortunately for him, he was able to put his money where his mouth was... Finished the season with 19½ sacks, second only to the Vikings' Chris Doleman... Had 72 tackles, including 68 unassisted... Led the team with four forced fumbles... Pro Bowl starter in his first trip to Honolulu... Recorded a diving interception off a Reggie White tip in the Pro Bowl... Has led the Packers in sacks in each of his four seasons in the league... Has 47½ sacks in his career... A steal on the fourth round of the 1986 draft out of Memphis State... Born Sept. 10, 1964, in Birmingham, Ala... Earned $600,000 last year.

BRENT FULLWOOD 26 5-11 209 — Running Back

Enjoyed his best year as a pro and began to live up to the high expectations that came with his first-round selection in 1987... Went to his first Pro Bowl... Rushed for 821 yards on 204 carries with five touchdowns... His rushing yardage was the most by a Packer since 1981... Added 19 receptions for 214 yards... Returned 11 kickoffs, averaging 22.1 yards per return... In 1988, led the Packers in rushing (483 yards), touchdowns (8) and kickoff returns (20.0 avg.)... Had a terrible rookie season... Rushed for only 274 yards, with no run longer than 18 yards... Was a unanimous All-American at Auburn... Led the SEC in rushing with 1,391 yards as a senior... Born Oct. 10, 1963, in Kissimmee, Fla.... Earned $300,000 last year.

CHRIS JACKE 23 5-11 197 — Kicker

Lived up to his billing as the top collegiate kicker in 1988... Led the Packers in scoring with 108 points... Nailed 22 of 28 field-goal attempts (78.6 percent) and was perfect on 42 extra points... Didn't miss a field-goal attempt until Week 5... Only Jan Stenerud has had better field-goal percentages in a Packers' uniform... Remarkably accurate from 40-49 yards (7 of 9)... Extremely accurate in college, hit on 27 of 29 field-goal attempts as a senior... Including his extra points, he was successful on 71 of 73 kicks... Sixth-round draft choice out of UTEP... Born May 9, 1967, in Richardson, Tex.

GREEN BAY PACKERS 89

KEITH WOODSIDE 26 5-11 213 — Running Back

His considerable achievements were overshadowed by Brent Fullwood... Though he carried the ball only 46 times, he gained 273 yards... His 5.9-yard average was among the league leaders... Greatest asset is his pass-catching ability... Caught 59 passes for 527 yards... Now has 98 receptions in his first two years in the league... Had the Packers' longest run of the season, a 68-yard touchdown... Solid rookie season in 1988 ... Rushed for 195 yards and caught 39 passes for 352 yards... Broke the SWC career receptions record with 109... Third-round draft choice out of Texas A&M... Born July 29, 1964, in Natchez, Miss... Earned $140,000 last year.

MARK MURPHY 32 6-2 201 — Strong Safety

Ageless wonder who has gotten better and better since becoming thirty-something... Finished third on the team in tackles with 93, including 79 unassisted... Intercepted three passes to bring his career total to 14... Had his most productive season in 1988, leading the Packers with 111 tackles and five interceptions ... Had six interceptions in his first seven seasons and has eight in his last two... Though he shaves his head, Murphy has a collection of over 300 hats to hide his bald pate... Came to the Packers as a free agent out of unheralded West Liberty State... Broke his hand prior to rookie season and wasn't activated until the final game of the year... Had a second rookie season in 1981 and was voted Packers' Rookie of the Year by his teammates... Born April 22, 1958, in Canton, Ohio... Earned $375,000 last year.

TONY MANDARICH 24 6-5 315 — Tackle

The highly touted offensive lineman turned into the biggest bust of the class of 1989... During his extended training-camp holdout, Mandarich threatened to throw away his football career and fight Mike Tyson... Missed the first two games of the year and struggled the rest of the way... Never started, but saw more and more action as the year went on... He has vowed to break into the starting lineup this season... Worked closely with offensive line coach Charlie Davis during the offseason... Has unbelievable speed (4.65 40-yard dash) for his size... Had a remarkable career at Michigan State... Though there are few statistics that reflect an offensive lineman's contributions, Mandarich shattered all the school records for "pancake blocks," blocks where the defender is knocked on his butt... Consumes 15,000 calories a day... Born Sept. 23, 1966, in Canada... Signed a five-year deal worth $5.15 million.

PERRY KEMP 28 5-11 170   **Wide Receiver**

This USFL refugee has found a home in Green Bay... Played for Lindy Infante at Jacksonville... Though he was overshadowed by Sterling Sharpe, Kemp was also a favored target for Majkowski... Caught 48 passes for 611 yards (12.7 yards per catch)... Caught two TD passes... Ran the ball five times for 43 yards... Had virtually identical stats in 1988, when he caught 48 passes for 620 yards... Came to the Packers as a free agent prior to the 1988 season... Played three games with the Browns in 1987, catching 12 passes for 224 yards... Played two years with Jacksonville Bulls of the USFL and then was out of a football job in 1986... Division II star at California University (Pa.)... Eleventh-round draft pick of the Bulls in 1984 ... Born Dec. 31, 1961, in McDonald, Pa.

JEFF QUERY 23 5-11 165   **Wide Receiver**

One of the sleepers of the 1989 draft, Query had a solid rookie season... Excellent speed (4.3 in the 40) combined with good hands... Caught 23 passes for 350 yards (15.2 yards per catch)... Established himself as the No. 1 punt-return man... Averaged 8.2 yards on 30 punt returns... Lasted until the fifth round of the 1989 draft because he played for tiny Milikin University in Illinois... In his four-year college career, averaged 21.4 yards per catch, had 28 TD catches, one TD run, three TDs on kick returns and two on punt returns... Born March 7, 1967, in Maroa, Ill.

COACH LINDY INFANTE: Give this man credit for one of the biggest turnarounds since Ronald Reagan left the Democratic Party... Started with a 4-12 team and a useless first-round pick, and still managed to lead the Packers to a 10-6 record in only his second year with the team... One of the great offensive minds in the game, Infante quickly took one of the worst offenses and turned it into one of the best... The Packers were at their best in close games... Prior to coming to the Packers, spent two years as the Browns' offensive coordinator... His last head-coaching job was with Jacksonville in the USFL... Did his college coaching at Florida, Memphis State and Tulane... Joined the pro coaching ranks with the Giants in 1977, then went to the Bengals... All-SEC defensive back at Florida... Played for Hamilton in the CFL... Born May 27, 1940, in Miami.

LONGEST PASS PLAY

TOBIN ROTE TO BILLY GRIMES

The Packers went to San Francisco on Dec. 10, 1950, hoping the final game of the season would bring an end to their six-game losing streak. The Packers were 3-8, the 49ers 2-9.

Green Bay got off to a big start early in the first quarter when Tobin Rote, on the Packer four-yard line, threw a screen pass to Billy Grimes, whose wall of blockers opened up a huge hole in the middle. Grimes went the distance for a 96-yarder.

But the 49ers scored the next four touchdowns and cruised to a 30-14 victory. The Rote-Grimes club record was small consolation.

INDIVIDUAL PACKER RECORDS

Rushing

Most Yards Game:	186	Jim Taylor, vs N.Y. Giants, 1961
Season:	1,474	Jim Taylor, 1962
Career:	8,207	Jim Taylor, 1958-66

Passing

Most TD Passes Game:	5	Cecil Isbell, vs Cleveland, 1942
	5	Don Horn, vs St. Louis, 1969
	5	Lynn Dickey, vs New Orleans, 1981
	5	Lynn Dickey, vs Houston, 1983
Season:	32	Lynn Dickey, 1983
Career:	152	Bart Starr, 1956-71

Receiving

Most TD Passes Game:	4	Don Hutson, vs Detroit, 1945
Season:	17	Don Hutson, 1943
Career:	99	Don Hutson, 1935-45

Scoring

Most Points Game:	33	Paul Hornung, vs Baltimore, 1961
Season:	176	Paul Hornung, 1960
Career:	823	Don Hutson, 1935-45
Most TDs Game:	5	Paul Hornung, vs Baltimore, 1961
Season:	19	Jim Taylor, 1962
Career:	105	Don Hutson, 1935-45

LOS ANGELES RAMS

TEAM DIRECTORY: Pres.: Georgia Frontiere; Exec. VP: John Shaw; VP-Media and Community Rel.: Marshall Klein; Dir. Operations: Dick Beam; Adm. Football Operations: Jack Faulkner; Dir. Player Personnel: John Math; Dir. Marketing: Pete Donovan; Dir. Pub. Rel.: John Oswald; Head Coach: John Robinson. Home field: Anaheim Stadium (69,007). Colors: Royal blue, gold and white.

Henry Ellard was fourth in NFL in reception yardage.

SCOUTING REPORT

OFFENSE: Can you find a weakness?

The passing game? Not with Jim Everett and his cannon.

The receivers? Are you kidding? With Henry Ellard and Flipper Anderson at the corners and Pete Holohan inside, Everett is like a kid in a candy store.

The running game? Well, the Rams felt they could afford to give up 1,000-yard Greg Bell. They've got Robert Delpino, who does everything, and young prospects in Cleveland Gary and Gaston Green. Throw ex-Seahawk Curt Warner into the game and you've got a dangerous backfield.

The offensive line? Sorry. This one is one of the best in the business. They've got three Pro Bowlers up front—Jackie Slater, Doug Smith and Tom Newberry. And their No. 1 pick was center Bern Brostek. You want a hole to run through? No problem. You want to sit in the pocket all day and look for a receiver? Take your time.

DEFENSE: Though this was one of the worst-rated defenses in the league (21st overall, 28th against the pass), they came through with brilliant efforts against the Eagles and the Giants in the playoffs.

Rookie Mike Piel was a pleasant addition to a weak defensive line. The Rams were able to cover up the inadequacies of the line by flooding the field with linebackers.

The secondary was considerably better than the statistics showed. Jerry Gray is a sensational cover man and Vince Newsome is a punishing hitter. The biggest problem will be filling LeRoy Irvin's considerable shoes. The addition of rookie safety Pat Terrell takes some of the sting out of the loss of Irvin.

KICKING: The Rams boast Mike Lansford (23-for-30), but the punting game is a major liability. The Rams are hoping that San Diego's Hank Ilesic will be a big improvement on Dale Hatcher.

The Rams' return games were neither a strength nor a liability. They pretty much gave up what they got. On kick returns, the Rams averaged 19.8 while giving up 19.4. On punt returns, the Rams edged the opposition 9.5 yards per return to 9.3.

THE ROOKIES: The Rams have always depended on a solid offensive line and kept up the tradition by taking Washington's 300-pound Brostek. They were shocked to find USC's Terrell,

RAMS VETERAN ROSTER

HEAD COACH—John Robinson. Assistant Coaches—Larry Brooks, Dick Coury, Artie Gigantino, Marv Goux, Gil Haskell, Hudson Houck, Steve Shafer, Fritz Shurmur, Norval Turner, Fred Whittingham, Ernie Zampese.

No.	Name	Pos.	Ht.	Wt.	NFL Exp.	College
83	Anderson, Willie	WR	6-0	172	3	UCLA
57	Bethune, George	LB	6-4	240	2	Alabama
88	Carter, Pat	TE	6-4	250	3	Florida State
84	Cox, Aaron	WR	5-9	178	3	Arizona State
72	Cox, Robert	T	6-5	285	5	UCLA
14	Craig, Paco	WR	5-10	170	2	UCLA
39	Delpino, Robert	RB	6-0	198	3	Missouri
80	Ellard, Henry	WR	5-11	180	8	Fresno State
11	Everett, Jim	QB	6-5	214	5	Purdue
51	Faryniarz, Brett	LB	6-3	235	3	San Diego State
43	Gary, Cleveland	RB	6-0	226	2	Miami
25	Gray, Jerry	CB	6-0	185	6	Texas
30	Green, Gaston	RB	5-11	192	3	UCLA
91	Greene, Kevin	LB	6-3	238	6	Auburn
70	Hawkins, Bill	DT	6-6	268	2	Miami
20	Henley, Darryl	CB	5-9	170	2	UCLA
9	Herrmann, Mark	QB	6-4	202	10	Purdue
28	Hicks, Clifford	CB	5-10	188	4	Oregon
81	Holohan, Pete	TE	6-4	232	10	Notre Dame
8	Ilesic, Hank	P	6-1	210	2	No college
31	Jackson, Alfred	CB	6-0	177	2	San Diego State
86	Johnson, Damone	TE	6-4	250	5	Cal Poly-SLO
52	Kelm, Larry	LB	6-4	240	4	Texas A&M
1	Lansford, Mike	K	6-0	190	9	Washington
67	Love, Duval	G	6-3	287	6	UCLA
90	McDonald, Mike	LB	6-1	235	6	Southern California
24	McGee, Buford	RB	6-0	210	7	Mississippi
71	Millnichik, Joe	G	6-5	275	4	North Carolina State
66	Newberry, Tom	G	6-2	285	5	Wisconsin-LaCrosse
26	Newman, Anthony	S	6-0	199	3	Oregon
22	Newsome, Vince	S	6-1	185	8	Washington
58	Owens, Mel	LB	6-2	240	10	Michigan
75	Pankey, Irv	T	6-5	295	11	Penn State
95	Piel, Mike	DT	6-4	263	2	Illinois
93	Reed, Doug	DE	6-3	265	7	San Diego State
78	Slater, Jackie	T	6-4	280	15	Jackson State
96	Smith, Brian	LB-DT	6-6	242	2	Auburn
56	Smith, Doug	C	6-3	260	13	Bowling Green
97	Smith, Sean	DT	6-4	275	4	Grambling
50	Stams, Frank	LB	6-2	240	2	Notre Dame
23	Stewart, Michael	S	6-0	195	4	Fresno State
53	Strickland, Fred	LB	6-2	250	3	Purdue
21	Warner, Curt	RB	5-11	205	8	Penn State
54	Wilcher, Mike	LB	6-3	245	8	North Carolina
99	Wright, Alvin	NT	6-2	285	5	Jacksonville State

TOP DRAFT CHOICES

Rd.	Name	Sel. No.	Pos.	Ht.	Wt.	College
1	Brostek, Bern	23	C	6-2	300	Washington
2	Terrell, Pat	49	DB	6-0	195	Notre Dame
3	Berry, Latin	78	RB	5-9	196	Oregon
6	Stallworth, Tim	161	WR	5-9	177	Washington State
7	Elmore, Kent	190	P	6-2	180	Tennessee

96 THE COMPLETE HANDBOOK OF PRO FOOTBALL

rated by many as the top safety in the draft, still available on the second round. Oregon halfback Latin Berry should strengthen an already strong running attack.

OUTLOOK: A huge improvement from the defense will be needed to challenge the 49ers again. On the other end, John Robinson's Rams (11-5 in '89) may have a tough time fending off the improving Saints and may even be in for a shock from the Falcons. Their out-of-division schedule is no piece of cake with games against the Giants, Eagles, Browns, Packers and Oilers.

RAM PROFILES

JIM EVERETT 27 6-5 214   Quarterback

While the 1980s belonged to Joe Montana, Everett is emerging as an early favorite for that title in the 1990s... Became the first Ram to throw for more than 4,000 yards as he completed 304 of 518 passes for 4,310 yards... Threw 29 touchdowns (tops in the league) and only 17 interceptions... Quarterback rating of 90.6 was the best of his career and the third-best in the league... Added another 737 yards in three playoff games... Threw for 454 yards in comeback overtime victory over the Saints... Completed 18 straight passes in regular-season victory over the Giants... Ran for only 31 yards on 25 carries... Came to the Rams at a premium. Rams gave up two first-round picks and a fifth-rounder in a trade with Houston in 1986... Born Jan. 3, 1963, in Emporia, Kan... Earned $450,000 last year.

CURT WARNER 29 5-11 205   Running Back

Slipped badly in seventh season with Seahawks and they didn't place him on their 37-man protected list... So the Rams, no doubt paying him less than the $1.1-million he got as a Seahawk, signed him as Plan-B free agent... Gained just 631 yards with a 3.3 average and three TDs in '89 following his fourth 1,000-yard season... Holds Seahawks records for

LOS ANGELES RAMS 97

carries (1,649), yards (6,705) and rushing TDs (55)... Has had 23 100-yard games... Missed all but part of opener in '84 because of severe knee injury... Made comeback in '85, gaining 1,094 yards... Played in '83 Pro Bowl as a rookie and was picked for Pro Bowl in '86 and '87 but didn't play because of injuries... First-round pick out of Penn State, where he set numerous records, including rushing yardage (3,398)... Scored 89 TDs in high school... Born March 18, 1961, in Wyoming, W. Va.

HENRY ELLARD 29 5-11 180   Wide Receiver

One of the league's great late bloomers... Proved that his 1988 Pro Bowl season was no fluke by having another spectacular year... Caught 70 passes for 1,382 yards (fourth in the NFL) while pulling down eight touchdowns... Averaged 19.7 yards per catch... Has gone to the Pro Bowl twice as a receiver and once as a punt-returner... Owns current streak of 50 games with at least one reception... Caught 12 passes for 230 yards and three touchdowns against the Colts... Season totals particularly impressive because he missed two games and was hampered in a third by a hamstring pull... Led the NFL in receiving yards in 1988 with a career-high 1,414... Second-round pick out of Fresno State in 1983... Born July 21, 1961, in Fresno, Cal.... Earned $375,000 last year.

FLIPPER ANDERSON 25 6-0 172   Wide Receiver

After a quiet rookie season, Flipper exploded on the scene in 1989... Caught 44 passes for 1,146 yards for a remarkable 26.0 average... Broke an NFL single-game record with 336 receiving yards (15 receptions) against the Saints... Caught two touchdown passes, including the game-winner in overtime, in the playoff victory over the Giants... Pulled down

two passes for 77 yards against the Eagles in the wild-card game
... Had only 11 receptions as a rookie in 1988, but made them count, averaging 29.0 yards per catch... Yes, he is named after the dolphin of TV fame... Unspectacular career at UCLA, but attracted scouts with his speed and hands... Taken on the second round of the 1988 draft... Born March 7, 1965, in Paulsboro, N.J... Earned $170,000 last year.

JACKIE SLATER 36 6-4 280   Tackle

Ageless wonder continues to get the job done... Though he's reached an age where most of his contemporaries are out of the game, he started all 16 games last year, and earned his sixth trip to the Pro Bowl in the last seven years... Ranks fifth on the Rams' all-time list in games played (195)... Can move into first place (past Merlin Olsen) if he plays in 15 games this year... Senior member of the team and offensive team captain... Took four years to break into the starting lineup and eight years to earn his first trip to the Pro Bowl... Third-round draft choice in 1976... Played at Jackson State, where he blocked for Walter Payton... Born May 27, 1954, in Jackson, Miss. ... Earned $400,000 last year.

JERRY GRAY 27 6-0 185   Cornerback

Capped off yet another excellent season by earning MVP honors in the Pro Bowl, where he picked off a Warren Moon pass and returned it 51 yards for a touchdown... Led the Rams with six interceptions during the regular season... Also led the team in unassisted tackles with 67 (second in overall tackles with 79)... Recorded a team-high 23 passes defensed... His Pro Bowl appearance was his fourth straight... Scored his second career touchdown against the Patriots in Week 16... Since becoming a starter in 1986, he has started all 60 non-strike games... Active in the NFLPA... Consensus All-American for two years at Texas... First-round choice in 1985 draft... Born Dec. 16, 1962, in Lubbock, Tex.... Earned $250,000 last year.

LOS ANGELES RAMS 99

KEVIN GREENE 28 6-3 238 — Linebacker

Yet another in a parade of Ram Pro Bowlers ... Earned his first trip to Honolulu with 16½ sacks and 64 tackles ... This was Greene's second straight 16½-sack season ... Added three sacks in the playoffs ... Greene hasn't gotten the credit he deserves because much of his sack production has been attributed to the Rams' gambling "Eagle Defense" ... Got season off on the right foot with a three-sack performance against the Falcons ... Recorded five sacks in two games against Atlanta ... Nothing has ever come easy for Greene ... A walk-on at Auburn who served three years as a backup before becoming a starter in 1988 ... Fifth-round draft choice in 1985 ... Born July 31, 1962, in Granite City, Ill. ... Earned $225,000 last year.

MIKE LANSFORD 32 6-0 190 — Kicker

One of the great clutch kickers in the history of football ... Hasn't cost his team with a miss with the game on the line since his sophomore year of high school ... Nailed 23 of 30 field goals and all 51 of his extra points ... Did not miss a field-goal attempt at home ... Finished the year with 120 points ... Beat the 49ers, 13-12, with a field goal with two seconds remaining ... Rams' all-time leading scorer with 702 points ... Off year from long distance, missing on all four of his tries from 50+ yards ... Signed as a free agent in 1982 after kicking for the University of Washington ... Born July 29, 1958, in Monterrey Park, Cal. ... Earned $195,000 last year.

DOUG SMITH 33 6-3 260 — Center

A perennial all-star, Smith earned his sixth straight trip to the Pro Bowl ... Started all 16 games and has now started in 136 of his 156 games with the Rams ... One of three Ram linemen to go to the Pro Bowl (along with Jackie Slater and Tom Newberry) ... Waited seven years for first Pro Bowl appearance ... Excellent run-blocker, he helped pave the way to Eric Dickerson's 2,105-yard season in 1984 ... Missed most of 1979 and 1980 with a knee injury ... Has started all but six games in the last nine years... Played at unheralded Bowling Green and was passed over in the 1978 draft... Holds a masters degree from Cal State-Fullerton... Born Nov. 25, 1956, in Columbus, Ohio ... Earned $400,000 last year.

ROBERT DELPINO 24 6-0 198   Fullback

Became a valuable member of the Rams' offense in just his second year in the league... Finished second on the team in rushing with 368 yards on 78 carries (4.7 yards per carry)... Dangerous receiver, catching 34 passes for 334 yards... His 334 yards in kick returns helped him top 1,000 yards in total offense... Led all Rams with 11 special-teams tackles... Killed the Giants with 34 yards rushing, 70 yards receiving and 38 yards in kick returns... Rams' special-teams Player of the Year as a rookie in 1988... Played wide receiver until his senior year at Missouri... Fifth-round pick in 1988... Born Nov. 2, 1965, in Dodge City, Kan... Earned $97,500 last year.

COACH JOHN ROBINSON:

In his last 18 years as a pro and college coach, Robinson has been involved with only one losing team... He has taken the Rams to the playoffs in six of his seven years... Last year, he took a wild-card team and led it to the NFC championship game before getting streamrolled by the 49ers ... Rams' coaching record improved to 71-50... Helped the Rams overcome a four-game losing streak midway through the season and got them back in the playoffs... Has a knack for coaching the running game... Coached Charles White and Marcus Allen at USC and Eric Dickerson, Greg Bell and White again with the Rams ... Joined the Rams in 1983 after compiling a 67-14-2 record at USC... Has the longest tenure of any Rams' coach... Assistant coach under John Madden with Raiders... Started his coaching career in 1960 at the University of Oregon, where he played end... Played briefly in the 1957 Rose Bowl... Born July 25, 1935, in Daly City, Cal.

LONGEST PASS PLAY

FRANK RYAN TO OLLIE MATSON

On the same day that Roger Maris was hitting his Babe Ruth, record-breaking 61st home run—Oct. 1, 1961—Ram backup quarterback Frank Ryan and Ollie Matson teamed for a smash hit of their own.

They couldn't steal the headlines from Maris, but they made their mark in a home game against the Steelers. With the score tied at 14 late in the fourth quarter and the ball on the Rams' four-yard line, Ryan, a replacement for the injured Zeke Bratkowski, passed to Matson at the Rams' 33 and this world-class sprinter went the rest of the way for the winning touchdown in a 24-14 decision.

Second-best to the Ryan-Matson 96-yarder is a Bill Munson-to-Bucky Pope 95-yarder in 1964.

INDIVIDUAL RAM RECORDS

Rushing

Most Yards Game:	248	Eric Dickerson, vs Dallas, 1985
Season:	2,105	Eric Dickerson, 1984
Career:	7,245	Eric Dickerson, 1983-87

Passing

Most TD Passes Game:	5	Bob Waterfield, vs N.Y. Bulldogs, 1949
	5	Norm Van Brocklin, vs Detroit, 1950
	5	Norm Van Brocklin, vs N.Y. Yanks, 1951
	5	Roman Gabriel, vs Cleveland, 1965
	5	Vince Ferragamo, vs New Orleans, 1980
	5	Vince Ferragamo, vs San Francisco, 1983
	5	Jim Everett, vs N.Y. Giants, 1988
Season:	31	Jim Everett, 1988
Career:	154	Roman Gabriel, 1962-72

Receiving

Most TD Passes Game:	4	Bob Shaw, vs Washington, 1949
	4	Elroy Hirsch, vs N.Y. Yanks, 1951
	4	Harold Jackson, vs Dallas, 1973
Season:	17	Elroy Hirsch, 1951
Career:	53	Elroy Hirsch, 1949-57

Scoring

Most Points Game:	24	Elroy Hirsch, vs N.Y. Yanks, 1951
	24	Bob Shaw, vs Washington, 1949
	24	Harold Jackson, vs Dallas, 1973
Season:	130	David Ray, 1973
Career:	702	Mike Lansford, 1982-89
Most TDs Game:	4	Elroy Hirsch, vs N.Y. Yanks, 1951
	4	Bob Shaw, vs Washington, 1949
	4	Harold Jackson, vs Dallas, 1973
Season:	20	Eric Dickerson, 1983
Career:	58	Eric Dickerson, 1983-87

MINNESOTA VIKINGS

TEAM DIRECTORY: Chairman: John Skoglund; Pres.: Wheelock Whitney; Exec. VP/GM: Mike Lynn; Dir. Finance: Harley Peterson; Dir. Football Operations: Jerry Reichow; Asst. GMs: Jeff Diamond, Bob Hollway; Dir. Pub. Rel.: Merrill Swanson; Head Coach: Jerry Burns. Home field: Hubert H. Humphrey Metrodome (63,000). Colors: Purple, white and gold.

Vikings need Herschel Walker to fulfill expectations.

SCOUTING REPORT

OFFENSE: Plenty of talent. How about some results for a change?

Herschel Walker rode into town as a savior, but ended the season as a pariah. Given a full training camp to work out the kinks, the Vikings should be able to utilize his talents much more effectively this year. Whatever the contributions of Rick Fenney, D.J. Dozier and Alfred Anderson, the key has to be Walker.

The passing game should also be better than it was in 1989. There shouldn't be a quarterback controversy this year. Wade Wilson proved that he can be a great quarterback in 1988; he just has to put 1989 behind him.

The receiving game is in excellent hands with Anthony Carter, Hassan Jones and Steve Jordan.

No complaints about the offensive line either. Randall McDaniel has been a great addition to a line that already had Gary Zimmerman and Keith Lowdermilk.

DEFENSE: Awesome. From end to end, the defensive line was the best in football. Keith Millard was the top defensive player in the league, while Chris Doleman was close behind.

There wasn't too much of a dropoff at linebacker, where Scott Studwell and Mike Merriweather shut down the oppositions' running games.

An excellent secondary was yet another reason why the Vikings have the top defense in the NFL. Carl Lee and Joey Browner may not have been the happiest players in the league, but they certainly were among the best.

KICKING GAME: Rich Karlis enjoyed a career-year, kicking for 120 points, including 31-for-39 FGs. Bucky Scribner wasn't quite so hot, averaging only 39.8 yards per punt.

The return game got a big boost with the addition of Walker, who averaged 28.8 yards on 13 kick returns. Leo Lewis ranked seventh in the conference, averaging 10.1 yards per return.

THE ROOKIES: Thanks to the Walker deal, the Vikings didn't get to pick until the third round, where they used their two selections to bolster two of the strongest parts of their team. Texas A&M's Mike Jones was one of the highest-rated tight ends in the country. Marion Hobb, a defensive end out of Tennessee, adds depth to an already deep defensive line.

VIKINGS VETERAN ROSTER

HEAD COACH—Jerry Burns. Assistant Coaches—Tom Batta, Maxie Baughan, Jerry Brown, John Brunner, John Michels, Tom Moore, Floyd Peters, Dick Rehbein, Bob Schnelker, Paul Wiggin.

No.	Name	Pos.	Ht.	Wt.	NFL Exp.	College
46	Anderson, Alfred	RB	6-1	219	6	Baylor
50	Berry, Ray	LB	6-2	230	4	Baylor
68	Blair, Paul	T	6-4	280	3	Oklahoma State
53	Braxton, David	LB	6-1	232	2	Wake Forest
44	Brim, Michael	CB	6-0	186	3	Virginia Union
47	Browner, Joey	CB-S	6-2	212	8	Southern California
19	Burbage, Cornell	WR	5-10	189	4	Kentucky
81	Carter, Anthony	WR	5-11	175	6	Michigan
33	Clark, Jessie	RB	6-0	223	8	Arkansas
71	Clarke, Ken	DT	6-2	281	12	Syracuse
56	Doleman, Chris	DE	6-5	250	6	Pittsburgh
42	Dozier, D. J.	RB	6-0	198	4	Penn State
59	Dusbabek, Mark	LB	6-3	230	2	Minnesota
31	Fenney, Rick	RB	6-1	240	4	Washington
62	Foote, Chris	C	6-4	265	8	Southern California
29	Fullington, Darrell	S	6-1	183	3	Miami
51	Galvin, John	LB	6-3	226	2	Boston College
16	Gannon, Rich	QB	6-3	197	4	Delaware
80	Gustafson, Jim	WR	6-1	181	5	St. Thomas (Minn.)
74	Habib, Brian	T	6-7	282	2	Washington
89	Hillary, Ira	WR	5-11	190	4	South Carolina
82	Hilton, Carl	TE	6-3	232	4	Houston
72	Huffman, David	G	6-6	283	10	Notre Dame
76	Ingram, Darryl	TE	6-2	230	2	California
76	Irwin, Tim	T	6-6	289	10	Tennessee
84	Jones, Hassan	WR	6-0	195	5	Florida State
83	Jordan, Steve	TE	6-3	230	9	Brown
69	Kalis, Todd	G	6-5	269	3	Arizona State
30	Karlis, Rich	K	6-0	180	9	Cincinnati
77	Knight, Shawn	DT-DE	6-6	280	4	Brigham Young
39	Lee, Carl	CB	5-11	183	8	Marshall
87	Lewis, Leo	WR	5-8	171	9	Missouri
63	Lowdermilk, Kirk	C	6-3	263	6	Ohio State
49	Lyons, Robert	S	6-1	195	2	Akron
78	Marrone, Doug	C-G	6-5	295	3	Syracuse
79	Martin, Doug	DE	6-3	270	10	Washington
64	McDaniel, Randall	G	6-4	275	3	Arizona State
26	McMillan, Audray	CB	6-0	190	5	Houston
57	Merriweather, Mike	LB	6-2	221	8	Pacific
75	Millard, Keith	DT	6-5	262	6	Washington State
18	Newsome, Harry	P	6-0	188	6	Wake Forest
85	Novosetsky, Brent	TE	6-2	238	3	Pennsylvania
99	Noga, Al	DT	6-1	245	3	Hawaii
52	Rasmussen, Randy	C-G	6-1	254	6	Minnesota
36	Rice, Allen	RB	5-10	203	7	Baylor
48	Rutland, Reggie	S	6-1	195	4	Georgia Tech
12	Salisbury, Sean	QB	6-5	215	3	Southern California
17	Schillinger, Andy	WR	5-11	186	2	Miami, Ohio
60	Schreiber, Adam	C-G	6-4	285	7	Texas
13	Scribner, Bucky	P	6-0	205	5	Kansas
27	Stills, Ken	S	5-10	196	6	Wisconsin
94	Strauthers, Thomas	DE	6-4	265	7	Jackson State
55	Studwell, Scott	LB	6-2	230	14	Illinois
97	Thomas, Henry	NT	6-2	268	4	Louisiana State
34	Walker, Herschel	RB	6-1	223	5	Georgia
11	Wilson, Wade	QB	6-3	203	10	East Texas State
73	Wotley, Craig	G-T	6-1	270	11	Syracuse
65	Zimmerman, Gary	T	6-6	277	5	Oregon

TOP DRAFT CHOICES

Rd.	Name	Sel. No.	Pos.	Ht.	Wt.	College
3	Jones, Mike	54	TE	6-3	255	Texas A&M
3	Hobby, Marion	75	DE	6-4	277	Tennessee
4	Hampton, Alonzo	104	DB	5-10	197	Pittsburgh
5	Thornton, Reggie	116	WR	5-10	166	Bowling Green
5	Smith, Cedric	131	RB	5-10	223	Florida

OUTLOOK: Last year, the Vikings had their hands full with the Packers before taking the Central Division title. This year, they will repeat as champions, barely edging out the upstart Lions and resurgent Bears.

VIKING PROFILES

KEITH MILLARD 28 6-5 262 — Defensive Tackle

Associated Press Defensive Player of the Year... His 18 sacks tied a league record for sacks by a tackle... Ranked third in the NFL and second on the Vikings to Chris Doleman's league-leading 21... Earned second straight trip to the Pro Bowl, where he scored a touchdown on an eight-yard fumble recovery... Began the season at a record-breaking pace, with 12 sacks after only six games... One of the most tenacious pass-rushers in the game... Biggest problem is drinking and driving... Drafted by Vikings out of Washington State in first round in 1984, but opted for a season with the Jacksonville Bulls in the USFL... Born March, 18, 1962, in Pleasonton, Cal.... Earned $850,000 last year.

HERSCHEL WALKER 28 6-1 223 — Running Back

Huge disappointment after gaining 148 yards in his first game as a Viking... Running style wasn't suited to the Vikings' trap-blocking offense... Finished the year with 915 yards on 250 carries... Caught 40 passes for 423 yards... Scored 10 touchdowns (7 rushing, 2 receiving, 1 return)... Came from Dallas in 12-for-1 deal that gave Cowboys Darrin Nelson, Jesse Solomon, David Howard, Issiac Holt, Alex Stewart and seven future draft choices... Led NFC in rushing in 1988 with 1,502 yards... Two-time Pro Bowler... Signed with the Cowboys as a free agent out of the USFL in 1986... Was MVP in USFL playing for Donald Trump and the New Jersey Generals in 1985... Gained 7,046 yards in three seasons in USFL... Won Heisman Trophy in 1982 at Georgia... Born March 3, 1962, in Wrightsville, Ga.... Earned $900,000 last year.

MINNESOTA VIKINGS 107

CHRIS DOLEMAN 28 6-5 250 — Defensive End

Led the NFL in sacks with 21... Now has 43 for five-year career... Went to the Pro Bowl for the third year in a row... Utilizes a rare combination of size and speed... Combined with Keith Millard for best one-two sack punch ever (39)... Forced five fumbles and recovered five fumbles... Spent most of his first two seasons as an outside linebacker, but has thrived since moving to the defensive line... Fourth man taken in the 1985 draft... All-American at Pittsburgh... Born Oct. 16, 1961, in Indianapolis, Ind... Earned $325,000 last year.

RICH KARLIS 31 6-0 180 — Kicker

Had a spectacular season after being picked up on waivers from the Broncos... Didn't arrive until Week 4, but still managed to lead the Vikings with 120 points... Hit on 31 of 39 field goals and 27 of 28 extra points... His 31 field goals established a team record... Made nine of 15 attempts from over 40 yards... Lost his job in the Broncos' training camp to Scott Treadwell... Has now scored over 100 points in five of the last six seasons... Joined the Broncos as a free agent in 1982... Kicked for three years at the University of Cincinnati... Born May 23, 1959, in Salem, Ohio... Earned $225,000 last year.

WADE WILSON 31 6-3 203 — Quarterback

Horrendous follow-up to 1988 Pro Bowl season... Completed 194 of 362 passes for 2,543 yards... Threw only nine touchdown passes while giving up 12 interceptions... Ranked ninth in the NFC with a quarterback rating of 70.5... In 1988, Wilson led the NFC with a quarterback rating of 91.5... Caught up in quarterback controversy with the now-departed Tommy Kramer... Rushed for 132 yards on 32 carries... Ran for one touchdown... Threw for only 84 yards in playoff loss to the 49ers before being benched... Eighth-round draft choice in 1981 after starring at tiny East Texas State... Born Feb. 1, 1959, in Greenville, Tex.... Signed a four-year, $4.35-million contract before '89 season and earned only a small fraction of it.

ANTHONY CARTER 29 5-11 175   Wide Receiver

Topped the 1,000-yard mark for the second straight season, though he failed to live up to 1988 production... Caught 65 passes for 1,066 yards... Had four receptions for 44 yards in the playoff loss to the 49ers... Recorded career highs for receptions (72) and yards (1,225) in 1988... Reception yardage established team record... Went to the Pro Bowl after 1987 and 1988 seasons... Broke NFL playoff records in 1987 with most receiving yards in a game (227 against the 49ers) and most punt-return yardage (143 against the Saints)... Spent three seasons with the Michigan Panthers and Oakland Invaders of the USFL... Drafted by the Dolphins on 12th round of 1983 draft... Three-time All-American at Michigan... Born Sept. 17, 1960, in Riviera Beach, Fla.... Earned $450,000 last year.

STEVE JORDAN 29 6-4 230   Tight End

Continues to be one of best tight ends in the league... Named to fourth consecutive Pro Bowl after catching 35 passes for 506 yards and three touchdowns... Production suffered after training camp holdout... Saved biggest day for the playoffs, catching nine passes for 149 yards against the 49ers... Seventh-round choice out of Brown in 1982... Earned degree in civil engineering... In high school, Jordan lettered twice in football and three times in tennis... Born Jan. 10, 1961, in Phoenix, Ariz.... Earned $950,000 last year.

SCOTT STUDWELL 36 6-2 230   Linebacker

Defies the clock as he enters 14th season... Led the Vikings in tackles (172) for the eighth time in his career... Topped the 100-tackle mark for the 11th straight season, including two strike-shortened seasons... Didn't get picked for Pro Bowl after going to Honolulu in the two previous two seasons... Career-high 230 tackles in 1981... All-time Viking leader in total tackles (1,872), solo tackles (1,246) and assists (626)... Broke Dick Butkus' tackling records at Illinois... Ninth-round draft choice in 1977... Born Aug. 27, 1954, in Evansville, Ind.

MINNESOTA VIKINGS 109

JOEY BROWNER 30 6-2 212 — Safety

His respect in the league can best be shown by five straight Pro Bowl appearances... Led Vikings with five interceptions and now has 25 for career that began in 1983... Finished second on the team with 112 tackles (a career high)... Recorded one sack... Had three interceptions in 1988 playoffs... Has not missed a start in the last five seasons... Played strong safety, free safety and cornerback at USC, where he was a second-team All-American... The 19th player taken in 1983 draft... Brothers Ross, Jim and Keith have all played in NFL... Owns black belt in martial arts... Born May 15, 1960, in Warren, Ohio ... Earned $350,000 last year.

RANDALL McDANIEL 25 6-4 275 — Guard

In only two years, McDaniel has established himself as one of the top guards in the league.. Earned Pro Bowl honors last year... Excellent pass-blocker and solid run-blocker... Replaced injured Dave Huffman in the first week of 1988 and started the final 15 games... Unanimous pick for 1988 All-Rookie team... Taken in the first round of 1988 draft (19th pick) after career at Arizona State, where he was All-American in 1987 ... Competitive weight-lifter... Held the NCAA record in the deadlift... Born Dec. 19, 1964, in Phoenix, Ariz... Earned $150,000 last year.

CARL LEE 29 5-11 183 — Cornerback

Earned second straight Pro Bowl appearance ... Lee has thrived since moving from safety to cornerback three years ago... Though he had only two interceptions, it didn't reflect the job he did as a cover man... Finished eighth on the team with 57 tackles... Started all 16 games... Led the Vikings with eight interceptions in 1988... Taken in the seventh round of the 1983 draft... Was the 35th defensive back taken, following four-year starting role at Marshall University... Born April 6, 1961, in South Charleston, W.Va.... Earned $775,000 last year.

COACH JERRY BURNS: Has done everything in the last two seasons except find a way to beat the 49ers in the playoffs ... In the last two years, the Vikings have lost twice to the 49ers in the conference semifinals by a combined score of 75-22 ... Took over as the Vikings' head coach in 1986 and has led the team to four winning seasons and three playoff berths ... Has had trouble deciding on a starting quarterback and was accused of underutilizing Herschel Walker's considerable talents ... Career records stands at 38-25 in regular-season games and 3-3 in the playoffs ... Served as the Vikings' offensive coordinator from 1968-1985 ... Coached under Vince Lombardi at Green Bay ... Played quarterback at Michigan ... Head coach at Iowa (1961-65) and served as an assistant at Hawaii, Whittier and Iowa ... Born Jan. 24, 1927, in Detroit.

LONGEST PASS PLAY

FRAN TARKENTON TO CHARLEY FERGUSON

It shouldn't come as a surprise that the longest pass play in Viking history began with a throw from Hall of Famer Fran Tarkenton. What was surprising was the fact that Tarkenton completed only six of 23 passes for 173 yards that day, Nov. 11, 1962, at Chicago.

Three of the passes went for touchdowns by running back Charley Ferguson, and the longest of these was a club-record 89-yarder that the Tennessee State product caught at midfield. Ferguson and Bear defensive back Bennie McRae arrived simultaneously and Ferguson wrestled the ball out of McRae's hands, then beat Rich Petitbon to the goal line.

The Bears wound up winning the game, 31-30, on a last-minute field goal by Roger Leclerc.

INDIVIDUAL VIKING RECORDS

Rushing

Most Yards Game:	200	Chuck Foreman, vs Philadelphia, 1976
Season:	1,155	Chuck Foreman, 1976
Career:	5,879	Chuck Foreman, 1973-79

Passing

Most TD Passes Game:	7	Joe Kapp, vs Baltimore, 1969
Season:	26	Tommy Kramer, 1981
Career:	239	Francis Tarkenton, 1961-66, 1972-78

Receiving

Most TD Passes Game:	4	Ahmad Rashad, vs San Francisco, 1979
Season:	11	Jerry Reichow, 1961
Career:	50	Sammy White, 1976-85

Scoring

Most Points Game:	24	Chuck Foreman, vs Buffalo, 1975
	24	Ahmad Rashad, vs San Francisco, 1979
Season:	132	Chuck Foreman, 1975
Career:	1,365	Fred Cox, 1963-77
Most TDs Game:	4	Chuck Foreman, vs Buffalo, 1975
		Ahmad Rashad, vs San Francisco, 1979
Season:	22	Chuck Foreman, 1975
Career:	76	Bill Brown, 1962-74

112 THE COMPLETE HANDBOOK OF PRO FOOTBALL
NEW ORLEANS SAINTS

TEAM DIRECTORY: Owner: Tom Benson; Pres./GM: Jim Finks; VP-Administration: Jim Miller; Bus. Mgr./Controller: Bruce Broussard; Dir. Media Rel.: Rusty Kasmiersky; Head Coach: Jim Mora. Home field: Superdome (69,065). Colors: Old gold, black and white.

SCOUTING REPORT

OFFENSE: The 9-7 Saints enter the 1990 season with a bona fide quarterback controversy. Bobby Hebert's performances ran the gamut from spectacular to horrendous, while journeyman John

Running and receiving, Dalton Hilliard led NFL in TDs (18).

Fourcade turned in one of the best relief performances this side of Mark Davis.

Things are much more settled at running back, where Dalton Hilliard was simply marvelous both as a runner and receiver.

The receiving corps is anchored by Eric Martin, one of the most underrated players in the league. Lonzell Hill is a fine No. 2 target.

DEFENSE: An excellent group that will be even better in 1990. While the Saints are known for the best linebacking corps in football, their defensive line and secondary aren't exactly cajun-style chopped liver.

Rickey Jackson should be even better this year, as he has fully recovered from the auto accident that nearly ended his career. Pat Swilling should improve on his impressive sack totals, since he won't have to go through another extended holdout.

Last year's rookie class provided two major additions, cornerback Robert Massey and defensive end Wayne Martin. This year's crop brings two of the same quality, end Renaldo Turnbull and cornerback Vince Buck. The biggest loss to the defense came when the 49ers snapped up safety Dave Waymer, who was inexplicably left unprotected.

KICKING GAME: Despite an off year (20-for-29) in 1989, Morten Andersen remains among the all-time elite. The punting game is something else, with Tommy Bernhardt ranking 10th in the conference.

The Saints' return game was only adequate, averaging 20.4 yards per kick return and only 8.1 yards per punt return. Fortunately, their coverage was excellent, holding the opposition to only 17.9 yards per kick return and 7.0 yards per punt return (No. 2 in the NFL).

THE ROOKIES: The Saints needed help on the defensive line and that's precisely what they got. West Virginia All-American Turnbull should make an immediate impact. In the third round, they got another top defensive end in Western Michigan's Joel Smeenge. The spot vacated by the loss of Dave Waymer should be filled nicely by Central State's Buck.

OUTLOOK: Things can never look too bright when you play in the same division as the 49ers and Rams, but if Jim Mora resolves the quarterback controversy early, the Saints could be in the fight for a wild-card berth.

SAINTS VETERAN ROSTER

HEAD COACH—Jim Mora. Assistant Coaches—Paul Boudreau, Dom Capers, Vic Fangio, Joe Marciano, Russell Paternostro, John Pease, Steve Sidwell, Jim Skipper, Carl Smith, Steve Walters.

No.	Name	Pos.	Ht.	Wt.	NFL Exp.	College
7	Andersen, Morten	K	6-2	200	9	Michigan State
28	Atkins, Gene	S	6-1	200	4	Florida A&M
6	Barnhardt, Tommy	P	6-2	207	4	North Carolina
85	Brenner, Hoby	TE	6-5	245	10	Southern California
67	Brock, Stan	T	6-6	292	11	Colorado
41	Cook, Toi	CB	5-11	188	4	Stanford
79	Derby, Glenn	T	6-6	290	2	Wisconsin
72	Dombrowski, Jim	T	6-5	298	5	Virginia
63	Edelman, Brad	G	6-6	270	9	Missouri
52	Forde, Brian	LB	6-3	225	3	Washington State
11	Fourcade, John	QB	6-1	215	4	Mississippi
74	Haverdink, Kevin	T	6-5	285	2	Western Michigan
3	Hebert, Bobby	QB	6-4	215	6	NW Louisiana
34	Heyward, Craig	RB	5-11	260	3	Pittsburgh
61	Hilgenberg, Joel	C-G	6-2	252	7	Iowa
87	Hill, Lonzell	WR	5-11	189	4	Washington
21	Hilliard, Dalton	RB	5-8	204	5	Louisiana State
57	Jackson, Rickey	LB	6-2	239	10	Pittsburgh
53	Johnson, Vaughan	LB	6-3	245	5	North Carolina State
89	Jones, Mike	WR	5-11	180	7	Tennessee State
23	Jordan, Buford	RB	6-0	223	5	McNeese State
60	Korte, Steve	C	6-2	271	8	Arkansas
24	Mack, Milton	CB	5-11	182	4	Alcorn State
84	Martin, Eric	WR	6-1	195	6	Louisiana State
93	Martin, Wayne	DE	6-5	275	2	Arkansas
40	Massey, Robert	CB	5-10	182	2	North Carolina Central
39	Maxie, Brett	S	6-2	194	6	Texas Southern
36	Mayes, Rueben	RB	5-11	200	4	Washington State
51	Mills, Sam	LB	5-9	225	5	Montclair State
35	Morse, Bobby	RB	5-10	213	3	Michigan State
80	Perriman, Brett	WR	5-9	180	3	Miami
43	Phillips, Kim	CB	5-9	188	2	North Texas
83	Scales, Greg	TE	6-4	253	3	Wake Forest
56	Swilling, Pat	LB	6-3	242	5	Georgia Tech
82	Tice, John	TE	6-5	249	8	Maryland
54	Toles, Alvin	LB	6-1	234	5	Tennessee
65	Trapilo, Steve	G	6-5	281	4	Boston College
88	Turner, Floyd	WR	5-11	188	2	NW Louisiana
73	Warren, Frank	DE	6-4	285	10	Auburn
94	Wilks, Jim	NT	6-5	275	10	San Diego State
18	Wilson, Dave	QB	6-3	206	9	Illinois
69	Woods, Tony	DE	6-4	274	2	Oklahoma

TOP DRAFT CHOICES

Rd.	Name	Sel. No.	Pos.	Ht.	Wt.	College
1	Turnbull, Renaldo	14	DE	6-4	248	West Virginia
2	Buck, Vince	44	DB	6-0	195	Central State
3	Smeenge, Joel	71	DE	6-5	245	Western Michigan
4	Winston, DeMond	98	LB	6-2	239	Vanderbilt
5	Arbuckle, Charles	125	TE	6-2	238	UCLA

SAINT PROFILES

DALTON HILLIARD 26 5-8 204 — Running Back

Made the leap into the league's elite... Dangerous as a runner and receiver, he finished third in the NFC with 1,262 yards rushing and added 52 receptions for 514 yards... Led the NFL with 18 touchdowns (13 rushing, 5 receiving)... Established team records for touchdowns and consecutive games with touchdowns (6)... First non-kicker in team history to score more than 100 points (108)... Despite lack of height, Hilliard is one of most powerful runners in the league... Rushed for 823 yards to lead Saints in 1988... Finished LSU career as the No. 3 rusher in SEC history (behind Herschel Walker and Bo Jackson)... Drafted in the second round of the 1986 draft... Born Jan. 21, 1964, in Patterson, La.... Earned $500,000 last year.

VAUGHN JOHNSON 28 6-3 245 — Linebacker

Finally won a berth in the Pro Bowl... Now all four Saints' starting linebackers have been to the Pro Bowl... One of the premier inside linebackers, he finished second on the team in tackles (83) after leading the Saints in each of the previous two seasons... Along with Sam Mills, they were regarded as the best pair of linebackers in the league... Recorded 108 tackles in 1988 and 86 in 1987... Chosen by the Saints in 1984 supplemental draft, but opted to play in the USFL with the Jacksonville Bulls for two seasons... Signed by Saints in 1986... Attended North Carolina State... Born March 4, 1962, in Morehead City, N.C.... Earned $335,000 last year.

PAT SWILLING 25 6-3 242 — Linebacker

Recovered from a slow start to have an exceptional season... Recorded 16½ sacks for team record, all in the final 12 games... Terrorized Atlanta's Chris Miller with 3½ sacks... Earned first trip to Pro Bowl... Finished sixth on the team with 56 tackles... Forced five fumbles and intercepted one pass... Remarkably fast for his size... Excellent at tracking down running backs as well as QBs... Now has 38 sacks in four years... Had an off year in 1988, but suffered with an abdominal pull for much of the season... Played defensive end at Georgia Tech... One of three third-round picks in 1986 draft... Born Oct. 25, 1964, in Toccoa, Ga.... Earned $350,000 last year.

ERIC MARTIN 28 6-1 195   Wide Receiver

Led Saints in receiving for third straight year... Caught 68 passes for 1,090 yards... Broke his own team record for receiving yards set in 1988 (1,083)... Established team record with five games with more than 100 yards receiving... Caught nine passes for 120 yards and two touchdowns in upset of the Eagles... Had five catches for 131 yards and two touchdowns against the Jets... Caught eight touchdown passes on the year... Starred at LSU, where he established an SEC career record for receiving yards... Seventh-round draft pick in 1985... Born Nov. 8, 1961, in Van Vleck, Tex.... Earned $450,000 last year.

BOBBY HEBERT 30 6-4 215   Quarterback

Suffered through a roller-coaster season and was benched for the final three games of the year... Completed 222 of 353 passes for 2,686 yards (62.9 percent established a team record)... Threw for 15 touchdowns and 15 interceptions... Completed 31 of 49 passes for 308 yards and two touchdowns against the 49ers... Completed 23 of 32 for 282 yards and three touchdowns against the Packers... Named NFC Offensive Player of the Month for October... After losing consecutive games to the Rams and Lions late in the season, Hebert was benched... Played three years in the USFL, leading the Michigan Panthers to the title in 1983... Signed with the Saints as a free agent in 1985... Graduated from Northwestern Louisiana... Born Aug. 19, 1960, in Galliano, La.... Earned $650,000 last year.

JOHN FOURCADE 29 6-1 215   Quarterback

The man who brings new meaning to the term journeyman may have found a home in New Orleans... Started the final three games of the season, leading the Saints to victories over the Bills, Eagles and Colts... Owned a 102.6 quarterback rating in those three games... Entered 1990 training camp in a bona fide battle for the starting quarterback job with Bobby Hebert... Finished season with a rating of 92.0... Completed 61 of 107 passes for 930 yards with seven touchdowns and four interceptions... Played for the Saints' replacement team in 1987 ... Had shoulder surgery following 1988 season after playing in only one game in 1988... Since leaving the University of Mississippi, Fourcade has played in the CFL, USFL and even Arena Football... Broke most of Archie Manning's passing records at Mississippi... Born Oct. 11, 1960, in New Orleans, La.... Earned $100,000 last year.

RICKEY JACKSON 32 6-2 239　　　　　Linebacker

Chalked up another solid year... Finished ninth on the Saints with 47 tackles... Had 7½ sacks to increase his career total to 79½, the most in the history of the franchise... Ranked second on the team with three forced fumbles ... Extremely durable, Jackson has started in all 131 games he's been in... Went to the Pro Bowl four straight years from 1983-86... Known as a punishing hitter, Jackson has forced 21 fumbles in his nine-year career... Starred for a Pitt team that had 19 players from the class of 1981 drafted... Played defensive end in college ... Drafted in the second round... Passing his name along to son Rickeem and daughter Rickeyah... Born March 20, 1958, in Pahokee, Fla.... Earned $350,000 last year.

MORTEN ANDERSEN 30 6-2 200　　　　　Kicker

This was an off season for one of the best kickers in the history of the game... Andersen hit on 44 of 45 PATs, but nailed only 20 of 29 field-goal attempts... His 104 points marked the fifth straight season over 100 points... Went 0-for-4 from 50+ yards, the first time since 1982 that he failed to kick one from that distance... Fell into second place in the all-time field-goal accuracy list... He has hit on 171 of 222 career field-goal attempts (.770), while Kansas City's Nick Lowery has hit on 224 of 289 (.775)... Over the last five years, Andersen has scored more points (563) and kicked the most field goals (131) of anyone in the NFL... Fourth-round draft pick in 1982 after All-American career at Michigan State... Came to America from Denmark as an exchange student in 1977... Sings and acts during the offseason... Born Aug. 19, 1960, in Struer, Denmark... Earned $500,000 last year.

ROBERT MASSEY 23 5-10 182   Cornerback

Enjoyed an excellent rookie season... Finished fourth on the team in tackles with 80 and interceptions with five... Intercepted two Jim Everett passes... Led Saints with 18 passes defensed... His five interceptions tied him with Atlanta's Deion Sanders and New England's Maurice Hurst for the top total by a rookie... Teams tried to take advantage of the rookie corner early, but soon discovered he was no easy mark... Surprisingly good cover man when you consider that he was drafted for his abilities as a hitter... Excellent special-teams player, he blocked 12 kicks in college at North Carolina Central ... Second-round draft choice in 1989... Born Feb. 17, 1966, in Charlotte, N.C.

SAM MILLS 31 5-9 225   Linebacker

Though he led the Saints in tackles (95), Mills failed to make this year's Pro Bowl team after starting for the NFC in 1988... Shortest and one of best inside linebackers in the league... Recorded three sacks... Forced two fumbles, while recovering one... Began his career in the USFL, where he also played under Jim Mora... Played college ball at Division II Montclair State... NFL scouts had little faith in a 5-9 linebacker out of a Division II school... Not surprisingly, Mills was ignored in the 1981 draft... Signed by the Browns as a free agent, but failed to make the team... Taught photography at East Orange (N.J.) High School before joining the Philadelphia Stars... Born June 3, 1959, in Neptune, N.J.... Earned $229,200 last year.

COACH JIM MORA:

Led the Saints to their third straight winning season despite playing in a division with the 49ers and Rams... Took a team that had finished 5-11 in 1985 and improved them to 7-9 in his first season... The next year, Mora earned NFL Coach-of-the-Year honors, leading the Saints to a 12-3 record and a wild-card berth... Saints finished at 10-6 in 1988, missing the playoffs in a tie-breaker

... Needed three straight victories at the end of last season to finish at 9-7... Owns a 38-26 record with the Saints, by far the best record of any Saints coach... Came to the Saints after a three-year stint in the USFL, where he led the Philadelphia/Baltimore Stars to two league championships... Played tight end at Occidental College, where his teammate and roommate was quarterback-turned-politician Jack Kemp... After graduation, spent the next seven years coaching at Occidental... From there, Mora went to Stanford, Colorado, UCLA and Washington before coming to the NFL as a defensive line coach with the Seattle Seahawks... Coached with the New England Patriots briefly before going to the USFL... Born May 24, 1935, in Glendale, Cal.

LONGEST PASS PLAY

BILLY KILMER TO FLEA ROBERTS

The longest pass play in the history of the Saints came on one of the longest afternoons in a long and dismal opening season (3-11) for the franchise.

The Saints had high hopes for the game at Philadelphia on Nov. 19, 1967, because they had beaten the Eagles earlier in the year for their first-ever victory. Not only didn't the Saints come up with their second victory, they suffered a 48-21 thrashing.

The only bright spot in the loss was the club-record 96-yard bomb from Billy Kilmer to Flea Roberts. The Saints lined up at their own three-yard line, Klimer hit Roberts with the pass, but Flea ran out of gas and was brought down at the Eagles' one-yard line. Kilmer then hit Danny Abromowicz with a one-yard buttonhook pass for the final score of the game.

INDIVIDUAL SAINT RECORDS
Rushing

Most Yards Game:	206	George Rogers, vs St. Louis, 1983
Season:	1,674	George Rogers, 1981
Career:	4,267	George Rogers, 1981-84

Passing

Most TD Passes Game: 6   Billy Kilmer, vs St. Louis, 1969
Season: 23   Archie Manning, 1980
Career: 155   Archie Manning, 1971-81

Receiving

Most TD Passes Game: 3   Dan Abramowicz, vs San Francisco, 1971
Season: 9   Henry Childs, 1977
Career: 37   Dan Abramowicz, 1967-72

Scoring

Most Points Game:
- 18 Walt Roberts, vs Philadelphia, 1967
- 18 Dan Abramowicz, vs San Francisco, 1971
- 18 Archie Manning, vs Chicago, 1977
- 18 Chuck Muncie, vs San Francisco, 1979
- 18 George Rogers, vs Los Angeles, 1981
- 18 Wayne Wilson, vs Atlanta, 1982
- 18 Dalton Hilliard, vs L.A. Rams, 1989

Season: 121   Morten Andersen, 1987
Career: 750   Morten Andersen, 1982-89

Most TDs Game:
- 3 Walt Roberts, vs Philadelphia, 1967
- 3 Dan Abramowicz, vs San Francisco, 1971
- 3 Archie Manning, vs Chicago, 1977
- 3 Chuck Muncie, vs San Francisco, 1979
- 3 George Rogers, vs Los Angeles, 1981
- 3 Wayne Wilson, vs Atlanta, 1982
- 3 Dalton Hilliard, vs L.A. Rams, 1989

Season: 18   Dalton, Hilliard, 1989
Career: 37   Dan Abramowicz, 1967-72

NEW YORK GIANTS

TEAM DIRECTORY: Pres.: Wellington Mara; VP/Treasurer: Timothy Mara; VP/GM: George Young; Dir. Pro Personnel: Tom Boisture; Dir. Pub. Rel.: Ed Croke; Head Coach: Bill Parcells. Home field: Giants Stadium (76,891). Colors: Blue, red and white.

SCOUTING REPORT

OFFENSE: The Giants' offense did just enough to get the team into the playoffs, but not quite enough to get them beyond the first round.

It's almost impossible to predict how the Giants' offense will perform this year. Going into training camp, the team had a re-

Despite ankle, Lawrence Taylor made ninth Pro Bowl in row.

122 THE COMPLETE HANDBOOK OF PRO FOOTBALL

markable number of questions for a defending division champion:
 • How much more punishment can Phil Simms take?
 • Is rookie Rodney Hampton durable enough to anchor the Giants' running game in the 1990s? Where do sophomores David Meggett and Lewis Tillman fit into the picture? Is this the end of Joe Morris and Ottis Anderson?
 • What about the receivers? Is Lionel Manuel over the hill? Will Mark Ingram and Odessa Turner ever live up to their potential? Is Mark Bavaro ready to return to Pro Bowl form?

The one area where there are more answers than questions is the offensive line. After investing their top two picks in the 1988 and 1989 drafts on the line, the payoffs should begin in earnest this year with Eric Moore, Jumbo Elliott, Brian Williams and Bob Kratch.

DEFENSE: The healthy return of Eric Dorsey should be a big help to the defensive line, as should a full year of starting experience for Erik Howard. Leonard Marshall is getting on in years, but he shows no signs of letting up. The Giants are expecting big things out of rookies Mike Fox and Greg Mark.

The linebacking corps is in excellent shape with Lawrence Taylor and Carl Banks on the wings and Pepper Johnson, Steve DeOssie and Gary Reasons in the middle.

The defensive backfield should soon rank among the league's best. Mark Collins continues to excel, while Myron Guyton, Sheldon White and Greg Jackson are three talented young players. Dallas vet Everson Walls provides depth.

KICKING: Sean Landeta was voted as the punter of the decade of the 1980s and should get off to a good start in the 1990s. Raul Allegre is an excellent kicker, but his history of injuries always casts a shadow over the kicking game. The return game was greatly bolstered by the addition of Meggett. He went to the Pro Bowl on the strength of his punt- and kick returns and figures to be even better in 1990. The special teams got a huge boost with the addition of hit men Reyna Thompson and DeOssie.

THE ROOKIES: Georgia's Hampton, the third-leading runner in Bulldog history and a junior, should make both Morris and Anderson expendable. Second-rounder Fox (West Virginia) and third-rounder Mark (Miami), were excellent defensive linemen playing in the shadows of All-American linemates. The Giants' fifth-round pick was QB Craig Kupp out of tiny Pacific Lutheran.

GIANTS VETERAN ROSTER

HEAD COACH—Bill Parcells. Assistant Coaches—Bill Belichick, Tom Coughlin, Romeo Crennel, Ron Erhardt, Al Groh, Ray Handley, Fred Hoaglin, Lamar Leachman, Johnny Parker, Mike Pope, Mike Sweatman, Charlie Weis.

No.	Name	Pos.	Ht.	Wt.	NFL Exp.	College
2	Allegre, Raul	K	5-10	167	8	Texas
24	Anderson, Ottis	RB	6-2	225	12	Miami
85	Baker, Stephen	WR	5-8	160	4	Fresno State
58	Banks, Carl	LB	6-4	235	7	Michigan State
89	Bavaro, Mark	TE	6-4	245	6	Notre Dame
44	Carthon, Maurice	RB	6-1	225	6	Arkansas State
25	Collins, Mark	CB	5-10	190	5	Cal-Fullerton
96	Cooks, Johnie	LB	6-4	251	9	Mississippi State
87	Cross, Howard	TE	6-5	245	2	Alabama
99	DeOssie, Steve	LB	6-2	248	7	Boston College
77	Dorsey, Eric	DE	6-5	280	5	Notre Dame
76	Elliott, John	T	6-7	305	3	Michigan
	Feggins, Howard	CB	5-10	190	3	NC-Charlotte
29	Guyton, Myron	CB-S	6-1	205	2	Eastern Kentucky
15	Hostetler, Jeff	QB	6-3	212	6	West Virginia
74	Howard, Erik	NT	6-4	268	5	Washington State
82	Ingram, Mark	WR	5-10	188	4	Michigan State
47	Jackson, Greg	S	6-1	200	2	Louisiana State
54	Jiles, Dwayne	LB	6-4	245	6	Texas Tech
52	Johnson, Pepper	LB	6-3	248	5	Ohio State
61	Kratch, Bob	G	6-3	288	2	Iowa
5	Landeta, Sean	P	6-0	200	5	Towson State
86	Manuel, Lionel	WR	5-11	180	7	Pacific
70	Marshall, Leonard	DE	6-3	285	8	Louisiana State
30	Meggett, David	RB	5-7	180	2	Towson State
60	Moore, Eric	T	6-5	290	3	Indiana
20	Morris, Joe	RB	5-7	195	9	Syracuse
	Mrosko, Robert	TE	6-5	270	2	Penn State
65	Oates, Bart	C	6-3	265	6	Brigham Young
55	Reasons, Gary	LB	6-4	234	7	NW Louisiana
72	Riesenberg, Doug	T	6-5	275	4	California
66	Roberts, William	T	6-5	280	6	Ohio State
81	Robinson, Stacy	WR	5-11	186	6	North Dakota State
22	Rouson, Lee	RB	6-1	222	6	Colorado
11	Simms, Phil	QB	6-3	214	11	Morehead State
56	Taylor, Lawrence	LB	6-3	243	10	North Carolina
21	Thompson, Reyna	CB	6-0	193	5	Baylor
34	Tillman, Lewis	RB	6-0	195	2	Jackson State
83	Turner, Odessa	WR	6-3	205	4	NW Louisiana
73	Washington, John	DE	6-4	275	5	Oklahoma State
36	White, Adrian	S	6-0	200	4	Florida
39	White, Sheldon	CB-S	5-11	188	3	Miami (Ohio)
59	Wiliams, Brian	C-G	6-5	300	2	Minnesota
23	Williams, Perry	CB	6-2	203	7	North Carolina State

TOP DRAFT CHOICES

Rd.	Name	Sel. No.	Pos.	Ht.	Wt.	College
1	Hampton, Rodney	24	RB	5-11	217	Georgia
2	Fox, Mike	51	DT	6-6	272	West Virginia
3	Mark, Greg	79	DE	6-2	252	Miami
4	Whitmore, David	107	DB	6-0	235	Stephen F. Austin
5	Kupp, Craig	135	QB	6-4	230	Pacific Lutheran

OUTLOOK: Though Bill Parcell's team lost virtually all of its depth through Plan B, there is still enough talent around to make the Giants a favorite to repeat the Eastern Division champion. But a tough non-division schedule, including games against the 49ers, Bills, Vikings and Rams, will make it tough to repeat their 12 victories of 1989.

GIANT PROFILES

LAWRENCE TAYLOR 31 6-3 243   Linebacker

Earned an unprecedented ninth straight trip to the Pro Bowl despite playing much of the season on a broken ankle... Led the team in sacks with 15... The ankle and severe back spasms didn't keep him from two sacks of Jim Everett in the playoffs... Survived the season with no further drug problems... A two-time violator of the NFL's drug policy, Taylor was suspended for four games at the start of the 1988 season... NFL MVP in 1986... Unanimous selection to the NFL Team of the Decade... The second selection of the 1981 draft after outstanding career at North Carolina... An avid golfer... Born Feb. 4, 1959, in Williamsburg, Va.... Earned $1.1 million last year.

DAVID MEGGETT 24 5-7 180   Halfback

Was the steal of the 1989 draft... Made it to the Pro Bowl as a rookie and caught an 11-yard touchdown pass... Broke the Giants' team record with 1,806 total yards.... Ranked second in receiving yardage (531 yards) and accounted for the team's three longest touchdowns of the year... A 76-yard punt return for a touchdown was the first touchdown return by a Giant since 1978.... Proved himself as a blocker.... Must overcome propensity for fumbling in critical spots... Fifth-round pick out of tiny Towson State, where he had a 100-yard kickoff return... May be only player in NCAA history to be named captain at two different four-year colleges.... He started off at Morgan State... MVP for North in Senior Bowl... Born April 30, 1966, in Charleston, S.C.... Earned $127,500 last year.

NEW YORK GIANTS 125

CARL BANKS 28 6-4 235 — Linebacker

Rebounded well after disappointing 1988 season... Finished the year as the team's second-leading tackler (98)... Broke a team record by forcing six fumbles... Following the retirement of Harry Carson and George Martin, emerged as a team leader in 1989... Began his 1988 season with an extended holdout, but signed a multiyear $3.2-million contract immediately prior to season opener... Led the Giants in tackles in 1986 and 1987... Only Pro Bowl appearance came after the 1987 season... Consensus All-American at Michigan State... Aiming for a post-football career in broadcasting... Born Aug. 29, 1962, in Flint, Mich.... Earned $800,000 last year.

PHIL SIMMS 34 6-3 214 — Quarterback

Based on 1989, Simms may be in the twilight of his career... Plagued by injuries to his ankle, chest and thumb, Simms could never get on track... Unfortunately, he saved his worst outings for the biggest games... Had a bad one in the Giants' overtime playoff loss to the Rams... Completed 228 of 405 passes for 3,061 yards... The usually accurate Simms threw as many touchdown passes (14) as interceptions... Had the best game in the history of the Super Bowl when he completed 22 of 25 with three touchdowns against the Broncos in Super Bowl XXI... Was a surprise first-round pick out of Morehead State in 1979... Born Nov. 3, 1955, in Springfield, Ky.... Earned $1.3 million last year.

MYRON GUYTON 23 6-1 205 — Safety

Had exceptional rookie season, leading the Giants with 99 tackles... Broke into the starting lineup in Week 2 and never left... A great natural tackler who showed excellent abilities as a cover man... Proved a steal on the eighth round of the 1989 draft, outperforming several first- and second-round DBs... Was a starter for four years at Eastern Kentucky, initially as a cornerback, then as a strong safety... But never was more than honorable mention on the Ohio Valley Conference team... Giant scouts followed him closely and Bill Parcells liked what he saw at the spring workout... Played basketball and competed in track,

126 THE COMPLETE HANDBOOK OF PRO FOOTBALL

in addition to football, at Central High School in Thomasville, Ga.... Born Aug. 26, 1967, in Metcalf, Ga.

MARK BAVARO 27 6-4 245   Tight End

For the second straight year, injuries prevented Bavaro from playing anywhere close to his prior Pro Bowl form.... Played in only seven games before a season-ending knee injury in San Diego... Caught 22 passes for 278 yards and three touchdowns... Underwent complex reconstructive surgery two days prior to playoff loss.... No stranger to the operating room, Bavaro had three minor operations following the 1988 season... Arrested in 1988 offseason for activities relating to his anti-abortion stance... Not overly impressive in career at Notre Dame... Lasted until the fourth round of the 1985 draft... Nicknamed "Rambo"... Born April 23, 1963, in Winthrop, Mass.... Earned $650,000 last year.

LEONARD MARSHALL 28 6-3 285   Defensive End

Continued to get the job done in 1989... The only defensive lineman on the team with any success in getting to the opposing quarterback... Ranked second on the team with 9½ sacks and now has 61 for his career... Finished eighth on the team with 58 tackles... Forced two fumbles and recorded four passes defensed... Two-time Pro Bowler... Led the team in sacks in 1985 with 15½... Named 1985 Defensive Lineman of the Year by NFLPA... Marshall has been plagued by a series of minor injuries throughout his career... Second-round draft pick in 1983 out of LSU... Born Oct. 22, 1961, in Franklin, La.... Earned $425,000 last year.

SEAN LANDETA 28 6-0 200   Punter

Enjoyed one of his best seasons... Led the NFL with a net punting average of 37.8... Second in the conference with an average of 43.1 yards per kick despite kicking in the cold and wind of Giants Stadium... Snubbed by the Pro Bowl voters, but named the top punter in the league by the Associated Press... Great comeback after missing virtually the entire

1988 season following a holdout and back injury in Week 1... Best year was in 1986 when he led the NFL with a 44.8 average and went to the Pro Bowl... Has had only one punt blocked in his career... Began his professional career in the USFL... Played at Towson State... Led all Division II punters in 1980 with a 43.4 average... Longtime friend of tabloid darling Marla Maples... Born Jan. 6, 1962, in Baltimore... Earned $330,000 last year.

OTTIS ANDERSON 32 6-2 225   Running Back

Rose from the ashes to run for 1,023 yards last year... Nevertheless, was left unprotected by the Giants... NFL Comeback Player of the Year... Also left unprotected to Plan-B free agency in 1988 but nobody called... Established a record for the lowest per-carry average (3.1 yards) of any player to exceeding 1,000 yards in a season.... Recorded a career-high 14 touchdowns during the regular season and one more in the playoffs.... Topped off season by rushing for 120 yards against the Rams in the playoffs... Caught 28 passes for 268 yards... Prior to 1989, Anderson had rushed for a total of 932 yards in the previous four seasons.... Was a first-round pick by the Cardinals in 1979 and had five 1,000-yard seasons in his first six years... He came to the Giants early in 1986 season for second- and seventh-round picks in '87 draft... Born Nov. 19, 1957, in West Palm Beach, Fla.... Earned $250,000 last year.

JOE MORRIS 29 5-7 195   Running Back

It wasn't exactly a banner year for Morris... He broke his foot during the preseason and was on injured reserve for the entire year.... Stewed because he was physically able to play long before the season was over... His slashing running style may no longer be suited to the Giants' new power running game... Prior to injury, Morris had rushed for over 1,000 yards in three of the previous four seasons... Giants' all-time leading rusher with 5,296 yards... Set a team record with 1,516 yards in 1986... All-time leading rusher in Syracuse history, surpassing such stars as Jim Brown and Larry Csonka... Born Sept. 16, 1960, in Fort Bragg, N.C.... Earned $530,000 last year.

MARK COLLINS 26 5-10 190   Cornerback

Finished fourth on the team with 84 tackles and ranked third with 12 passes defensed... Pulled down only two interceptions during the regular season... Had mixed success in the playoffs against the Rams, making one end-zone interception to prevent a touchdown, but was beaten by Flipper Anderson on the game-winning overtime touchdown... It was later revealed that Collins had broken his ankle three plays earlier... Set school record for interceptions at Cal State-Fullerton... Born Jan. 16, 1964, in St. Louis... Earned $215,000 last year.

COACH BILL PARCELLS:

Took a team in transition and turned them into a 12-4 playoff contender... Went to playoffs for the fourth time in seven-year career... The Giants Stadium loss to the Rams was his first home playoff loss ever... Raised his career record to 57-37... Was one of the most daring fourth-down coaches, succeeding on 17 of 22 fourth-down attempts... Decided to all but abandon the passing game, relying on a powerful straight-ahead running game to wear down the opposition... Was NFL Coach of the Year in 1986 after leading Giants to their only Super Bowl championship... Played linebacker at Wichita State and earned all-conference honors... Coached at West Point, Wichita State, Florida State, Vanderbilt, and Texas Tech before getting first head-coaching job at Air Force Academy... Spent a year with the Patriots as linebackers coach... Joined Giants in 1981 as defensive coordinator... Appointed head coach after Ray Perkins left in 1983... Born Aug. 22, 1941, in Englewood, N.J.

LONGEST PASS PLAY

EARL MORRALL TO HOMER JONES

It was opening day, Sept. 11, 1966. Giants at Pittsburgh.

Early in the game Giant quarterback Earl Morrall connected on a 75-yard touchdown pass to Homer Jones, but the Giants trailed the Steelers, 31-20, in the fourth quarter.

Now Morrall was sacked on his own two-yard line. On third down he dropped deep into the end zone and heaved a 60-yard pass to Jones, who caught the ball at the Steelers' 36 and blew by cornerback Brady Keys, the same victim on Jones' earlier score, for a Giant-record 98-yarder.

With the score tied at 34 late in the fourth quarter, Morrall tried another deep pass to Jones, but this time Keys picked the ball off to preserve the tie.

INDIVIDUAL GIANT RECORDS

Rushing

Most Yards Game:	218	Gene Roberts, vs Chicago Cardinals, 1950
Season:	1,516	Joe Morris, 1986
Career:	5,296	Joe Morris, 1982-89

Passing

Most TD Passes Game:	7	Y. A. Tittle, vs Washington, 1962
Season:	36	Y. A. Tittle, 1963
Career:	173	Charlie Conerly, 1948-61

Receiving

Most TD Passes Game:	4	Earnest Gray, vs St. Louis, 1980
Season:	13	Homer Jones, 1967
Career:	48	Kyle Rote, 1951-61

Scoring

Most Points Game:	24	Ron Johnson, vs Philadelphia, 1972
	24	Earnest Gray, vs St. Louis, 1980
Season:	127	Ali Haji-Sheikh, 1983
Career:	646	Pete Gogolak, 1966-74
Most TDs Game:	4	Ron Johnson, vs Philadelphia, 1972
	4	Earnest Gray, vs St. Louis, 1980
Season:	21	Joe Morris, 1985
Career:	78	Frank Gifford, 1952-60, 1962-64

PHILADELPHIA EAGLES

TEAM DIRECTORY: Owner: Norman Braman; Pres/CEO: Harry Gamble; VP-Finance: Mimi Box; VP-Marketing: Decker Uhlhorn; Dir. Player Personnel: Joe Woolley; Dir. Pub. Rel.: Ron Howard; Head Coach: Buddy Ryan. Home field: Veterans Stadium (65,356). Colors: Kelly green, white and silver.

SCOUTING REPORT

OFFENSE: Randall Cunningham, one of the most dangerous offensive weapons in football, has some new targets. Buddy Ryan used his second, third and fourth picks of the draft to get wide receivers, the most intriguing of whom is Mike Bellamy, Jeff George's favorite receiver at Illinois.

With some quality wide receivers, Keith Jackson should be even more threatening. Jackson was the best receiving tight end in football despite getting double and triple attention.

One thing Ryan didn't do was get a running back to give the Eagles' offense some desperately needed balance. Buddy apparently has more faith in Keith Byars and Anthony Toney than the Eagles' fans have.

The offensive line won't be the Eagles' downfall, but it won't be their salvation either.

DEFENSE: No real complaints. The Eagles led the NFL with 56 takeaways. They intercepted 30 passes and recovered 26 fumbles. Much of the credit has to go to one of the most feared defensive lines in the league. Reggie White's numbers were cut down by double- and triple-teaming, but Clyde Simmons, Jerome Brown and Mike Pitts picked up the slack, combining for 33 sacks.

The linebacking corps doesn't begin to compare with the defensive line, but it is strong enough not to be a liability.

The secondary played especially well. Led by Pro Bowl star Eric Allen, who topped the NFC with eight interceptions, the Eagles picked off 30 passes. No. 1 pick Ben Smith was named a starter on the day he was drafted.

KICKING GAME: Not much to be encouraged about here. Roger Ruzek was dropped by the Cowboys and he hit on eight of 11 field-goal attempts. John Teltschik is a solid, if unspectacular punter. It was Cunningham, of course, who got off the longest punt of the season, a 91-yarder.

PHILADELPHIA EAGLES 131

Reggie White revels as a menace on powerful line.

EAGLES VETERAN ROSTER

HEAD COACH—Buddy Ryan. Assistant Coaches—Dave Atkins, Tom Bettis, Jeff Fisher, Dale Haupt, Ronnie Jones, Rich Kotite, Dan Neal, Al Roberts, Doug Scovil, Bill Walsh.

No.	Name	Pos.	Ht.	Wt.	NFL Exp.	College
72	Alexander, David	C-T	6-3	282	4	Tulsa
21	Allen, Eric	CB	5-10	181	3	Arizona State
49	Bell, Todd	S	6-1	215	9	Ohio State
99	Brown, Jerome	DT	6-2	292	4	Miami
41	Byars, Keith	RB	6-2	230	5	Ohio State
80	Carter, Cris	WR	6-3	196	4	Ohio State
6	Cavanaugh, Matt	QB	6-2	210	13	Pittsburgh
12	Cunningham, Randall	QB	6-4	192	6	Nevada-Las Vegas
78	Darwin, Matt	T	6-4	275	5	Texas A&M
36	Drummond, Robert	RB	6-1	205	2	Syracuse
84	Edwards, Anthony	WR-KR	5-11	195	2	New Mexico Highlands
56	Evans, Byron	LB	6-2	235	4	Arizona
33	Frizzell, William	CB-S	6-3	206	7	North Carolina Central
86	Garrity, Gregg	WR	5-10	175	8	Penn State
83	Giles, Jimmie	TE	6-3	245	14	Alcorn State
90	Golic, Mike	DT	6-5	275	5	Notre Dame
54	Hager, Britt	LB	6-1	222	2	Texas
95	Harris, Al	LB	6-5	265	11	Arizona State
73	Heller, Ron	T	6-6	280	7	Penn State
34	Hoage, Terry	S	6-3	201	7	Georgia
48	Hopkins, Wes	S	6-1	215	7	Southern Methodist
88	Jackson, Keith	TE	6-2	250	3	Oklahoma
46	Jenkins, Izel	CB	5-10	191	3	North Carolina State
85	Johnson, Ron	WR	6-3	190	6	Long Beach State
31	Jones, Tyrone	S	6-4	223	2	Arkansas State
59	Joyner, Seth	LB	6-2	248	5	Texas-El Paso
94	Kaufusi, Steve	DE-DT	6-4	274	2	Brigham Young
87	Le Bel, Harper	TE	6-4	251	2	Colorado State
37	Lilly, Sammy	CB	5-9	178	2	Georgia Tech
74	Pitts, Mike	DT	6-5	277	8	Alabama
82	Quick, Mike	WR	6-2	195	9	North Carolina State
66	Reeves, Ken	T-G	6-5	270	6	Texas A&I
50	Rimington, Dave	C-G	6-3	285	8	Nebraska
7	Ruzek, Roger	K	6-1	195	4	Weber State
79	Schad, Mike	G	6-5	290	3	Queens (Canada)
51	Shaw, Ricky	LB	6-4	240	3	Oklahoma State
23	Sherman, Heath	RB-KR	6-0	190	2	Texas A&I
96	Simmons, Clyde	DE	6-6	275	5	Western Carolina
68	Singletary, Reggie	G-T	6-3	285	4	North Carolina State
52	Small, Jessie	LB	6-3	239	2	Eastern Kentucky
65	Solt, Ron	G	6-3	288	6	Maryland
61	Tamburello, Ben	G-C	6-3	278	3	Auburn
10	Teltschik, John	P	6-2	210	5	Texas
25	Toney, Anthony	RB	6-0	227	5	Texas A&M
20	Waters, Andre	S	5-11	185	7	Cheyney State
47	Werner, Greg	TE	6-4	236	2	DePauw
92	White, Reggie	DE	6-5	285	6	Tennessee

TOP DRAFT CHOICES

Rd.	Name	Sel. No.	Pos.	Ht.	Wt.	College
1	Smith, Ben	22	DR	5-10	183	Georgia
2	Bellamy, Mike	50	WR	6-0	196	Illinois
3	Barnett, Fred	77	WR	6-0	203	Arkansas State
5	Williams, Calvin	133	WR	5-11	181	Purdue
6	Thompson, Kevin	162	DR	5-10	191	Oklahoma

PHILADELPHIA EAGLES 133

The Eagles had no success with their kick-return games, giving up 21.8 yards per return, while averaging only 16.9. The outlook improves with the addition of Bellamy, 30.9 as an Illinois senior. The punt-return numbers were substantially better, as the Eagles averaged 8.9 yards per return and allowed a measly 5.8 yards, the lowest total in the league.

THE ROOKIES: Georgia's Smith, a devastating hitter, will replace Wes Hopkins at free safety. Bellamy, 50th pick in the draft, led Illinois in receiving and kickoff returns. Ryan followed with selections of wide receivers Fred Barnett of Arkansas State and Calvin Williams of Purdue.

OUTLOOK: With the Giants improving and the Redskins on a roll, the 11-5 Eagles will be hard-pressed to get back into the playoffs. Give them that one elusive running back, though, and you are looking at a division winner with expectations of even greater things.

EAGLE PROFILES

RANDALL CUNNINGHAM 27 6-4 192   Quarterback

Brooded through much of the year... Attacked anyone who claimed that he wasn't one of three best quarterbacks in football.... Completed 290 of 532 passes for 3,400 yards... Threw 21 touchdown passes and was intercepted 15 times... Ranked 14th in the NFL with a rating of 75.5.... Led Eagles in rushing with 621 yards on 104 carries for 6.0 average... Became the first quarterback in the modern era to lead his team in rushing three consecutive years... Completed 24 of 40 passes for 238 yards in playoff loss to the Rams... Named 1988 NFL Player of the Year by the Maxwell Club... Was 1988 Pro Bowl MVP ... Second-round draft pick in 1985 out of UNLV... Was an All-American punter in college.... Had a 91-yard punt last year against the Giants... Born March 27, 1963, in Santa Barbara, Cal.... In second season of seven-year, $17.94-million contract.

REGGIE WHITE 28 6-5 285   Defensive End

After leading the NFL in sacks in 1987 and '88, White recorded the lowest sack total (11) of his career... Complained bitterly, and not without basis, that he was being held all year long... First time he failed to lead the Eagles in sacks... Led the team with 78 quarterback hurries... Recorded 119 tackles... A practicing Baptist minister, he is nicknamed "The Minister of Defense"... Was named 1988 NFL Player of the Year by the Washington Touchdown Club... Played two years for the Memphis Showboats (USFL)... Claimed by the Eagles in the first round of the 1984 supplemental draft... Attended Tennessee... Born Dec. 19, 1961, in Chattanooga, Tenn.... Earned $1.65 million last year.

CLYDE SIMMONS 26 6-6 275   Defensive End

Led the Eagles with 15½ sacks... Nearly doubled his total of 16 for his first three years in the league... Was the beneficiary of much of the double-teaming of Reggie White.... Finished fourth on the team with 122 tackles... Had 52 quarterback pressures and three forced fumbles... Was All-Southern Conference at Western Carolina University, but only a ninth-round selection in 1986... Which makes him one of the biggest draft steals of the decade... Babe Ruth League teammate of Michael Jordan... Played scholastic basketball against Michael... Born Aug. 4, 1964, in Lanes, S.C.... Earned $325,000 last year.

KEITH JACKSON 25 6-2 250   Tight End

Managed to earn his second straight trip to the Pro Bowl despite missing much of the season... Led all NFL tight ends with 63 receptions and 648 yards... Had 12-catch games against Washington and Minnesota... NFC Rookie of the Year in 1988... Caught 81 passes for 869 yards as a rookie... Had more receptions in each of his first two years as a professional than in his entire career at Oklahoma... Excellent cello player... While most college football players struggle to get their degrees in five years, Jackson earned his in three-and-a-half... Born

PHILADELPHIA EAGLES 135

April 19, 1965, in Little Rock, Ark.... Earned $312,000 last year.

ERIC ALLEN 24 5-10 181   Cornerback

Has been a starter since the first day of his career with the Eagles ... Earned all-rookie honors in 1988 and was named to his first Pro Bowl in 1989 ... Led the NFC with eight interceptions ... Sprained his ankle while horsing around in the Eagles' locker room with teammate Sammy Lilly ... As a result, was hampered through the final three games and in the playoffs ... Has 13 interceptions in his first two seasons ... A second-round draft choice out of Arizona State, where he was a four-year starter ... Had 15 interceptions in college, including one against Michigan in the 1986 Rose Bowl ... Born Nov. 22, 1965, in San Diego ... Earned $215,000 last year.

ANTHONY TONEY 27 6-0 227   Fullback

Led all Eagles' running backs with 582 yards, but couldn't beat out Randall Cunningham for team lead ... Rushed for a career-high 582 yards on 172 carries ... Caught 19 passes for 124 yards ... Best day came in final regular-season game, when he rushed for 82 yards against the Cards ... Scored the winning touchdown against the Giants in Week 5 and also set up another score with a 44-yard romp on a fake reverse ... Rushed for 502 yards in 1988 ... Shared fullback duties with Roger Vick at Texas A&M ... All-SWC selection as a senior ... Second-round draft choice in 1986 ... Enjoys making his own lip-synch videos ... Born Sept. 23, 1962, in Salinas, Cal.... Earned $225,000 last season.

ANDRE WATERS 28 5-11 185   Safety

Season got off on a bad foot when he lost his starting job following an extended training-camp holdout ... Regained starting job in Week 4 after Todd Bell broke his leg ... Still managed to finish third on the team with 129 tackles ... A punishing hitter, Waters forced four fumbles ... He also had one interception and one sack ... Led the team in tackles from

1986 to 1988... Came to the Eagles in 1984 as a free agent... Made the team on the strength of his special-teams play... Unheralded college player out of Cheyney State... Born March 10, 1962, in Belle Glade, Fla.... Earned $410,000 last year.

WES HOPKINS 28 6-1 215   Safety

He'd proved his knee problems (three operations) were behind him in '88, and last year he finished second on the team with 131 tackles... Had missed a season and a half, including all of '87... Was a Pro Bowl starter and the team's defensive MVP in '85... A first-round pick in '83 out of SMU, where he began as a walk-on and finished as career interception leader... Played in 1983 Hula Bowl... Born Sept. 26, 1961, in Birmingham, Ala.... Earned $500,000 last year.

KEITH BYARS 26 6-1 230   Running Back

Billed as the solution to the Eagles' running problems when he arrived as a first-round pick in 1986, Byars has yet to live up to expectations... Though he was the second-leading ground-gainer in Ohio State history, Byars has made his greatest contributions as a receiver... Emerged as Randall Cunningham's favorite target last year, catching 68 passes for 721 yards... Led Eagles in receptions and receiving yardage... Ran for 452 yards on 133 carries (3.4 average)... Ranked third among NFL running backs in receptions... Buddy Ryan calls him the best player he's ever seen at making catches out of the backfield... Broke his foot in each of his first two training camps... Born Oct. 14, 1963, in Dayton, Ohio... Earned $475,000 last year.

JEROME BROWN 25 6-2 292   Defensive Tackle

Ranked third on the Eagles with 10½ sacks (11th in the NFC)... Emerging as one of the league's top defensive tackles... Earned his first trip to the Pro Bowl... Has 19½ sacks in his first three seasons.... Had 123 tackles and 40 quarterback hurries... Tied for the team lead with four forced fumbles... Was the ninth player selected in the 1987 draft out of the University of Miami, where he was an All-American.... Reggie

White was his counselor when he attended the University of Tennessee's football camp for high-school players... Born Feb. 4, 1965, in Brooksville, Fla.... Earned $302,000 last year.

COACH BUDDY RYAN: It was a difficult fourth year at the Eagles' helm for Ryan... He was in the middle of a "bounty hunting" controversy for allegedly putting price tags on the heads of Troy Aikman and Luis Zendejas... Led the 11-5 Eagles to their second straight playoff berth, but they have yet to win a single playoff game under him... Easily the most colorful coach in the game... Given to honesty and that always draws a response... Buddy's coached for 22 years in the NFL... Created the "46" defense as the defensive coordinator of the Bears and also coached for the Vikings and the Jets... Has a long-standing feud with Mike Ditka ... Played offensive guard at Oklahoma State... Born Feb. 17, 1934, in Frederick, Okla.... Entered the Army at 16, served in Korea for two years and wound up as a master sergeant—perfect for role as coaching taskmaster... Regular-season mark is 33-29-2.

LONGEST PASS PLAY

RON JAWORSKI TO MIKE QUICK

The Eagles had squandered a 17-10 fourth-quarter lead and now it was 17-17 and they were in overtime against the visiting Saints on Nov. 10, 1985.

The Falcons had first shot, but failed to move the ball. Rick Donnelly got off a 62-yard punt that went out of bounds inches from the Eagles' goal line.

After an incomplete pass, offensive coordinator Ted Marchibroda called for a post pattern from Ron Jaworski to Mike Quick, who responded with a 99-yard play that meant a 23-17 Eagle victory and a place in the team and NFL record book.

INDIVIDUAL EAGLE RECORDS

Rushing

Most Yards Game:	205	Steve Van Buren, vs Pittsburgh, 1949
Season:	1,512	Wilbert Montgomery, 1979
Career:	6,538	Wilbert Montgomery, 1977-84

Passing

Most TD Passes Game:	7	Adrian Burk, vs Washington, 1954
Season:	32	Sonny Jurgensen, 1961
Career:	167	Ron Jaworski, 1977-85

Receiving

Most TD Passes Game:	4	Joe Carter, vs Cincinnati, 1934
	4	Ben Hawkins, vs Pittsburgh, 1969
Season:	13	Tommy McDonald, 1960 and 1961
	13	Mike Quick, 1983
Career:	79	Harold Carmichael, 1971-83

Scoring

Most Points Game:	25	Bobby Walston, vs Washington, 1954
Season:	116	Paul McFadden, 1984
Career:	881	Bobby Walston, 1951-62
Most TDs Game:	4	Joe Carter, vs Cincinnati, 1934
	4	Clarence Peaks, vs St. Louis, 1958
	4	Tommy McDonald, vs N.Y. Giants, 1959
	4	Ben Hawkins, vs Pittsburgh, 1969
	4	Wilbert Montgomery, vs Washington, 1978
	4	Wilbert Montgomery, vs Washington, 1979
Season:	18	Steve Van Buren, 1945
Career:	79	Harold Carmichael, 1971-83

PHOENIX CARDINALS

TEAM DIRECTORY: Pres.: William V. Bidwill; GM: Larry Wilson; VPs-Administration: Curt Mosher, Joe Rhein; VP-Communications: Terry Bledsoe; Dir. Pro Personnel: Erik Widmark; Dir. Pub. Rel.: Paul Jensen. Head Coach: Joe Bugel. Home field: Sun Devil Stadium (72,000). Colors: Cardinal red, white and black.

Sprained knee couldn't keep Luis Sharpe out of Pro Bowl.

SCOUTING REPORT

OFFENSE: After a dismal season (5-11) in which injuries decimated the running and passing games, it's hard to say exactly where the offense stands in 1990. The passing game is up in the air. The Cards must decide whether the time has come to put the ball in the hands of Timm Rosenbach, Tom Tupa or go to old standby Gary Hogeboom.

The running game is also in disarray. Stump Mitchell is making a remarkable recovery from what appeared to be a career-ending knee injury, but it's doubtful that he will be his old dominant self. Without Mitchell, the Cards went an entire season without producing a single 100-yard rushing effort. Heisman Trophy runnerup Anthony Thompson will have ample opportunity to make his presence felt.

The Cards still possess two of the best receivers in the game in Roy Green and J.T. Smith, but they're well into their thirties. That's one reason for the drafting of wide receiver Richard Proehl.

The offensive line is the one area of the offense the Cards can count on. Luis Sharpe is a Pro Bowler, Tootie Robbins is close and Joe Wolf is on his way.

DEFENSE: The Cardinals ranked 26th in the league in team defense, hardly an encouraging figure. The defensive line was destroyed by injuries, substance abuse and incompetence. The Cards were forced to use 10 different starting defensive fronts. Hopefully, Freddie Joe Nunn can stay clean in 1990 and everyone else can remain healthy.

The linebacking corps, at least, was cause for encouragement. Ken Harvey, Anthony Bell and Eric Hill give the Cards youth, speed and talent in the middle of the defense.

In the secondary, All-Pro safety Tim McDonald is the one bright spot. The Cards were particularly thin at cornerback last year, but they've made two major Plan-B acquisitions in Lorenzo Lynch (Bears) and Tracy Eaton (Oilers).

KICKING GAME: Easily the best part of the Cardinals' package. Rich Camarillo punted his way into the Pro Bowl, while Al Del Greco was a model of consistency (28-29 PATs, 18-of-26 FGs).

The Cards' return game is never a problem so long as Vai Sikahema is on the field. Pro Bowler Ron Wolfley is one of the most dangerous special-teams tacklers and blockers in the league.

CARDINALS VETERAN ROSTER

HEAD COACH—Joe Bugel. Assistant Coaches—Tod Cottrell, Bobby Hammond, Jim Johnson, Mike Murphy, Joe Pascale, Ted Plumb, Jerry Rhome, Pete Rodriguez, Bob Rogucki, Tom Lovat.

No.	Name	Pos.	Ht.	Wt.	NFL Exp.	College
80	Awalt, Robert	TE	6-5	244	4	San Diego State
44	Baker, Tony	RB	5-10	190	4	East Carolina
55	Bell, Anthony	LB	6-3	235	5	Michigan State
71	Bostic, Joe	G	6-3	276	11	Clemson
16	Camarillo, Rich	P	5-11	185	10	Washington
45	Carr, Lydell	RB	6-1	228	2	Oklahoma
41	Carter, Carl	CB	5-11	189	5	Texas Tech
79	Clasby, Bob	DT	6-5	276	5	Notre Dame
17	Del Greco, Al	K	5-10	198	7	Auburn
21	Eaton, Tracey	S	6-1	190	3	Portland State
65	Galloway, David	DE	6-3	259	9	Florida
81	Green, Roy	WR	6-0	195	12	Henderson State
73	Hadd, Gary	DT	6-4	278	3	Minnesota
56	Harvey, Ken	LB	6-2	230	3	California
5	Hogeboom, Gary	QB	6-4	208	11	Central Michigan
83	Holmes, Don	WR	5-10	177	5	Mesa
53	Jax, Garth	LB	6-2	229	5	Florida State
86	Jones, Ernie	WR	5-11	191	3	Indiana
32	Jordan, Tony	RB	6-2	220	3	Kansas State
57	Kauahi, Kani	C	6-2	270	8	Hawaii
70	Kennard, Derek	C-G	6-3	309	5	Nevada-Reno
52	Kirk, Randy	LB	6-2	231	4	San Diego State
51	Lewis, Bill	C	6-7	275	5	Nebraska
29	Lynch, Lorenzo	CB	5-9	199	3	Cal State-Sacramento
47	Mack, Cedric	CB	6-0	185	8	Baylor
46	McDonald, Tim	CB-S	6-2	207	4	Southern California
54	McKenzie, Reggie	LB	6-1	242	5	Tennessee
30	Mitchell, Stump	RB	5-9	188	10	Citadel
78	Nunn, Freddie Joe	DE	6-4	250	6	Mississippi
89	Reeves, Walter	TE	6-3	249	2	Auburn
63	Robbins, Tootie	T	6-5	307	9	East Carolina
3	Rosenbach, Timm	QB	6-2	210	2	Washington State
72	Saddler, Rod	DE	6-5	280	4	Texas A&M
67	Sharpe, Luis	T	6-4	260	9	UCLA
36	Sikahema, Vai	RB-KR	5-9	191	5	Brigham Young
84	Smith, J. T.	WR	6-2	185	13	North Texas State
61	Smith, Lance	T-G	6-2	278	6	Louisiana State
27	Taylor, Jay	CB	5-9	170	2	San Jose State
19	Tupa, Tom	QB-P	6-4	220	3	Ohio State
23	Turner, Marcus	CB-S	6-0	191	2	UCLA
66	Wahler, Jim	DT	6-3	268	2	UCLA
60	Walker, Jeff	T	6-4	295	4	Memphis State
68	Wolf, Joe	T-G	6-5	279	2	Boston College
24	Wolfley, Ron	RB	6-0	222	6	West Virginia
43	Young, Lonnie	CA-S	6-1	191	6	Michigan State
38	Zordich, Mike	CB-S	5-11	197	4	Penn State

TOP DRAFT CHOICES

Rd.	Name	Sel. No.	Pos.	Ht.	Wt.	College
2	Thompson, Anthony	31	RB	5-11	207	Indiana
3	Proehl, Ricky	58	WR	5-10	181	Wake Forest
4	Davis, Travis	85	DT	6-0	274	Michigan State
5	Centers, Larry	115	RB	5-10	203	Stephen F. Austin
6	Shavers, Tyrone	142	WR	6-2	205	Lamar

THE ROOKIES: The Cards lost their top pick when they took Rosenbach in last year's supplemental draft. They still got some value in the draft, taking Indiana's Thompson, the nation's leading rusher, in the second round. Proehl, a possession receiver out of Wake Forest, caught 51 passes, with eight TDs, in 1989.

OUTLOOK: Bleak to terrible for new coach Joe Bugel. No chance of catching the Giants, Eagles or Redskins. The Cardinals will even have their hands full holding off the Cowboys.

CARDINAL PROFILES

GARY HOGEBOOM 32 6-4 208   **Quarterback**

Established career highs for passing yards, completions and touchdown passes... Completed 204 of 364 passes for 2,591 yards... Threw 14 touchdown passes and 19 interceptions... His 19 interceptions was a career high ... Had four of his first eight passes intercepted in loss to Giants... Best game came against the Seahawks when he completed 18 of 24 passes for 298 yards and four touchdowns... Signed as a Plan-B free agent after the 1988 season... Spent three injury-plagued seasons with the Colts... Started only 12 games in three years ... Drafted by the Cowboys in the fifth round of the 1980 draft out of Central Michigan... Born Aug. 21, 1958, in Grand Rapids, Mich.... Earned $970,000 last year.

TIM McDONALD 25 6-2 207   **Strong Safety**

Made it to his first Pro Bowl in only his second season as a starter... Recorded 155 tackles, including 102 solos... Led the Cards in tackles for the second consecutive year... Ranked second on the team with 16 passes defensed... Ranked second in the NFC and first on the Cards with seven interceptions... Led the NFC with 170 interception return yards... Recorded four interceptions over a two-week span in games against the Giants and Cowboys... Had 16 tackles against the Redskins... As a rookie in 1987, he broke his ankle and missed all but the final four games... Second-round pick out of USC... Born Jan. 6, 1965, in Fresno, Cal.... Earned $190,000 last year.

PHOENIX CARDINALS 143

LUIS SHARPE 30 6-4 260 — Tackle

Returned to the Pro Bowl for the third straight year despite playing much of the season on a sprained knee... Injury forced Sharpe to miss the first two games of his eight-year career... One of the best pass-blockers in the league... Played in 44 games during a 16-month stretch from 1984-85... Started all 16 games for the Cardinals in 1984, then 12 games with the Memphis Showboats of the USFL in the spring of 1985, then 16 games with the Cards in 1985... First-round pick out of UCLA in 1982 and started every game as a rookie... Born June 16, 1960, in Havana, Cuba, he moved to Detroit at age six.... Has a degree in political science... Earned $640,000 last year.

RON WOLFLEY 28 6-0 222 — Fullback

Earned his fourth straight trip to the Pro Bowl as a special-teams player... May have made it to the Pro Bowl on reputation alone last year... Had only 13 special-teams tackles, 17 less than teammate Garth Jax... Fearless, known for his kamakaze efforts and disregard for injury and pain... An excellent special-teams blocker as well... Ran the ball only 13 times for 36 yards and caught five passes for 38 yards... Fourth-round pick out of West Virginia in 1985... Born Oct. 14, 1962, in Hamburg, N.Y.... Earned $237,500 last year.

KEN HARVEY 25 6-2 225 — Linebacker

Emerging as one of the top young linebackers... In only his first year as a starter, ranked second on the team in tackles with 120... Led the Cards with seven sacks... Recorded 16 tackles (15 solo) against the Broncos... Also contributed on special teams... Didn't start as a rookie in 1988, but still managed to record 36 tackles and six sacks... Defensive Player of the Game in the 1988 East-West Shrine Game... Extremely strong, set a weight-lifting record at the University of California... Dropped out of high school to work at McDonald's but returned and went on to play at Laney (Tex.) JC before attending California... Twelfth player selected in '88... Born May 6, 1965, in Austin, Tex.... Earned $255,000 last year.

RICH CAMARILLO 31 5-11 185 — Punter

Saw his career rise from the ashes... Earned his second trip to the Pro Bowl... Led the NFL with an average of 43.3 yards per punt... Had 21 punts inside the opposition's 20-yard line... Picked up by the Cards as a free agent after spending one year with the Rams and eight with the Patriots... Went to his first Pro Bowl in 1983, when he led the NFL in net punting average (37.1 yards) and was second in gross yardage (44.6 yards)... Played at the University of Washington... Born Nov. 29, 1959, in Whittier, Cal.... Earned $152,500 last year.

JOE WOLF 24 6-5 279 — Tackle/Guard

Made everybody's all-rookie team after an excellent first season... Effective as both a run- and pass-blocker... Started the final 15 games... With injuries all over the Cards' offensive line, Wolf was forced to start at left tackle (two games), right tackle (seven games) and left guard (six games)... Honorable mention All-American guard at Boston College... At 18, he was the youngest member of the Doug Flutie-quarterbacked Cotton Bowl team in 1984... Brother Mike was a center at Penn State... First guard and 17th player overall taken in the 1989 draft... Born Dec. 28, 1966, in Allentown, Pa.

J.T. SMITH 34 6-2 185 — Wide Receiver

Suffered ankle and knee sprains against the Giants and missed the final seven weeks of the season... Smith was on a pace to shatter Art Monk's single-season reception mark... Recorded 62 receptions for 778 yards and five touchdowns in only nine games... He was leading the NFL in receptions at the time of the injuries... Caught 11 passes for 123 yards against the Chargers and caught three touchdown passes against the Redskins... Went to the Pro Bowl (as an alternate) after the 1988 season... Signed with the Cardinals as a free agent in 1985... Originally signed as a free agent by the Redskins in 1978 after playing at North Texas State... Born Oct. 29, 1955, in Leonard, Tex.... Earned $450,000 last year.

PHOENIX CARDINALS 145

ROY GREEN 33 6-0 195 — Wide Receiver

Yet another member of the Cardinals' corps of walking wounded... Broke his collarbone in Week 5 and missed the next four games... Finished with only 44 receptions for 703 yards... Still managed to catch seven touchdown passes... Had a huge game in Week 2, catching eight passes for 166 yards and three touchdowns against the Seahawks... His 1,555 receiving yards in 1984 is the fourth-highest total in league history... Went to the Pro Bowl in 1983 and 1984... In 1984, averaged 45.3 yards for each of his 12 touchdown receptions... Began his career as a defensive back... Caught a touchdown pass and made an interception in the same game against the Redskins in 1981... Born June 30, 1957, in Magnolia, Ark.... Earned $740,000 last year.

STUMP MITCHELL 31 5-9 188 — Running Back

Suffered a career-threatening knee injury against the Giants... Underwent reconstructive surgery and missed the final 13 games of the season... Rushed for 165 yards on 43 carries.... Though he played in only three games, finished third on the team in rushing... Failed to rush for 100 yards in any game, but had a 95-yard effort (18 carries) against the Seahawks.... Prior to 1989, he had four straight years of 700+ yards rushing... Rushed for 145 yards in first career start in 1983 against the Eagles... Had a career-high 1,006 rushing yards in 1985... Ninth-round draft choice out of the Citadel in 1981... Born March 15, 1959, in Kingsland, Ga.... Earned $440,000 last year.

VAI SIKAHEMA 27 5-9 191 — Kick Returner

Finished third in the NFC in punt returns, averaging 11.7 yards per return... Ranked 12th in conference in kickoff returns, averaging 20.3 yards per return... Injuries in backfield gave Sikahema two starts at halfback... Rushed for 145 yards on 38 carries... Caught 23 passes for 245 yards... Voted to the Pro Bowl in 1986 and 1987 after leading the league in punt-returning... Tenth-round pick out of Brigham Young in 1986... In the 1986 season finale against Tampa Bay, he became only the fifth player in NFL history to return two punts for touchdowns in one game... Born Aug. 29, 1962, in Nyku' Alofa, Tonga... Earned $185,000 last year.

COACH JOE BUGEL: After four college and three pro jobs, Bugel gets his first shot at a head-coaching position this year... He made his greatest impact with the Washington Redskins, where he spent the last nine seasons, most recently as "Assistant Head Coach-Offense" ... His area of expertise has been the offensive line... Four Redskins' offensive linemen earned Pro Bowl honors under Bugel's tutelage... He should have some fun working with the Cardinals' passing game, but will have to use all of his talents to re-establish the running attack... Served as the offensive line coach with both the Lions (1975-76) and the Oilers (1977-80) ... Coached at Ohio State, Iowa State, Navy and Western Kentucky... Played guard at Western Kentucky, where he earned his Masters degree in counseling... Born March 10, 1940, in Pittsburgh.

LONGEST PASS PLAYS

DOUG RUSSELL TO GAYNELL TINSLEY

OGDEN COMPTON TO DICK LANE

JIM HART TO BOBBY MOORE (AHMAD RASHAD)

Three tandems share the Cardinals' record for longest pass play.
Playing against the Browns on Nov. 27, 1938, Gaynell Tinsley's 98-yard reception highlighted the Chicago Cardinals' 31-17 victory over the Browns. A year earlier, Tinsley had been on the receiving end of a 97-yarder from Pat Coffee against the Bears in a 16-7 defeat.

Rookie Ogden Compton hooked up with Dick Lane on a 98-yarder against the Packers on Nov. 13, 1955, as the Packers drubbed the Chicago Cardinals, 31-14.

PHOENIX CARDINALS 147

The St. Louis Cardinals pulled off a 24-14 upset of the L.A. Rams on Dec. 10, 1972, and the highlight of the game was the longest pass play in league history that didn't result in a touchdown. The Cardinals' Jim Hart connected with Bobby Moore (Ahmad Rashad) on a play that began at the Cards' one-yard line and ended at the Rams' one. Another 98-yarder.

INDIVIDUAL CARDINAL RECORDS

Rushing

Most Yards Game:	203	John David Crow, vs Pittsburgh, 1960
Season:	1,605	Ottis Anderson, 1979
Career:	7,999	Ottis Anderson, 1979-86

Passing

Most TD Passes Game:	6	Jim Hardy, vs Baltimore, 1950
	6	Charley Johnson, vs Cleveland, 1965
	6	Charley Johnson, vs New Orleans, 1969
Season:	28	Charley Johnson, 1963
	28	Neil Lomax, 1984
Career:	205	Jim Hart, 1966-82

Receiving

Most TD Passes Game:	5	Bob Shaw, vs Baltimore, 1950
Season:	15	Sonny Randle, 1960
Career:	60	Sonny Randle, 1959-66

Scoring

Most Points Game:	40	Ernie Nevers, vs Chicago, 1929
Season:	117	Jim Bakken, 1967
	117	Neil O'Donoghue, 1984
Career:	1,380	Jim Bakken, 1962-78
Most TDs Game:	6	Ernie Nevers, vs Chicago, 1929
Season:	17	John David Crow, 1962
Career:	60	Sonny Randle, 1959-66

148 THE COMPLETE HANDBOOK OF PRO FOOTBALL
SAN FRANCISCO 49ERS

TEAM DIRECTORY: Owner/Pres.: Edward J. DeBartolo Jr.; Exec. VP-Front Office/League Relations: Carmen Policy; VP-Football Administration: John McVay; Dir. Pub. Rel.: Jerry Walker. Head Coach: George Seifert. Home field: Candlestick Park (61,499). Colors: 49er gold and scarlet.

SCOUTING REPORT

OFFENSE: Enough weapons to be classified as a Super Power. Joe Montana has established himself as one of the best, if not the best, quarterbacks ever. The only question is: how much longer can he go? Based on last year's performance and the protection

Roger Craig was as vital as ever in 49ers' super year.

he's been getting, the answer is: as long as he wants to.

Give at least some of the credit for Montana's success to an awesome group of receivers. Jerry Rice is as good as anyone in football and John Taylor is well on his way to stardom. Brent Jones is about everything one could hope for in a tight end.

The running game is in great hands with the Nebraska duo of Roger Craig and Tom Rathman, both as dangerous catching the ball as they are carrying it. And the No. 1 pick was Dexter Carter, a speedy running back and kickoff-returner.

The offensive line doesn't get nearly the credit it deserves. Only Guy McIntyre went to the Pro Bowl, but Harris Barton will be there soon.

DEFENSE: It can be frustrating to play defense on a team known for its offense. Nevertheless, the defensive unit happens to be one of the best in the league. The defensive line will be helped by the healthy return of Michael Carter, who missed eight games last year. Pierce Holt is emerging as a top young pass-rusher, while Daniel Stubbs is coming on strong.

The line will be even stronger this year with the addition of Plan-B nose tackle Fred Smerlas from the Bills and rookie tackle Dennis Brown.

The linebacking corps is underrated. Charles Haley has become one of the top pass-rushing linebackers in the league, while Michael Walter is an imposing presense on the inside.

The 49ers' solid pass defense should also be improved in 1990. At safety, Ronnie Lott and Chet Brooks will be helped out this year by the Plan-B acquisition of Dave Waymer (New Orleans), while cornerbacks Darryl Pollard and Don Griffin will get some backup help from another Plan-B acquisition, Hanford Dixon (Cleveland).

KICKING: Nothing to kick about here either. Mike Cofer was deadly from inside 40 yards, missing only one of 20 tries. If there was any weakness, it was the punting game. Barry Helton averaged 40.5 yards per punt. Perhaps the 49ers' offense just didn't give him enough practice.

THE ROOKIES: The 49ers picked up a reliable third-down back in Florida State's Carter. An excellent receiver out of the backfield, he should fit in perfectly with the 49ers' offense. Washington's Brown, a projected first-rounder, should bolster the middle of the 49ers' defensive line. Jacksonville State's Eric Davis could fill in quickly at cornerback.

49ERS VETERAN ROSTER

HEAD COACH—George Seifert. Assistant Coaches—Jerry Attaway, Tommy Hart, Mike Holmgren, Al Lavan, Sherman Lewis, John Marshall, Bobb McKittrick, Bill McPherson, Ray Rhodes, Lynn Stiles, Bob Zeman.

No.	Name	Pos.	Ht.	Wt.	NFL Exp.	College
67	Aronson, Doug	G	6-4	278	2	San Diego State
79	Barton, Harris	T	6-4	280	4	North Carolina
13	Bono, Steve	QB	6-4	215	6	UCLA
65	Bregel, Jeff	G	6-4	280	4	Southern California
31	Brooks, Chet	S	5-11	191	3	Texas A&M
64	Burt, Jim	NT	6-1	270	10	Miami
95	Carter, Michael	NT	6-2	285	7	Southern Methodist
6	Cofer, Mike	K	6-1	190	3	North Carolina State
69	Collie, Bruce	G-T	6-6	275	6	Texas-Arlington
38	Cox, Greg	S	6-0	217	3	San Jose State
33	Craig, Roger	RB	6-0	224	8	Nebraska
68	Cullity, Dave	T	6-7	275	2	Utah
59	DeLong, Keith	LB	6-2	235	2	Tennessee
28	Dixon, Hanford	CB	6-0	185	10	Southern Mississippi
50	Ellison, Riki	LB	6-2	225	7	Southern California
75	Fagan, Kevin	DE	6-4	265	4	Miami
55	Fahnhorst, Jim	LB	6-4	230	7	Minnesota
49	Fuller, Jeff	S	6-2	216	7	Texas A&M
96	Goss, Antonio	LB	6-4	228	2	North Carolina
29	Griffin, Don	CB	6-0	176	5	Middle Tenn. State
94	Haley, Charles	LB-DE	6-5	230	5	James Madison
65	Hamilton, Steve	DE	6-4	275	5	East Carolina
9	Helton, Barry	P	6-3	205	3	Colorado
30	Henderson, Keith	RB	6-1	220	2	Georgia
56	Hendrickson, Steve	LB	6-0	245	2	California
46	Holmoe, Tom	S	6-2	195	7	Brigham Young
78	Holt, Pierce	DE	6-4	280	3	Angelo State
4	Horne, Greg	P	6-0	190	3	Arkansas
40	Jackson, Johnny	S	6-1	204	2	Houston
84	Jones, Brent	TE	6-4	230	4	Santa Clara
57	Kennedy, Sam	LB	6-2	235	2	San Jose State
67	Kugler, Pete	DE	6-4	255	7	Penn State
60	Lockett, Danny	LB	6-2	250	3	Arizona
42	Lott, Ronnie	S	6-0	200	10	Southern California
62	McIntyre, Guy	G	6-3	265	7	Georgia
54	Millen, Matt	LB	6-2	245	11	Penn State
16	Montana, Joe	QB	6-1	195	12	Notre Dame
77	Paris, Bubba	T	6-6	306	8	Michigan
26	Pollard, Darryl	CB	5-11	187	4	Weber State
76	Putzier, Rollin	NT	6-4	279	3	Oregon
57	Radloff, Wayne	C	6-5	277	6	Georgia
44	Rathman, Tom	RB	6-1	232	5	Nebraska
80	Rice, Jerry	WR	6-2	200	6	Miss. Valley State
91	Roberts, Larry	DE	6-3	275	5	Alabama
53	Romonowski, Bill	LB	6-4	231	3	Boston College
61	Sapolu, Jessie	C	6-4	260	5	Hawaii
71	Shannon, John	DE	6-3	270	3	Kentucky
88	Sherrard, Mike	WR	6-2	187	2	UCLA
72	Smerias, Fred	NT	6-4	291	12	Boston College
32	Swoope, Craig	S	6-2	210	4	Illinois
24	Sydney, Harry	RB	6-0	217	4	Kansas
66	Tausch, Terry	G	6-4	278	9	Texas
82	Taylor, John	WR	6-1	185	4	Delaware State
47	Tennell, Derek	TE	6-5	248	4	UCLA
60	Thomas, Chuck	C	6-3	280	5	Oklahoma
23	Tillman, Spencer	RB	5-11	206	4	Oklahoma
58	Turner, Keena	LB	6-2	222	11	Purdue
74	Wallace, Steve	T	6-5	276	5	Auburn
89	Walls, Wesley	TE	6-5	246	2	Mississippi
99	Walter, Michael	LB	6-3	238	8	Oregon
51	Washington, Chris	LB	6-4	240	6	Iowa State
43	Waymer, Dave	S	6-1	188	11	Notre Dame
81	Williams, Jamie	TE	6-4	245	8	Nebraska
85	Wilson, Mike	WR	6-3	215	10	Washington State
21	Wright, Eric	CB	6-1	185	9	Missouri
8	Young, Steve	QB	6-2	200	6	Brigham Young

TOP DRAFT CHOICES

Rd.	Name	Sel. No.	Pos.	Ht.	Wt.	College
1	Carter, Dexter	25	RB	5-8	168	Florida State
2	Brown, Dennis	47	DT	6-3	308	Washington
2	Davis, Eric	53	DB	5-10	176	Jacksonville State
3	Lewis, Ron	68	WR	5-11	172	Florida State
4	Caliguire, Dean	92	C	6-3	265	Pittsburgh

49ER PROFILES

JOE MONTANA 34 6-1 195 Quarterback

Statistically speaking, at least, Montana had the best year ever turned in by a quarterback... Established a record for quarterback rating (112.4) and had the second-highest completion percentage (70.2) in the history of the game... Completed 271 of 386 passes for 3,521 yards... Threw 26 touchdowns and only eight interceptions... Ranked third on the team in rushing with 227 yards on 49 carries... Ran for three touchdowns... And how could he top a postseason in which he completed 26 of 30 passes against the Rams in the NFC championship game, then completed 22 of 29 for 297 yards and five touchdowns against the Broncos in the Super Bowl?... Earned a record-breaking third Super Bowl MVP... NFL career leader for quarterback rating and completion percentage... The third draft pick in 1979, out of Notre Dame, he enters his 12th season... Born June 11, 1956, in New Eagle, Pa.... Earned $1.2 million last year.

TOM RATHMAN 27 6-1 232 Fullback

Emerged in 1989 as one of the top pure fullbacks in the league... Great blocker and exceptional pass-receiver... Led all NFC running backs with 73 receptions (616 yards)... Rushed 79 times for 305 yards... Capped off his best season with a two-touchdown performance in the Super Bowl... Has played his entire professional and collegiate career in the shadow of other great backs... Used almost exclusively as a blocking back at Nebraska... Was the first of three 49er third-round picks in 1986 (along with Tim KcKyer and John Taylor)... Born Oct. 7, 1962, in Grand Island, Neb.... Earned $500,000 last year.

152 THE COMPLETE HANDBOOK OF PRO FOOTBALL

JERRY RICE 27 6-2 200 — Wide Receiver

Keeps getting better... Caught 82 passes for 1,483 yards (18.1 average)... Led the league with 17 touchdown receptions... Ran five times for 33 yards... Earned his fourth straight trip to the Pro Bowl... His 1989 totals for catches, yards and touchdowns all ranked second in his career... Enjoyed a fantastic postseason capped off by a three-touchdown effort in the Super Bowl... Angry when he wasn't named as the Super Bowl MVP... NFL MVP in 1987... Super Bowl MVP in 1988... Rice has an uncanny ability to turn a short pass into a huge gain... Set 18 Division I-AA records at Mississippi Valley State... First-round pick in 1985... Part of a class that included fellow receivers Al Toon, Eddie Brown and Andre Reed... Born Oct. 13, 1962, in Starkville, Miss.... Earned $950,000 last year.

ROGER CRAIG 30 6-0 224 — Running Back

The most valuable player on almost any other team, Craig is just one of a crowd of stars with the 49ers... Rushed for 1,054 yards on 271 carries... Caught 49 passes for 473 yards... Ranked third on the team with seven TDs... Needs only nine catches this year to move into first place on the NFL's all-time list for receptions by a running back... Set a team record in 1988 with 1,502 rushing yards... In 1985, became the first player in league history to surpass 1,000 yards rushing and receiving... Owns the NFL single-season record for receptions by a running back (92 in 1985)... Second-round draft pick in 1983... Overshadowed at Nebraska by Heisman Trophy winner Mike Rozier... Won't mess with his brother-in-law, boxer Michael Nunn... Born July 10, 1960, in Preston, Miss.... Earned $650,000 last year.

JOHN TAYLOR 28 6-1 185 — Wide Receiver

Enjoyed his most productive season, catching 60 passes for 1,077 yards and 10 touchdowns... Had his best day as a pro, catching 11 passes for 286 yards against the Rams... This included a 95-yard touchdown grab... Topped off his season with a 35-yard touchdown reception in the Super Bowl... Returned from a substance-abuse suspension in 1988 to make the winning touchdown catch in the final seconds of Super Bowl XXIII.... Averaged 11.6 yards per punt return... Earned his second straight Pro Bowl berth, first selection as a receiver... Led the NFL in punt returns in 1988... Third-round pick in 1986 out of Delaware State... Born March 31, 1962, in Pennsauken, N.J.... Earned $200,000 last year.

MIKE COFER 26 6-1 190 — Kicker

Led the NFL in scoring with 138 points... Not bad for a guy with a sketchy employment record until he became a 49er... Hit on 29 of 36 field-goal attempts during the regular season... Added 49 of 51 extra points... Missed only one kick inside 40 yards... Had a rough time in the playoffs, missing three of four tries from 30-39 yards... Made seven of eight extra points in the Super Bowl... Led the NFC in scoring in 1988 with 121 points... Made two of four field-goal attempts in Super Bowl XXIII... Broke all North Carolina State kicking records and was signed as a free agent in 1987 by the Browns... Was cut before he got to play a game, then signed with the Saints for two "replacement" games that year and released again... Signed with 49ers in 1988 and finally found a steady job... Born Feb. 19, 1964, in Columbia, S.C.... Earned $92,500 last year.

GUY McINTYRE 29 6-3 265 — Guard

Earned first trip to the Pro Bowl in only his second season as a starter... Missed a month of training camp because of contractual problems and was a backup until he reclaimed starting berth on Oct. 1 against the Rams... Excellent run- and pass-blocker... Has been plagued by injuries throughout his career... Caught a 17-yard touchdown pass against the Falcons in 1988... Low point came with fumble on unexpected kick return against the Dolphins in Super Bowl XIX... Scored the first touchdown of his career on recovery of fumbled snap on a punt against the Lions in 1985... Third-round pick out of Georgia in 1984... Born Feb. 17, 1961, in Thomasville, Ga.... Earned $360,000 last year.

154 THE COMPLETE HANDBOOK OF PRO FOOTBALL

MICHAEL WALTER 29 6-3 238　　　　　　Linebacker

Has somehow remained relatively anonymous despite being the leading tackler on the world champions for the third straight year... Finished with a career-high 103 tackles... Intercepted his only pass of the year in the Super Bowl, setting up Jerry Rice's 28-yard touchdown catch early in the third quarter... What is turning out to be an excellent career began horribly... He was a second-round pick by the Cowboys, out of Oregon, in 1983, but lasted only one year... Waived five days prior to the start of 1984 season and was immediately picked up by the 49ers... Born Nov. 3, 1960, in Eugene, Ore.... Earned $450,000 last year.

CHARLES HALEY 26 6-5 230　　　　　　Linebacker

Only disappointment of an otherwise excellent season was being passed over for the Pro Bowl... Tied for team lead with 10½ sacks... Now has 40 sacks in his four-year career.... Ranked fourth on the team with 57 tackles... Forced three fumbles, best on the team... Recorded six passes defensed... Earned trip to the Pro Bowl in 1988 after leading the 49ers with 11.5 sacks... Surprised the experts as a fourth-round pick out of James Madison in 1986... In rookie year he recorded 12 sacks as a pass-rush specialist... Born Jan. 6, 1964, in Gladys, Va.... Earned $450,000 last year.

RONNIE LOTT 31 6-0 200　　　　　　Free Safety

Simply put, the best free safety in the league... Earned his eighth trip to the Pro Bowl as he led the 49ers in interceptions with five... Recorded 42 solo tackles... His five interceptions moved him into first place on the 49ers' all-time list with 48... Led the NFL with 10 interceptions in 1986... While his statistics reveal him to be a great cover man, Lott has also made his reputation on his punishing hitting... First-round draft choice out of USC in 1981... Born May 8, 1959, in Albuquerque, N.M.... Earned $825,000 last year.

COACH GEORGE SIEFERT: Rookie head coach led the 49ers to the best record in the NFL, then to the most dominant playoff run since the beginning of the Super Bowl years. . . . In three postseason games, the 49ers outscored the opposition 126-26 . . . Credited for creating a warmer, closer atmosphere in the aftermath of the Bill Walsh years . . . Spent nine years with the 49ers before getting his chance at the helm . . . Considered to be one of the best defensive minds in the game, but the offense actually improved last year, with more players involved . . . Coached at the college level for 15 years, including head-coaching stints at Westminster College (Utah) and Cornell University . . . After three victories in two seasons at Cornell (including a loss to Columbia), nobody would have guessed a promising future for Siefert . . . Played end and guard at Utah . . . As a schoolboy, he served as an usher for 49er games at Kezar Stadium . . . Born Jan. 22, 1940, in San Francisco.

LONGEST PASS PLAY

JOE MONTANA TO JERRY RICE

It was supposed to be a mismatch, but the Chargers were giving the 49ers fits early in the game on Nov. 27, 1988. While the Chargers were moving the ball easily, the visiting 49ers couldn't get on track. In their first two possessions, the 49ers' total offense was negative three yards.

The 49ers began their third possession at their own four-yard line after Rolf Mojsiejenko nailed a coffin-corner punt. On first down, Jerry Rice lined up wide to the right and drew double coverage from cornerback Gil Byrd and safety Martin Bayless. But Rice ran a simple fly pattern and Joe Montana put the ball on target. Rice caught it at the 49ers' 42 and raced untouched the remaining 58 yards for a team-record 96-yarder.

The touchdown opened the floodgates as the 49ers scored on seven of their next eight possessions and routed the Chargers, 48-10.

156 THE COMPLETE HANDBOOK OF PRO FOOTBALL

Tom Rathman capped great year with two Super Bowl TDs.

INDIVIDUAL 49ER RECORDS

Rushing

Most Yards Game:	194	Delvin Williams, vs St. Louis, 1976
Season:	1,502	Roger Craig, 1988
Career:	7,344	Joe Perry, 1948-60, 1963

Passing

Most TD Passes Game:	5	Frank Albert, vs Cleveland (AAC), 1949
	5	John Brodie, vs Minnesota, 1965
	5	Steve Spurrier, vs Chicago, 1972
	5	Joe Montana, vs Atlanta, 1985
	5	Joe Montana, vs Philadelphia, 1989
Season:	31	Joe Montana, 1987
Career:	216	Joe Montana, 1979-89

SAN FRANCISCO 49ERS

Receiving

Most TD Passes Game:	3	Alyn Beals, vs Brooklyn (AAC), 1948
	3	Alyn Beals, vs Chicago (AAC), 1949
	3	Gordy Soltau, vs Los Angeles, 1951
	3	Bernie Casey, vs Minnesota, 1962
	3	Dave Parks, vs Baltimore, 1965
	3	Gene Washington, vs San Diego, 1972
	3	Jerry Rice, vs Indianapolis, 1986
	3	Jerry Rice, vs St. Louis, 1986
	3	Jerry Rice, vs Tampa Bay, 1987
	3	Jerry Rice, vs Cleveland, 1987
	3	Jerry Rice, vs Chicago, 1987
	3	Jerry Rice, vs Tampa, 1988
	3	Jerry Rice, vs Minnesota, 1988
Season:	22	Jerry Rice, 1987
Career:	66	Jerry Rice, 1985-89

Scoring

Most Points Game:	26	Gordy Soltau, vs Los Angeles, 1951
Season:	138	Jerry Rice, 1987
Career:	896	Ray Wersching, 1977-86
Most TDs Game:	4	Bill Kilmer, vs Minnesota, 1961
Season:	23	Jerry Rice, 1987
Career:	70	Jerry Rice, 1985-89

TAMPA BAY BUCCANEERS

TEAM DIRECTORY: Owner-Pres.: Hugh Culverhouse; VP: Joy Culverhouse; VP-Head Coach: Ray Perkins; VP-Administration: Gay Culverhouse; Asst. to Pres.: Phil Krueger; Dir. Player Personnel: Jerry Angelo; Dir. Pub. Rel.: Rick Odioso; Home field: Tampa Stadium (74,296). Colors: Florida orange, white and red.

SCOUTING REPORT

OFFENSE: Whatever hopes the 5-11 Bucs have for 1990 ride on the strength of the offensive unit.

Slowly but surely, Vinny Testaverde is developing into a legitimate NFL quarterback. He's nowhere near where the Bucs hoped he would be when they made him the first pick of the 1987 draft, but he's getting better.

Finding receivers is no problem. In Mark Carrier and Bruce Hill, the Bucs have one of the best tandems in the league.

The running game received a huge boost in the offseason. First came the deal that brought Gary Anderson from San Diego. Then came the addition of Reggie Cobb, potentially the best runner in the draft.

The offensive line is good and getting better, with Paul Gruber one of the top young tackles, and there are no glaring weaknesses.

DEFENSE: The Bucs ranked 27th in the league last year, but there is relief in sight via linebacker Keith McCants, fourth overall in the draft.

The defensive line was adequate-to-poor, the linebacking corps was average and the secondary gave up 29 touchdown passes. The Bucs aren't sure if they'll be going with their 3-4 defense or moving Broderick Thomas to defensive end and switching to the 4-3.

The secondary was led by safeties Harry Hamilton and Mark Robinson, but the Bucs got horrendous play from their corners.

KICKING: Donald Igwebuike (22-for-28) is an excellent kicker. Punter Chris Mohr was named as last year's All-Rookie punter by default (he was the only rookie punter in the league). Willie Drewrey averaged 11.0 yards per punt return, but the Bucs averaged only 17.0 per kick return, while giving up 20.7 yards per return.

Mark Carrier caught acclaim as Bucs' MVP.

THE ROOKIES: Alabama's McCants, a junior, is either the biggest draft steal since the 49ers got Joe Montana on the third round or a resounding bust. McCants comes with knee, agent and attitude problems. Lawrence Taylor calls McCants the L.T. of the '90s. The Bucs also rolled the dice on the second round, grabbing Tennessee's Cobb, who has a history of alleged drug abuse.

BUCCANEERS VETERAN ROSTER

HEAD COACH—Ray Perkins. Assistant Coaches—John Bobo, Tommy Brasher, Fred Bruney, Joel Collier, Sylvester Croom, Jeff Fitzgerald, Kent Johnston, Joe Kines, Mike Shula, Rodney Stokes, Richard Williamson.

No.	Name	Pos.	Ht.	Wt.	NFL Exp.	College
40	Anderson, Gary	RB	6-0	184	5	Arkansas
56	Anno, Sam	LB	6-2	235	4	Southern California
75	Bax, Carl	G	6-4	290	2	Missouri
11	Bell, Kerwin	QB	6-3	205	3	Florida
55	Bob, Adam	LB	6-3	255	2	Texas A&M
69	Bruhin, John	G	6-3	285	3	Tennessee
78	Cannon, John	DE	6-5	265	9	William & Mary
88	Carrier, Mark	WR	6-0	182	4	Nicholls State
53	Coleman, Sidney	LB	6-2	250	3	Southern Mississippi
23	Cooper, Evan	CB-S	5-11	195	7	Michigan
71	Cooper, Mark	T	6-5	280	8	Miami
79	Davis, Reuben	DE	6-4	285	3	North Carolina
76	Dill, Scott	T	6-5	285	3	Memphis State
87	Drewrey, Willie	WR	5-7	170	6	West Virginia
42	Everett, Eric	CB-S	5-10	170	3	Texas Tech
12	Ferguson, Joe	QB	6-1	200	18	Arkansas
36	Futrell, Bobby	CB-S	5-11	190	5	Elizabeth City State
94	Goff, Robert	DE	6-3	270	3	Auburn
65	Graham, Dan	C	6-2	270	2	Northern Illinois
60	Grimes, Randy	C	6-4	275	8	Baylor
74	Gruber, Paul	T	6-5	290	3	Wisconsin
45	Haddix, Wayne	RB	6-1	205	3	Liberty
82	Hall, Ron	TE	6-4	245	4	Hawaii
39	Hamilton, Harry	CB-S	6-0	195	7	Penn State
20	Harris, Odie	CB-S	6-0	190	3	Sam Houston State
84	Hill, Bruce	WR	6-0	180	4	Arizona State
43	Howard, William	RB	6-0	240	3	Tennessee
1	Igwebuike, Donald	K	5-9	185	6	Clemson
95	Jarvis, Curt	NT	6-2	270	3	Alabama
22	Jones, Rod	CB-S	6-0	185	5	Southern Methodist
38	Lawson, Jamie	RB	5-10	240	2	Nicholls State
97	Lee, Shawn	NT	6-2	285	3	North Alabama
99	Marve, Eugene	LB	6-2	240	9	Saginaw Valley State
73	McHale, Tom	G	6-4	280	4	Cornell
41	Mitchell, Alvin	RB	6-0	235	2	Auburn
5	Mohr, Chris	P	6-4	220	2	Alabama
58	Moss, Winston	LB	6-3	235	4	Miami
59	Murphy, Kevin	LB	6-2	235	5	Oklahoma
57	Najarian, Pete	LB	6-2	235	3	Minnesota
96	Newton, Tim	NT	6-0	275	6	Florida
86	Parks, Jeff	TE	6-4	245	4	Auburn
83	Peebles, Danny	WR	5-11	180	2	North Carolina State
80	Pillow, Frank	WR	5-10	170	3	Tennessee State
54	Randle, Ervin	LB	6-1	250	6	Baylor
29	Reynolds, Ricky	CB-S	5-11	190	4	Washington State
31	Rice, Rodney	CB-S	5-8	180	2	Brigham Young
30	Robinson, Mark	CB-S	5-11	200	7	Penn State
24	Stamps, Sylvester	RB	5-7	180	6	Jackson State
70	Swayne, Harry	T	6-5	270	4	Rutgers
34	Tate, Lars	RB	6-2	215	3	Georgia
72	Taylor, Rob	T	6-6	290	7	Northwestern
14	Testaverde, Vinny	QB	6-5	218	4	Miami
51	Thomas, Broderick	LB	6-4	245	2	Nebraska
85	Walker, Jackie	TE	6-5	255	5	Jackson State
23	Williams, Keith	RB	5-10	175	2	Southwest Missouri

TOP DRAFT CHOICES

Rd.	Name	Sel. No.	Pos.	Ht.	Wt.	College
1	McCants, Keith	4	LB	6-4	254	Alabama
2	Cobb, Reggie	30	RB	6-0	217	Tennessee
4	Anderson, Jesse	87	TE	6-1	240	Mississippi State
4	Mayberry, Tony	108	C	6-4	270	Wake Forest
5	Beckles, Ian	114	G	6-1	295	Indiana

OUTLOOK: Grim. The Vikings, Bears, Packers and Lions all have more talent than Ray Perkins' Bucs. It would take a minor miracle to keep Tampa out of last place. There's little encouragement in the likelihood that the Bucs will be in the race for the first pick in the 1991 draft.

BUCCANEER PROFILES

VINNY TESTAVERDE 26 6-5 218　　　　Quarterback

He's still young enough to develop into one of the better passers in the league... Completed 258 of 480 passes for 3,133 yards... Threw a team-record 20 touchdowns while coughing up 22 interceptions... His quarterback rating of 68.9 was a 20-point boost over a horrendous 1988... Finished seventh in the NFC in passing yards despite missing three games... Ran the ball 25 times for 139 yards... Threw 35 interceptions in 1988, blaming much of his trouble on "color blindness"... Heisman Trophy winner out of Miami and first player selected in the 1987 draft... Born Nov. 13, 1963, in Brooklyn, N.Y.... Earned $1.16 million last year.

MARK CARRIER 24 6-0 182　　　　Wide Receiver

A bright spot in a less than bright season for the Bucs... Earned team MVP honors by catching 86 passes for 1,422 yards and nine touchdowns... Tied with Art Monk for third in the NFL in receptions, while taking third place in receiving yards... His catches and receiving yards both set team records... Led the NFL with nine 100-yard receiving games... Finished season with four straight 100+ efforts... Named as an alternate to the Pro Bowl... Just missed the 1,000-yard plateau in 1988, catching 57 passes for 970 yards... Had a team-record 212-yard effort against the Saints as a rookie... Third-round pick out of Nicholls State in 1987... Established school records for receptions (132) and yards (2,407)... Born Oct. 28, 1965, in Lafayette, La.... Earned $175,000 last year.

LARS TATE 24 6-2 215   Running Back

Led the Bucs in rushing for the second straight year... Carried 167 times for 589 yards and eight touchdowns... Showed some abilities as a pass-receiver, catching 11 passes for 75 yards and one touchdown... Tied for team lead with nine touchdowns... Excellent leaping ability makes him particularly valuable near the goal line... Strong power runner, but lacks breakaway speed... Rushed for 467 yards as a rookie... Tate was the second-leading rusher in Georgia history (3,017 yards), trailing only Herschel Walker... Led the Bulldogs in rushing (954 yards), receiving (22 catches) and scoring (102 points) as a senior... Second-round pick (from San Francisco) in the 1988 draft... Born Feb. 2, 1966, in Indianapolis, Ind.... Earned $170,000 last year.

PAUL GRUBER 25 6-5 290   Tackle

The Bucs raised some eyebrows when they invested the fourth pick of the 1988 draft in a tackle, but the gamble paid off quickly... Gruber is quickly establishing himself as one of the best linemen in the game... Has started all 32 games since coming to the Bucs... Excellent run-blocker, just needs a runner worth blocking for... All-Rookie performer in 1988 ... First offensive lineman taken in 1988... All-American at Wisconsin... Signed a five-year, $3.8 million deal, then the highest ever by a rookie lineman... Born Feb. 24, 1965, in Madison, Wis.... Earned $425,000 last year.

HARRY HAMILTON 27 6-0 195   Safety

Had another excellent year... Tied for third in the NFC with six interceptions... Tied for team lead in interceptions with Mark Robinson, a teammate at Penn State... Finished fifth on the team with 90 tackles and third with 17 passes defensed... Picked up from the Jets on waivers in 1988 and proceeded to record 107 tackles and six interceptions... Despite his reputation as a hard hitter and smart player, he found his way into Joe Walton's doghouse and never escaped... Led the Jets in interceptions in 1987... Seventh-round draft choice in 1984... Two-time academic All-American, he graduated with a 3.65

grade-point average... Pursuing his law degree in the offseason ... Born Nov. 29, 1962, in Jamaica, N.Y.... Earned $250,000 last year.

MARK ROBINSON 27 5-11 200 — Safety

In his first injury-free season as a starter, Robinson put up impressive numbers... Tied for team lead with six interceptions (tied for third in NFC)... Finished third on the team in tackles with 104... Led the Bucs with 22 passes defensed... Forced three fumbles and recorded 2½ sacks... Came to the Bucs in a trade that sent Steve DeBerg to the Chiefs... Immediately won a starting job in 1988, but missed seven games with injuries... Fourth-round pick by the Chiefs in 1984 draft... All-American as a junior at Penn State, but had his draft value plummet after breaking his ankle as a senior... Born Sept. 13, 1962, in Washington, D.C.... Earned $275,000 last year.

BRUCE HILL 26 6-0 180 — Wide Receiver

Teamed with Mark Carrier to give the Bucs a tough one-two punch... After leading the Bucs in receiving in 1988, he had to adjust to his new role as the No. 2 target... Caught 50 passes for 673 yards and five touchdowns... Caught 58 passes for 1,040 yards in 1988... Played in only eight games as a rookie, but finished the year with 17 catches for 329 yards over the final four weeks... Taken on the fourth round of the 1987 draft with one of the selections received from the 49ers in the Steve Young deal... Spent his first two years at Arizona State as a cornerback before moving to offense... Born on Feb. 29, 1964, in Fort Dix, N.J.... Earned $125,000 last year.

EUGENE MARVE 30 6-2 240 — Linebacker

The Bucs got a windfall when they stole Marve from the linebacker-laden Buffalo Bills in 1988 ... Finished second on the team in tackles with 106 last season... Went over the 100-tackle mark for the sixth time in his career... One of the most durable inside linebackers in the game, Marve has started all 32 games for the Bucs ... Broke into the Bills' starting lineup as a rookie in 1982... Led the Bucs in tackles in 1988 with 121 after coming in the trade for a seventh-round 1989 draft choice... Led the Bills in tackles three times, with a high of 200 in 1983... Lost his starting job with the Bills after dislocating his elbow in 1987... Third-round pick in 1982 out of Saginaw (Mich.) Valley State... Born Aug. 14, 1960, in Flint, Mich.... Earned $375,000 last year.

DONALD IGWEBUIKE 29 5-9 185   Kicker

Relatively unsung, Igwebuike is emerging as one of the most accurate kickers in the game... Recorded a career-high 99 points on 33 of 35 extra points and 22 of 28 field goals (a team-record 78.6 percent)... Has never missed a field goal under 35 yards in his career (42 for 42)... One of the strongest legs in the league, Igwebuike has connected on 9 of 17 attempts of 50 yards or longer... Played soccer and football at Clemson... Considering the difficulty in pronouncing his name (IgwayBWEEkay), it's not surprising that his teammates call him "Iggy" and his coach calls him "Donald Kicker"... Grew up in Anambra, Nigeria, as a member of the Ibo tribe... Became a U.S. citizen in 1988... Born Dec. 27, 1960, in Anambra... Earned $290,000 last year.

GARY ANDERSON 29 6-0 184   Running Back

San Diego's best running back sat out 1989 season after failing to come to contract terms, and now he's a Buccaneer following trade for third-round draft choice in 1990 and 1991... Voted Charger MVP in '88 after rushing for 1,119 yards, his first 1,000-yard NFL season... He gained 217 yards in '88 finale... Threat to catch passes, too, he has 1,978 receiving yards in four NFL seasons... Spent three seasons with Tampa Bay Bandits of USFL, rushing for 2,731 yards... Twentieth player chosen in '83 NFL draft after starring at Arkansas... Was MVP in three bowl games... Born April 18, 1961, in Columbia, Mo.

COACH RAY PERKINS: Perkins always predicts big things for the Bucs, but keeps coming up short... Led his team to their second straight 5-11 season after going 4-12 in his first year with the team... "We went in with some high expectations which I helped create and we did not achieve them," Perkins admitted ... Highlight of season were two victories over the Bears... Came to the Bucs after four-year stint at Alabama... Finished with a record of 32-15-1... Had the impossible job of following in Bear Bryant's footsteps... Previously compiled a 23-34 record in four years (1979-82) as the Giants' head coach... Had served as an assistant with San Diego and New England... As a wide receiver at Alabama, Perkins was Joe Namath's primary target... Played on two national championship teams and earned All-American honors as a senior... Played five seasons with the Baltimore Colts before injuries ended his career... Born Nov. 6, 1941, in Mount Olive, Miss.... Regular-season pro mark is 37-67.

LONGEST PASS PLAY

DOUG WILLIAMS TO KEVIN HOUSE

The Bucs and the Lions, tied atop the NFC's Central Division with records of 8-7, were meeting in the final game of the regular season at Detroit on Dec. 20, 1981. The winner would go to the playoffs.

The Lions were leading, 7-3, early in the second quarter and were threatening deep in Tampa territory. On third and six from the Bucs' 10-yard line, Eric Hipple's pass for Fred Scott was picked off at the three-yard line by Cedric Brown, who returned it to the Bucs' 16.

Quarterback Doug Williams wasted no time in taking advantage of the turnover. Kevin House ran a simple fly pattern down the right side of the field, then blew by cornerback Jimmy Allen. Williams hit House in full stride at the Lions' 46 and House raced untouched into the end zone for the team-record 84-yard TD. The Bucs eventually won, 20-17, and made the playoffs.

INDIVIDUAL BUCCANEER RECORDS

Rushing

Most Yards Game:	219	James Wilder, vs Minnesota, 1983
Season:	1,544	James Wilder, 1984
Career:	5,957	James Wilder, 1981-89

Passing

Most TD Passes Game:	5	Steve DeBerg, vs Atlanta, 1987
Season:	20	Doug Williams, 1980
	20	Vinnie Testaverde, 1989
Career:	73	Doug Williams, 1978-82

Receiving

Most TD Passes Game:	4	Jimmie Giles, vs Miami, 1985
Season:	9	Kevin House, 1981
	9	Bruce Hill, 1988
	9	Mark Carrier, 1989
Career:	34	Jimmie Giles, 1978-86

Scoring

Most Points Game:	24	Jimmie Giles, vs Miami, 1985
Season:	99	Donald Igwebuike, 1989
Career:	416	Donald Igwebuike, 1985-89
Most TDs Game:	4	Jimmie Giles, vs Miami, 1985
Season:	13	James Wilder, 1984
Career:	43	James Wilder, 1981-88

WASHINGTON REDSKINS 167

WASHINGTON REDSKINS

TEAM DIRECTORY: Chairman/CEO: Jack Kent Cooke; Exec. VP: John Kent Cooke; GM: Charley Casserly; Asst. GM: Bobby Mitchell; Dir. Pro Scouting: Joe Mack; Dir. Pro Player Personnel: Kirk Mee; Dir. College Scouting: George Saimes; VP-Communications: Charlie Dayton; Dir. Information: Jamie Crittenberger; Dir. Media Rel.: Mike McCall. Head Coach: Joe Gibbs. Home field: Robert F. Kennedy Stadium (55,672). Colors: Burgundy and gold.

Mark Rypien proved his mettle in late-season surge.

SCOUTING REPORT

OFFENSE: The passing game lived and died with Mark Rypien's up-and-down season. At his best, Rypien ranks among the league's best. At his worst, he doesn't even belong in football.

Finding targets is the least of Rypien's problems. Art Monk, Ricky Sanders and Gary Clark (each with over 1,000 yards receiving) are as tough a threesome as you'll find.

There's plenty of help in the backfield, as Earnest Byner and Gerald Riggs gave the Skins both excellent running and receiving production.

The biggest problem with the Redskins' offense is an aging and injured offensive line. Mark Adickes, fresh from Kansas City, could step into the starting lineup. So might rookie guard Mohammed Elewonibi.

DEFENSE: Age and injuries forced Joe Gibbs into major mid-season changes on defense. The infusion of new blood was one of the main reasons why the 10-6 Skins won their final five. Tracy Rocker showed promise at DT, playing next to Charles Mann on the left side.

At linebacker, Ravin Caldwell broke into the starting lineup early in the season and ended up fourth on the team in tackles behind fellow outside linebacker Wilber Marshall. Rookie linebacker Andre Collins brings all-around skills.

There was a huge turnover in the secondary, where rookie A. J. Johnson and first-year man Martin Mayhew took over the starting cornerback jobs.

KICKING GAME: Chip Lohmiller (29-for-40) was outstanding from inside 40 yards, but struggled on his long-range kicks. Ralf Mojsiejenko had a big season, fourth in the NFC with 43.0 yards per punt.

The Redskins' return game was only adequate (20.3 yards per kick return as opposed to 20.7 for the opposition and 8.7 yards per punt return, while giving up 11.3 yards per return). Things should be different in 1990 with the addition of Walter Stanley, who led the NFL as a Lion in punt returns last year.

THE ROOKIES: Despite the absence of a first-round pick, the Redskins may have done well. Second-rounder Collins played safety at Penn State, but will play linebacker in the pros. Outland Trophy winner Elewonibi (Brigham Young), the top-rated guard

REDSKINS VETERAN ROSTER

HEAD COACH—Joe Gibbs. Assistant Coaches—Don Breaux, Jack Burns, Bobby DePaul, Rod Dowhower, Jim Hanifan, Larry Peccatiello, Richie Petitbon, Dan Riley, Wayne Sevier, Warren Simmons, Charley Taylor, Emmitt Thomas, LaVern Torgeson

No.	Name	Pos.	Ht.	Wt.	NFL Exp.	College
61	Adickes, Mark	G	6-4	275	5	Baylor
56	Bonner, Brian	LB	6-2	225	2	Minnesota
53	Bostic, Jeff	C	6-2	260	11	Clemson
23	Bowles, Todd	S	6-2	203	5	Temple
29	Branch, Reggie	RB	5-11	235	6	East Carolina
46	Brandes, John	TE	6-2	250	4	Cameron University
67	Brown, Ray	T	6-5	280	5	Arkansas State
38	Brown, Tom	RB	6-1	228	2	Pittsburgh
24	Bryant, Kelvin	RB	6-2	195	4	North Carolina
21	Byner, Earnest	RB	5-10	215	7	East Carolina
50	Caldwell, Ravin	LB	6-3	229	4	Arkansas
84	Clark, Gary	WR	5-9	173	6	James Madison
51	Coleman, Monte	LB	6-2	230	12	Central Arkansas
34	Davis, Brian	CB	6-2	190	4	Nebraska
26	Davis, Wayne	CB	5-11	180	6	Indiana State
25	Dupard, Reggie	RB	5-11	205	5	Southern Methodist
27	Edwards, Brad	S	6-2	196	3	South Carolina
97	Geathers, James	DE	6-7	290	6	Wichita State
54	Gouveia, Kurt	LB	6-1	227	4	Brigham Young
77	Grant, Darryl	DT	6-1	275	10	Rice
28	Green Darrell	CB	5-8	170	8	Texas A&I
68	Grimm, Russ	G	6-3	275	10	Pittsburgh
59	Harbour, Dave	C	6-4	265	3	Illinois
75	Hodge, Milford	DT	6-3	278	5	Washington State
80	Howard, Joe	WR	5-8	170	3	Notre Dame
16	Humphries, Stan	QB	6-2	223	2	NE Louisiana
66	Jacoby, Joe	T	6-7	310	10	Louisville
47	Johnson, A.J.	CB	5-8	176	2	S.W. Texas State
88	Johnson, Jimmie	TE	6-2	246	2	Howard
74	Koch, Markus	DE	6-5	275	5	Boise State
79	Lachey, Jim	T	6-6	290	6	Ohio State
22	Lockett, Charles	WR	6-0	185	3	Long Beach State
8	Lohmiller, Chip	K	6-3	213	3	Minnesota
71	Mann, Charles	DE	6-6	270	8	Nevada-Reno
91	Manusky, Greg	LB	6-1	242	3	Colgate
58	Marshall, Wilber	LB	6-1	230	7	Florida
73	May, Mark	G-T	6-6	295	10	Pittsburgh
35	Mayhew, Martin	CB	5-8	172	2	Florida State
57	McArthur, Kevin	LB	6-2	250	2	Lamar
63	McKenzie, Raleigh	C-G	6-2	270	5	Tennessee
48	Middleton, Ron	TE	6-2	255	5	Auburn
62	Mitz, Alonzo	DE	6-3	275	5	Florida
2	Mojsiejenko, Ralf	P	6-2	212	6	Michigan State
81	Monk, Art	WR	6-3	209	11	Syracuse
87	Orr, Terry	TE	6-3	227	5	Texas
35	Profit, Eugene	CB	5-10	175	3	Yale
37	Riggs, Gerald	RB	6-1	232	9	Arizona State
99	Rocker, Tracy	DT	6-3	288	2	Auburn
10	Rutledge, Jeff	QB	6-1	195	12	Alabama
11	Rypien, Mark	QB	6-4	234	4	Washington State
83	Sanders, Ricky	WR	5-11	180	5	SW Texas State
69	Schlereth, Mark	G	6-3	285	2	Idaho
76	Simmons, Ed	T	6-5	300	4	Eastern Washington
89	Stanley, Walter	WR	5-9	180	6	Mesa
60	Stokes, Fred	DE	6-3	262	4	Georgia Southern
64	Swoopes, Pat	DT	6-3	280	3	Mississippi State
86	Tice, Mike	TE	6-7	247	10	Maryland
31	Vaughn, Clarence	S	6-0	202	4	Northern Illinois
40	Walton, Alvin	S	6-0	180	5	Kansas
85	Warren, Don	TE	6-4	242	12	San Diego State
82	Whisenhunt, Ken	TE	6-3	240	5	Georgia Tech
45	Wilburn, Barry	CB	6-3	186	6	Mississippi
32	Wilder, James	RB	6-3	225	10	Missouri

TOP DRAFT CHOICES

Rd.	Name	Sel. No.	Pos.	Ht.	Wt.	College
2	Collins, Andre	46	LB	6-1	224	Penn State
3	Elewonibi, Mohammed	76	G	6-4	282	Brigham Young
4	Conklin, Cary	86	QB	6-4	215	Washington
4	Labbe, Rico	109	DB	5-11	202	Boston College
5	Mitchell, Brian	130	RB	5-10	195	SW Louisiana

in the draft, somehow lasted until the third round. Washington QB Cary Conklin is a project.

OUTLOOK: The Skins have the talent and the coaching to sneak up on the Giants and Eagles and steal the Eastern Division title. If they win those typical two-point games with the Giants instead of lose them, the title can be theirs.

REDSKIN PROFILES

MARK RYPIEN 27 6-4 234   Quarterback

Finished third in the NFC with a rating of 88.1 ... Completed 280 of 476 passes for 3,768 yards ... Threw 22 touchdowns and only 13 interceptions ... Excelled during five-game, season-ending winning streak, completing 108 of 166 passes for 1,430 yards ... Had a huge day against the Bears, throwing for 401 yards on 30 of 47 ... Slumped during middle of the season and was benched for two games. . . . Distributed the ball well, as the Skins became only the second team in league history to have three 1,000-yard receivers. . . . Sixth-round pick in 1986 out of Washington State ... Spent his first two years on injured reserve ... Born Oct. 2, 1962, in Calgary, Canada ... Earned $275,000 last year.

ART MONK 32 6-3 209   Wide Receiver

Moved into third place on the all-time receiving list, passing his good friend and coach Charley Taylor to get there ... Career total up to 662 receptions ... Tied for fourth in the NFL with 86 receptions (1,186 yards) ... Caught eight touchdown passes. . . . His 86 catches were the third-highest total of his career ... Set a single-season record in 1984 with 106 receptions. . . . Needs 155 catches to move into first place on the all-time receiving list ... Most productive game last year came against the Bears—nine passes for 152 yards and two touchdowns ... First-round pick out of Syracuse in 1980 ... Born Dec. 5, 1957, in White Plains, N.Y. . . . Earned $800,000 last year.

GERALD RIGGS 29 6-1 232 — Running Back

Huge acquisition gave the Redskins the running game they so desperately needed... Ran for 834 yards on 201 carries with four touchdowns ... Caught seven passes for 67 yards... Obtained April 23, 1989, from the Falcons in exchange for first-, second- and fifth-round selections... Set a career high for yards in a game (221) against the Eagles... Was the only runner to top 100 yards (111) against the Giants last year... Hampered by injuries and missed four games... Rushed for 658 yards in first seven games and had only 176 over the final nine weeks... First-round pick out of Arizona State in 1982... Born Nov. 6, 1960, in Tullos, Cal.... Earned $530,000 last year.

CHARLES MANN 29 6-6 270 — Defensive End

Yet another big season... Led the Skins with 9½ sacks and added 31 quarterback pressures ... Forced two fumbles and recovered one... Ranked sixth on the team with 96 tackles... Recognized as one of the toughest and best defensive ends in football... Won his third straight trip to the Pro Bowl... Upped career sack total to 60 (seven seasons)... Third-round pick out of Nevada-Reno... Sells real estate in the offseason and does modeling... Born April 12, 1961, in Sacramento, Cal.... Earned $525,000 last year.

RICKY SANDERS 28 5-11 180 — Wide Receiver

Established a career high with 80 catches and 1,138 yards... Had three games where he topped 140 yards in receptions... Caught 12 passes for 158 yards and a touchdown against the Raiders... Led the NFC with 12 touchdown receptions in 1988... Biggest game of his career came in Super Bowl XXII, when he caught nine passes for 193 yards, including touchdowns of 50 and 80 yards... Caught 104 passes in 1984 while playing with the Houston Gamblers of the USFL... Was a running back at Southwest Texas State... Redskins got him in 1986 from New England in 1986 in exchange for an '87 third-round draft choice... Born Aug. 30, 1962, in Temple, Tex.... Earned $550,000 last year.

172 THE COMPLETE HANDBOOK OF PRO FOOTBALL

GARY CLARK 28 5-9 173 — Wide Receiver

Topped the 1,000 yard-receiving mark for the third time in five-year career... Caught 79 passes for 1,229 yards and nine touchdowns... Led the Redskins in touchdowns... Upped career reception total to 340... Only Art Monk (360) and Jerry Rice (344) have more receptions in the last five years... John Madden paid him the highest compliment, saying that if he had to start a team, Clark would be the first wide receiver he'd take... Played two years with the Jacksonville Bulls in the USFL... Caught 128 passes for 1,686 yards... Signed May 13, 1985, by the Redskins... All-time leading receiver at James Madison... Born May 1, 1962, in Dublin, Va.... Earned $575,000 last year.

WILBER MARSHALL 28 6-1 230 — Linebacker

Finished third on the team with 108 tackles... Led with eight tackles behind the line of scrimmage... Recorded four sacks and 14 quarterback hurries... Had only one interception and one forced fumble.... Signed as a Bears' free agent in 1987, becoming a "Six-Million Dollar Man" with a five-year deal... Two-time Pro Bowler with the Bears... Bears' first-round draft choice out of Florida in 1984... Played high-school ball with Cris Collinsworth of the Bengals... Born April 18, 1962, in Titusville, Fla.... Comes from a family of 12 children... Earned $1 million last year.

ALVIN WALTON 26 6-0 180 — Safety

Was having an excellent season before he was sidelined by a shoulder injury in Week 12... Still led the team in tackles with 137... Tied for lead with four interceptions and deflected five passes... Extremely hard hitter... Has a total of 474 tackles in his four-year career... Has led the Redskins in tackles in each of the last three years... Lasted until third round of 1986 draft after he was academically ineligible for his senior year at Kansas... Born March 14, 1964, in Riverside, Cal.... Earned $310,000 last year.

WASHINGTON REDSKINS 173

TODD BOWLES 29 6-2 203   **Safety**

One of only five Skins to start all 16 games... Finished second on the team with 130 tackles... Intercepted two passes... Calls the signals for the secondary... Had a career-high 141 tackles in 1988... Earned a starting job in 1987... Played his college ball at Temple... Dislocated a wrist during his senior season and it cost him a shot at getting drafted... Signed by the Skins as a free agent... He was so sure he wasn't going to make the team that he bet a teammate $10 that he'd be cut... Born Nov. 18, 1960, in Elizabeth, N.J.... Earned $255,000 last year.

ERNEST BYNER 27 5-10 215   **Running Back**

Dangerous double-threat for the Redskins... Had only a limited role as a runner (134 rushes, 580 yards), but was particularly valuable in short-yardage situations... Greatest contributions came as a receiver out of the backfield... Caught 54 passes for 458 yards... Tied for the team lead in touchdowns (9)... Moved to starting running back in Week 12 and the Redskins never lost another game... Traded to the Redskins from the Browns in '89 in exchange for Mike Oliphant... Rushed for 100 yards on 14 carries against the Cardinals... Caught nine passes for 75 yards in loss to the Cowboys... Born Sept. 15, 1962, in Milledgeville, Ga.... An avid golfer... Earned $610,000 last year.

COACH JOE GIBBS: Considered calling it quits midway through a frustrating season.... He changed his mind after leading his team to five consecutive victories to end the year... The Redskins' 10-6 could have been much better if they hadn't lost two heartbreakers to the Giants and weren't the victims of a huge letdown in the Cowboys' only victory of the year... Gibbs' regular-season record stands at 102-46... Since taking over as head coach in 1981, he has led the Redskins to two Super Bowl titles, three NFC championships and four division titles... AP Coach of the Year in 1982 and 1983... Served as offensive coordinator at Tampa Bay and San Diego... Played tight end for Don Coryell at San Diego State... College coaching experience began at San Diego State, then to Florida State, USC and Arkansas... National champion racquetball player (35 and over) in 1976... Born Nov. 25, 1940, in Mocksville, N.C.

LONGEST PASS PLAYS

FRANK FILCHOCK TO ANDY FARKAS
GEORGE IZO TO BOBBY MITCHELL
SONNY JURGENSEN TO GERRY ALLEN

The Redskins' Frank Filchock, filling in for the injured Sammy Baugh, made the most of his relief appearance in Washington on Oct. 15, 1939.

With the Skins leading the Steelers, 19-14, and on their own one-foot mark, Filchock threw to Andy Farkas at the four-yard line. Farkas weaved through the Steelers' porous defense and raced for a touchdown in what turned into a 44-14 romp.

It was the first 99-yard pass completion in NFL history.

George Izo, replacing the benched Norm Snead, completed a 99-yarder to Bobby Mitchell against the Browns at Cleveland on Sept. 15, 1963. It happened late in a 37-14 loss to Cleveland.

A Brig Owens interception of the Bears' Jack Concannon in Chicago on Sept. 15, 1968, gave the Skins the ball on their own one-yard line. Then Sonny Jurgensen hit Gerry Allen at the Skins' 31 and he took it all the way. The 99-yarder highlighted the Skins' 38-28 triumph.

INDIVIDUAL REDSKIN RECORDS
Rushing

Most Yards Game:	221	Gerald Riggs, vs Philadelphia, 1989
Season:	1,347	John Riggins, 1983
Career:	7,472	John Riggins, 1976-79, 1981-85

WASHINGTON REDSKINS 175

Passing

Most TD Passes Game:	6	Sam Baugh, vs Brooklyn, 1943
	6	Sam Baugh, vs St. Louis, 1947
Season:	31	Sonny Jurgensen, 1967
Career:	187	Sammy Baugh, 1937-52

Receiving

Most TD Passes Game:	3	Hugh Taylor (5 times)
	3	Jerry Smith, vs Los Angeles, 1967
	3	Jerry Smith, vs Dallas, 1969
	3	Hal Crisler
	3	Joe Walton
	3	Pat Richter, vs Chicago, 1968
	3	Larry Brown, vs Philadelphia, 1973
	3	Jean Fugett, vs San Francisco, 1976
	3	Alvin Garrett, vs Lions, 1982
	3	Art Monk, vs Indianapolis, 1984
Season:	12	Hugh Taylor, 1952
	12	Charley Taylor, 1966
	12	Jerry Smith, 1967
	12	Ricky Sanders, 1988
Career:	79	Charley Taylor, 1964-77

Scoring

Most Points Game:	24	Dick James, vs Dallas, 1961
	24	Larry Brown, vs Philadelphia, 1973
Season:	161	Mark Moseley, 1983
Career:	1,176	Mark Moseley, 1974-85
Most TDs Game:	4	Dick James, vs Dallas, 1961
	4	Larry Brown, vs Philadelphia, 1973
Season:	24	John Riggins, 1983
Career:	90	Charley Taylor, 1964-77

INSIDE THE AFC

By BRIAN WHITE

PREDICTED ORDER OF FINISH

EAST	CENTRAL	WEST
Buffalo	Cincinnati	Kansas City
Miami	Cleveland	Denver
Indianapolis	Houston	L.A. Raiders
New England	Pittsburgh	San Diego
New York Jets		Seattle

AFC Champion: Buffalo

Parity is alive and well in the AFC, which means there isn't a club in the conference that doesn't honestly believe it has a shot at reaching the Super Bowl. Not after watching the Bengals put things together in their magical 1988 season, then fall back to last place. And not after seeing the no-name Steelers fall a few yards short of reaching last year's AFC championship.

This year, things will be different, for the Broncos must face a rising monster in the East, a nasty four-way battle in the Central and rising teams in the West.

The Bills would like to forget 1989, a year injuries destroyed their talented defense and controversy dogged their versatile offense. Cornelius Bennett, Shane Conlan and others were hurting and the offense was feuding, but the Bills still squeaked by to win the East. That means, of course, that this year they should win it handily.

The Dolphins appear to be the best of the rest, but only because

---

Brian White of the Ft. Myers News Press *follows the Dolphins and everything else that swims in NFL waters.*

the Patriots and the Jets are starting over with new coaches and the Colts are as unpredictable as Eric Dickerson's emotions. The Dolphins' fortunes hinge on the development of running back Sammie Smith. The Pats need several defenders to bounce back from injuries as well as a return to form by running back John Stephens.

The Jets should be exciting with Bruce Coslet's Bengal-like offense and rookie Blair Thomas. Many feel the Colts put Buffalo on Easy Street with their baffling draft-day trade for the rights to quarterback Jeff George.

The Central is fiercely competitive once again. The Bengals were last with an 8-8 record in '89, but you could argue they were the AFC's best team at season's end. Even if Ickey Woods doesn't return to full form, Cincy's talent is overwhelming. Cleveland proved to be tough in the clutch even though quarterback Bernie Kosar was ailing.

The Browns' chances hinge on Kosar returning to full health. If new Oiler coach Jack Pardee can oversee a smooth offensive transition, Warren Moon and Co. will be in the playoffs again. Last year's playoff treat made the young Steelers hungry for more, but Merril Hoge and Tim Worley both will have to play like Supermen all year long for Pittsburgh to make it out of the division again.

After years of weakness, the West is ready to regain respect. Don't be surprised if the Chiefs and human locomotive Christian Okoye ram the Broncos out of contention. Once KC's quarterback position achieves consistency, Marty Schottenheimer's defensive-minded team can flourish.

The Chargers have excited their fans once again with a ferocious pass rush. Jim McMahon and Gary Anderson are gone, making room for a new era. Art Shell has the Raiders relaxed and confident again, especially when the ball is under Bo Jackson's big arms. Seattle is the only team in the division that seems to be off the pace. Finding the next Curt Warner is important.

Look for Buffalo and Cincinnati to win division titles early, then for Kansas City to edge out Denver in a battle to the end in the West. The Bills and Bengals will escape the crowded playoffs, with Buffalo's frigid home-field advantage helping to send its heroes to the Super Bowl.

BUFFALO BILLS

TEAM DIRECTORY: Pres.: Ralph Wilson; GM/VP-Administration: Bill Polian; Dir. Pro Personnel: Bob Ferguson; Mgr. Media Rel.: Scott Berchtold; Dir. Pub. and Community Rel.: Denny Lynch; Head Coach: Marv Levy. Home field: Rich Stadium (80,290). Colors: Scarlet red, royal blue and white.

SCOUTING REPORT

OFFENSE: Quarterback Jim Kelly's griping and shoulder injury gained much of the ink in Buffalo last year, but it was running back Thurman Thomas who emerged as a star. Thomas, once a draft-day gamble, led the NFL with 1,913 total yards and 12 touchdowns.

The Bills (9-7) are never going to have a wide-open offense, so Kelly won't have the stats of other high-profile quarterbacks. But his strong arm and the outstanding talent of wideout Andre Reed (AFC-leading 88 receptions) provide a nice mix of pass and run. Reed's numbers are more impressive when you consider he is not teamed with another star receiver and that Kelly missed three weeks because of injury.

Bills' coaches should keep in mind that the team was 6-0 in games in which bowling-ball fullback Larry Kinnebrew carried nine times or more. Rookie fullback Carwell Gardner could be a factor.

Kent Hull is the Bills' best lineman. Right tackle Howard Ballard has been inconsistent and has drawn the public wrath of Kelly.

DEFENSE: Marv Levy's biggest task with this group is to keep the stars healthy. With linebackers Cornelius Bennett and Shane Conlan out with knee injuries, the Bills' defense was an average unit. Darryl Talley emerged as a standout in their absence.

The big-name defender is right end Bruce Smith, who had 13 sacks but didn't defend the run as well as he chased quarterbacks. Still, he has shown he can still dominate a game single-handedly. The loss of nose tackle Fred Smerlas (to 49ers as a Plan-B free agent) will hurt, as will the aging of Art Still.

Nate Odomes is the lone standout in the defensive backfield. Safeties Leonard Smith and Mark Kelso have deficiencies but hit hard and have good instincts. The Bills expect a lot from rookie cornerback J.D. Williams.

BUFFALO BILLS 179

Thurman Thomas proved explosive with 1,913 total yards.

As a unit, the Bills dropped from a No. 4 ranking to No. 11, including a mediocre No. 14 against the run.

KICKING GAME: Scott Norwood made 23-of-30 field-goal attempts, missing 5-of-15 from 40-49 yards. A punter is needed because John Kidd signed with San Diego.

Mickey Sutton arrived in Week 5 and handled punt-return duties well, turning in an 8.9-yard average. The Bills' kickoff coverage (15.8 avg.) was the best in the NFL for the third straight year.

THE ROOKIES: Fresno State's Williams is an outstanding athlete with 4.29 speed and a 38-inch vertical leap. He should start along with Odomes and learn the pro game with the luxury of a

BILLS VETERAN ROSTER

HEAD COACH—Marv Levy. Assistant Coaches—Tom Bresnahan, Walt Corey, Glenn Headmond, Bruce DeHaven, Chuck Dickerson, Rusty Jones, Don Lawrence, Chuck Lester, Ted Marchibroda, Nick Nicolau, Elijah Pitts, Dick Roach.

No.	Name	Pos.	Ht.	Wt.	NFL Exp.	College
54	Balley, Carlton	LB	6-2	237	3	North Carolina
75	Ballard, Howard	T	6-6	315	3	Alabama A&M
24	Barnes, Lew	WR	5-8	170	2	Oregon
55	Bennett, Cornelius	LB	6-2	235	4	Alabama
50	Bentley, Ray	LB	6-2	235	5	Central Michigan
	Brady, Kerry	K	6-1	200	2	Hawaii
61	Burton, Leonard	T	6-3	277	5	South Carolina
90	Cofield, Timmy	LB	6-2	242	5	Elizabeth City State
58	Conlan, Shane	LB	6-3	235	4	Penn State
79	Davis, John	T	6-4	310	4	Georgia Tech
23	Davis, Kenneth	RB	5-10	209	5	Texas Christian
45	Drane, Dwight	S	6-2	205	5	Oklahoma
85	Franklin, Darryl	WR	5-11	185	2	Washington
59	Frerotte, Mitch	G	6-3	280	3	Penn State
7	Gilbert, Gale	QB	6-3	210	3	California
22	Hagy, John	S	5-11	190	3	Texas
67	Hull, Kent	C	6-5	275	5	Mississippi State
47	Jackson, Kirby	CB	5-10	180	4	Mississippi State
12	Kelly, Jim	QB	6-3	215	5	Miami
38	Kelso, Mark	S	5-11	185	5	William & Mary
28	Kinnebrew, Larry	RB	6-2	256	7	Tennessee State
63	Lingner, Adam	C	6-4	268	8	Illinois
80	Lofton, James	WR	6-3	190	13	Stanford
84	McKeller, Keith	TE	6-4	245	3	Jacksonville State
74	Mesner, Bruce	NT	6-5	280	4	Maryland
88	Metzelaars, Pete	TE	6-7	250	9	Wabash
36	Mitchell, Devon	S	6-1	198	3	Iowa
57	Monger, Matt	LB	6-1	240	5	Oklahoma State
39	Mueller, Jamie	RB	6-1	230	4	Benedictine
11	Norwood, Scott	K	6-0	207	6	James Madison
37	Odomes, Nate	CB	5-10	188	4	Wisconsin
94	Pike, Mark	DE	6-4	272	4	Georgia Tech
97	Radecic, Scott	LB	6-3	236	7	Penn State
83	Reed, Andre	WR	6-1	190	6	Kutztown State
14	Reich, Frank	QB	6-4	210	4	Maryland
40	Riddick, Robb	RB	6-0	195	8	Millersville State
51	Ritcher, Jim	G	6-3	273	11	North Carolina State
87	Rolle, Butch	TE	6-4	245	5	Michigan State
96	Seals, Leon	DE	6-5	267	4	Jackson State
78	Smith, Bruce	DE	6-4	280	6	Virginia Tech
30	Smith, Don	RB	5-11	200	4	Mississippi State
46	Smith, Leonard	S	5-11	202	8	McNeese State
20	Sutton, Mickey	CB-S-KR	5-9	172	5	Montana
56	Talley, Darryl	LB	6-4	235	8	West Virginia
89	Tasker, Steve	WR	5-9	185	6	Northwestern
34	Thomas, Thurman	RB	5-10	198	3	Oklahoma State
69	Wolford, Will	T	6-5	290	5	Vanderbilt
91	Wright, Jeff	NT	6-2	270	3	Central Missouri State

TOP DRAFT CHOICES

Rd.	Name	Sel. No.	Pos.	Ht.	Wt.	College
1	Williams, James	16	DB	5-9	172	Fresno State
2	Gardner, Carwell	42	RB	6-1	232	Louisville
3	Parker, Glenn	69	T	6-5	301	Arizona
4	Fuller, Eddie	100	RB	5-9	199	LSU
6	Nies, John	154	P	6-2	199	Arizona

standout pass rush. Arizona tackle Glenn Parker has little football experience but has the athletic ability to get better with time. Louisville's Gardner is a former defensive end who can catch the ball.

OUTLOOK: The Bills' offense has proven it can provide the versatility to complement its defense. Replacing Smerlas is important. The Bills should rebound from a rocky year and win the AFC East again.

BILL PROFILES

JIM KELLY 30 6-3 215   Quarterback

After controversy-filled season, Kelly became NFL's highest-paid player. He signed a seven-year, $20-million deal that begins in 1991... Bills' offense struggled as Kelly and teammates feuded... Physical talent is unquestioned. He threw for 3,130 yards in 13 games in '89... Missed three games with shoulder injury. Bills were 3-0 in those games... Tossed 25 TD passes, second in Bills' history only to Joe Ferguson's 26 in 1983 ... Threw TDs in 12 of 13 games he played and has 81 in his career, second to Ferguson's 181... Upped QB rating to 86.2 from career-low 78.2 in '88... Starred in 1984-85 in USFL... Was first-round pick out of Miami in '83, but didn't join the Bills until '86... Involved heavily in charity work... 1989 salary: $1.3 million. 1990 salary: $1.4 million... Born Feb. 14, 1960, in East Brady, Pa.

BRUCE SMITH 27 6-4 280   Defensive End

Can dominate a game with quickness... Had 13 sacks to become Bills' all-time sack leader in '89, surpassing Ben Williams' 51... Finished second in AFC sacks for fourth straight year... Has 57.5 sacks in five seasons... Named NFL Defensive Lineman of the Year for second consecutive season by NFL Players Association... Named Pro Bowl starter, his third trip to the game... Made 88 tackles in '89, fourth on club ... Missed time in '88 because of violation of NFL substance-abuse policy... 1985 Outland Trophy winner, out of Virginia Tech, he was first player taken in draft... 1989 salary: $1.3 million. 1990 salary: $1.7 million... Born June 18, 1963, in Norfolk, Va.

CORNELIUS BENNETT 24 6-2 235   Linebacker

Injuries prevented Bennett from returning to Pro Bowl... Played in 12 games, making 54 tackles, 5.5 sacks and two interceptions... Missed Weeks 12-15. Bills went 1-3 in those games... His presence in lineup makes Bills' defense one of best in NFL... Acquired in 1987 in three-team Eric Dickerson trade involving Colts and Rams... Colts made him second player picked in '87 draft but couldn't sign him... NFL Players Association AFC Linebacker of Year in '88... Made 287 tackles in career at Alabama... 1990 salary: $600,000... Born Aug. 25, 1966, in Birmingham, Ala.

ANDRE REED 26 6-1 190   Wide Receiver

No secret anymore, he became Bills' all-time leading receiver in sensational '89 season... Caught 88 passes for 1,312 yards and 9 TDs... Led AFC in receptions and yards. Only Green Bay's Sterling Sharpe, with 90, caught more passes in NFL... Named to Pro Bowl for second straight year... Has 317 career receptions, surpassing Elbert Dubenion in '89... Had three consecutive 100-yard games... Caught 13 passes for 157 yards vs. Denver... Pulled in 78-yard TD from Kelly at Houston... Fourth-round draft choice out of Kutztown (Pa.) University in 1985 and became immediate starter... Was high-school quarterback... Born Jan. 29, 1964, in Philadelphia.

THURMAN THOMAS 24 5-10 198   Running Back

Had spectacular season, leading NFL in total yards from scrimmage with 1,913 (1,244 rushing, 669 receiving)... Those all-purpose yards rank third in club history, behind O.J. Simpson's 2,243 in '75 and 2,073 in '73... Named to Pro Bowl as a reserve... Set club record for receptions by a running back with 60... Rushed for more than 100 yards seven times.

Bills were 7-0 in those games... Tied Christian Okoye for AFC scoring lead (non-kickers) with 72 points... Was third among AFC rushers... Ran for 881 yards as a rookie in '88, when a leg injury prevented him from gaining 1,000 yards... Was considered a gamble when drafted in second round because of history of knee problems... Gained 4,595 yards at Oklahoma State, including 1,613 yards and 18 TDs as senior... Born July 16, 1966, in Missouri City, Tex.

SHANE CONLAN 26 6-3 235   Linebacker

Missed seven games in '89 with knee injury suffered in Monday night game against Denver ... Came back and played final seven games of season... Made 50 tackles in 10 games, ranking ninth on club... Still, selected to Pro Bowl as a reserve... Second straight year an injury has hampered his season... NFL Rookie of the Year in '87, when he led club with 114 tackles... Made 84 stops in '88 and was All-Pro... First-round draft pick out of Penn State, where he was a consensus All-American and led Nittany Lions to 12-0 record and national title ... Joe Paterno has called him best linebacker ever at Penn State ... Grew up in Frewsburg, N.Y., about 70 miles from Buffalo's Rich Stadium... 1990 salary: $302,500... Born April 3, 1964, in Olean, N.Y.

NATE ODOMES 25 5-10 188   Cornerback

Former second-round draft choice is regarded as Bills' best man-to-man defender... Thrives when Bills' tremendous pass rush hurries quarterbacks... Has started every Bills' game since his arrival, a streak of 44... Had five interceptions and 46 tackles... Set up winning drive in season opener at Miami with clutch interception of Dan Marino... As a rookie in '87, took over position that had been held down by Charles Rhomes from 1978-86... Had just two interceptions his first two seasons... Also starred in track at Wisconsin, running 4 x 100 relay and competing in long jump... Was second in Big Ten long jump to Rod Woodson, now of Steelers... Born Aug. 25, 1965, in Columbus, Ga.

DARRYL TALLEY 30 6-4 235　　　　　　　　Linebacker

With injuries dropping players all around him, Talley was steady... Named team's defensive MVP after finishing second with 97 tackles... Had six sacks, second to Smith's 13 on team... Forced a fumble... Started 16 games at right outside linebacker... Has started for four straight seasons but has been underrated playing with the likes of Smith, Bennett and Conlan... Second-round draft pick out of West Virginia in 1983... Was All-American for the Mountaineers... As a senior, had 135 tackles, seven sacks and two interceptions... In four years at WVU, had 484 tackles, 19 sacks and five interceptions... Born July 10, 1960, in Cleveland.

KENT HULL 29 6-5 275　　　　　　　　　　　Center

Finally an established NFL star... Named to Pro Bowl for second straight year... Also made *Sporting News*' All-Pro Team... Started 16 games and helped clear way for Thurman Thomas' spectacular season... Played three years with New Jersey in USFL before going to Bills in '86... Hasn't missed a start in seven pro seasons... Four-year starter at Mississippi State who was a seventh-round pick by New Jersey in USFL draft... Has degree in business administration, but owns farm in Greenwood, Miss., and raises cows... Father Charles is Mississippi's director of agriculture... Born Jan. 13, 1961, in Ponotoc, Miss.

LARRY KINNEBREW 30 6-2 256　　　　　　　Fullback

Burly fullback added punch to Bills' running attack in '89... Signed as free agent after sitting out 1988 in contract dispute with Cincinnati... Bills' second-leading rusher with 533 yards and six touchdowns... Averaged 4.1 yards per carry... Caught five passes for 60 yards... Rushed for 121 yards against Miami, the fifth 100-yard game of his career... Has rushed for more than 3,000 yards in six NFL seasons... Played for Bengals from 1983-87... Best year was '84, when he had 623 yards and nine TDs... Averaged four yards per carry at Tennessee State... Born June 11, 1960, in Rome Ga.

COACH MARV LEVY: The NFL's professor of coaches, he has Master's degree in English history from Harvard... Was thought to have overhauled Bills into a power but team stumbled to 9-7 in '89... Is 31-25 in four years in Buffalo... In his 14th year as NFL head coach... Was director of football operations for Montreal Alouettes of Canadian Football League when Bills hired him to replace Hank Bullough Nov. 3, 1986... Coached one year in USFL, going 5-13 with the Chicago Blitz in 1984... Guided Kansas City Chiefs from 1977-82 and Montreal Alouettes from 1973-77... Won two CFL titles in Montreal... Was 31-41 with Chiefs, and career NFL record is 62-67... Was college head coach at New Mexico, California and William & Mary... Was a running back at Coe College... Avid fan of boxing and the Chicago Cubs... Born Aug. 3, 1928, in Chicago.

LONGEST PASS PLAY

JACK KEMP TO GLENN BASS

It wasn't often that the 1964 Bills' heroics came through the air, but Jack Kemp and Glenn Bass helped put away the Houston Oilers at Houston on Oct. 11 with a team-record 94-yard bomb in a 48-17 victory. The victory made the Bills 5-0 and they went 9-0 on the way to a 12-2 record and their first AFL championship.

Bass was the Bills' leading receiver that season and scored a career-high seven touchdowns. Kemp also holds the Chargers' club record for longest pass play, a 91-yard touchdown strike to Keith Lincoln in the club's 1961 championship season.

The Chargers tried to slip Kemp, who had a broken hand, through waivers before the '62 season, but the Bills claimed him for $100. The Bills' fortunes rose quickly, and Kemp stayed in Buffalo until 1969. He is second to Joe Ferguson on most Bills' all-time passing lists.

After football, Kemp entered the political arena. He became a U.S. congressman from New York and today is Secretary of Housing and Urban Development in President George Bush's cabinet.

INDIVIDUAL BILL RECORDS

Rushing

Most Yards Game:	273	O. J. Simpson, vs Detroit, 1976
Season:	2,003	O. J. Simpson, 1973
Career:	10,183	O. J. Simpson, 1969-77

Passing

Most TD Passes Game:	5	Joe Ferguson, vs N.Y. Jets, 1979
	5	Jim Kelly, vs Houston, 1989
Season:	26	Joe Ferguson, 1983
Career:	181	Joe Ferguson, 1973-84

Receiving

Most TD Passes Game:	4	Jerry Butler, vs N.Y. Jets, 1979
Season:	10	Elbert Dubenion, 1964
Career:	35	Elbert Dubenion, 1960-67

Scoring

Most Points Game:	30	Cookie Gilchrist, vs N.Y. Jets, 1963
Season:	138	O. J. Simpson, 1975
Career:	465	Scott Norwood, 1985-89
Most TDs Game:	5	Cookie Gilchrist, vs N.Y. Jets, 1963
Season:	23	O. J. Simpson, 1975
Career:	70	O. J. Simpson, 1969-77

CINCINNATI BENGALS

TEAM DIRECTORY: Chairman: Austin E. Knowlton; Pres.: John Sawyer; VP/GM: Paul Brown; Asst. GM: Michael Brown; Dir. Player Personnel: Pete Brown; Dir. Pub. Rel.: Allan Heim; Bus. Mgr.: Bill Connelly; Head Coach: Sam Wyche. Home field: Riverfront Stadium (59,754). Colors: Orange, black and white.

SCOUTING REPORT

OFFENSE: The powerful Bengals have such depth and so much talent on offense that injuries don't seem to knock them far off track. Fullback Ickey Woods, a rookie phenom in 1988, missed

Boomer Esiason led AFC with 28 TD passes, 92.1 rating.

most of 1989 with a severe knee injury. So what did the Bengals do? They led the NFL in rushing. Thanks to James Brooks, who rushed for 1,239 yards and a league-leading 5.6-yard average at age 31, the Bengals (8-8) were explosive once again. If Woods' rehab is slow, Craig Taylor and Eric Ball will try to help Brooks. So will rookie running back Harold Green and Paul Palmer, the Plan-B signee from the Cowboys.

Boomer Esiason won his second consecutive AFC passing title, throwing 28 touchdowns and just 11 interceptions for a 92.1 rating. Speedster Tim McGee finally has developed into a star who complements Eddie Brown.

There is some uncertainty on the line. Pro Bowl guard Max Montoya fled to the Raiders in Plan B, leaving a huge void in Cincinnati's pass-blocking. Brian Blados is expected to step in.

No problem at tight end; Rodney Holman is the AFC's best.

The offense will be back in Sam Wyche's hands more now that offensive coordinator Bruce Coslet signed on as head coach of the Jets. Don't expect any slowdown, and that includes, as always, the performance of nine-time Pro Bowler Anthony Munoz.

DEFENSE: The Bengals were hurt last year on the line, turning in a No. 26 ranking against the run. Nose tackle Tim Krumrie made a gallant comeback from a broken leg but wasn't at his All-Pro level. He should be back strong this year.

The Bengals still don't have a game-breaking pass-rusher. Jason Buck led the club with six sacks, followed by Jim Skow's 4½.

Safety David Fulcher is a star, and with a decent pass rush the secondary could be outstanding.

Perhaps the Bengals' biggest task is replacing linebacker Reggie Williams, who retired after 14 splendid seasons. A big step in that direction was the drafting of James Francis.

KICKING GAME: Special teams was a problem once again in Cincy. Kicker Jim Breech brought some consistency when he was brought back during the season and hit 12-of-14 field-goal attempts. He is a sure thing from short range. Punter Lee Johnson had an acceptable 40.1 average, but his net of 30.2 was last in the NFL.

The Bengals didn't do much better fielding punts, ranking last in the league with a 5.8 return average. The next lowest average was 6.4 yards. Stanford Jennings (20.2) is good on kickoffs, but the Bengals averaged just 17.4 as a club.

BENGALS VETERAN ROSTER

HEAD COACH—Sam Wyche. Assistant Coaches—Jim Anderson, Dana Bible, Marv Braden, Bill Johnson, Dick LeBeau, Jim McNally, Dick Selcer, Mike Stock, Chuck Studley, Kim Wood.

No.	Name	Pos.	Ht.	Wt.	NFL Exp.	College
42	Ball, Eric	RB	6-2	211	2	UCLA
35	Barber, Chris	S	6-0	187	3	North Carolina A&T
86	Barber, Mike	WR	5-10	172	2	Marshall
53	Barker, Leo	LB	6-2	227	7	New Mexico State
24	Billups, Lewis	CB	5-11	179	5	North Alabama
74	Blados, Brian	G	6-5	296	7	North Carolina
55	Brady, Ed	LB	6-2	236	7	Illinois
3	Breech, Jim	K	5-6	161	12	California
21	Brooks, James	RB	5-10	180	10	Auburn
81	Brown, Eddie	WR	6-0	185	6	Miami
99	Buck, Jason	DE	6-5	258	4	Brigham Young
27	Bussey, Barney	S	6-0	206	5	South Carolina State
34	Carey, Richard	CB	5-9	185	2	Idaho
29	Dixon, Rickey	S	5-11	196	3	Oklahoma
7	Esiason, Boomer	QB	6-5	215	7	Maryland
33	Fulcher, David	S	6-3	234	5	Arizona State
48	Garrett, John	WR	5-11	180	2	Princeton
16	Gelbaugh, Stan	QB	6-3	205	3	Maryland
98	Grant, David	NT	6-4	288	4	West Virginia
71	Hammerstein, Mike	DE	6-4	272	4	Michigan
40	Holifield, John	RB	6-0	202	2	West Virginia
82	Holman, Rodney	TE	6-3	238	9	Tulane
37	Jackson, Robert	S	5-10	186	8	Central Michigan
36	Jennings, Stanford	RB	6-1	209	7	Furman
68	Jetton, Paul	G	6-4	288	2	Texas
11	Johnson, Lee	P-K	6-2	200	6	Brigham Young
77	Jones, Scott	T	6-5	278	2	Washington
84	Kattus, Eric	TE	6-5	241	5	Michigan
58	Kelly, Joe	LB	6-2	235	5	Washington
64	Kozerski, Bruce	C	6-4	287	7	Holy Cross
69	Krumrie, Tim	NT	6-2	267	8	Wisconsin
88	Martin, Mike	WR	5-10	181	8	Illinois
72	McClendon, Skip	DE	6-7	283	4	Arizona
85	McGee, Tim	WR	5-10	179	5	Tennessee
73	Moyer, Ken	T	6-6	292	2	Toledo
78	Muñoz, Anthony	T	6-6	284	11	Southern California
23	Palmer, Paul	RB	5-9	181	4	Temple
75	Reimers, Bruce	T	6-7	294	7	Iowa State
87	Riggs, Jim	TE	6-5	245	4	Clemson
15	Schonert, Turk	QB	6-1	196	11	Stanford
70	Skow, Jim	DE	6-3	243	5	Nebraska
83	Smith, Kendal	WR	5-9	189	2	Utah State
20	Taylor, Craig	RB	5-11	224	2	West Virginia
22	Thomas, Eric	CB	5-11	181	4	Tulane
96	Tuatagaloa, Natu	DE	6-4	265	2	California
59	Walker, Kevin	LB	6-3	233	3	Maryland
63	Walter, Joe	T	6-6	290	6	Texas Tech
51	White, Leon	LB	6-3	237	5	Brigham Young
41	Wilcots, Solomon	CB	5-11	190	4	Colorado
4	Wilhelm, Erik	QB	6-3	210	2	Oregon State
30	Woods, Ickey	RB	6-2	232	3	Nevada-Las Vegas
91	Zander, Carl	LB	6-2	235	6	Tennessee

TOP DRAFT CHOICES

Rd.	Name	Sel. No.	Pos.	Ht.	Wt.	College
1	Francis, James	12	LB	6-4	243	Baylor
2	Green, Harold	38	RB	6-1	216	South Carolina
3	Clark, Bernard	65	LB	6-1	250	Miami
4	Brennan, Mike	91	T	6-4	267	Notre Dame
5	James, Lynn	122	WR	6-1	185	Arizona State

THE ROOKIES: Linebacker Francis is an impact player who combines speed and tackling power. He is an outstanding athlete who played basketball at Baylor and blocked eight kicks on the football field. The versatility of South Carolina's Green fits in perfectly with the Bengals' offense and provides insurance in case Woods' recovery is slow.

OUTLOOK: The Bengals went from last in '87 to first in '88, then again to last in '89 with an 8-8 record. With all that talent and a fourth-place schedule, another reversal is possible.

BENGAL PROFILES

BOOMER ESIASON 29 6-5 215   **Quarterback**

Won second consecutive AFC passing title, recording a 92.1 quarterback rating... Passed for 3,525 yards and 28 touchdowns with just 11 interceptions... Ranked second in NFL to Joe Montana's 112.4 rating... Selected to Pro Bowl... Nearly matched his NFL MVP season of '88, when he threw for 3,572 yards and had a 97.4 rating... Only Dan Marino, Warren Moon and Bernie Kosar threw for more yards in the AFC in '89 ... A fiery leader who is a student of the game... Second-round draft pick out of Maryland in 1984... Became starter early in '85 season... Holds all Maryland passing records, including 42 TD passes... 1989 salary: $1.2 million... Full name is Norman Julius Esiason... Born April 17, 1961, in East Islip, N.Y.

JAMES BROOKS 31 5-10 180   **Running Back**

Selected as Pro Bowl starter after gaining 1,545 all-purpose yards, second in AFC to Buffalo's Thurman Thomas... Led AFC in average per rushing attempt (5.6) while rushing for 1,239 yards and seven TDs... Rushing output was a club record and his best in nine NFL seasons ... His previous high was 1,087 in '86... Accomplished such stats despite absence of running mate Ickey Woods... Named offensive MVP by teammates

... Made third Pro Bowl appearance... Went to Bengals in '84 from San Diego in a trade for Pete Johnson... Led NFL in total yards with Chargers in '81 and '82... Chargers' first-round draft choice out of Auburn in 1981... 1989 salary: $550,000... Born Dec. 28, 1958, in Warner Robbins, Ga.

DAVID FULCHER 25 6-3 234   Safety

Sure to become a regular in the Pro Bowl... Named to the all-star contest for the second straight year and was NFL All-Pro along with 49ers' Ronnie Lott... Led Bengals with 107 tackles (70 solo, 37 assists) and eight interceptions... Interception total was second in AFC to Cleveland's Felix Wright... Recovered four fumbles... Big and fast, resembling a linebacker on the field... Has started since he was a third-round draft pick out of Arizona State in '86... Nicknamed "Rock" for his punishing hits... Left ASU early after being named an All-American... Born Sept. 28, 1964, in Los Angeles.

ANTHONY MUNOZ 32 6-6 284   Tackle

As usual, had phenomenal season... Named to Pro Bowl for ninth consecutive season... Some consider him to be the best tackle ever... One of most athletic players ever at his position... Has caught four touchdown passes in his career and is a standout softball player... "He's the best athlete I've ever been around," said Bengal line coach Jim McNally. "He could be a linebacker or tight end."... Munoz considers 1986 to be his best season... Has appeared in two movies, including "The Right Stuff"... First-round pick out of Southern California... 1989 salary: $565,000... Born Aug. 19, 1958, in Ontario, Cal.

RODNEY HOLMAN 30 6-3 238   Tight End

The top tight end in the AFC... Made second straight Pro Bowl appearance... Finished third among Bengal receivers with 50 catches for 736 yards and nine TDs... All were career highs... Ideal combination of strength and speed makes him difficult to cover... Takes immense pride in his blocking... Won team's Ed Block Courage Award in 1987, when he played with an injured knee... Third-round draft pick out of Tulane in 1982 ... He is Tulane's all-time leading receiver and coaches alma mater during spring practice... Cousin of former NFL running back Preston Pearson... 1989 salary: $558,300... Born April 20, 1960, in Ypsilanti, Mich.

EDDIE BROWN 27 6-0 185   Wide Receiver

Dropped off from his sensational 1988 season when he led AFC with 1,273 receiving yards ... 1989 stats: 52 receptions, 814 yards, six TDs... Has been picture of consistency since being drafted in first round out of Miami in 1985... Has caught more than 50 passes in four of his five seasons... Has scored six or more TDs in three different seasons... Was NFL Offensive Rookie of Year in '85, when he caught 53 passes for 942 yards and eight TDs... Shouldn't have been a surprise after coming out of University of Miami's high-flying offense... Was first Hurricane to gain 1,000 yards in a season... 1989 salary: $800,000... Born Dec. 18, 1962, in Miami.

TIM KRUMRIE 30 6-2 267   Nose Tackle

Made stirring comeback from broken leg suffered in Super Bowl in Jan. 1989... Was determined to overcome doubts and surprised everybody with training-camp participation... Was ready for season-opener and finished third on club with 45 tackles... Also had three sacks and a fumble recovery... It was the first time in five years he didn't lead club in tackles... Had 152 tackles in phenomenal 1988 season... His relentless style is known league-wide. "He's a shark out there who smells blood," said former teammate Cris Collinsworth... A lesson in dedication, a 10th-round draft choice who beat all odds to stardom... Was All-American at Wisconsin, but pro scouts thought he was too slow and too small to make it in the NFL... Born May 20, 1960, in Eau Claire, Wis.

CINCINNATI BENGALS 193

TIM McGEE 26 5-10 179 — Wide Receiver

Speedy receiver had by far his best NFL season, leading club with 65 receptions for 1,211 yards... Catches ranked eighth in AFC, yards fourth... Previous highs were 36 for 686 in '87... Scored eight TDs and averaged 18.6 yards per reception... Second to James Brooks in team voting for offensive MVP... Became a starter in 1988... Returned kicks in 1986 and '87 for an average of 21.5 yards... First-round draft pick out of Tennessee in 1986... Vols' all-time leading receiver with 123 receptions for 2,042 yards and 15 TDs... Born Aug. 7, 1964, in Cleveland.

ICKEY WOODS 24 6-2 232 — Running Back

Trying to come back from serious knee injury suffered early in 1989 season... Had only 29 carries for 94 yards before the setback... Determined to prove that surprising 1988 rookie year was no fluke... That year, he rushed for 1,066 yards for a 5.3-yard average and 15 touchdowns... Combined with James Brooks to give Bengals one of best rushing attacks in football... Big question upon his return will be his cutback ability, which he used so effectively as rookie... Second-round draft pick out of Nevada-Las Vegas who was considered a risk despite leading nation with 1,658 yards as senior... First name is Elbert... Born Feb. 28, 1966, in Fresno, Cal.

ERIC THOMAS 25 5-11 181 — Cornerback

Underrated defender who has 11 interceptions the past two seasons... Had four in '89, second on club to David Fulcher's eight... Seventh on team with 47 tackles... Had two sacks... Made the Pro Bowl in '88 after making seven pickoffs... Had two interceptions in 1988 playoffs... Started as a rookie... Second-round draft choice in '87 out of Tulane, alma mater of teammate Rodney Holman... Was an immediate starter... Attended Pasadena City College before going to Tulane... Hobbies are track, basketball and weightlifting... Born Sept. 11, 1964, in Sacramento, Cal.

COACH SAM WYCHE: Made headlines several ways in 1989, most notably with his mouth... Drew criticism when he locked reporters out of Bengal locker room after a game... After Bengals' 61-7 victory over Houston, Wyche lambasted Oilers' coach Jerry Glanville in front of media... Seems secure in Cincinnati, whose fans wanted him fired in 1987 ... Will be on the spot because of departure of offensive coordinator Bruce Coslet, who left to coach New York Jets... That should be no problem, for Wyche is known as one of football's most innovative coaches... Has 49-46 record since replacing Forrest Gregg in 1984... Named NFL Coach of Year after leading Bengals to Super Bowl in 1988 ... Was assistant with 49ers from 1979-82 and head coach at Indiana University in 1983, when he turned in a 3-8 record ... Was a walk-on at Furman... Played quarterback for Bengals, Redskins, Lions, Cardinals and Bills... Ran sporting good store for three years after retiring, then switched to coaching... Has gained national attention for his work for the homeless... Born Jan. 5, 1945, in Atlanta.

LONGEST PASS PLAY

KEN ANDERSON TO BILLY BROOKS

The longest pass in Bengal history was thrown by the team's best quarterback ever. Ken Anderson, who threw for 4,475 yards from 1971-86, hit Billy Brooks for a 94-yard touchdown on Nov. 13, 1977. The score was Cincinnati's only touchdown in a 42-10 loss to the Vikings.

Brooks, a first-round draft pick out of Oklahoma, played for the Bengals from 1976-79. The previous longest Bengal pass was 90 yards, from Virgil Carter to Speedy Thomas against Philadelphia in 1971. Sam Wyche, the current Bengals' coach, ranks fifth in team annals, with two passes of 80 yards to Bob Trumpy—against Miami in 1968, Kansas City in 1969.

The 1977 Bengals-Vikings game was also significant because Minnesota quarterback Fran Tarkenton broke his leg after completing 17 of 18 passes. His 94-percent completion rate would have beaten out Anderson's NFL single-game record of 90.91 on 20-of-22 against Pittsburgh in 1974. But the league requires 20 attempts to qualify for the record book.

INDIVIDUAL BENGAL RECORDS

Rushing

Most Yards Game:	163	James Brooks, vs New England, 1986
Season:	1,087	James Brooks, 1986
Career:	5,421	Pete Johnson, 1977-83

Passing

Most TD Passes Game:	5	Boomer Esiason, vs N.Y. Jets, 1986
	5	Boomer Esiason, vs Tampa Bay, 1989
Season:	29	Ken Anderson, 1981
Career:	196	Ken Anderson, 1971-85

Receiving

Most TD Passes Game:	3	Bob Trumpy, vs Houston, 1969
	3	Isaac Curtis, vs Cleveland, 1973
	3	Isaac Curtis, vs Baltimore, 1979
Season:	10	Isaac Curtis, 1974
Career:	53	Isaac Curtis, 1973-83

Scoring

Most Points Game:	24	Larry Kinnebrew, vs Houston, 1984
Season:	115	Jim Breech, 1981
Career:	875	Jim Breech, 1981-89
Most TDs Game:	4	Larry Kinnebrew, vs Houston, 1984
Season:	16	Pete Johnson, 1981
Career:	70	Pete Johnson, 1977-83

CLEVELAND BROWNS

TEAM DIRECTORY: Owner/Pres.: Art Modell; Exec. VP-Legal Administration: Jim Bailey; VP-Football Operations: Ernie Accorsi; VP-Pub. Rel.: Kevin Byrne; Head Coach: Bud Carson. Home field: Cleveland Stadium (80,098). Colors: Seal brown, orange and white.

Eric Metcalf's rookie year gives promise of great career.

SCOUTING REPORT

OFFENSE: Quarterback Bernie Kosar's durability is a question. He played hurt once again late last season, and while he was effective, he wasn't enough to carry the Browns (9-6-1) through the playoffs.

Kosar has a slew of receivers, led by Webster Slaughter and Reggie Langhorne. Also, second-year player Lawyer Tillman should be better with a full training camp. Of course, Kosar always has the exciting Eric Metcalf to dump off to. As a rookie, Metcalf had 1,030 yards from scrimmage. Tight end Ozzie Newsome returns for a 13th season.

Metcalf is up and down as a running back, meaning the Browns need Kevin Mack to forget his off-field troubles and play well for a full season. Cleveland ranked 21st in rushing last year. Rookie Leroy Hoard should improve that ranking.

The line got a boost when center Mike Baab was re-acquired from New England. His absence was felt.

The Browns have got to learn to start fast. They were shut out 11 times in the first quarter in 1989.

DEFENSE: It was no surprise the Browns ranked seventh in total defense last year. Simply put, Bud Carson's teams can play defense.

Some interesting things happened during the offseason to a quality defensive backfield. Hanford Dixon, who fell out of favor with Carson, was unprotected and signed with the 49ers. However, the club signed former All-Pro cornerback Raymond Clayborn from the Patriots. Cleveland should come out ahead in the switch.

The Browns intercepted an AFC-high 27 passes last year, led by safety Felix Wright's nine. He and Thane Gash provide good help to cornerback Frank Minnifield, whose best days are behind him.

Michael Dean Perry keys the line while Clay Matthews leads the linebackers. It will be interesting to see how Lawrence McGrew, signed in Plan B from New England, fits into Carson's defense.

KICKING GAME: Gerald McNeil ranked second in the AFC with a 10.1-yard average on punt returns, then signed with Houston. Speedy Mike Oliphant is expected to replace "The Cube." Metcalf handled kickoff-return duties well, turning in a 23.2 average.

Punter Bryan Wagner averaged just 39.4 yards, but landed an

BROWNS VETERAN ROSTER

HEAD COACH—Bud Carson. Assistant Coaches—Zeke Bratkowski, Mike Faulkiner, Hal Hunter, Stan Jones, Paul Lanham, Richard Mann, Joe Popp, Dan Radakovich, George Sefcik, Jim Shofner, Lionel Taylor, John Teerlinck, Jim Vechiarella.

No.	Name	Pos.	Ht.	Wt.	NFL Exp.	College
61	Baab, Mike	C	6-4	270	9	Texas
8	Bahr, Matt	K	5-10	175	12	Penn State
60	Baker, Al	DE	6-6	250	13	Colorado State
97	Banks, Robert	DE	6-5	255	3	Notre Dame
64	Baugh, Tom	C	6-4	290	5	Southern Illinois
24	Blaylock, Tony	CB	5-10	190	3	Winston-Salem State
77	Bolden, Rickey	T	6-4	280	7	Southern Methodist
36	Braggs, Stephen	CB	5-9	180	4	Texas
86	Brennan, Brian	WR	5-10	155	7	Boston College
94	Buczkowski, Bob	DT-DE	6-5	250	2	Pittsburgh
58	Charlton, Clifford	LB	6-3	245	3	Florida
43	Clack, Darryl	RB	5-10	220	5	Arizona State
25	Clayborn, Raymond	CB	6-1	188	14	Texas
49	Dilliahunt, Ellis	S	5-11	196	2	East Carolina
67	Dunn, K.D.	TE	6-3	237	6	Clemson
74	Farren, Paul	T-G	6-5	270	8	Boston University
69	Fike, Dan	G	6-7	255	6	Florida
30	Gash, Thane	S	5-11	200	3	East Tennessee State
16	Gay, Everett	WR	6-2	209	2	Texas
71	Gibson, Tom	DE	6-7	250	2	Northern Arizona
56	Grayson, David	LB	6-2	235	4	Fresno State
78	Hairston, Carl	DT	6-2	275	15	Maryland-E. Shore
23	Harper, Mark	CB	5-9	185	5	Alcorn State
51	Johnson, Eddie	LB	6-1	225	10	Louisville
59	Johnson, Mike	LB	6-1	225	5	Virginia Tech
95	Jones, Marlon	DE	6-4	260	3	Central State, Ohio
66	Jones, Tony	T	6-5	285	3	Western Carolina
19	Kosar, Bernie	QB	6-5	210	6	Miami
40	Kramer, Kyle	S	6-3	190	2	Bowling Green
88	Langhorne, Reggie	WR	6-2	200	5	Elizabeth City State
75	Lucas, Jeff	T	6-7	282	2	West Virginia
34	Mack, Kevin	RS	6-0	230	6	Clemson
42	Manoa, Tim	RB	6-1	240	4	Penn State
57	Matthews, Clay	LB	6-2	235	13	Southern California
53	McGrew, Lawrence	LB	6-5	233	10	Southern California
21	Metcalf, Eric	RB	5-10	185	2	Texas
31	Minnifield, Frank	CB	5-9	180	7	Louisville
62	Newsome, Ozzie	TE	6-2	232	13	Alabama
89	Oliphant, Mike	WR-KR	5-9	170	2	Puget Sound
10	Pagel, Mike	QB	5-2	211	9	Arizona State
87	Patchan, Matt	T	6-3	275	3	Miami
92	Perry, Michael Dean	DE	6-0	280	3	Clemson
75	Pike, Chris	DT	5-8	290	2	Tulsa
73	Rakoozy, Gregg	C	5-8	290	4	Miami
35	Redden, Barry	RB	5-10	219	9	Richmond
52	Rose, Ken	LB	6-1	216	4	Nevada-Las Vegas
84	Slaughter, Webster	WR	6-0	170	5	San Diego State
71	Smith, Dave	T	6-7	290	2	Southern Illinois
96	Stewart, Andrew	DE	6-5	285	2	Cincinnati
85	Tillman, Lawyer	WR	6-5	230	2	Auburn
15	Wagner, Bryan	P	6-2	200	4	Cal State-Northridge
50	Walters, Van	LB	6-4	245	3	Indiana
91	Weston, Rhondy	DT	6-5	275	2	Florida
27	Wright, Charlie	CB-S	5-10	178	3	Tulsa
22	Wright, Felix	S	6-2	195	5	Drake

TOP DRAFT CHOICES

Rd.	Name	Sel. No.	Pos.	Ht.	Wt.	College
2	Hoard, Leroy	45	RB	6-0	222	Michigan
3	Pleasant, Anthony	73	DE	6-4	238	Tennessee State
4	Barnett, Harlon	101	DB	5-11	199	Michigan State
5	Burnett, Rob	129	DE	6-3	270	Syracuse
6	Hilliard, Randy	157	DB	5-10	162	NW Louisiana

NFL-high 32 inside the 20. Matt Bahr hit 16-of-24 field-goal attempts and never seemed to get into a comfortable groove.

THE ROOKIES: Michigan's Hoard is a tough inside runner who can learn from Mack or serve as insurance. He loves to block and can be used as a receiver. Tennessee defensive end Anthony Pleasant is a speed rusher from the outside. Michigan State end Rob Burnett had a disappointing senior year but was a sack artist early in his college career.

OUTLOOK: The Browns were ugly in victory last year. They have a nice mix of youth and experience, but all hope hinges on Kosar surviving the season.

BROWN PROFILES

BERNIE KOSAR 26 6-5 210 Quarterback

Battled through a sore arm and led Browns to playoffs, as he has done in each of his five NFL seasons... Was No. 4 passer in AFC with 80.3 rating... Completed 303 of 513 passes for 3,533 yards and 18 TDs... Threw 14 interceptions... Had worst day of career on Oct. 15 against Pittsburgh, completing 15 of 41 passes with four interceptions... Had streak of 181 passes without an interception broken against Denver... 1990 salary: $1.5 million. Has a seven-year contract for $16.3 million, an average of $2.33 million per year, ranking him third in NFL behind Jim Kelly and Randall Cunningham... Considered one of smartest players in NFL... Won AFC passing title in 1987 with 95.4 rating... Picked in supplemental draft in 1985 after starring at Miami for two years... Born Nov. 25, 1963, in Boardman, Ohio.

CLAY MATTHEWS 34 6-2 235 Linebacker

Named as starter in Pro Bowl, his fifth selection in 12 NFL seasons... Fourth on team with 113 tackles... Had four sacks, nine passes defensed, two fumble recoveries, three forced fumbles and one interception... Switched from right outside linebacker to strong-side linebacker in team's new 4-3 defense... Nearly lost crucial season finale at Houston on

Dec. 23 when he tried to lateral after recovering a fumble. The Oilers recovered, but Cleveland pulled out the game... Has averaged more than 100 tackles over last nine seasons... Has blocked four field goals in career... First-round draft choice out of Southern California in 1978... Brother Bruce is an offensive lineman for Houston... 1989 salary: $650,000... Born March 15, 1956, in Palo Alto, Cal.

ERIC METCALF 22 5-10 185   Running Back

Son of former NFL star Terry Metcalf proved just as elusive, leading Browns with 633 yards... Also broke team's rookie receiving record with 54 catches for 397 yards... Scored 10 TDs, including nine in last 12 games... Also passed for a TD... Dazzling move against Cincinnati for a TD on Monday Night Football made all highlight films... Cleveland traded four draft picks to Denver to make Metcalf the 13th player taken in '89 draft... Fourth running back selected in draft... While at Texas, set Southwest Conference all-purpose yardage record with 5,705 yards... Two-time NCAA long-jump champion... 1989 salary: $250,000. 1990 salary: $350,000... Born Jan. 23, 1968, in Seattle.

KEVIN MACK 28 6-0 230   Running Back

Survived troubled season with strong finish... Didn't join team until Nov. 27... Spent 30 days in jail for illegal substance abuse... Also had knee surgery on Sept. 25... Saw first game action on Dec. 3... Scored winning TD with 39 seconds left in season finale at Houston to clinch division... Gained 130 yards on 37 carries in '89... Missed all or part of 10 games in '88 because of neck, shoulder, calf and knee injuries... Has been to Pro Bowl twice and has 4.1 career average... Has nine career 100-yard games... Browns are 13-0 when he has rushed for 90 or more yards... Finished second in AFC with 10 TDs in '86 despite missing four games... Broke Jim Brown's club rookie rushing mark with 1,104 yards in 1985... First-round pick out of Clemson in '84 supplemental draft... Born Aug. 9, 1962, in Kings Mountain, N.C.

MICHAEL DEAN PERRY 25 6-0 280   Nose Tackle

Has surpassed all expectations and has proven to be better than his famous brother, The Fridge ... Named to start Pro Bowl after leading Browns' linemen with 92 tackles and 49 quarterback pressures ... Was second on team with seven sacks ... Plays crooked nose-tackle position, angling himself for quick pursuit ... Named All-Pro lineman along with Minnesota's Keith Millard ... Was in on 76 plays vs. Jets on Sept. 17 ... Second-round draft pick out of Clemson in 1988 ... Started two games as a rookie, recording six sacks ... That total was more than brother William, of the Bears, has had any season ... Clemson's all-time sack leader with 28 ... One of 12 children ... Active in anti-drug causes ... Born Aug. 27, 1965, in Aiken, S.C.

WEBSTER SLAUGHTER 25 6-0 170   Wide Receiver

Four-year veteran enjoyed record-breaking year ... Set club receiving mark with 1,236 yards on 65 catches ... Yardage total was third in AFC behind Andre Reed and Anthony Miller ... Had four 100-yard games in '89 and was named to Pro Bowl ... Had eight receptions for 186 yards against Chicago, including 97-yard TD ... Previous high for a season was 47 catches in 1987 ... Second-round draft pick out of San Diego State in 1986 ... Missed seven games in '88 because of broken arm ... Did not play football until senior year of high school ... Excellent basketball and saxaphone player ... Born Oct. 19, 1964, in Stockton, Cal.

FRANK MINNIFIELD 30 5-9 180   Cornerback

Aggressive defender who doesn't roll up big numbers but is considered among the best cornerbacks in the game ... Has been to four consecutive Pro Bowls, the last three as a starter ... Had three interceptions in '89 and has never had more than four in a season ... Had 17 passes defensed, one less than team leader Mark Harper ... Missed parts of two games with a groin injury ... Has been starter since fourth game of his rookie 1984 season ... Played in 1983 with Chicago of USFL ... Went undrafted in NFL selection because of his USFL contract... Made Louisville's team as a walk-on and started three years... Led nation in kickoff returns as a junior... 1989 salary: $625,000... Born Jan. 1, 1960, in Lexington, Ky.

REGGIE LANGHORNE 27 6-2 200   Wide Receiver

Teams with Webster Slaughter to give Browns tough tandem... Set a career high with 60 receptions for 749 yards... Was first time in team history two wide receivers caught 60 passes in same year... Had three or more receptions in 13 of 16 games... Played in season-opener despite having an emergency appendectomy performed a few weeks before... Initial medical reports said he wouldn't be able to play until the third game... Runs 40-yard dash in 4.4 seconds... Seventh-round pick out of Elizabeth City State in 1985... Born April 7, 1963, in Suffolk, Va.

OZZIE NEWSOME 34 6-2 232   Tight End

Surprised most when he announced in March that he wasn't retiring after 12 seasons... Is NFL's fifth-leading receiver of all time and the most prolific tight end ever with 639 receptions for 7,740 yards and 45 TDs... Stated desire to win Super Bowl as a reason for returning... Honored on "Thanks, Ozzie" day at Cleveland by fans and teammates who thought he was quitting... Had no receptions vs. Houston on Oct. 29, ending streak of 150 games in which he caught a pass... First-round pick out of Alabama in 1978... Born March 16, 1956, in Muscle Shoals, Ala.

FELIX WRIGHT 31 6-2 195   Safety

NFL leader with nine interceptions, four more than career high... Ended up one shy of club record set by Thom Darden in 1978... Had six interceptions in last eight games... Third on club with 118 tackles... Has seven interceptions off Houston's Warren Moon and five on Monday Night Football... Made switch from free safety to strong safety during training camp... Signed as free agent in 1985 after three years in Canadian

Football League... Was cut by Houston in 1982... Never missed a game in four years at Drake... Has degrees in physical education and history... License plate reads "Flex 22"... Born June 22, 1959, in Carthage, Mo.

COACH BUD CARSON: Eighth Browns' head coach inherited experienced team when hired away in 1989 from the New York Jets, for whom he was defensive coordinator... Made smashing debut with 51-0 rout of Pittsburgh in season-opener... Known for his defensive knowledge, he was openly critical of his offense during the season... Last time he was a head coach was 1971, when he concluded a five-year stay at Georgia Tech... Was 27-27 at Tech. "I made all the mistakes I could make," he said. "I was no more ready to be a head coach than to fly."... Served as defensive coordinator for Pittsburgh, Los Angeles Rams, Indianapolis and Kansas City... Directed Steelers' "Steel Curtain" from 1972-77... Has coached in three Super Bowls, two with Steelers and one with Rams... Spent 30 years in Marines after being defensive back at North Carolina... Born April 28, 1931, in Freeport, Pa.

LONGEST PASS PLAY

BERNIE KOSAR TO WEBSTER SLAUGHTER

The Browns' Webster Slaughter capped a sensational Monday Night Football performance with a play that put away a 27-7 victory over the Bears on Oct. 23, 1989.

With Cleveland leading 17-0 early in the fourth quarter, Chicago had first-and-goal at the Browns' seven but was unable to score. Quickly, Bernie Kosar hit Slaughter on a 97-yard touchdown that sent the Cleveland Stadium fans into a frenzy. The reception was the longest ever on Monday Night Football.

Slaughter was unstoppable against the Bears, catching eight passes for 186 yards, both career highs. He also caught TD passes of 80 and 77 yards in 1989. The previous Cleveland pass record was 87 yards from Bill Nelsen to Milt Morin against Philadelphia in 1968.

INDIVIDUAL BROWN RECORDS

Rushing

Most Yards Game:	237	Jim Brown, vs Los Angeles, 1957
	237	Jim Brown, vs Philadelphia, 1961
Season:	1,863	Jim Brown, 1963
Career:	12,312	Jim Brown, 1957-65

Passing

Most TD Passes Game:	5	Frank Ryan, vs N.Y. Giants, 1964
	5	Bill Nelsen, vs Dallas, 1969
	5	Brian Sipe, vs Pittsburgh, 1979
Season:	30	Brian Sipe, 1980
Career:	154	Brian Sipe, 1974-83

Receiving

Most TD Passes Game:	3	Mac Speedie, vs Chicago, 1951
	3	Darrell Brewster, vs N.Y. Giants, 1953
	3	Ray Renfro, vs Pittsburgh, 1959
	3	Gary Collins, vs Philadelphia, 1963
	3	Reggie Rucker, vs N.Y. Jets, 1976
	3	Larry Poole, vs Pittsburgh, 1977
	3	Calvin Hill, vs Baltimore, 1978
Season:	13	Gary Collins, 1963
Career:	70	Gary Collins, 1962-71

Scoring

Most Points Game:	36	Dub Jones, vs Chicago Bears, 1951
Season:	126	Jim Brown, 1965
Career:	1,349	Lou Groza, 1950-59, 1961-67
Most TDs Game:	6	Dub Jones, vs Chicago Bears, 1951
Season:	21	Jim Brown, 1965
Career:	126	Jim Brown, 1957-65

DENVER BRONCOS

TEAM DIRECTORY: Owner: Patrick D. Bowlen; GM: John Beake; Dir. Media Rel.: Jim Saccomano; Head Coach: Dan Reeves. Home field: Mile High Stadium (76,273). Colors: Orange, blue and white.

SCOUTING REPORT

OFFENSE: Critics ripped into John Elway last year for his mediocre statistics, but all the blond bomber had to do was point to the standings for proof that the Broncos' (11-5) offense was work-

Bobby Humphrey burst into pros with 1,000-yard season.

ing. Thanks to surprise rookie running back Bobby Humphrey, balance now has a home in Denver, former site of nothing but unlimited passing.

Humphrey gained 1,151 yards behind a beefed-up line, and the Broncos ranked sixth in rushing and 23rd in passing. His backup this year should be Lorenzo Hampton, a versatile former first-round pick of Miami who was signed in Plan B.

Expect Mark Jackson to rebound from an off year and Ricky Nattiel to show up recovered from knee surgery. The two will give Vance Johnson some help, and balls will fly in Denver again.

Elway threw 18 touchdown passes and 18 interceptions, but stepped his game up a notch in the playoffs. His Super Bowl disaster remains a mystery.

DEFENSE: Denver's switch in personality was as drastic on defense, where Wade Phillips changed things up and dominated with relative no-names. The Broncos' defense ranked third in the NFL, allowing the fewest points. That is not counting, of course, the Super Bowl fiasco.

Denver was No. 2 in the AFC with 47 sacks, but how long the line can hold up is a question. Free agents Alphonso Carreker and Ron Holmes are 27 and 26, respectively. Karl Mecklenberg gets all the publicity at linebacker, but Simon Fletcher quietly amassed 12 sacks last year. Rookie linebacker Jeroy Robinson is a powerful addition.

Second-year safety Steve Atwater will be a star for several years, and he teams well with veteran Dennis Smith. Denver's first draft pick was Alton Montgomery, a speedy safety. The Broncos' new aggressive mentality resulted in 22 opponents' fumbles recovered, tops in the AFC.

KICKING GAME: The fuss over Rich Karlis' departure didn't last long because of a steady performance by David Treadwell, who hit 27-of-33 tries, including 24-of-25 from inside 42 yards. Mike Horan averaged 40.4 yards per punt.

Ken Bell returned both punts and kickoffs, proving just adequate at both. Denver allowed 13.2 yards per punt return, worst in the AFC.

THE ROOKIES: Houston University's Montgomery is a smart, hard-hitting player who can learn from Smith. Texas A&M's Robinson is brutally strong and has ability to chase down ball-carriers. Family ties: Southern Cal center Brad Leggett's father, Earl, is a

BRONCOS VETERAN ROSTER

HEAD COACH—Dan Reeves, Assistant Coaches—Marvin Bass, Barney Chavous, Mo Forte, Chan Gailey, George Henshaw, Earl Leggett, Pete Mangurian, Al Miller, Mike Nolan, Wade Phillips, Harold Richardson, Mike Shanahan, Charlie Waters.

No.	Name	Pos.	Ht.	Wt.	NFL Exp.	College
57	Allert, Ty	LB	6-2	238	5	Texas
40	Alexander, Jeff	RB	6-0	232	2	Southern University
27	Atwater, Steve	S	6-3	217	2	Arkansas
35	Bell, Ken	RB	5-10	190	5	Boston College
54	Bishop, Keith	C-G	6-3	290	10	Baylor
32	Bratton, Melvin	RB	6-1	225	2	Miami
34	Braxton, Tyrone	CB	5-11	185	4	North Dakota State
56	Brooks, Michael	LB	6-1	235	4	Louisiana State
92	Carreker, Alphonso	DE	6-6	272	5	Florida State
29	Carrington, Darren	CB	6-1	189	2	Northern Arizona
25	Corrington, Kip	S	6-0	175	2	Texas A&M
58	Curtis, Scott	LB	6-1	230	3	New Hampshire
55	Dennison, Rick	LB	6-3	220	8	Colorado State
7	Elway, John	QB	6-3	215	8	Stanford
85	Embree, Jon	TE	6-3	235	3	Colorado
73	Fletcher, Simon	LB	6-6	240	6	Houston
69	Hamilton, Darrell	T	6-5	298	2	North Carolina
20	Hampton, Lorenzo	RB	5-11	208	6	Florida
36	Haynes, Mark	CB	5-11	195	11	Colorado
24	Henderson, Wymon	CB	5-9	186	4	Nevada-Las Vegas
68	Henke, Brad	DE	6-3	275	2	Arizona
90	Holmes, Ron	DE	6-4	265	6	Washington
2	Horan, Mike	P	5-11	190	7	Long Beach State
26	Humphrey, Bobby	RB	6-1	201	2	Alabama
80	Jackson, Mark	WR	5-9	180	4	Purdue
81	Johnson, Jason	WR	5-10	178	3	Illinois State
82	Johnson, Vance	WR	5-11	185	6	Arizona
66	Juriga, Jim	G-T	6-6	275	4	Illinois
72	Kartz, Keith	C	6-4	270	4	California
88	Kay, Clarence	TE	6-2	237	7	Georgia
71	Kragen, Greg	NT	6-3	265	6	Utah State
8	Kubiak, Gary	QB	6-0	192	8	Texas A&M
76	Lanier, Ken	T	6-3	290	10	Florida State
98	Little, David	TE	6-2	226	7	Middle Tenn. State
59	Lucas, Tim	LB	6-3	230	4	California
97	Mraz, Mark	DE	6-4	260	3	Utah State
96	McCullough, Jake	DE	6-5	270	2	Clemson
77	Mecklenburg, Karl	LB	6-3	240	8	Minnesota
89	Mobley, Orson	TE	6-5	259	5	Salem College
51	Munford, Marc	LB	6-2	231	4	Nebraska
84	Nattiel, Ricky	WR	5-9	180	4	Florida
60	Perry, Gerald	T	6-6	305	3	Southern University
91	Powers, Warren	DE	6-6	287	2	Maryland
74	Provence, Andrew	NT	6-3	270	6	South Carolina
48	Robbins, Randy	S	6-2	189	7	Arizona
30	Sewell, Steve	RB	6-3	210	6	Oklahoma
49	Smith, Dennis	S	6-3	200	10	Southern California
65	Smith, Monte	G	6-4	270	2	North Dakota
50	Stephens, Rod	LB	6-1	237	2	Georgia Tech
61	Townsend, Andre	DE-NT	6-3	265	7	Mississippi
9	Treadwell, David	K	6-1	175	2	Clemson
86	Verhulst, Chris	TE	6-2	249	3	Chico State
70	White, Robb	DE	6-4	270	3	South Dakota
67	Widell, Doug	G	6-4	287	2	Boston College
23	Winder, Sammy	RB	5-11	203	9	Southern Mississippi
83	Young, Mike	WR	6-1	183	6	UCLA

TOP DRAFT CHOICES

Rd.	Name	Sel. No.	Pos.	Ht.	Wt.	College
2	Montgomery, Alton	52	DB	6-0	198	Houston
4	Robinson, Jeroy	82	LB	6-1	238	Texas A&M
5	Davidson, Jeff	111	G	6-4	306	Ohio State
5	Lang, Le-Lo	136	DB	5-10	184	Washington
6	Haliburton, Ronnie	164	TE	6-4	230	LSU

Bronco assistant coach, and Savannah State receiver Shannon Sharpe's brother is Sterling of the Packers.

OUTLOOK: The Broncos bounced back nicely from an off year, then were exposed in the Super Bowl. They finally are heading the right direction in style of play, but the AFC West is getting better. Elway and friends might be sorry they blew their championship chances.

BRONCO PROFILES

JOHN ELWAY 30 6-3 215   Quarterback

Frustrations of season seemed to be forgotten as he put game together to rally Broncos to Super Bowl... MVP two years ago, finished ninth in AFC passing for second straight year ... Threw for 3,051 yards, 18 TDs and 18 interceptions... Gained national publicity and criticism when complained of being "smothered" by own celebrity... Year ended on a downer with awful Super Bowl performance... Is 0-3 in Super Bowls... Only player in NFL history with 3,000 passing yards and 200 rushing yards in five consecutive seasons... Has thrown for more than 300 yards 14 times... Ranks seventh on Bronco all-time rushing list with 1,675 yards... Stanford All-American was first player picked in '83 draft, by Colts... Didn't want to play in Baltimore and was traded to Denver... 1989 salary: $1.425 million... Born June 28, 1960, in Port Angeles, Wash.

BOBBY HUMPHREY 23 6-1 201   Running Back

Broken foot made drafting Humphrey a risk, but Broncos hit jackpot... Brought diversity Bronco offense has been looking for since John Elway's arrival... Named team's offensive MVP after rushing for 1,151 yards... First Bronco rookie ever to break 1,000... Fifth among AFC rushers... Had five 100-yard games, most by a Bronco since 1974... Gained 102 yards in first pro start... Selected out of Alabama in first round of supplemental draft... How much of a risk was he? College coach and close friend Ray Perkins of Tampa Bay passed on him... Sat out '88 season after breaking foot in spring practice ... Gained 3,783 yards in three seasons... Born Oct. 11, 1966, in Birmingham, Ala.

STEVE ATWATER 23 6-3 217 — Safety

No rookie surprise here. The first safety picked in draft, he made immediate impact in starting lineup... His 129 tackles was second on team behind Karl Mecklenberg's 143... Bruising hitter who's always around the ball... Made three interceptions... Arkansas' all-time interception leader with 15... Went to Arkansas as wishbone quarterback... Has degree in business administration... Cousin of Giants' receiver Mark Ingram ... Nickname is H2O... 1989 salary: $225,000. 1990 salary: $275,000... Born Oct. 28, 1966, in Chicago.

VANCE JOHNSON 27 5-11 185 — Wide Receiver

Was busy man as two other Amigos, Mark Jackson and Ricky Nattiel, were having off years... Caught career-high 76 passes, third in AFC and most by a Bronco in 24 years... Caught 48 more passes than Bronco runnerup Jackson... Scored seven TDs... Had first 1,000-yard season... Led Broncos in '88 with 68 catches... Caught 51 passes as rookie, when he ran a club-record 4.36-second 40-yard dash... Second-round draft pick out of Arizona in '85... Played tailback in college and led Pac-10 with 13 TDs as a junior... Won Pac-10 long-jump title in '82 and was alternate on '84 Olympic team... An accomplished artist... Born March 13, 1963, in Trenton, N.J.

KARL MECKLENBURG 30 6-3 240 — Linebacker

Returned to All-Pro form under Wade Phillips' new defense... Led Bronco tacklers with 143 ... Made 7½ sacks after recording just 1½ in '88... Went to Pro Bowl for fourth time and was placed on All-Pro team along with Chicago's Mike Singletary... Was AFC Defensive Player of Month in November... Recovered four fumbles and scored first pro TD on a 23-yard recovery and return... His 47½ sacks rank fourth in Bronco history... Unassuming, brainy player who holds degree in biology from Minnesota... Twelfth-round draft pick in '83... Began college career at Augustana (S.D.)... 1989 salary: $700,000... Born Sept. 1, 1960, in Edina, Minn.

DENNIS SMITH 31 6-3 200 — Safety

Had outstanding year playing alongside rookie Steve Atwater... Named to third Pro Bowl... Selected defensive MVP by teammates... Had 82 tackles and two interceptions... Constantly overshadowed by longtime friend Ronnie Lott of 49ers but has gained respect of peers... Made 13 tackles in Super Bowl XXII... Coaches have used him occasionally as wide receiver because of his great jumping ability... First-round draft choice out of Southern Cal in '81... Lettered three times as high jumper in college... 1989 salary: $620,000... Born Feb. 3, 1959, in Santa Monica, Cal.

MARK JACKSON 27 5-10 180 — Wide Receiver

Casualty of great years turned in by Vance Johnson and Bobby Humphrey... Caught just 26 passes for 446 yards, both second on club... Dropoff from 46 receptions, 852 yards and six TDs in '88... Both TDs came against Raiders in season-opener... Came on with fine performance in playoffs... Always seems to shine in postseason... Had 80-yard TD in '87 AFC title game and another crucial score in '86 title game... Sixth-round pick in '86 out of Purdue, where he played with Jim Everett of Rams... Only made honorable mention All-Big Ten... Born May 23, 1963, in Chicago but grew up in Terre Haute, Ind.

TYRONE BRAXTON 25 5-11 185 — Cornerback

Went from special-teams player to club interception leader in third NFL season... Picked off six passes, fifth in AFC... Started every game... Had two interceptions and a sack in '88... Revealed a few days before Super Bowl that he was dedicating season to his brother, who was jailed in Green Bay for robbery... Said he came from troubled background and wanted to use his earnings to straighten family's life... Twelfth-round draft choice out of North Dakota State in '87... Standout

DENVER BRONCOS 211

defensive back, punt-returner and member of conference champion 400-meter relay team in college... Born Dec. 12, 1964, in Madison, Wis.

SIMON FLETCHER 28 6-6 240   Linebacker

Keeps getting better as linebacker after playing defensive end for first two seasons... Led club with career-high 12 sacks, ranking fourth in AFC... Made 105 tackles... Was team's defensive MVP in '88, when he had nine sacks... Saw spot playing time DE in '85 and '86, then was moved to LB because of his agility... Wasn't his first position switch, as he moved from tackle to end in college... Second-round pick out of Houston in '85... Born Feb. 18, 1962, in Bay City, Tex.

RICKY NATTIEL 24 5-9 180   Wide Receiver

Hoping to bounce back from knee injury that slowed him in '89... Limited to just 10 receptions for 183 yards and a TD... Underwent surgery on Feb. 13 to have pins placed in crack in kneecap... Was coming off best of his two previous seasons... Caught 46 passes for 574 yards and had 9.7-yard punt return average in '88... First-round draft choice out of Florida in '87... Gators' No. 2 all-time receiver with 2,086 yards... Participated in NFL Fastest Man competition in '87... Has worked as rehab counselor in Florida... 1989 salary: $200,000... Born Jan. 25, 1966, in Gainesville, Fla.

COACH DAN REEVES:

Fantastic coaching career marred by inability to win a Super Bowl... Doesn't take those losses lightly, either. He admitted he worked harder than ever preparing for latest title game, only to get blown out once again... Has displayed incredible diversity, revamping coaching staff and style of offense and still finishing on top of AFC... Was UPI AFC Coach of Year... Has participated in NFL-record eight Super Bowls as player or coach... NFL career record is 91-54-1, a .627 winning clip... Only four active coaches have won more. They are Don Shula, Chuck Noll, Chuck Knox and Joe Gibbs.... Was youngest coach in NFL (37) when he was hired by Broncos in '81... Dallas Cowboys' fifth-leading rusher with 1,990 yards and 25 TDs ... Played quarterback at South Carolina... Began coaching career as player-assistant for Cowboys in '70... Spent '73 out of football before returning to Dallas in '74... Born Jan. 19, 1944, in Americus, Ga.

LONGEST PASS PLAY

GEORGE SHAW TO JERRY TAAR

The Broncos' George Shaw and Jerry Taar spent one unspectacular year in the NFL, but their names still stand in the team's record book. In a 41-16 loss at Boston on Sept. 21, 1962, Shaw hit Tarr for a 97-yard touchdown. The play broke the team record of 96 yards set a week earlier by quarterback Frank Tripucka and halfback Al Frazier at Buffalo.

Tarr's reception was one of just eight receptions he made all year. A 17th-round draft pick out of Oregon, Tarr finished with 211 yards and two touchdowns. Shaw was Tripucka's backup and was 49-for-110 for 783 yards and four touchdowns. Craig Morton and Steve Watson turned in the third- and fourth-longest Bronco receptions—95 yards against San Diego and 93 against Detroit, both in 1981.

INDIVIDUAL BRONCO RECORDS

Rushing

Most Yards Game:	183	Otis Armstrong, vs Houston, 1974
Season:	1,407	Otis Armstrong, 1974
Career:	6,323	Floyd Little, 1967-75

Passing

Most TD Passes Game:	5	Frank Tripucka, vs Buffalo, 1962
	5	John Elway, vs Minnesota, 1984
Season:	24	Frank Tripucka, 1960
Career:	120	John Elway, 1983-89

DENVER BRONCOS 213

Receiving

Most TD Passes Game:	3	Lionel Taylor, vs Buffalo, 1960
	3	Bob Scarpitto, vs Buffalo, 1966
	3	Haven Moses, vs Houston, 1973
	3	Steve Watson, vs Baltimore, 1981
Season:	13	Steve Watson, 1981
Career:	44	Lionel Taylor, 1960-66
	44	Haven Moses, 1972-81

Scoring

Most Points Game:	21	Gene Mingo, vs Los Angeles, 1960
Season:	137	Gene Mingo, 1962
Career:	736	Jim Turner, 1971-79
Most TDs Game:	3	Lionel Taylor, vs Buffalo, 1960
	3	Don Stone, vs San Diego, 1962
	3	Bob Scarpitto, vs Buffalo, 1966
	3	Floyd Little, vs Minnesota, 1972
	3	Floyd Little, vs Cincinnati, 1973
	3	Haven Moses, vs Houston, 1973
	3	Otis Armstrong, vs Houston, 1974
	3	Jon Keyworth, vs Kansas City, 1974
	3	Steve Watson, vs Baltimore, 1981
	3	Gerald Willhite, vs Dallas, 1986
	3	Gerald Willhite, vs Kansas City, 1986
Season:	13	Floyd Little, 1972
	13	Floyd Little, 1973
	13	Steve Watson, 1981
Career:	54	Floyd Little, 1967-75

HOUSTON OILERS

TEAM DIRECTORY: Pres./Owner: K.S. (Bud) Adams; GM/Exec. VP: Mike Holovak; Exec. VP/Adm.: Mike McClure; Dir. College Scouting: Dick Corrick; Dir. Business Oper.: Lewis Mangum; Dir. Media Services and Broadcasting: Chip Namias; Dir. Marketing: Gregg Stengel; Head Coach: Jack Pardee. Home field: Astrodome (60,502). Colors: Scarlet, Columbia blue and white.

SCOUTING REPORT

OFFENSE: Jack Pardee and his run-and-shoot offense at Houston U. move across town this year, and, scary as it may seem, Warren Moon may improve. Moon was the AFC's No. 2-rated passer last year and now will have targets all over the field.

There's no doubt the Oilers (9-7) have the talent to light up a scoreboard. Pardee probably will arrange to have Drew Hill, Ernest Givins, Curtis Duncan and others all on the field at the same time. And running backs? For the past few years, this has been where former All-Americans go to waste away. Somehow, the team with Mike Rozier, Allen Pinkett, Lorenzo White and Alonzo Highsmith ranked 12th in rushing in '89. Look for Pardee to loosen things up and key on one or two backs.

Surely, there are holes to run through. Bruce Matthews and Mike Munchak form the best guard tandem in the NFL, and their help isn't too shabby. Pardee might be the man to finally unleash all this talent.

DEFENSE: Once again, the Oilers showed flashes of defensive progress, but blowups were frequent. Houston allowed 23 or more points 11 times and 412 points for the season, most in the AFC.

The Oilers will switch to a 4-3 alignment this year, and they should have the linemen to fit in. Ray Childress (8½ sacks) is a star, and William Fuller and Sean Jones are quality players. Houston picked up veteran defensive end Ezra Johnson from Indianapolis in Plan B. And their top draft picks were linebacker Lamar Lathon and defensive lineman Jeff Alm.

The Oilers lost starting safety Jeff Donaldson to the Chiefs but signed Terry Kinard from the Giants. Bubba McDowell had a stellar rookie season at strong safety. It will be interesting to watch the progress of the Class of '89 safeties—McDowell, Steve Atwater, Louis Oliver and Carnell Lake.

How high the Moon? Warren's figures keep mounting.

KICKING GAME: Punter Greg Montgomery boosted his average from 38.8 yards to 43.3 and led the AFC in both gross and net (36.1) average. For some reason, the Oilers are excellent in kick coverage but awful on returns. They ranked last in the AFC in kick (17.4) and punt (6.4) returns. Gerald McNeil, signed in Plan B from Cleveland, should help.

Tony Zendejas made 25-of-37 field goals, including just 9-of-14 from 30-39 yards. He was, however, 2-for-2 beyond 50 yards.

Houston blocked three punts in '89, giving them eight in the last two seasons.

THE ROOKIES: Houston University's Lathon should help the Oilers' switch to a 4-3 defense. He missed much of his senior

OILERS VETERAN ROSTER

HEAD COACH—Jack Pardee. Assistant Coaches—Jim Eddy, Kevin Gilbride, Frank Novak, Chris Palmer, Richard Smith, Jim Stanley, Pat Thomas, Steve Watterson, Bob Young.

No.	Name	Pos.	Ht.	Wt.	NFL Exp.	College
29	Allen, Patrick	CB	5-10	182	7	Utah State
31	Arnold, David	S	6-3	210	2	Michigan
33	Bell, Billy	CB	5-10	170	2	Lamar
58	Brantley, John	LB	6-2	240	2	Georgia
24	Brown, Steve	CB	5-11	187	8	Oregon
71	Byrd, Richard	NT	6-4	273	6	Southern Mississippi
67	Camp, Reggie	DE	6-4	270	6	California
14	Carlson, Cody	QB	6-3	194	4	Baylor
79	Childress, Ray	NT-DE	6-6	276	6	Texas A&M
77	Davis, Bruce	T	6-6	315	12	UCLA
28	Dishman, Cris	CB	6-0	178	3	Purdue
80	Duncan, Curtis	WR	5-11	184	4	Northwestern
51	Fairs, Eric	LB	6-3	238	5	Memphis State
88	Ford, Bernard	WR	5-10	171	2	Central Florida
95	Fuller, William	DE	6-3	269	5	North Carolina
97	Garalczyk, Mark	NT	6-5	272	3	Western Michigan
81	Givins, Ernest	WR	5-9	172	5	Louisville
59	Grimsley, John	LB	6-2	238	7	Kentucky
83	Harris, Leonard	WR	5-8	162	5	Texas Tech
32	Highsmith, Alonzo	RB	6-1	234	4	Miami
85	Hill, Drew	WR	5-9	174	11	Georgia Tech
86	Jackson, Kenny	WR	6-0	183	7	Penn State
84	Jeffires, Haywood	WR	6-2	201	4	North Carolina State
90	Johnson, Ezra	DE	6-4	255	14	Morris Brown
23	Johnson, Richard	CB	6-1	195	6	Wisconsin
22	Jones, Quintin	S	5-11	194	2	Pittsburgh
96	Jones, Sean	DE	6-7	273	7	Northeastern
27	Kinard, Terry	S	6-1	196	8	Clemson
21	Knight, Leander	CB-S	6-1	196	2	Montclair State
56	Kozak, Scott	LB	6-3	226	2	Oregon
93	Lyles, Robert	LB	6-1	230	7	Texas Christian
78	Maggs, Don	T-G	6-5	285	4	Tulane
74	Matthews, Bruce	G	6-5	286	8	Southern California
25	McDowell, Bubba	S	6-1	195	2	Miami
89	McNeil, Gerald	WR-KR	5-8	144	5	Baylor
91	Meads, Johnny	LB	6-2	232	7	Nicholls State
94	Montgomery, Glenn	NT	6-0	274	2	Houston
9	Montgomery, Greg	P	6-4	217	3	Michigan State
1	Moon, Warren	QB	6-3	210	7	Washington
63	Munchak, Mike	G	6-3	284	9	Penn State
52	Pennison, Jay	C	6-1	282	5	Nicholls State
20	Pinkett, Allen	RB	5-9	192	5	Notre Dame
96	Reese, Jerry	NT-DE	6-2	275	2	Kentucky
66	Robison, Tommy	G-T	6-4	295	3	Texas A&M
30	Rozier, Mike	RB	5-10	213	6	Nebraska
53	Seale, Eugene	LB	5-10	250	4	Lamar
54	Smith, Al	LB	6-1	240	2	Utah State
99	Smith, Doug	NT	6-6	286	6	Auburn
70	Steinkuhler, Dean	T	6-3	287	7	Nebraska
44	White, Lorenzo	RB	5-11	218	3	Michigan State
73	Williams, David	T	6-5	292	2	Florida
69	Williams, Doug	G-T	6-6	295	3	Texas A&M
7	Zendejas, Tony	K	6-8	165	6	Nevada-Reno

TOP DRAFT CHOICES

Rd.	Name	Sel. No.	Pos.	Ht.	Wt.	College
1	Lathon, Lamar	15	LB	6-3	240	Houston
2	Alm, Jeff	41	DT	6-5	260	Notre Dame
3	Peguese, Willis	72	DE	6-3	262	Miami
4	Still, Eric	99	G	6-2	277	Tennessee
5	Newbill, Richard	126	LB	6-1	240	Miami

HOUSTON OILERS 217

season with a knee injury, but has seemingly recovered. He is an amazing athlete. Notre Dame's Alm is a strong, disciplined player, but not spectacular. Miami (Fla.) end Willis Peguese is a fine athlete who was overshadowed at star-studded Miami.

OUTLOOK: It might be time the Oilers traded in some of their foolish aggressiveness for common sense. Pardee walks into a nice situation, but faces a rugged AFC Central. How quickly his offense takes hold will determine the Oilers' fate.

OILER PROFILES

WARREN MOON 33 6-3 210   Quarterback

Star quarterback continues to be outstanding player and citizen... Set career highs for completions (280), yards (3,631), TDs (23), completion percentage (60.3) and QB rating (88.9) ... Only Dan Marino threw for more yards in the AFC... Had career-best day on Dec. 23 against Cleveland with 32-for-51 for 424 yards, most by an Oiler in 28 years... Pro Bowl starter and *Football News*' AFC Player of Year... Named Traveler's NFL Man of Year for charity work... Threw just seven interceptions in last 351 attempts... Ranks second to George Blanda on Oilers' all-time yardage list... Came to Houston in '84 after six seasons in CFL... Starred at University of Washington and was MVP of 1978 Rose Bowl win over Michigan... Has four years left on contract... 1989 salary: $1.5 million... Born Nov. 18, 1956, in Los Angeles.

DREW HILL 33 5-9 174   Wide Receiver

Has led club in receiving each of his five years in Houston... Career statistics are fairly consistent... In '89, caught 66 passes for 938 yards and eight touchdowns... Missed out on chance for fourth 1,000-yard season in last five years when he sat out final 2½ games with back injury... Had three 100-yard games, upping his career total to 23, 20 with the Oilers...

Played five seasons with the Rams after being picked in the 12th-round out of Georgia Tech... Oilers traded fourth- and seventh-round picks for him in '85... Has degree in industrial management... Played in Super Bowl XIV as rookie... Born Oct. 5, 1956, in Newnan, Ga.

ALONZO HIGHSMITH 25 6-1 234   Fullback

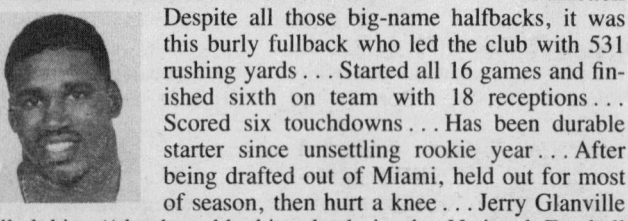

Despite all those big-name halfbacks, it was this burly fullback who led the club with 531 rushing yards... Started all 16 games and finished sixth on team with 18 receptions... Scored six touchdowns... Has been durable starter since unsettling rookie year... After being drafted out of Miami, held out for most of season, then hurt a knee... Jerry Glanville called him "the best blocking back in the National Football League."... Rushed for 106 yards as rookie and 466 in '88... Learned versatility in Miami's pro-set offense... Finished with 1,873 rushing yards in college, second to O.J. Anderson in Hurricane history... 1989 salary: $400,000... Born Feb. 26, 1965, in Bartow, Fla.

MIKE ROZIER 29 5-10 213   Running Back

Started final 11 games of season but seemed to get lost in shuffle of talented halfbacks... Finished with 301 yards, a dropoff from 1,000-yard 1988 season... Missed opener because of holdout and Weeks 3-5 because of a knee injury... Has 3,384 yards to rank third on club's all-time rushing list behind Earl Campbell and Hoyle Granger... Was superb in '88 with 1,002 yards and 11 TDs, most by an Oiler since Campbell's 12 in '83... Went to Oilers from USFL in '85... Played two seasons for Jacksonville Bulls after winning Heisman Trophy at Nebraska... Rushed for 4,780 yards and 49 TDs in three years of college ball... 1989 salary: $650,000... Born March 1, 1961, in Camden, N.J.

HOUSTON OILERS 219

ERNEST GIVINS 25 5-9 172 — Wide Receiver

In just four seasons, has climbed to fourth on Oilers' all-time reception and yardage lists... Has caught 229 passes for 3,765 yards... Had 55 receptions for 794 yards in '89, both second to Drew Hill... Moon's deep threat, his 14.4 average led team... Second-round draft pick out of Louisville in 1986... Played at Northeast Oklahoma Junior College before joining the Cardinals... Accounted for 34 percent of Louisville's total yardage as senior... Runs 4.36-second 40-yard dash... Was a baseball prospect, but says he decided to concentrate on football after facing Dwight Gooden in high-school baseball game... 1989 salary: $220,000... Born Sept. 3, 1964, in St. Petersburg, Fla.

BRUCE MATTHEWS 29 6-5 286 — Guard

Established among elite offensive linemen in NFL... Pro Bowl starter for second straight year... Also was first-time All-Pro... Started all 16 games for second consecutive year... Brother Clay plays linebacker for Cleveland. Father Clay Sr. played linebacker for 49ers... Bruce and Clay are only brother tandem to be selected for Pro Bowl in same year, and they have done it twice... Switched positions often early in career... First-round pick out of Southern Cal in '83, ninth overall... 1989 salary: $400,000... Born Aug. 8, 1961, in Raleigh, N.C.

MIKE MUNCHAK 30 6-3 284 — Guard

Pencil him in for the Pro Bowl... Has gone five times, three times as a starter, including 1989... Teams with Bruce Matthews to give Oilers best guard tandem in league... Suffered severe knee injury in '86 while blocking William Perry, but fought back and made Pro Bowl in '87... Eighth player taken in 1982 draft... Starred at Penn State... Was first of three consecutive first-round picks Oilers invested in offensive linemen... Others were Matthews in '83 and Dean Steinkuhler in '84... Didn't play offensive line until college... Has degree in business logistics... 1989 salary: $650,000... Born March 5, 1960, in Scranton, Pa.

RAY CHILDRESS 27 6-6 276   Defensive End

Outstanding season was cut short by broken leg in Week 14 . . . Still, tied career-high with 8½ sacks . . . Has led Oiler linemen in tackles (57 in '89) in each of his five NFL seasons and has led or shared team sack lead the past four . . . Injury ended streak of 76 consecutive starts . . . Was named to Oilers' 30th Anniversary "Dream Team" . . . Recovered just one fumble after grabbing seven in '88 . . . Made career-high 172 tackles in '86 . . . Third player picked in '85 draft . . . All-American at Texas A&M . . . A financial buff who owns a construction business, and is involved in apartment syndications and cattle ranching . . . Born Oct. 20, 1962, in Memphis, Tenn.

ALLEN PINKETT 26 5-9 192   Running Back

Finally started to become big part of Houston offense, but coaching switch may change things . . . Made career-high six starts and was second in rushing with 449 yards . . . His 4.8-yard average was best on team . . . Top receiving back on club with 31 receptions for 239 yards . . . Broke a 60-yard run against Chicago . . . Gained 513 yards in '88 while starting two games . . . Had just 225 and 149 yards in first two NFL seasons . . . Third-round draft pick out of Notre Dame in '86 . . . Irish's all-time leading rusher with 4,131 yards and 49 TDs . . . Has degree in marketing and has served on NCAA Committee on Recruiting . . . Born Jan. 25, 1964, in Washington, D.C.

BUBBA McDOWELL 23 6-1 195   Safety

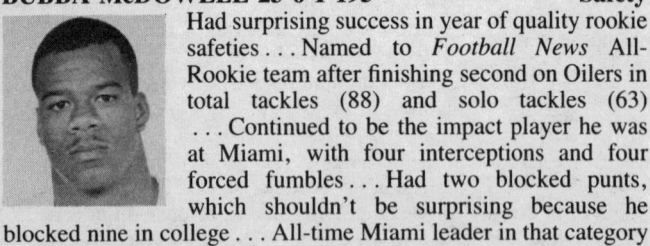

Had surprising success in year of quality rookie safeties . . . Named to *Football News* All-Rookie team after finishing second on Oilers in total tackles (88) and solo tackles (63) . . . Continued to be the impact player he was at Miami, with four interceptions and four forced fumbles . . . Had two blocked punts, which shouldn't be surprising because he blocked nine in college . . . All-time Miami leader in that category . . . Made 181 tackles and four interceptions in four Miami seasons . . . Third-round draft pick . . . Born Nov. 4, 1966, in Fort Gaines, Ga.

HOUSTON OILERS

COACH JACK PARDEE: Moved across town from University of Houston, where he went 22-11-1 in three seasons... Coached Heisman Trophy winner Andre Ware in '89... Replaced Jerry Glanville to become 14th head coach in club's 30-year history... Signed five-year contract... His Run 'N Shoot offense led the nation in total yards (624.9), passing yards (511.3) and scoring (53.5) in '89... Coached USFL Houston Gamblers, with quarterback Jim Kelly, in 1984-85, going 23-12... Was defensive coordinator for Chargers in 1981 and head coach for the Redskins from 1978-80... Named AP NFL Coach of Year after going 10-6 in '79... Coached Bears from 1975-77 (NFC Coach of the Year in '76) after leading bankrupt Florida Blazers to the first, and last, World Football League title game... Career NFL record: 44-46... Born April 19, 1936, in Exira, Iowa, but grew up in West Texas... Played 15 years as linebacker for Los Angeles and Washington after college ball at Texas A&M under Bear Bryant.

LONGEST PASS PLAY

JACKY LEE TO WILLARD DEWVEALL

Jacky Lee never was the Oilers' leading passer, but he is in the team's record book three times for long-range tosses. As George Blanda's backup, a draft choice out of Cincinnati in 1960, Lee holds the Oiler record with a 98-yard touchdown pass to Willard Dewveall in a 33-27 victory over San Diego at Houston on Nov. 25, 1962.

The play broke the record of 92 yards, which Lee set in 1960 with a touchdown pass to Bill Groman against Denver. Only Blanda topped Lee's second-best effort, with a 95-yard pass to Dick Compton against Buffalo in 1965. Lee played for Houston from 1960-63 and again from 1966-67. After the '63 season, Denver traded for Lee, who is seventh on the Oilers' all-time passing list with 3,291 yards and 25 touchdowns.

Dewveall led the Bears in receiving in 1960, then played at Houston from 1961-64. His best year in Houston was 1963, when he caught 58 passes for 752 yards and seven touchdowns.

INDIVIDUAL OILER RECORDS

Rushing

Most Yards Game:	216	Billy Cannon, vs N.Y. Jets, 1961
Season:	1,934	Earl Campbell, 1980
Career:	8,574	Earl Campbell, 1978-84

Passing

Most TD Passes Game:	7	George Blanda, vs N.Y. Jets, 1961
Season:	36	George Blanda, 1961
Career:	165	George Blanda, 1960-66

Receiving

Most TD Passes Game:	3	Bill Groman, vs N.Y. Jets, 1960
	3	Bill Groman, vs N.Y. Jets, 1961
	3	Billy Cannon, vs N.Y. Jets, 1961
	3	Charlie Hennigan, vs San Diego, 1961
	3	Charlie Hennigan, vs Buffalo, 1963
	3	Charles Frazier, vs Denver, 1966 (twice)
	3	Dave Casper, vs Pittsburgh, 1981
	3	Drew Hill, vs Washington, 1988
Season:	17	Bill Groman, 1961
Career:	51	Charlie Hennigan, 1960-66

Scoring

Most Points Game:	30	Billy Cannon, vs N.Y. Jets, 1961
Season:	115	George Blanda, 1960
	115	Tony Zendejas, 1989
Career:	596	George Blanda, 1960-66
Most TDs Game:	5	Billy Cannon, vs N.Y. Jets, 1961
Season:	19	Earl Campbell, 1979
Career:	73	Earl Campbell, 1978-84

INDIANAPOLIS COLTS

TEAM DIRECTORY: Pres./Tres.: Robert Irsay; VP/GM: Jim Irsay; VP/Gen. Counsel: Michael Chernoff; Dir. Player Personnel: Jack Bushofsky; Dir. Pub. Rel.: Craig Kelley; Head Coach: Ron Meyer. Home field: Hoosier Dome (60,127). Colors: Royal blue and white.

SCOUTING REPORT

OFFENSE: The Colts (8-8) are not prepared for life without Eric Dickerson. If the star running back doesn't have a change of heart

Colts shelled out $15 million for Illini QB Jeff George.

and follows through with retirement plans, Ron Meyer's club could be doomed. Dickerson, who rushed for 1,311 yards in '89, had a career-low 4.17-yard average, but nobody can do the things he can when he's healthy.

What's left? An offense that ranked 23rd in the league with Dickerson didn't sign any Plan-B free-agent runners or blockers and is left with Albert Bentley, Ivy Joe Hunter and rookie second-round fullback Anthony Johnson. Bentley is a versatile player who thrived when opponents paid attention to Dickerson.

There was no star at quarterback until the Colts made Jeff George the No. 1 pick and a millionaire in the draft deal that cost them Andre Rison and Chris Hinton. Chris Chandler had shown flashes, but a knee injury ended his '89 season in the third game. Jack Trudeau is an adequate backup who was booed often but played well enough to be named team MVP. Can the rich rookie from Illinois take over right away and be all they hope he'll be?

The Colts still have Bill Brooks, a consistent veteran who has averaged 58 receptions over the last four years, and they can count on veteran All-Pro center Ray Donaldson.

Dickerson complained in '89 about his linemen, who slipped a notch, and now with Hinton gone—and maybe Dickerson as well—what happens to a team that rushed for only 11 TDs in '89?

DEFENSE: The Colts finally generated a pass rush in 1989 and also might have uncovered a rising star in linebacker Jeff Herrod. Indy notched 46 sacks, up from 30 in '88. End Jon Hand had 10 and Ezra Johnson 8½, but Johnson was lost to Houston in Plan B.

Herrod was surrounded by household names but led the team in tackles. If Fredd Young returns to his old form, the foursome that includes Duane Bickett and Chip Banks, back from a 1½-year layoff, is formidable.

The Colts made 21 interceptions last year, thanks to seven by reserve Keith Taylor. Still, they have trouble covering swift receivers man-to-man when the rest of the defense takes risks. Once again, opposing passers completed nearly 60 percent of their passes.

KICKING GAME: Dean Biasucci is a reliable kicker who has made 51 of his last 55 attempts from inside 45 yards. Last year, he was 21-for-27 overall. Rohn Stark ranked second among AFC punters with a 42.9-yard average but his net was just 32.9

The Colts are solid on returns with speedy Clarence Verdin, who led the AFC on punts (12.9) and averaged 19.5 on kickoffs.

COLTS VETERAN ROSTER

HEAD COACH—Ron Meyer. Assistant Coaches—Leon Burtnett, George Catavolos, Milt Jackson, Larry Kennan, Bill Muir, Dante Scarnecchia, Brad Seely, Rick Venturi, Tom Zupancic.

No.	Name	Pos.	Ht.	Wt.	NFL Exp.	College
97	Alston, O'Brien	LB	6-6	241	3	Maryland
79	Armstrong, Harvey	NT	6-3	282	7	Southern Methodist
62	Baldinger, Brian	G	6-4	272	8	Duke
31	Ball, Michael	CB-S	6-0	217	3	Southern University
51	Banks, Chip	LB	6-4	235	8	Southern California
36	Baylor, John	CB-S	6-0	203	2	Southern Mississippi
81	Beach, Pat	TE	6-4	252	8	Washington State
95	Benson, Mitchell	NT	6-3	302	2	Texas Christian
20	Bentley, Albert	RB	5-11	214	6	Miami
4	Blasucci, Dean	K	6-0	189	6	Western Carolina
50	Bickett, Duane	LB	6-5	251	6	Southern California
87	Bouza, Matt	WR	6-3	211	9	California
80	Brooks, Bill	WR	6-0	185	5	Boston University
71	Call, Kevin	T	6-7	308	7	Colorado State
17	Chandler, Chris	QB	6-4	218	3	Washington
91	Clancy, Sam	DE	6-7	264	7	Pittsburgh
38	Daniel, Eugene	CB	5-11	188	7	Louisiana State
29	Dickerson, Eric	RB	6-3	224	8	Southern Methodist
69	Dixon, Randy	G	6-3	302	4	Pittsburgh
53	Donaldson, Ray	C	6-3	292	11	Georgia
67	Eisenbooth, Stan	T-G	6-5	290	3	Towson State
37	Goode, Chris	CB	6-0	195	4	Alabama
78	Hand, Jon	DE	6-7	301	5	Alabama
54	Herrod, Jeff	LB	6-0	246	3	Mississippi
45	Hunter, Ivy Joe	RB	6-0	237	2	Kentucky
63	Knight, Steve	T	6-4	326	2	Tennessee
59	Larson, Kurt	LB	6-4	236	2	Michigan State
96	McDonald, Quintus	LB	6-3	240	2	Penn State
73	Moss, Zefross	T	6-6	315	2	Alabama State
39	Prior, Mike	CB-S	6-10	210	5	Illinois State
49	Pruitt, James	WR	6-3	201	5	Cal-Fullerton
14	Ramsey, Tom	QB	6-1	185	6	UCLA
3	Stark, Rohn	P	6-3	203	9	Florida State
10	Strock, Don	QB	6-5	225	17	Virginia Tech
27	Taylor, Keith	CB-S	5-11	206	3	Illinois
99	Thompson, Donnell	DE	6-4	280	10	North Carolina
10	Trudeau, Jack	QB	6-3	219	5	Illinois
83	Verdin, Clarence	WR	5-8	170	5	SW Louisiana
56	Young, Fredd	LB	6-1	235	7	New Mexico State

TOP DRAFT CHOICES

Rd.	Name	Sel. No.	Pos.	Ht.	Wt.	College
1	George, Jeff	1	QB	6-4	221	Illinois
2	Johnson, Anthony	36	RB	6-0	216	Notre Dame
4	Simmons, Stacey	83	WR	5-9	183	Florida
4	Schultz, Bill	94	G	6-4	280	USC
4	Grant, Alan	103	DB	6-0	185	Stanford

THE ROOKIES: Most personnel directors doubt George is worth the $15 million the Colts gave him. He must play every day the way he did when he wowed scouts in a postseason workout. Notre Dame's Johnson is a good blocker and receiver. Notre Dame coach Lou Holtz said Johnson was one of the nation's most underrated players.

OUTLOOK: Word was that Meyer was feeling some heat. But without Dickerson, Vince Lombardi would have trouble winning with what's left. To slip into the expanded playoffs, the Colts must avoid a slow start, something that killed them the past two years.

COLT PROFILES

ERIC DICKERSON 29 6-3 224   Running Back

Having the league's best running back is not without its problems... Dickerson continues to taint greatness with gripes, claiming displeasure with his offensive line, seeking a trade and threatening retirement... All this after a 1,311-yard season... Only running back in NFL history to record seven consecutive 1,000-yard seasons... His production was down from 1,659 yards in '88... Was third behind Christian Okoye and Barry Sanders in NFL in '89... Selected to Pro Bowl as a reserve... Surpassed 10,000 yards in 91 games. Quickest previously was Jim Brown in 98 contests... Acquired from Rams in 1987 trade... Holds NFL single-season rushing record of 2,105 yards... Played at SMU and was second pick, by Rams, in '83 draft... 1989 salary: $1.31 million. 1990 salary: $1.45 million... Born Sept. 2, 1960, in Sealy, Tex.

RAY DONALDSON 32 6-3 292   Center

Upped his starting streak to 193 non-strike games... Made fourth straight Pro Bowl, third straight as a starter... Was a standout long before Dwight Stephenson's career-ending injury and Eric Dickerson's arrival, but didn't get noticed... Voted team captain by teammates... Second-round draft pick out of Georgia in 1980... Became starter in '81... Planned to play

INDIANAPOLIS COLTS 227

linebacker for Bulldogs, but switched to offense as a sophomore
... 1989 salary: $500,000 ... Born May 18, 1958, in Rome, Ga.

CHIP BANKS 30 6-4 235 Linebacker

Colts took gamble by trading for troubled linebacker... Acquired from San Diego on Oct. 17 and started final 10 games of season at left outside linebacker... Finished with 42 tackles and a sack after ending 1½-year layoff due to drug problems... Traded from Cleveland to San Diego in '87 and was second among Chargers with 71 tackles... When his life is in order, he's an All-Pro... Made the Pro Bowl four times (1982-83, '85 and '87), with three starts... NFL Defensive Rookie of Year with San Diego in '82... First-round draft choice out of Southern California... Born Sept. 18, 1959, in Fort Lawton, Okla.

JACK TRUDEAU 27 6-3 219 Quarterback

Eric Dickerson got all the publicity, but Trudeau was named team MVP... Started 12 games and played through several injuries... Threw for 2,317 yards, 15 TDs and 13 interceptions... Only Steve Grogan of New England had a lower quarterback rating in AFC than Trudeau's 71.3... Got starting job when Chris Chandler suffered season-ending knee injury in Week 3... Rallied Colts to victory over Atlanta after entering game in third quarter... Earned starting spot in '88 but suffered season-ending knee injury in Week 3... Came to '89 camp and posted career bests in 40 (4.9) and squats (465)... Was 0-11 as rookie starter in '86... Second-round draft choice out of Illinois ... Born Sept. 9, 1962, in Forest Lake, Minn.

CHRIS CHANDLER 24 6-4 218 Quarterback

Hoping to duplicate Trudeau's successful return from knee surgery... Tore anterior cruciate ligament on Sept. 24, marking fourth straight season Colts lost starting QB in first four games of season... Season stats: 39-80 for 537 yards, two TDs and three interceptions... Was 20-for-33 for 266 yards, one TD and one interception against Rams... Led Colts to all nine of their victories in '88, but was knocked out of four games that year with injuries... Third-round draft choice out of Washington in '88... Threw for 4,161 yards in college... Has degree in economics... Born Oct. 12, 1965, in Everett, Wash.

DUANE BICKETT 27 6-5 251   Linebacker

Steady performer at right outside linebacker... Failed to lead team in tackles for first time in three years... Ranked fourth on club with 100 stops, 54 behind leader Jeff Herrod... Outstanding year rushing quarterbacks, turning in eight sacks and 11 pressures... Made Pro Bowl in '87, when he led club with 113 tackles and eight sacks... Named NFL Defensive Rookie of Year in '85... First-round pick out of Southern Cal in '85... Scored seven TDs as tight end and averaged 12 tackles per game as high-school senior... 1989 salary: $750,000... Born Dec. 1, 1962, in Los Angeles.

BILL BROOKS 26 6-0 185   Wide Receiver

Underrated speedster nearly matched his career-best rookie season... Led Colts with 63 receptions for 919 yards and four TDs... Nearly became only player in Colts' history to post two 1,000-yard receiving seasons... Caught 65 passes for 1,131 yards in '86... Had three 100-yard games in '89, including two in consecutive weeks... Did not make a reception on Sept. 24 vs. Atlanta, only the second game he has been shut out... Fourth-round pick out of Boston University in '86... 1989 salary: $132,000... Born April 6, 1964, in Boston.

JEFF HERROD 24 6-0 246   Linebacker

Surrounded by former Pro Bowlers, this former ninth-round pick flourished... Led Colts with 154 tackles, 104 unassisted... Had two sacks... Was in double digits in tackles eight times, including five consecutive games... Played left inside linebacker... Was outstanding against Patriots on Dec. 3, making 19 tackles... Made just 22 tackles as a rookie but stood out on kickoff coverage... Ninth-round pick out of Mississippi in '88... Made 23 tackles vs. Arkansas State as senior... Had 150 for the season... Born July 29, 1966, in Birmingham, Ala.

FREDD YOUNG 28 6-1 235   Linebacker

Former Pro Bowl selection has yet to make impact expected when Colts traded two No. 1 picks to Seattle in '88 to get him... Still productive, though, finishing second on club in '89 with 122 tackles, including 89 solo... Also had two interceptions and forced three fumbles... Had four 12-tackle games... Named to Pro Bowl in each of his first four NFL seasons, all with Seattle... Third-round draft choice out of New Mexico State in 1984... 1989 salary: $725,000... Born Nov. 14, 1961, in Dallas.

ALBERT BENTLEY 30 5-11 214   Running Back

Dependable veteran whose accomplishments are smothered by attention given to Eric Dickerson... Plays his role without complaint, contributing in all phases of game... Rushed for 299 yards and caught 52 passes in '89, both second-best on club.... Returned 17 kickoffs for a 19.3 average... Colts use him as a surprise when teams key on Dickerson... Led AFC with 1,578 all-purpose yards in 1987... Played two years in USFL, then went to Colts in '84 supplemental draft... Three-year letterman at Miami... 1989 salary: $260,000... Born Aug. 15, 1960, in Immokalee, Fla.

COACH RON MEYER: Struggle of '89 curtailed his turnaround in Indy... Is 29-22 in two-plus years with Colts... Endured dissension problems that, this time, thanks to Eric Dickerson, weren't his doing... Motivated Colts to strong finish in '89... Has been a success at all coaching stops—UNLV, SMU and New England... Patriots fired him in '84 even though team was 5-3... Players weren't comfortable with his discipline... Brought New England from 2-14 to the playoffs... Has coached all levels and even worked as a sports agent... Was a walk-on defensive back at Purdue... Born Feb. 17, 1941, in Westerville, Ohio... Regular-season career mark in pros is 47-36.

LONGEST PASS PLAY

BERT JONES TO ROGER CARR

The Bert Jones-to-Roger Carr connection was a successful one in November 1975. On Nov. 16, just seven days after tying the Colts' club record with an 89-yard bomb at Buffalo, Jones and Carr topped that with a 90-yard touchdown in a 52-19 victory over the New York Jets at Baltimore.

At the time, long-range passing typified the Colts, who won nine consecutive games to end the regular season. The victory over the Jets was No. 4 in that streak and would have been more of a rout had Jones not left the game in the third quarter with a rib injury. He was 16-of-22 for 277 yards and three touchdowns before exiting.

The bomb to Carr surpassed an 89-yard pass from John Unitas to John Mackey against the Rams in 1966.

INDIVIDUAL COLT RECORDS

Rushing

Most Yards Game:	198	Norm Bulaich, vs N.Y. Jets, 1971
Season:	1,659	Eric Dickerson, 1988
Career:	5,487	Lydell Mitchell, 1972-77

Passing

Most TD Passes Game:	5	Gary Cuozzo, vs Minnesota, 1965
	5	Gary Hogeboom, vs Buffalo, 1987
Season:	32	John Unitas, 1959
Career:	287	John Unitas, 1956-72

Receiving

Most TD Passes Game:
- 3 Jim Mutscheller, vs Green Bay, 1957
- 3 Raymond Berry, vs Dallas, 1960
- 3 Raymond Berry, vs Green Bay, 1960
- 3 Jimmy Orr, vs Washington, 1962
- 3 Jimmy Orr, vs Los Angeles, 1964
- 3 Roger Carr, vs Cincinnati, 1976

Season: 14 Raymond Berry, 1959
Career: 68 Raymond Berry, 1955-67

Scoring

Most Points Game:
- 24 Lenny Moore, vs Chicago, 1958
- 24 Lenny Moore, vs Los Angeles, 1960
- 24 Lenny Moore, vs Minnesota, 1961
- 24 Lydell Mitchell, vs Buffalo, 1975
- 24 Eric Dickerson, vs Denver, 1988

Season: 120 Lenny Moore, 1964
Career: 678 Lenny Moore, 1956-67

Most TDs Game:
- 4 Lenny Moore, vs Chicago, 1958
- 4 Lenny Moore, vs Los Angeles, 1960
- 4 Lenny Moore, vs Minnesota, 1961
- 4 Lydell Mitchell, vs Buffalo, 1975
- 4 Eric Dickerson, vs Denver, 1988

Season: 20 Lenny Moore, 1964
Career: 113 Lenny Moore, 1956-67

KANSAS CITY CHIEFS

TEAM DIRECTORY: Owner: Lamar Hunt; Pres./COO/GM: Carl Peterson; Exec. VP-Adm.: Tim Connolly; Player Personnel Dir.: Whitey Dovell; Dir. Pub. Rel.: Robert Moore; Head Coach: Marty Schottenheimer. Home field: Arrowhead Stadium (78,094). Colors: Red and gold.

SCOUTING REPORT

OFFENSE: Unless you're a fan of bruising, straight-ahead, ball-control football, the Chiefs' offense is not exciting. But with the quick-learning Christian Okoye, it is effective.

When Marty Schottenheimer took over the Chiefs (8-7-1) last year, he handed the ball to Okoye, who still is relatively new to the game but led the NFL with 1,480 yards. Running behind

Nobody had more rushing yards than Christian Okoye.

a huge offensive line, Okoye helped the Chiefs rank fourth in the league in rushing after ranking no higher than 19th from 1981-88.

Okoye also took attention off the Chiefs' muddled quarterback situation. Well-traveled veteran Steve DeBerg finished the season and was 6-4 as a starter. But Steve Pelluer was acquired at midseason and could be a factor this year. There's also Mike Elkins, whose rookie year was hampered by a back injury. The Chiefs threw for just 14 touchdowns last year.

The receiving corps is adequate. Stephone Paige led the way with 44 receptions but just two TDs.

DEFENSE: Kansas City defenders got awful antsy standing on the sidelines while Okoye's ball-control show was in action, and the result was a revved-up attack that flourished under Schottenheimer.

The Chiefs' defense ranked No. 2 in the NFL, behind Minnesota, and was led by the outstanding play of rookie Derrick Thomas, who showed signs of becoming the next Lawrence Taylor. Thomas started strong with 10 sacks in the first 10 games. He went without one in the final six weeks, but special attention paid to him opened things up for ends Neil Smith and Leonard Griffin. Nose tackle Bill Maas broke his left arm last year, but Plan-B free agent Dan Saleaumua played well in his place. The presence of both will make the KC defense even more versatile. And their first draft pick was linebacker Percy Snow.

Dan Marino was the only QB to pass for over 300 yards against the Chiefs in 1989. Kevin Ross and Albert Lewis are outstanding cornerbacks, but for the first time in several years, there is some question at safety. Long-time star Deron Cherry underwent knee surgery in December, prompting the Chiefs to sign Jeff Donaldson away from Houston.

KICKING GAME: This is a problem for the Chiefs. Nick Lowery made just 24-of-33 field-goal attempts, including 10-of-14 from 30-39 yards. General Manager Carl Peterson said he signed Bjorn Nittmo from the Giants in Plan B because of his deep kickoffs.

Punter Kelly Goodburn (40.1 avg.) is nothing special. Punt (7.5 avg.) and kickoff (17.6) returns need a boost.

THE ROOKIES: The Chiefs' already-tough defense got better with the addition of Snow, who was a dominant inside player at Michigan State. He made 164 tackles as a junior. Notre Dame's

CHIEFS VETERAN ROSTER

HEAD COACH—Marty Schottenheimer. Assistant Coaches—Bruce Arians, Russ Ball, Bill Cowher, Tony Dungy, Jim Erkenbeck, Howard Mudd, Joe Pendry, Tom Pratt, Dave Redding, Al Saunders, Kurt Schottenheimer, Darvin Wallis.

No.	Name	Pos.	Ht.	Wt.	NFL Exp.	College
76	Alt, John	T	6-7	300	7	Iowa
54	Ashley, Walker Lee	LB	6-0	231	7	Penn State
77	Baldinger, Rich	G-T	6-4	292	9	Wake Forest
99	Bell, Mike	DE	6-4	262	10	Colorado State
34	Burruss, Lloyd	S	6-0	205	10	Maryland
70	Cannon, Mark	C	6-3	258	7	Texas-Arlington
20	Cherry, Deron	S	5-11	203	10	Rutgers
62	Chilton, Gene	C-G	6-3	286	4	Texas
55	Cooper, Louis	LB	6-2	238	6	Western Carolina
25	Copeland, Danny	S-KR	6-2	210	2	Eastern Kentucky
17	DeBerg, Steve	QB	6-3	214	14	San Jose State
42	Donaldson, Jeff	S	6-0	190	7	Colorado
75	Eatman, Irv	T	6-7	298	5	UCLA
10	Elkins, Mike	QB	6-3	225	2	Wake Forest
22	Gamble, Kenny	RB-KR	5-10	204	2	Colgate
2	Goodburn, Kelly	P	6-2	201	4	Emporia State
49	Griffin, James	S	6-2	203	8	Middle Tenn. State
96	Griffin, Leonard	DE	6-4	272	5	Grambling
56	Hackett, Dino	LB	6-3	228	5	Appalachian State
26	Harmon, Kevin	RB	6-0	190	3	Iowa
73	Harris, Michael	C-G	6-4	306	2	Grambling
86	Harry, Emile	WR	5-11	178	4	Stanford
85	Hayes, Jonathan	TE	6-5	254	6	Iowa
44	Heard, Herman	RB	5-10	194	7	Southern Colorado
41	Hill, Willie	S	6-0	200	2	Bishop
7	Jaworski, Ron	QB	6-1	202	16	Youngstown State
91	Jones, Rod	TE	6-4	245	4	Washington
3	Karcher, Ken	QB	6-3	205	3	Tulane
29	Lewis, Albert	CB	6-2	196	8	Grambling
8	Lowery, Nick	K	6-4	189	11	Dartmouth
72	Lutz, David	G-T	6-6	303	8	Georgia Tech
63	Maas, Bill	NT-DE	6-5	277	7	Pittsburgh
89	Mandley, Pete	WR	5-10	195	7	Northern Arizona
57	Martin, Chris	LB	6-2	232	8	Auburn
92	McCabe, Jerry	LB	6-2	225	3	Holy Cross
50	McGovern, Rob	LB	6-2	223	2	Holy Cross
48	McNair, Todd	RB-KR	6-1	185	2	Temple
69	Meisner, Greg	DE-NT	6-3	271	10	Pittsburgh
68	Morris, Michael	C	6-5	275	3	NE Missouri State
64	Neville, Tom	G	6-5	300	3	Fresno State
9	Nittmo, Bjorn	K	5-11	179	2	Appalachian State
35	Okoye, Christian	RB	6-1	260	4	Azusa Pacific
83	Paige, Stephone	WR	6-2	185	8	Fresno State
24	Pearson, Jayice	CB	5-11	185	5	Washington
11	Pelleur, Steve	QB	6-4	212	7	Washington
45	Petry, Stan	CB	5-11	175	2	Texas Christian
27	Porter, Kevin	S	5-10	219	3	Auburn
87	Roberts, Alfredo	TE	6-3	246	3	Miami
31	Ross, Kevin	CB	5-9	182	7	Temple
97	Saleaumua, Dan	NT	6-0	289	4	Arizona State
21	Saxon, James	RB	5-11	215	3	San Jose State
90	Smith, Neil	DE	6-4	271	3	Nebraska
52	Snipes, Angelo	LB	6-0	228	4	West Georgia
58	Thomas, Derrick	LB	6-3	234	2	Alabama
47	Thomas, Johnny	CB-S	5-9	185	3	Baylor
81	Thomas, Robb	WR	5-11	171	2	Oregon State
94	Ward, David	LB	6-2	232	3	Southern Arkansas
19	Ware, Timmie	WR	5-10	175	4	Southern California
46	Washington, Charles	CB-S	6-1	206	2	Cameron
53	Webster, Mike	C	6-2	260	17	Wisconsin
65	Winters, Frank	C-G	6-3	280	4	Western Illinois
84	Worthen, Naz	WR	5-8	177	2	North Carolina State

TOP DRAFT CHOICES

Rd.	Name	Sel. No.	Pos.	Ht.	Wt.	College
1	Snow, Percy	13	LB	6-2	244	Michigan State
2	Grunhard, Tim	40	C	6-2	291	Notre Dame
4	Jones, Fred	96	WR	5-8	175	Grambling
5	Graham, Derrick	124	T	6-4	312	Appalachian State
5	Hackemack, Ken	127	T	6-8	300	Texas

offensive lineman Tim Grunhard is a powerful run-blocker who might be the Chiefs' next center.

OUTLOOK: The Chiefs won four of their last five in '89. They didn't make the playoffs but served notice they'll be a factor in the race for the Super Bowl for years to come. The defense is solid. Schottenheimer must find stability at the quarterback position before injuries or defenses catch up to Okoye.

CHIEF PROFILES

CHRISTIAN OKOYE 29 6-1 260   Running Back

An amazing story of someone picking up the game quickly... The native of Nigeria led the NFL with 1,480 rushing yards, a team record... Didn't play football until he attended Azusu Pacific on track scholarship... Led NFL with eight 100-yard games, including 170 vs. Dallas... Also had games of 95 and 98 yards... First Chief Pro Bowl running back since Joe Delaney in 1981... A bruising, straight-ahead runner who was Chiefs' workhorse with league-leading 370 carries... Scored 12 TDs... Missed all of preseason with neck injury and missed one game with thigh bruise... Had just 1,133 yards and six TDs in first two seasons... Missed seven games in '88 with various injuries... Holds African discus record and runs 4.46-second 40-yard dash... Second-round draft pick in '87... Born Aug. 16, 1961, in Enugu, Nigeria.

DERRICK THOMAS 23 6-3 234   Linebacker

An instant force in the NFL with 10 sacks, most by a Chief linebacker since '73, when stat was first kept... Named Associated Press Defensive Rookie of Year and named Pro Bowl starter... First Chief OLB to go to Pro Bowl since Bobby Bell in '73... Made 75 tackles and forced three fumbles... Started all 16 games... Made all 10 sacks in first 10 games... Fourth player selected in '89 draft... Recorded 52 sacks at Alabama... Runs 4.52-second 40-yard dash... Replaced Cornelius Bennett for Crimson Tide as junior... Father Robert was Air

236 THE COMPLETE HANDBOOK OF PRO FOOTBALL

Force pilot whose plane was shot down in Vietnam... 1989 salary: $300,000... Born Jan. 1, 1967, in Miami.

ALBERT LEWIS 29 6-2 198   Cornerback

Another excellent season rewarded with third straight Pro Bowl selection... Named All-Pro along with Rams' Jerry Gray... Had four interceptions, his most since '86... Forced three fumbles... Had sixth blocked punt of his career... Led team in passes defensed for third consecutive year with 17... Had just two interceptions in 1987-88 after making 12 the previous two years... Made six interceptions in final three games of '85 to give him AFC-leading eight... Was nickel back as rookie after being drafted in third-round of '83 draft... Intercepted 11 passes in final two seasons at Grambling... Has degree in political science... 1989 salary: $600,000... Born Oct. 6, 1960, in Mansfield, La.

KEVIN ROSS 28 5-9 182   Cornerback

Approaching the level of backfield mates Albert Lewis and Deron Cherry... Named to first Pro Bowl in '89 after tying Lewis with team-leading four interceptions and 13 deflections... Led Chiefs with 57 solo tackles... Missed one game and parts of three others with sore ankle... Has been a starter since his first NFL game in '84, when he was a seventh-round pick out of Temple... Made six interceptions as a rookie and has 21 in six seasons... Had 13 interceptions and 249 tackles in college... Nicknamed "Rock"... Born Jan. 16, 1962, in Camden, N.J.

STEVE DeBERG 36 6-3 214   Quarterback

Veteran was big part of Chiefs' strong 1989 finish... Overcame rough start, which saw him benched in October and again in November... Was 6-4 as starter, and his 60.5 completion percentage was third-highest in NFL... Ability to play-fake to Christian Okoye kept defenses off-guard... Threw for 2,529 yards and 11 TDs but tossed 16 interceptions... In 13 seasons, has thrown 143 TDs and 171 interceptions... Traded from Tampa Bay in 1987... Has been benched in career in favor of Joe Montana at San Francisco, John Elway at Denver and Vinny Testaverde at Tampa Bay. Now, Mike Elkins and Steve Pelluer lurk... Cowboys drafted him out of San Jose State in 10th round of 1977 draft. Was cut and signed by 49ers... Born Jan. 19, 1954, in Oakland.

DERON CHERRY 30 5-11 203 — Safety

One of game's best safeties finally missed out on Pro Bowl after six consecutive trips... Was named an alternate... Had two interceptions, his lowest total since '82 and a dropoff from seven in '88... Led Chiefs with 87 tackles... Has 14 career fumble recoveries, one shy of team record... Made team-record six fumble recoveries in '88... Originally signed with Chiefs as free-agent punter in '81 but switched to secondary in training camp... Was cut and re-signed during the season... Played nickel back in '82 and became starter in '83... Played safety and punted at Rutgers... Has degree in biology... 1989 salary: $775,000... Born Sept. 12, 1959, in Palmyra, N.J.

NEIL SMITH 24 6-4 271 — Defensive End

Made up for rocky rookie season... Started 15 games and recorded 7½ sacks... Forced four fumbles and recovered two... Scored first NFL TD on three-yard fumble recovery... Finished strong with 29 tackles, four sacks, four forced fumbles and two recoveries in final six games... Second player picked in '88 draft but was slowed by injuries... Started seven games as rookie... Had 14½ sacks at Nebraska, 7½ as a senior... Entered school as 208-pound freshman who ran 40 in 5.09 seconds and left at 260 pounds with 4.59 speed... Increased vertical leap five inches in that time... Has wing span of 7 feet, 1½ inches ... 1990 salary: $425,000... Born April 10, 1966, in New Orleans.

MIKE WEBSTER 38 6-2 260   Center

Fooled everybody by dropping retirement plans to anchor Chiefs' line... Nine-time Pro Bowl pick who started all 16 games... Joined Chiefs as assistant line coach but decided to return shortly before training camp... Played 15 seasons with Pittsburgh, winning four Super Bowls... Has played in 236 games and has 200 starts... Has been to more Pro Bowls than any offensive lineman in history... Was Steelers' offensive captain for his final nine years there... Fifth-round draft pick out of Wisconsin in 1974... Born March 18, 1952, in Tomahawk, Wis.

STEVE PELLUER 28 6-4 212   Quarterback

Expects to push Steve DeBerg for starting spot... Chiefs traded draft choices to Cowboys on Oct. 17 for Pelluer, who had missed training camp in contract dispute... With Troy Aikman and Steve Walsh in Dallas, Pelluer was expendable... Started five games for Chiefs, throwing for 301 yards and a TD... Hurt knee on Nov. 19 and missed remainder of season... Was inconsistent as starter in Dallas in '88, when he threw for 17 TDs and 19 interceptions... Fifth-round pick out of Washington in 1984... School's No. 2 all-time passer with 4,603 yards... Born July 29, 1962, in Yakima, Wash.

STEPHONE PAIGE 28 6-2 185   Wide Receiver

Had little chance to shine in run-oriented offense, but led club with 44 receptions for 759 yards... Totals were his lowest since '84 and his two TDs were lowest ever... Missed two games because of late signing... Those were first games he has missed in seven-year career... Had three 100-yard games... Rams' Flipper Anderson broke his 309-yard record-breaker set in '85... Signed in 1983 as undrafted free agent out of Fresno State... College teammate of Henry Ellard... Played two years at Saddleback (Cal.) Junior College... Born Oct. 15, 1961, in Slidell, La.

COACH MARTY SCHOTTENHEIMER: Has put excitement back into Chiefs' football... Many scoffed when he set goal of winning Super Bowl in '89, but he nearly rallied Chiefs to playoffs... Was first of his five NFL seasons he didn't make playoffs... Has instilled bruising running game he loves so much... Came to Chiefs after '88 season because of dispute with Browns' owner Art Modell, who once predicted Schottenheimer would become "the next great coach in football."... Was only NFL coach to win division titles each year from 1985-88... Took over Chiefs for Frank Gansz, who was 8-22-1 in two seasons... First head coach in Chiefs' history with previous head-coaching experience... Career NFL coaching record is 44-26-1... Was AFC Coach of Year in '86... Originally joined Browns as defensive coordinator in '80... Served as an assistant with Giants and Lions in NFL and Portland in WFL... Was All-American linebacker at Pitt who played six years in NFL... Born Sept. 23, 1943, in Canonsburg, Pa.

LONGEST PASS PLAY

MIKE LIVINGSTON TO OTIS TAYLOR TO ROBERT HOLMES

The 1969 Chiefs gained glory on the ground while Len Dawson and Mike Livingston shared the quarterback duties. Livingston came up with the longest play of the year, but needed some extra help to do so. On Oct. 19, in a 17-10 victory over the Dolphins, Livingston hit receiver Otis Taylor, who ran 79 yards, then lateraled to fullback Robert Holmes. Holmes carried the ball the final 14 yards of the bizarre 93-yard scoring play.

It was one of the few times Livingston, a Chief from 1968-79, landed atop Hall of Famer Dawson in the club's record book. Livingston, a second-round draft choice out of Southern Methodist, ranks third among Kansas City passers behind Dawson and Bill Kenney. Dawson has the next five longest Chief passes—92 (twice), 90 and 89 yards. The latter was to Taylor in 1966.

INDIVIDUAL CHIEF RECORDS

Rushing

Most Yards Game:	193	Joe Delaney, vs Houston, 1981
Season:	1,480	Christian Okoye, 1989
Career:	4,451	Ed Podolak, 1969-77

Passing

Most TD Passes Game:	6	Len Dawson, vs Denver, 1964
Season:	30	Len Dawson, 1964
Career:	237	Len Dawson, 1962-75

Receiving

Most TD Passes Game:	4	Frank Jackson, vs San Diego, 1964
Season:	12	Chris Burford, 1962
Career:	57	Otis Taylor, 1965-75

Scoring

Most Points Game:	30	Abner Haynes, vs Oakland, 1961
Season:	129	Jan Stenerud, 1968
Career:	1,231	Jan Stenerud, 1967-79
Most TDs Game:	5	Abner Haynes, vs Oakland, 1961
Season:	19	Abner Haynes, 1962
Career:	60	Otis Taylor, 1965-75

LOS ANGELES RAIDERS   241

LOS ANGELES RAIDERS

TEAM DIRECTORY: President: Al Davis; Exec. Asst.: Al LoCasale; Sr. Exec.: John Herrera; Sr. Administrator: Morris Bradshaw; Business Mgr.: Dave Houghton; Publications: Mike Taylor; Head Coach: Art Shell. Home field: Los Angeles Memorial Coliseum (92,487). Colors: Silver and black.

SCOUTING REPORT

OFFENSE: First-year coach Mike Shanahan was the offensive whiz. Jay Schroeder was to be the answer at quarterback. After turmoil at the beginning of the 1989 season, the Raiders (8-8)

Foes shudder at thought of Bo Jackson in a full season.

went back to the drawing board with a new coach, Art Shell, and a new quarterback, Steve Beuerlein.

Beuerlein is expected to be the starter this year. The Raiders will try to survive the first half of the season so as to be in good shape when Bo Jackson arrives after the baseball season. Jackson continues to amaze all. The Kansas City Royals' slugger rushed for 950 yards and four touchdowns in half of a season in '89. The Raiders expect help from 1,000-yarder Greg Bell, ex-Ram, but Marcus Allen (293 yards) is a question mark.

Mervyn Fernandez stood out in '89 with 57 receptions for 1,069 yards and nine TDs. He teamed with Willie Gault, and the Raiders hope Tim Brown makes a successful return from knee surgery.

Big news came in Plan B with the arrival of Pro Bowl guard Max Montoya from Cincinnati. He's among the best in the game and should help a mediocre line.

DEFENSE: The Raiders survive with a nasty line and aggressive hitting. Howie Long returned to form after missing much of the 1988 and anchored a solid line. Greg Townsend benefited from Long's return, registering 10½ sacks. Now add Arizona defensive end Anthony Smith, the team's first draft pick.

The Raiders need more consistent play from their linebackers. Like the L.A. offense, the names are there but the production sometimes isn't. Veterans Jerry Robinson, Linden King and Thomas Benson played most of the time while Ricky Hunley and Emanuel King, two players once thought to be headed for stardom, are reserves. There's clearly an opening for rookie outside linebacker Aaron Wallace of Texas A&M

KICKING GAME: Brown's absence was felt on special teams. If he returns, the Raiders will have their game-breaker back. Also in the picture is speedster Ron Brown, signed in Plan B from the Rams. Brown, normally a receiver, will be tried as a defensive back.

Jeff Jaeger made just 23-of-34 field-goal attempts, including just 5-of-12 from 40-49 yards. Jeff Gossett ranked in the middle of the AFC with a 40.5-yard average.

THE ROOKIES: Arizona's Smith isn't as big as most ends and is coming off knee surgery. But his quickness and strength enticed the Raiders into drafting him. The speedy Wallace set Texas A&M's career record of 42 sacks. Defensive back Torin Dorn played running back his first three years at North Carolina.

RAIDERS VETERAN ROSTER

HEAD COACH—Art Shell. Assistant Coaches—Dave Adolph, Fred Biletnikoff, Sam Gruiesen, Kim Helton, Steve Ortmayer, Terry Robiskie, Joe Scanella, Jack Stanton, Bill Urbanik, Tom Walsh, Mike White, Doug Wilkerson.

No.	Name	Pos.	Ht.	Wt.	NFL Exp.	College
44	Adams, Stefon	WR	5-10	185	5	East Carolina
89	Alexander, Mike	WR	6-3	195	2	Penn State
32	Allen, Marcus	RB	6-2	205	9	Southern California
33	Anderson, Eddie	CB	6-1	200	5	Fort Valley State
	Bell, Greg	RB	5-11	210	7	Notre Dame
54	Benson, Tom	LB	6-2	240	7	Oklahoma
7	Beuerlein, Steve	QB	6-2	205	3	Notre Dame
24	Brown, Ron	CB	5-11	185	7	Arizona State
81	Brown, Tim	WR	6-0	195	2	Notre Dame
50	Burton, Ron	LB	6-2	245	4	North Carolina
99	Campbell, Joe	DE	6-3	240	3	New Mexico State
29	Carter, Russell	S	6-2	200	7	Southern Methodist
23	Crudup, Derrick	RB	6-2	210	2	Oklahoma
70	Davis, Scott	DE	6-7	275	3	Illinois
84	Dyal, Mike	TE	6-2	240	2	Texas A&I
86	Fernandez, Mervyn	WR	6-3	200	4	San Jose State
73	FitzPatrick, James	T	6-7	300	5	Southern California
83	Gault, Willie	WR	6-1	180	8	Tennessee
63	Gesek, John	G	6-5	280	4	Cal State-Sacramento
79	Golic, Bob	DT	6-2	275	11	Notre Dame
6	Gossett, Jeff	P	6-2	195	9	Eastern Illinois
85	Graddy, Sam	WR	5-10	175	3	Tennessee
60	Graves, Rory	T	6-6	290	3	Ohio State
45	Harden, Mike	S	6-1	195	11	Michigan
22	Haynes, Mike	CB	6-2	195	15	Arizona State
61	Hellestrae, Dale	G	6-5	285	4	Southern Methodist
88	Horton, Ethan	TE	6-4	240	4	North Carolina
96	Hunley, Ricky	LB	6-2	250	7	Arizona
34	Jackson, Bo	RB	6-1	225	4	Auburn
18	Jaeger, Jeff	K	5-11	195	3	Washington
53	Jordan, Darin	LB	6-1	235	2	Northeastern
87	Junkin, Trey	TE	6-2	240	8	Louisiana Tech
92	King, Emanuel	LB	6-4	250	6	Alabama
52	King, Linden	LB	6-4	250	13	Colorado State
97	Klostermann, Bruce	LB	6-4	230	4	South Dakota State
25	Land, Dan	CB	6-0	190	2	Albany State
75	Long, Howie	DE	6-5	265	10	Villanova
36	McDaniel, Terry	CB	5-10	175	2	Tennessee
26	McElroy, Vann	S	6-2	195	9	Baylor
65	Montoya, Max	G	6-5	275	12	UCLA
72	Mosebar, Don	C	6-6	280	8	Southern California
42	Mueller, Vance	RB	6-0	215	5	Occidental
43	Patterson, Elvis	CB	5-11	195	7	Kansas
74	Peat, Todd	T	6-2	310	3	Northern Illinois
71	Pickel, Bill	DT	6-5	260	8	Rutgers
31	Porter, Kerry	RB	6-1	215	3	Washington State
20	Price, Dennis	CB	6-1	175	3	UCLA
57	Robinson, Jerry	LB	6-2	225	12	UCLA
78	Rother, Tim	T	6-7	275	2	Nebraska
13	Schroeder, Jay	QB	6-4	215	7	UCLA
35	Smith, Steve	RB	6-1	235	4	Penn State
39	Strachan, Steve	RB	6-1	225	6	Boston College
27	Streeter, George	S	6-1	205	2	Notre Dame
93	Townsend, Greg	DE	6-3	250	8	Texas Christian
67	Turk, Dan	C	6-4	270	5	Wisconsin
48	Washington, Lionel	CB	6-0	185	7	Tulane
68	Wilkerson, Bruce	T	6-5	285	4	Tennessee
90	Wise, Mike	DE	6-7	270	4	California-Davis
76	Wisniewski, Steve	G	6-4	280	2	Penn State
66	Wright, Steve	T	6-6	280	8	Northern Illinois

TOP DRAFT CHOICES

Rd.	Name	Sel. No.	Pos.	Ht.	Wt.	College
1	Smith, Anthony	11	DE	6-5	257	Arizona
2	Wallace, Aaron	37	LB	6-3	236	Texas A&M
4	Dorn, Torin	95	DB	6-0	194	North Carolina
5	*Smagala, Stan	123	DB	5-9	189	Notre Dame
6	Wilson, Marcus	149	RB	6-1	205	Virginia
7	Lewis, Garry	173	DB	5-11	180	Alcorn State

*Traded to Dallas

OUTLOOK: The Raiders seem at ease with Shell in charge. They are hurt, however, by questions at quarterback, offensive line and on defense as well as by Bo's half-year absence. On talent alone, count L.A. in contention for a wild-card spot.

RAIDER PROFILES

BO JACKSON 27 6-1 225   **Running Back**

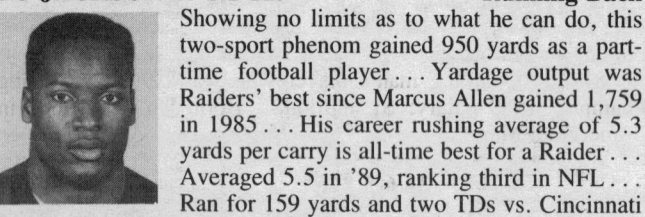

Showing no limits as to what he can do, this two-sport phenom gained 950 yards as a part-time football player... Yardage output was Raiders' best since Marcus Allen gained 1,759 in 1985... His career rushing average of 5.3 yards per carry is all-time best for a Raider... Averaged 5.5 in '89, ranking third in NFL... Ran for 159 yards and two TDs vs. Cincinnati on Nov. 5, including 92-yard TD... Started ahead of Allen after midseason arrival from Kansas City Royals... Was baseball All-Star Game hero last year... Gained 554 and 580 yards in first two pro seasons... Won 1985 Heisman Trophy and was drafted by Tampa Bay... After a season of baseball, Raiders picked him in seventh round of '86 draft, one of the all-time steals in sports... Rushed for 1,786 yards as a senior at Auburn... 1989 football salary: $1.356 million... Born Nov. 30, 1962, in Bessemer, Ala.

MARCUS ALLEN 30 6-2 205   **Running Back**

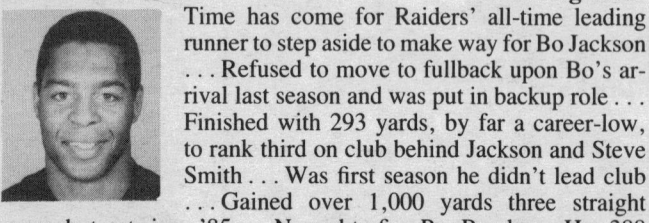

Time has come for Raiders' all-time leading runner to step aside to make way for Bo Jackson... Refused to move to fullback upon Bo's arrival last season and was put in backup role... Finished with 293 yards, by far a career-low, to rank third on club behind Jackson and Steve Smith... Was first season he didn't lead club... Gained over 1,000 yards three straight years, but not since '85... Named to five Pro Bowls... Has 388 receptions in eight seasons, fourth-best in Raider history... Has rushed for 7,275 yards... Club's all-time leader with 80 TDs... Once rushed for over 100 yards in NFL-record 11 consecutive games... MVP of Super Bowl XVIII with 191 yards rushing... Tenth player taken in '82 draft after winning Heisman Trophy at Southern Cal... 1989 salary: $1.1 million... Born March 22, 1960, in San Diego.

LOS ANGELES RAIDERS 245

HOWIE LONG 30 6-5 265   Defensive End

Came back strong from calf injury that sidelined him for final 10 games of '88... That injury ended a streak of five straight Pro Bowls... Finished with five sacks and 44 tackles in '89, 11th on the club... Recorded 54½ sacks in first six pro seasons but just 12 in the past three years... Has played 121 games with the Raiders. Club record is 217 by Gene Upshaw... Draws regular double-team blocking... NFL Defensive Lineman of Year in '84 and '86... Had career-best 13 sacks in '83, including five in one game... Second-round pick out of Villanova in '81... A working man's player who was collegiate boxing champ... 1989 salary: $1 million... Born Jan. 6, 1960, in Somerville, Mass.

MAX MONTOYA 34 6-5 275   Guard

The surprise of the NFL's 1989 Plan B movement... Pro Bowl guard was left unprotected by Bengals, who figured he'd stay put because of business interests in the city... Couldn't refuse offer to return to hometown, especially after Raiders offered $650,000 for '89... Has been picked for Pro Bowl three times... Better blocking for the pass than for the run... At one point in '88, he had allowed opponent to hit, not sack, quarterback just once in 237 passes... Was seventh-round draft choice out of UCLA in '79... Owns two restaurants in Cincinnati area, but will now have to run them from afar... Born May 12, 1956, in Montebello, Cal.

MERVYN FERNANDEZ 30 6-3 200   Wide Receiver

Swervin' Mervyn blew away other Raider receivers in '89 with 57 catches for 1,069 yards and nine TDs... Closest teammate was Willie Gault, with 28 receptions... His nine TDs were most by a Raider since Todd Christensen scored 12 in '83... Only the sixth Raider receiver to top 1,000 yards in a season... Led NFL in '88 with 26 yards per catch... Has a reception in 30 consecutive games... Drafted by Raiders out of San Jose State in 10th round of '83 draft, but chose to play in Canadian Football League... Was CFL MVP in '85 and league's top receiver of '80s... Signed with Raiders in '87... Has caught on fast, gaining 236 yards in '87 and 805 in '88... Born Dec. 29, 1959, in Merced, Cal.

STEVE BEUERLEIN 25 6-2 205   Quarterback

Barring blockbuster trade, he figures to be the Raiders' signal-caller of the future after beating out Jay Schroeder at midseason... Started seven games, going 4-3... Completed 50 percent of his passes for 1,677 yards, 13 TDs and nine interceptions... Rating of 78.4 would have made him fifth in AFC if he'd qualified ... Smart player who doesn't make a lot of mistakes... Tossed two TDs in five different games... Played in 10 games in '88 with eight starts... Sat out '87 rookie season because of injury... Fourth-round draft choice out of Notre Dame in '87... Started four years for the Irish and holds career records for completions (473), attempts (850) and yards (6,527)... Threw 119 consecutive passes without an interception in '86... Born March 7, 1965, in Hollywood, Cal.

GREG TOWNSEND 28 6-3 250   Defensive End

Raiders' "designated pass-rusher"... Has 71½ sacks in seven pro seasons, plus 4½ more in playoff games... Led club with 10½ sacks in '89 and 11½ in '88... Sixth on team with 67 tackles... Made his mark early with 10½ sacks as a rookie... Also scored a 66-yard TD on a fumble recovery that year... Fourth-round pick out of Texas Christian in '83... Played both end and linebacker in college... Born Nov. 3, 1961, in Los Angeles.

JAY SCHROEDER 29 6-4 215   Quarterback

Strong-armed former Redskin was to be leader of a high-flying offense, but was benched after throwing eight TD passes and 13 interceptions ... Completed 47 percent of his passes for 1,550 yards and a 60.3 rating, lowest in league at the time... A disappointment because Raiders traded Pro Bowl tackle Jim Lachey for him before '88 season... Was benched after five starts in '88 ... Threw for team-high 290 yards at Denver on Sept. 24 ... Threw for over 300 yards twice in '88 ... Made Pro Bowl in '86 after passing for 4,109 yards and two TDs ... Started one game at UCLA, then switched to baseball ... Didn't make it in Toronto Blue Jays' system, and Skins drafted him in third round of '84 draft ... 1989 salary: $1 million ... Born June 28, 1961, in Milwaukee.

TIM BROWN 24 6-0 195   Wide Receiver

Knee injury in opener wiped out Brown's second season ... Recorded just one catch for eight yards before going down ... Big things are expected of '87 Heisman Trophy winner, especially after exciting rookie season in which he led the NFL in kick returns with 1,098 yards and a 26.8 average ... He, Mervyn Fernandez and Willie Gault provide tremendous deep threats ... Had 43 receptions for 725 yards as rookie ... Broke Gale Sayers' NFL record for most total yardage by rookie, 2,316 yards ... Third Raider rookie selected to Pro Bowl. Others were Marcus Allen and Ray Guy ... Holds Notre Dame records for receiving yards (2,493) and all-purpose yards (5,024) ... Lettered one year as sprinter on Irish track team ... Born July 22, 1966, in Dallas.

WILLIE GAULT 29 6-0 180   Wide Receiver

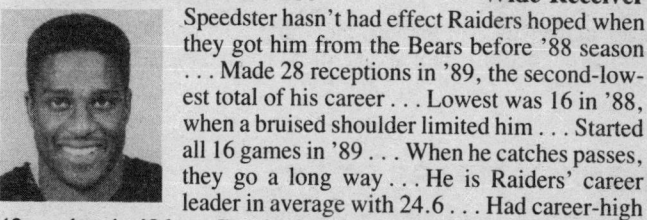

Speedster hasn't had effect Raiders hoped when they got him from the Bears before '88 season ... Made 28 receptions in '89, the second-lowest total of his career ... Lowest was 16 in '88, when a bruised shoulder limited him ... Started all 16 games in '89 ... When he catches passes, they go a long way ... He is Raiders' career leader in average with 24.6 ... Had career-high 42 catches in '86 ... Caught four passes for 129 yards in Super Bowl XX ... Was one of top hurdlers in nation and went to '88 Olympics as part of U.S. bobsled team ... Bears made him 18th pick in '83 draft ... Was football and track star at Tennessee ... Won '83 NCAA indoor title in 60-yard dash and high hurdles ... Ran second leg of world-record setting 400-meter team ... 1989 salary: $750,000 ... Born Sept. 5, 1960, in Griffin, Ga.

GREG BELL 28 5-11 210　　　　　　　　　　　Halfback

Traded by Rams in June after rushing for 1,137 yards on 272 carries (fourth in the NFC, ninth in the NFL)... Ran for 15 touchdowns... Caught 19 passes for 85 yards... Helped the Rams make the playoffs by rushing for 210 yards on 26 carries in Week 16 in a victory over the Patriots... Earned NFC Offensive Player of the Week honors for his effort... Had a career-high 221 yards against the Packers (28 carries)... Totaled 231 yards rushing in the playoffs... Came to Rams from the Bills as part of the Eric Dickerson deal on Oct. 31, 1987... World-class long-jumper at Notre Dame... Born Aug. 1, 1962, in Columbus, Ohio... Earned $500,000 last year.

COACH ART SHELL:

A player's coach from the start, Shell eased tensions at the Raiders' camp and turned the team into a winner... Took over for fired Mike Shanahan when club was 1-3 and went 7-5... Change was immediate, as players praised the Hall of Famer for letting them sit on their helmets at practice, something prohibited by Shanahan... Players seemed to have more fun under Shell, who players considered one of their own... Was a Raider assistant since 1983, when he retired after 15 standout seasons as a tackle with the team... Eight-time Pro Bowl selection who played in 207 games, including 23 playoff contests... Third-round draft choice out of Maryland State in 1968... Born Nov. 26, 1946, in Charleston, S.C.

LONGEST PASS PLAY

JIM PLUNKETT TO CLIFF BRANCH

Considering the Raiders' history of passing, it should come as no surprise that their longest pass play was as long as one can get. On Oct. 2, 1983, Jim Plunkett connected with Cliff Branch for a 99-yard touchdown in the Raiders' 37-35 loss to the Redskins, the team they would whip in the Super Bowl later that season.

In the loss at Washington, Plunkett threw for 372 yards, fourth-best in a Raider history that includes such quarterbacks as Daryle Lamonica, Ken Stabler, George Blanda and Tom Flores.

Blanda has the next-longest pass, a 94-yard touchdown strike to Warren Wells in 1968. Flores hit Dobie Craig for 93 yards in '63 and Marc Wilson hit Marcus Allen for 92 yards, but no touchdown, in '84.

INDIVIDUAL RAIDER RECORDS

Rushing

Most Yards Game:	221	Bo Jackson, vs Seattle, 1987
Season:	1,759	Marcus Allen, 1985
Career:	7,275	Marcus Allen, 1982-89

Passing

Most TD Passes Game:	6	Tom Flores, vs Houston, 1963
	6	Daryle Lamonica, vs Buffalo, 1969
Season:	34	Daryle Lamonica, 1969
Career:	150	Ken Stabler, 1970-79

Receiving

Most TD Passes Game:	4	Art Powell, vs Houston, 1963
Season:	16	Art Powell, 1963
Career:	76	Fred Biletnikoff, 1965-78

Scoring

Most Points Game:	24	Art Powell, vs Houston, 1963
	24	Marcus Allen, vs San Diego, 1984
Season:	117	George Blanda, 1968
Career:	863	George Blanda, 1967-75
Most TDs Game:	4	Art Powell, vs Houston, 1963
	4	Marcus Allen, vs San Diego, 1984
Season:	18	Marcus Allen, 1984
Career:	80	Marcus Allen, 1982-89

MIAMI DOLPHINS

TEAM DIRECTORY: Pres.: Timothy J. Robbie; Dir. Player Personnel: Charley Winner; Dir. Pro Personnel: Monte Clark; Dir. Media Relations: Harvey Greene; Head Coach: Don Shula. Home field: Joe Robbie Stadium (73,000). Colors: Aqua and orange.

SCOUTING REPORT

OFFENSE: Dan Marino's spectacular arm continues to get lost in Dolphin disarray. For years now, the Miami front office has talked about the need to have a running game to take pressure off Marino. The Dolphins (8-8) drafted Sammie Smith last year with that in mind, but the speedster out of Florida State found no holes, and the Dolphin rushing game ranked 27th. As Smith nursed injuries all season, the club managed just 1,330 yards on the ground.

Marino, meanwhile, faced his usual crowded defensive backfields while he tried to carry the team himself. Apparently, he's had enough. Tired of losing, the future Hall of Famer has asked for a trade. To make things worse, the line became thinner. One starter—Ronnie Lee—and the top three backups went elsewhere in Plan B. On the positive side, guard Harry Galbreath is quietly gaining respect around the league as a possible Pro Bowl selection.

There is hope at running back. Smith showed flashes of stardom, and Troy Stradford will provide versatility if he can rebound from a serious knee injury.

For all practical purposes, the Marks brothers have been cut in half. Mark Clayton is still as good as ever, but Mark Duper had another off year in '89. Duper, once a source of instant offense, has just one TD in each of the last two years. Jim Jensen is Marino's most reliable target. Tight end Farrell Edmunds failed to develop his immense talent further. The second-year player regressed, but somehow was selected to the Pro Bowl.

DEFENSE: Teams which like to run the ball like to play the Dolphins, whose rushing defense ranked 25th in the NFL. The Miami defense aged quickly in '89 because of the acquisition of linebackers Barry Krauss and E.J. Junior. Joining Hugh Green in calling themselves "The Graybeards," the crew was inspirational but couldn't prevent a late-season slide. The hard-nosed Krauss was the standout in the group, leading the club in tackles.

John Offerdahl is the only All-Pro on the Dolphin defense. End

Unhappy Dan Marino just missed fifth 4,000-yard season.

Jeff Cross (10 sacks) was a pleasant surprise last year. The young, hard-hitting safety tandem of Louis Oliver and Jarvis Williams will become the heart of the defense for years to come.

In a step toward solving the cornerback problems, Don Shula dealt for pass-swatting 49er cornerback Tim McKyer during the draft. William Judson, a starter at corner since '83, had signed with Detroit, leaving inconsistent Paul Lankford at one spot and untested Rodney Thomas at the other. If end John Bosa can com-

DOLPHINS VETERAN ROSTER

HEAD COACH—Don Shula. Assistant Coaches—George Hill, Tony Nathan, Tom Olivadotti, Mel Phillips, John Sandusky, Larry Seiple, Dan Sekanovich, Gary Stevens, Carl Taseff, Junior Wade, Mike Westoff.

No.	Name	Pos.	Ht.	Wt.	NFL Exp.	College
86	Banks, Fred	WR	5-10	180	5	Liberty
97	Bosa, John	DE	6-4	270	4	Boston College
82	Brown, Andre	WR	6-3	210	2	Miami
37	Brown, J.B.	CB	6-0	192	2	Maryland
59	Brudzinski, Bob	LB	6-4	235	14	Ohio State
83	Clayton, Mark	WR	5-9	184	8	Louisville
91	Cross, Jeff	DE	6-4	270	3	Missouri
65	Dellenbach, Jeff	T-C	6-6	282	6	Wisconsin
74	Dennis, Mark	T	6-6	290	4	Illinois
85	Duper, Mark	WR	5-9	190	9	NW Louisiana
80	Edmunds, Ferrell	TE	6-6	252	3	Maryland
	Elder, Donnie	CB	5-9	175	5	Memphis State
61	Foster, Roy	G	6-4	277	9	Southern California
62	Galbreath, Harry	G-C	6-1	275	3	Tennessee
79	Glesler, Jon	T	6-5	275	11	Michigan
	Glenn, Kerry	CB	5-9	175	4	Minnesota
99	Graf, Rick	LB	6-5	249	4	Wisconsin
55	Green, Hugh	LB	6-2	228	10	Pittsburgh
92	Griggs, David	LB	6-3	239	2	Virginia
84	Hardy, Bruce	TE	6-4	236	11	Arizona State
	Harvey, Stacy	LB	6-4	245	2	Arizona State
	Higgs, Mark	RB	5-7	188	3	Kentucky
29	Hobley, Liffort	S	6-0	202	5	Louisiana State
11	Jensen, Jim	WR-RB	6-4	224	10	Boston University
54	Junior, E.J.	LB	6-3	242	10	Alabama
88	Kinchen, Brian	TE	6-2	232	3	Louisiana State
58	Krauss, Barry	LB	6-3	260	12	Alabama
90	Kumerow, Eric	DE	6-7	268	3	Ohio State
44	Lankford, Paul	CB	6-1	190	9	Penn State
20	Logan, Marc	RB	5-11	220	4	Kentucky
13	Marino, Dan	QB	6-4	224	8	Pittsburgh
28	McNeal, Don	CB	6-0	195	10	Alabama
	Odorn, Cliff	LB	6-2	251	10	Texas-Arlington
56	Offerdahl, John	LB	6-3	240	5	Western Michigan
25	Oliver, Louis	S	6-2	226	2	Florida
	Paige, Tony	RB	5-10	235	7	Virginia Tech
	Reichenbach, Mike	LB	6-2	235	7	East Stroudsburg
4	Roby, Reggie	P	6-2	246	8	Iowa
81	Schwedes, Scott	WR-KR	6-0	182	4	Syracuse
9	Secules, Scott	QB	6-3	219	3	Virginia
33	Smith, Sammie	RB	6-2	226	2	Florida State
70	Sochia, Brian	NT	6-3	278	8	NW Oklahoma
18	Stoudt, Cliff	QB	6-4	218	12	Youngstown State
10	Stoyanovich, Pete	K	5-10	180	2	Indiana
23	Stradford, Troy	RB	5-9	192	4	Boston College
24	Thomas, Rodney	CB	5-10	190	3	Brigham Young
95	Turner, T.J.	DE	6-4	280	5	Houston
63	Uhlenhake, Jeff	C	6-3	282	2	Ohio State
26	Williams, Jarvis	S	5-11	198	3	Florida
	Wilson, Karl	DE	6-4	275	4	Louisiana State

TOP DRAFT CHOICES

Rd.	Name	Sel. No.	Pos.	Ht.	Wt.	College
1	Webb, Richmond	9	T	6-6	291	Texas A&M
2	Sims, Keith	39	G	6-2	310	Iowa State
3	Ogelsby, Alfred	66	DT	6-3	270	Houston
4	Mitchell, Scott	93	QB	6-6	231	Utah
5	Holt, Leroy	137	RB	5-10	236	USC

MIAMI DOLPHINS 253

plete his comeback from major knee surgery, the Dolphins finally can boast a consistent pass rush. End Eric Kumerow, a No. 1 pick two years ago, has yet to make an impact.

KICKING GAME: Punting is never a concern in Miami with Reggie Roby (42.4-yard average) on board. Shula gambled last year, cutting veteran Fuad Reveiz in favor of rookie Pete Stoyanovich, and the spunky former Hoosier came through with several clutch efforts and a 59-yard FG.

Miami found a gem in Plan-B free agent Marc Logan, who led the league in kickoff returns until a knee injury sidelined him late in the year. Using excellent decisions to make up for lack of blazing speed, Logan averaged 25.5, third-best in the NFL. Scott Schwedes, a straight-ahead runner, averaged 11.7 yards per punt return but was hurt for much of the season.

THE ROOKIES: With Marino aching and the running game going nowhere, the Dolphins drafted 600 pounds of bulk to add to the offensive line. First-round pick Richmond Webb of Texas A&M is sure to contribute soon, probably at left tackle. Second pick Keith Sims, an Iowa State guard, can be a solid pro if he controls his weight. Fourth-round pick QB Scott Mitchell is a lefty who will study under Marino.

OUTLOOK: The key to the Dolphins' success is Smith and his blockers. If he can stay healthy, he has the talent to be All-Pro and finally let Marino play against defenses not geared to play pass defense on every down. If given time, Marino is good enough to win with a mediocre defense.

DOLPHIN PROFILES

DAN MARINO 28 6-4 224   Quarterback

Survived injury-plagued season and still managed to put up big numbers... Led AFC in passing yardage (3,997) and was third with 24 TD passes, but tossed 22 interceptions. His plus-2 touchdown-to-interception differential and his 76.9 QB rating were career lows... Missed out on Pro Bowl for second straight year, the only two years of his career he wasn't selected... Played with elbow, rib and shoulder injuries... Expressed dissatisfaction with Dolphins during offseason when he asked team to explore trade possibilities... Went more than a year between sacks, finally getting caught by Buffalo's Jeff Wright on Oct. 29... Broke most of Bob Griese's team records in '89, including completions and yards... Was three yards shy of fifth 4,000-yard season. He is only NFL QB ever to throw for 4,000 yards in four seasons... 1989 salary: $1.45 million. 1990 salary: $1.5 million... Born Sept. 15, 1961, in Pittsburgh.

JIM JENSEN 31 6-4 224   Wide Receiver/Running Back

Gets better with age... Had best season of career in '89, catching 61 passes for 557 yards and six touchdowns... Second behind Mark Clayton among Dolphin receivers... Most versatile player on team, he is best special-teams player, started one game at fullback and threw a TD pass in his only attempt of season... Also plays tight end... Was part of TDs in three different ways in '89—passing, receiving and blocking a punt that resulted in Miami score... Specializes on third-down plays. In his career, he has touched the ball 64 times on third down (16 runs, 48 receptions) and has picked up first down 52 times... Nicknamed "Crash"... Drafted in the 11th round as a quarterback out of Boston University in 1981... Had just 45 receptions in his first seven seasons and 119 in last two... 1989 salary: $276,200... Born Nov. 14, 1958, in Abington, Pa.

JOHN OFFERDAHL 26 6-3 240   Linebacker

Selected Pro Bowl starter despite missing seven games because of a holdout... Made up for lost time quickly, finishing third on club with 72 tackles... Has been to Pro Bowl in each of his four NFL seasons, the third time as a starter... Only other Dolphin linebacker ever to be named to more than one Pro Bowl is Nick Buoniconti, in 1972 and '73... Settled holdout with one-year deal for $500,000... Voted Dolphins' Man of the Year for his charity work... Selected NFL Defensive Rookie of the Year in 1986, when he was a second-round draft choice out of Western Michigan... Born Aug. 17, 1964, in Wisconsin Rapids, Wis.

MIAMI DOLPHINS 255

MARK CLAYTON 29 5-9 184   Wide Receiver

Dolphins' best receiver... Production dropped off from '88, when he set club record with 86 catches... 1989 stats: 64 receptions, 1,011 yards, nine TDs... Missed all of training camp and season-opener because of contract dispute... Stepped right in after signing, catching six passes for 79 yards and a TD at New England after three days of practice... Has been hurt by Mark Duper's drastic dropoff in production... Second on Dolphins' all-time receiving list with 405. Leader Nat Moore has 510... Best athlete on Dolphins, Clayton is star of team's offseason basketball team.... Scored 60 points in a charity hoops game in Fort Myers... 1989 salary: $950,000. 1990 salary: $1 million, ranks second on team behind Marino... Eighth-round pick out of Louisville in 1983... Born April 8, 1961, in Indianapolis.

FERRELL EDMUNDS 25 6-6 252   Tight End

Named to Pro Bowl as reserve in second pro season, but still hasn't come close to physical potential... 1989 stats (32 receptions, 382 yards, 11.9 avg.) were down from '88 (33-575, 17.4)... Scored three TDs in '89, but two came in one game against Jets... First Miami tight end ever to make Pro Bowl... Didn't have fumbling problems he did as rookie... Extremely hard worker... Set Dolphin record for receptions by rookie tight end... Scored 80-yard TD in '88... Aspires to play like Kellen Winslow... Third-round draft pick out of Maryland in 1988... Four-year starter at Maryland... 1989 salary: $155,000. 1990 salary: $185,000... Born April 16, 1965, in South Boston, Va.

SAMMIE SMITH 23 6-2 226   Running Back

Showed flashes of greatness as rookie but was slowed by lengthy holdout and nagging injuries... Last rookie in NFL to sign, he missed all of training camp and the season-opener... Made 12 starts, gaining 659 yards and six TDs on 200 carries... Only Andra Franklin, with 711 yards in '81, topped Smith on the club's all-time rookie rushing list... Smith rushed for

167 yards in first five games, then 492 in last eight... Gained 123 yards against Colts, marking the first time a Dolphin topped 100 yards since '87... Frequent fumbling and slow adaptation to passing game has Dolphin coaches worried... Sprained ankle was most bothersome injury of season... Ninth player taken in '89 draft... Gained 2,539 yards at Florida State... 1989 salary: $850,000. 1990 salary: $890,000... Born May 16, 1967, in Orlando, Fla.

MARK DUPER 31 5-9 190   Wide Receiver

Coming off two worst seasons since becoming a regular in 1983... Has just two TDs in two years after scoring 19 in 1986-87... Third among Dolphin receivers in '89 with 49 catches for 717 yards... Had just 39 receptions in '88, when he was suspended for three games for violating NFL substance-abuse policy... Fourth Miami receiver to record 300 career receptions... Biggest game of '89 was at Cincinnati, where he had five receptions for 129 yards... Topped 100 yards twice in season ... Age might be starting to show. He was hobbled by ankle, calf and groin injuries in '89... Holds team record for 100-yard games with 24... Surprise second-round draft pick out of Northwestern (La.) State in 1982... In college, broke Joe Delaney's school-record in 100-meter dash with 10.21 seconds... 1989 salary: $650,000. 1990 salary: $700,000... Born Jan. 25, 1959, in Pineville, La.

LOUIS OLIVER 24 6-2 226   Safety

Fast, hard-hitting safety led Dolphins with four interceptions in '89... Started 14 games at free safety, missing two starts because of a shoulder injury... Injury limited him to passing downs for the last three games of season... Fifth among Miami tacklers with 62... Named AFC Defensive Player of the Week for performance against Cleveland in which he intercepted Bernie Kosar pass to force overtime... Highly-touted player at Florida who was outspoken about his displeasure at being selected 25th in the draft... Held that anger through contract negotiations, demanding to be paid more than Denver's Steve Atwater, the first

MIAMI DOLPHINS 257

safety taken in draft... Teamed at safety with former college teammate Jarvis Williams, who moved to strong safety to make room for Oliver... Made college team as walk-on, then became two-time All-American... Great intelligence allowed him to learn Dolphin defense quickly... Born March 9, 1966, in Belle Grade, Fla.... 1989 salary: $607,500. 1990 salary: $590,000.

BARRY KRAUSS 33 6-3 260   Linebacker

Battered veteran had surprising '89 season, leading Miami with 119 tackles after being let go to free agency by Indy and cut by Cleveland ... Started final 12 games of season... Reached 100 tackles for fifth time in his career ... Dolphins won seven of Krauss' 12 starts ... Led or tied for team lead in tackles eight times and was in double figures six times... Pro Bowl pick John Offerdahl said Krauss deserved the selection more than he did... Has made more than 1,000 career tackles and has played in 140 NFL games... Spent 10 seasons with Colts, who made him sixth player picked in '79 draft... All-American at Alabama... 1989 salary: $500,000. 1990 salary: $440,000... Born March 17, 1957, in Pompano Beach, Fla.

TROY STRADFORD 25 5-9 192   Running Back

Coming off severe knee injury suffered in seventh game of '89... Tore ligaments and cartilage in right knee but expects to be ready for this season... His jitterbug style will be tough on recovering knee... Finished as Miami's No. 2 rusher with 240 yards on 66 carries... Versatile back who can catch passes and return punts... Was leading Dolphin rushers at time of injury... Was having outstanding game against Green Bay when injured... Named NFL's Offensive Rookie of the Year in 1987 but leg injuries hampered his second season... Gained 619 yards as rookie but just 335 in '88... Fourth-round draft pick out of Boston College in '87... BC's all-time leading rusher, with 3,504 yards... 1989 salary: $125,000... Born Sept. 11, 1964, in Elizabeth, N.J.

COACH DON SHULA: Enters 28th season as NFL head coach, 21st with Miami... Regular-season career record: 268-119-6... Winningest active coach in league... Second on NFL all-time winning list, behind George Halas... Halas won 326 games in 40 years... Shula is more determined than ever to return Dolphins to playoff status... Bounced back from worst season of career in '89, but still was bitterly disappointed with 8-8 record and 1-4 finish... Has appeared in more Super Bowls (six) than any other coach, winning two... Only coach to win 100 games in his first decade as coach... Coached Baltimore before going to Miami ... Played running back at John Carroll and was a defensive back for seven years in the NFL with Browns, Colts and Redskins... Son David is an assistant at Dallas and son Mike is on the Tampa Bay staff... Born Jan. 4, 1930, in Grand River, Ohio.

LONGEST PASS PLAY

BOB GRIESE TO PAUL WARFIELD

When one thinks about big pass plays by the Dolphins, Dan Marino usually comes to mind. But it was Hall of Fame quarterback Bob Griese who recorded the Dolphins' longest throw, an 86-yard touchdown toss to Paul Warfield in a 24-21 victory over the Steelers in the Orange Bowl on Nov. 14, 1971.

This was after Griese spent the night before the game in a hospital with a stomach ailment. With the Dolphins trailing, 14-3, late in the first quarter, Griese entered the game. He fumbled on his first play to allow Pittsburgh to take a 21-3 lead. Griese recovered, however and hit Warfield on a 12-yard touchdown before hitting him again on the record-setting 86-yard pass just before halftime.

The two connected on a 60-yard TD in the fourth quarter for the victory. Marino and Mark Duper teamed for the second-longest Dolphin pass, twice going 85 yards for a touchdown. This happened against Baltimore in 1983 and against Houston in 1986.

MIAMI DOLPHINS

INDIVIDUAL DOLPHIN RECORDS

Rushing

Most Yards Game:	197	Mercury Morris, vs New England, 1973
Season:	1,258	Delvin Williams, 1978
Career:	6,737	Larry Csonka, 1968-74, 1979

Passing

Most TD Passes Game:	6	Bob Griese, vs St. Louis, 1977
	6	Dan Marino, vs N.Y. Jets, 1986
Season:	48	Dan Marino, 1984
Career:	220	Dan Marino, 1983-89

Receiving

Most TD Passes Game:	4	Paul Warfield, vs Detroit, 1973
Season:	18	Mark Clayton, 1984
Career:	74	Nat Moore, 1974-86

Scoring

Most Points Game:	24	Paul Warfield, vs Detroit, 1973
Season:	117	Garo Yepremian, 1971
Career:	830	Garo Yepremian, 1970-78
Most TDs Game:	4	Paul Warfield, vs Detroit, 1973
Season:	18	Mark Clayton, 1984
Career:	75	Nat Moore, 1974-86

260 THE COMPLETE HANDBOOK OF PRO FOOTBALL
NEW ENGLAND PATRIOTS

TEAM DIRECTORY: Chairman: Victor K. Kiam II; Vice Chairman: Francis W. Murray; Pres.: William Sullivan Jr.; VP: Bucko Kilroy; GM: Patrick J. Sullivan; Dir. Player Oper.: Joe Mendes; Dir. Media Rel.: Jim Oldham; Head Coach: Rod Rust. Home field: Sullivan Stadium (60,794). Colors: Red, white and blue.

SCOUTING REPORT

OFFENSE: Things usually start at quarterback, and nobody's QB situation was more confusing than the Patriots' in 1989. The

Patriots count on John Stephens' return to rookie figures.

New England (5-11) shuffle ended with Marc Wilson at the helm. That's the same Marc Wilson who spent a year out of football after being let go by the Raiders and Packers.

Playing quarterback is easy when John Stephens is playing well, but the stocky running back tailed off a bit from his rookie Pro Bowl season, gaining 883 yards for an unspectacular 3.4-yard average. The Pats need a return to form by Stephens.

A strong return is needed by receiver Irving Fryar, who was slowed by injury and by the quarterback problems last year. Eric Sievers, who made a team-leading 54 receptions, is established as the tight end, and Hart Lee Dykes finished his rookie year in strong fashion.

The Pats' line lacked cohesion last year, then lost center Mike Baab to Cleveland in Plan B. Guard Sean Farrell and tackle Bruce Armstrong are the team's best blockers.

DEFENSE: An outstanding defense fell to pieces last year, as injuries sidelined linebacker Andre Tippett, cornerback Ronnie Lippett and end Garin Veris. Tippett is the only certainty to come back at 100 percent, which is good news because he can change the face of a game.

When all the talent is assembled, the Patriot defense can put the club in contention. End Brent Williams had eight sacks in '89, and former Ram Gary Jeter had seven.

Plan B brought a big blow to the Patriots when star cornerback Raymond Clayborn signed with Cleveland, making Lippett's return to form a must.

KICKING GAME: Kicker Jason Staurovsky was called into action at midseason to replace Greg Davis. Staurovsky hit 14-of-17 attempts, including 5-of-5 from 44 yards and out. Jeff Feagles ranked at the bottom of the AFC with a 38-yard average, 1.4 yards below his closest competitor.

Sammy Martin once again was among the NFL leaders with a 24.3-yard kickoff-return average. Fryar's injuries hurt the Pats on punt returns. Opponent punt returns jumped from 5.9 yards in '88 to 9.1 in '89.

THE ROOKIES: Arizona linebacker Chris Singleton and North Carolina State defensive end Ray Agnew, both first-round picks, come to the aid of an injury-riddled defense. Singleton is steady against the run and had 10 sacks as a senior. Agnew is a hard worker who bench-presses 500 pounds. LSU quarterback Tom

PATRIOTS VETERAN ROSTER

HEAD COACH—Rod Rust. Assistant Coaches—Don Blackmon, Steve Crosby, Bobby Grier, Rod Humenuik, Dale Lindsey, Steve Nelson, John Polonchek, Jimmy Raye, Jerry Simmons, Charlie Sumner, Richard Wood.

No.	Name	Pos.	Ht.	Wt.	NFL Exp.	College
	Adams, George	RB	6-1	225	6	Kentucky
39	Allen, Marvin	RB	5-10	208	3	Tulane
78	Armstrong, Bruce	T	6-4	284	4	Louisville
28	Bowman, Jim	S	6-2	215	6	Central Michigan
59	Brown, Vincent	LB	6-2	245	3	Miss. Valley State
22	Coleman, Eric	CB	6-0	190	2	Wyoming
46	Cook, Marv	TE	6-4	234	2	Iowa
87	Dawson, Lin	TE	6-3	240	9	North Carolina State
67	Douglas, David	G-C	6-4	280	5	Tennessee
88	Dykes, Hart Lee	WR	6-4	218	2	Oklahoma State
66	Fairchild, Paul	G	6-4	270	7	Kansas
62	Farrell, Sean	G	6-3	260	9	Penn State
8	Feagles, Jeff	P	6-0	198	3	Miami
63	Feehery, Gerry	C	6-2	270	8	Syracuse
80	Fryar, Irving	WR-KR	6-0	200	7	Nebraska
	Gambol, Chris	T	6-6	303	3	Iowa
	Gannon, Chris	DE	6-6	265	2	SW Louisiana
	Gibson, Ernest	CB	5-10	185	7	Furman
72	Goad, Tim	NT	6-3	280	3	North Carolina
14	Grogan, Steve	QB	6-3	210	16	Kansas State
37	Hurst, Maurice	CB	5-10	185	2	Southern University
38	James, Roland	S	6-2	191	11	Tennessee
	Jarostchuk, Ilia	LB	6-3	236	4	New Hampshire
99	Jeter, Gary	DE	6-4	260	14	Southern California
	Johnson, Damian	T	6-5	290	5	Kansas State
83	Jones, Cedric	WR	6-1	184	9	Duke
93	Jordan, Tim	LB	6-3	226	4	Wisconsin
42	Lippett, Ronnie	CB	5-11	180	7	Miami
91	Lowry, Orlando	LB	6-4	236	7	Ohio State
31	Marion, Fred	S	6-2	191	9	Miami
82	Martin, Sammy	WR-KR	5-11	175	3	Louisiana State
23	McSwain, Rod	CB	6-1	198	7	Clemson
	Morris, Jamie	RB	5-7	188	3	Michigan
	Mowatt, Zeke	TE	6-3	240	8	Florida State
34	Perryman, Robert	RB	6-1	233	4	Michigan
52	Rembert, Johnny	LB	6-3	234	8	Clemson
95	Reynolds, Ed	LB	6-5	242	8	Virginia
51	Scholtz, Bruce	LB	6-6	244	9	Texas
85	Sievers, Eric	TE	6-4	238	10	Maryland
77	Sims, Kenneth	DE	6-5	271	8	Texas
4	Staurovsky, Jason	K	5-9	170	3	Tulsa
44	Stephens, John	RB	6-1	215	3	NW Louisiana
30	Tatupu, Mosi	RB	6-0	227	13	Southern California
49	Taylor, Kitrick	WR-KR	5-11	190	3	Washington State
56	Tippett, Andre	LB	6-3	241	8	Iowa
21	Tucker, Erroll	CB-KR	5-8	170	3	Utah
60	Veris, Garin	DE	6-4	255	5	Stanford
70	Viaene, David	T	6-5	300	2	Minnesota-Duluth
75	Villa, Danny	T	6-5	305	4	Arizona State
	White, Bob	C	6-5	273	4	Rhode Island
96	Williams, Brent	DE	6-4	275	5	Toledo
54	Williams, Ed	LB	6-4	244	6	Texas
15	Wilson, Marc	QB	6-5	205	10	Brigham Young
35	Wonsley, George	RB	5-10	219	7	Mississippi State
	Zackery, Tony	S	6-2	195	2	Washington

TOP DRAFT CHOICES

Rd.	Name	Sel. No.	Pos.	Ht.	Wt.	College
1	Singleton, Chris	8	LB	6-3	244	Arizona
1	Agnew, Ray	10	DE	6-3	281	NC State
3	Hodson, Tommy	59	QB	6-2	189	LSU
3	McMurtry, Greg	80	WR	6-1	204	Michigan
5	Robinson, Junior	110	DB	5-9	181	East Carolina

Hodson never met the expectations he prompted as a freshman and sophomore.

OUTLOOK: New coach Rod Rust steps into a jumbled situation. The Pats lost some valuable depth and some starters in Plan B and are hoping to forget the injuries of 1989. A super-talented roster needs a quarterback as well as direction and stability.

PATRIOT PROFILES

JOHN STEPHENS 24 6-1 215 — Running Back

Suffered dropoff from outstanding rookie season... Led club with 833 yards but average per rush dropped from 3.9 to 3.4... Had assortment of injuries, including thigh, ankle, neck and hip... Personality seemed to sour as year went on... Ranked seventh among AFC rushers... Topped 100 yards just twice... Went to Pro Bowl as a rookie after rushing for 1,168 yards... Second New England player to make Pro Bowl as rookie. Mike Haynes in '76 was the other... Has just seven percent body fat... First-round draft choice out of Northwestern (La.) State, where he holds all-time rushing mark of 3,057 yards.... Born Feb. 23, 1966, in Shreveport, La.

ANDRE TIPPETT 30 6-3 241 — Linebacker

Heart of Patriot defense never made it through the preseason, tearing up right shoulder in final exhibition, the same game that sidelined Garin Veris and Ronnie Lippett for season... Was shooting for sixth consecutive Pro Bowl appearance... Had seven sacks in '88 despite missing four games with groin injury... Was AFC Linebacker of Year in '87 and Defensive Player of Year in '85... Had 35 sacks in 1984-85 seasons, including career-high 18½ with 22 pressures in '84... Holds second-degree black belt in karate and earned teaching certificate in Japan... Second-round pick out of Iowa in '82... Born Dec. 27, 1959, in Birmingham, Ala.

264 THE COMPLETE HANDBOOK OF PRO FOOTBALL

STEVE GROGAN 37 6-3 210   Quarterback

Every time you count this balding vet out he comes back and finds a way to stand out... Opened the season third on the depth chart, and was starting by Week 7.... Started six games, going 2-4, before coach Raymond Berry switched to Marc Wilson... Berry told media not to count Grogan out for future... Completed 133 of 261 passes for team-high 1,697 yards, nine TDs and 14 interceptions in '89... Completed career-high 28 passes vs. Colts on Oct. 29, including 14 consecutive... Has thrown for more than 25,000 yards in career... Known throughout league as tough player who plays injured... Fifth-round draft choice out of Kansas State in '75... Born July 24, 1953, in San Antonio.

MARC WILSON 33 6-5 205   Quarterback

After a year out of football, he climbed to top of Patriots' bizarre quarterback derby... Couldn't hook up with team after being cut by Green Bay in '88, so spent year working in land development in Seattle... Patriots signed him on Feb. 15, 1989... Started final four games, going 1-3... Season stats: 75-for-150 for 1,006 yards, three TDs, five interceptions... Spent eight years with Raiders before being cut in '88... Was 31-19 as Raider starter and was fans' whipping boy... No. 5 passer in Raider history... Was 15th player taken in '80 draft... Set 11 NCAA passing records in three seasons at Brigham Young... Born Feb. 15, 1957, in Bremerton, Wash.

HART LEE DYKES 23 6-4 218   Wide Receiver

Rookie was one of few bright spots in Patriots' long season... Started slow but came on by leading club in receptions in four of last five games... Had just 10 receptions after nine games... Had four 100-yard games, all after Nov. 11... Finished second on team with 49 catches for 795 yards and five TDs... First receiver taken in draft, 16th player overall... Had 74 receptions for 1,278 yards as Ohio State senior... Runs 4.6 40 and has 34-inch vertical leap... Pitched for Buckeyes' baseball team as senior... Has 95 mph fastball and was drafted by Chicago White Sox in '88... 1989 salary: $225,000. 1990 salary: $275,000... Born Sept. 2, 1966, in Bay City, Tex.

ERIC SIEVERS 32 6-4 238   Tight End

Had shocking success in '89, leading Pats with 54 receptions... Previous high in nine-year career was 41 with Chargers in '84 and '85... Made 38 of his 54 receptions in final nine games... Had two 100-yard games, giving him four for his career... Only tight end in NFL to top Sievers' receptions was Eagles' Keith Jackson with 63... Failed to make Pro Bowl because team listed him as receiver, not tight end... Played 1981-88 with San Diego, but was claimed by Rams when Chargers tried to bring him off injured reserve on Dec. 7, 1988... Played in one regular-season game and one playoff game with Rams, then was unprotected in Plan B, where Pats got him... Fourth-round pick out of Maryland in '81... Born Nov. 9, 1957, in Urbana, Ill.

ROBERT PERRYMAN 25 6-1 233   Running Back

John Stephens' injury problems make this former Michigan standout important to Pats... Gained career-high 562 yards in '89, 15th in AFC... Led club in rushing four times... Hard-nosed player who doesn't mind clearing holes for Stephens... Gained 448 yards in '88 and 187 as rookie... Third-round draft pick in '87 after splitting time with Gerald White at Michigan... Wants to be a broadcaster after football... Born Oct. 16, 1964, in Raleigh, N.C.

IRVING FRYAR 27 6-0 200   Wide Receiver

Some wonder what he would do on a passing team... Missed five games because of knee injuries, but still made 29 receptions for 537 yards... His 18.5-yard average was career-high... Best season was '86, when he caught 43 passes... Caught Pats' only TD in Super Bowl XX... First player selected in '84 draft after All-American career at Nebraska, where career 1,196 yards receiving was second only to Johnny Rodgers' 2,479... Can play five musical instruments... Born Sept. 28, 1962, in Mount Holly, N.J.

SEAN FARRELL 30 6-3 260 Guard

A rare award-winner in New England, Farrell was named All-AFC by the *Football News*... Started 14 games, sitting out two because of an ankle injury... Came to Pats in '87 trade with Tampa Bay... New England gave up three draft picks... Has been a starter since he entered the league out of Penn State in '82... Was only offensive lineman finalist for '81 Lombardi Trophy and finished second to Dave Rimington for '81 Outland... Teamed with Oilers' Mike Munchak at Penn State to form dominating guard tandem... Born July 25, 1960, in Southhampton, N.Y.

FRED MARION 31 6-2 191 Safety

Quarterbacks around the NFL respect this eight-year vet's leadership of a tough defensive backfield... Aggressive player who had 123 tackles, second on team... His 94 solo stops led Patriots... Has been to Pro Bowl once, in 1985... Hasn't missed a game since 1984... Had two interceptions in '89, raising his career total to 23... Had seven in '85 for NFL-high 189 return yards... Is especially tough on Miami's Dan Marino, who always has trouble solving Patriots' defensive schemes... Fifth-round draft choice out of Miami, where he set school record with 16 interceptions... Born Jan. 2, 1959, in Gainesville, Fla.

COACH ROD RUST: Patriot defense should bounce back quickly under this familiar face... Respected defensive coach took over first NFL head coaching job when Raymond Berry was fired in offseason... This is a return for Rust, who served as Patriots' defensive coordinator from 1983-87... In that time, Pats finished in first or second place each year... His '85 unit ranked third in AFC... Left New England for Chiefs' staff in '88 and moved to Steelers in '89... Began NFL career with Eagles in '76 and spent 1978-82 with Chiefs... Coached CFL's Montreal Alouettes from 1973-75... Was head coach at North Texas State, where his

LONGEST PASS PLAY

TONY EASON TO CRAIG JAMES

In a preview of the season's Super Bowl, the Bears' defense manhandled the Patriots in a 20-7 victory at Chicago's Soldier Field on Sept. 15, 1985. A miserable New England offensive showing was brightened only when Craig James slipped through the Bear secondary and caught a 90-yard touchdown pass from Tony Eason. The play came with 5:57 remaining in the game and provided the final score.

The Bears flustered Eason all day, forcing the former Illinois quarterback into a 15-for-35 day with 234 yards, three interceptions and six sacks.

At the time, Eason appeared to be the Patriots' quarterback of the future, but he fell into disfavor rapidly. He now plays for the New York Jets. The play was one of James' two touchdown catches of the season. The previous Patriots' best was 88 yards from Jim Plunkett to Randy Vataha against the Baltimore Colts in 1971.

INDIVIDUAL PATRIOT RECORDS

Rushing

Most Yards Game:	212	Tony Collins, vs N.Y. Jets, 1983
Season:	1,458	Jim Nance, 1966
Career:	5,453	Sam Cunningham, 1973-79, 1981-82

Passing

Most TD Passes Game:	5	Babe Parilli, vs Buffalo, 1964
	5	Babe Parilli, vs Miami, 1967
	5	Steve Grogan, vs N.Y. Jets, 1979
Season:	31	Babe Parilli, 1964
Career:	178	Steve Grogan, 1975-89

Receiving

Most TD Passes Game:	3	Billy Lott, vs Buffalo, 1961
	3	Gino Cappelletti, vs Buffalo, 1964
	3	Jim Whalen, vs Miami, 1967
	3	Harold Jackson, vs N.Y. Jets, 1979
	3	Derrick Ramsey, vs Indianapolis, 1984
	3	Stanley Morgan, vs Seattle, 1986
Season:	12	Stanley Morgan, 1979
Career:	67	Stanley Morgan, 1977-89

Scoring

Most Points Game:	28	Gino Cappelletti, vs Houston, 1965
Season:	155	Gino Cappelletti, 1964
Career:	1,130	Gino Cappelletti, 1960-70
Most TDs Game:	3	Billy Lott, vs Buffalo, 1961
	3	Billy Lott, vs Oakland, 1961
	3	Larry Garron, vs Oakland, 1964
	3	Gino Cappelletti, vs Buffalo, 1964
	3	Larry Garron, vs San Diego, 1966
	3	Jim Whalen, vs Miami, 1967
	3	Sam Cunningham, vs Buffalo, 1974
	3	Mack Herron, vs Buffalo, 1974
	3	Sam Cunningham, vs Buffalo, 1975
	3	Harold Jackson, vs N.Y. Jets, 1979
	3	Tony Collins, vs N.Y. Jets, 1983
	3	Mosi Tatupu, vs L.A. Rams, 1983
	3	Derrick Ramsey, vs Indianapolis, 1984
	3	Stanley Morgan, vs Seattle, 1986
Season:	13	Steve Grogan, 1976
	13	Stanley Morgan, 1979
Career:	67	Stanley Morgan, 1977-89

NEW YORK JETS

TEAM DIRECTORY: Chairman: Leon Hess; Pres.: Steve Gutman; VP/GM: Dick Steinberg; Dir. Pro Personnel: Jim Royer; Dir. Pub. Rel.: Frank Ramos; Head Coach: Bruce Coslet. Home field: Giants Stadium (76,891). Colors: Kelly green and white.

SCOUTING REPORT

OFFENSE: The Jets' offense should begin to take shape under new coach Bruce Coslet, but new GM Dick Steinberg has to fill some big holes. Things will be interesting at quarterback, where

Erik McMillan's big plays led him to second Pro Bowl.

270 THE COMPLETE HANDBOOK OF PRO FOOTBALL

close friends Ken O'Brien and Tony Eason, a Patriot castoff, will battle it out. O'Brien, who hurt a shoulder last year, is the better player and a guy who has had to suffer over the years with weak surroundings.

The standout of the Jets (4-12) is receiver Al Toon, whose 1989 season was a washout because of a holdout and injuries. In his absence, JoJo Townsell emerged as a quality receiver. And the Jets drafted a prized receiver in Reggie Rembert.

With Freeman McNeil appearing to be on the downside of his career, leaving Johnny Hector as the key man, the Jets addressed the running-back situations by drafting Blair Thomas. Fullback Roger Vick has yet to make a big impact.

Outside of center Jim Sweeney, the Jets' line is a mess. Somehow, Coslet must find some stability. Otherwise, O'Brien will continue to be battered. The Jets allowed an incredible 62 sacks, worst in the league and up from 42 a year ago.

DEFENSE: It isn't easy to boast a unit of no-names while playing in the glare of the New York media, but the Jets have done so on defense. The Jet defense ranked 27th in the league in '89 and collected a league-low 28 sacks. End Dennis Byrd led the way with seven sacks.

The Jet secondary continued to make big plays as safety Erik McMillan and cornerback James Hasty made six and five interceptions, respectively. Both are gamblers who get beat too often but can turn games around with touchdowns.

First-round pick Jeff Lageman had a decent year at linebacker and doesn't appear to be the bust New York fans called him on draft day. Kyle Clifton is a steady player at inside linebacker while OLB Alex Gordon hasn't proved to be a game-changer yet.

KICKING GAME: Like the rest of the Jets, kicker Pat Leahy had an off year, making just 14-of-21 field-goal attempts. But he is a proven veteran who gives the Jets little reason for concern. Punter Joe Prokop (39.4 avg.) is inconsistent.

Townsell is solid returning punts and kickoffs. Bobby Humphery is another good kick-returner. The Jets allowed 7.6 yards per punt return to rank second in the AFC.

THE ROOKIES: Penn State's Thomas was the best running back and West Virginia's Reggie Rembert was the best receiver in the draft. Thomas is a can't-miss runner who has been timed at 4.48 in the 40. His versatility will fit the new offense perfectly.

JETS VETERAN ROSTER

HEAD COACH—Bruce Coslet. Assistant Coaches—Larry Beightol, Kippy Brown, Pete Carroll, Joe Daniels, Ed Donatell, Foge Fazio, Monte Kiffin, Greg Mackrides, Chip Myers, Greg Robinson, Bob Wylie.

No.	Name	Pos.	Ht.	Wt.	NFL Exp.	College
54	Benson, Troy	LB	6-2	235	5	Pittsburgh
42	Booty, John	CB-S	6-0	179	3	Texas Christian
80	Boyer, Mark	TE	6-4	252	6	Southern California
29	Brown, A.B.	RB	5-9	212	2	West Virginia
87	Burkett, Chris	WR	6-4	210	6	Jackson State
90	Byrd, Dennis	DE	6-5	270	2	Tulsa
31	Byrum, Carl	RB	6-0	237	4	Miss. Valley State
66	Cadigan, Dave	G-T	6-4	280	3	Southern California
59	Clifton, Kyle	LB	6-4	236	7	Texas Christian
61	Criswell, Jeff	T	6-7	290	4	Graceland
49	Curtis, Travis	S	5-10	180	4	West Virginia
84	Dressel, Chris	TE	6-4	245	6	Stanford
11	Eason, Tony	QB	6-4	212	8	Illinois
45	Egu, Patrick	RB	5-11	205	2	Nevada-Reno
91	Frase, Paul	DE-DT	6-5	267	3	Syracuse
55	Gordon, Alex	LB	6-5	246	4	Cincinnati
79	Haight, Mike	G	6-4	281	5	Iowa
40	Hasty, James	CB	6-0	197	3	Washington State
34	Hector, Johnny	RB	5-11	202	8	Texas A&M
28	Howard, Carl	CB-S	6-2	190	7	Rutgers
48	Humphery, Bobby	CB-KR	5-10	180	7	New Mexico State
81	Kelly, Pat	TE	6-6	252	3	Syracuse
57	Kohlbrand, Joe	LB	6-4	242	6	Miami
38	Konecny, Mark	RB	6-0	200	3	Alma
56	Lageman, Jeff	LB	6-5	250	2	Virginia
5	Leahy, Pat	K	6-0	196	17	St. Louis
93	Lyons, Marty	DE-DT	6-5	269	12	Alabama
15	Mackey, Kyle	QB	6-3	216	5	East Texas State
64	Matich, Trevor	C-G-T	6-4	270	6	Brigham Young
68	McElroy, Reggie	T	6-6	276	8	West Texas State
22	McMillan, Erik	S	6-2	197	3	Missouri
24	McNeil, Freeman	RB	5-11	209	10	UCLA
94	Mersereau, Scott	DT-DE	6-3	280	4	Southern Connecticut
36	Miano, Rich	S	6-0	200	5	Hawaii
72	Miller, Brett	T	6-7	300	8	Iowa
51	Mott, Joe	LB	6-4	253	2	Iowa
95	Naposki, Eric	LB	6-2	230	2	Connecticut
86	Neubert, Keith	TE	6-6	248	2	Nebraska
77	Nichols, Gerald	DT-DE	6-2	267	4	Florida State
7	O'Brien, Ken	QB	6-4	206	8	California-Davis
17	Parker, Carl	WR	6-2	201	3	Vanderbilt
6	Prokop, Joe	P	6-2	224	5	Cal Poly-Pomona
25	Radachowsky, George	S	5-11	195	6	Boston College
71	Rehder, Tom	T-G	6-7	280	3	Notre Dame
82	Shuler, Mickey	TE	6-3	231	13	Penn State
74	Singer, Curt	T	6-5	279	4	Tennessee
96	Stallworth, Ron	DE	6-5	262	2	Auburn
53	Sweeney, Jim	C	6-4	270	7	Pittsburgh
88	Toon, Al	WR	6-4	205	6	Wisconsin
83	Townsell, JoJo	WR-KR	5-9	180	6	UCLA
43	Vick, Roger	RB	6-3	235	4	Texas A&M
21	Washington, Brian	S	6-1	220	2	Nebraska
97	Washington, Marvin	DT-DE	6-6	260	2	Idaho
33	Williams, Terry	CB	5-11	204	3	Bethune-Cookman
76	Withycombe, Mike	T-G	6-5	300	3	Fresno State
63	Zawatson, Dave	G-T	6-5	275	2	California

TOP DRAFT CHOICES

Rd.	Name	Sel. No.	Pos.	Ht.	Wt.	College
1	Thomas, Blair	2	RB	5-11	190	Penn State
2	Rembert, Reggie	28	WR	6-3	195	West Virginia
3	Stargell, Tony	56	DB	5-11	179	Tennessee State
4	Taylor, Troy	84	QB	6-3	201	California
5	Savage, Tony	112	DT	6-2	306	Washington State

272 THE COMPLETE HANDBOOK OF PRO FOOTBALL

The Jets gained more speed in Rembert (4.45) and Tennessee State cornerback Tony Stargell (4.47).

OUTLOOK: With a new front office and coaching staff, the Jets finally are starting over. It's going to take time and some quality drafting to get this club back on track.

JET PROFILES

AL TOON 27 6-4 205 Wide Receiver

Super athlete who had his most frustrating season of career... Battled management in lengthy holdout, then ran into injury problems... Played in only six full games and parts of five others because of shoulder, thigh, ankle and head injuries... Still led club in receiving for fourth straight year... Caught 63 passes for 698 yards but just two TDs... Was coming off 93-catch, 1,067-yard season... Luckily, one of his few games was against Miami, whom he always seems to kill... Pulled off "double-triple" against Dolphins in Week 3 with 10 catches for 178 yards... Incredible streak of catching three passes in each of his NFL starts ended at 52 games in Week 4 vs. Colts... Has caught one pass in 64 straight games... Went to Pro Bowl three straight years from 1986-88... First Jet ever to be selected MVP three consecutive seasons... First-round pick out of Wisconsin in '85... Was All-American triple jumper in college... Top-paid receiver in NFL in '89 with salary of $1.35 million... Born April 30, 1963, in Newport News, Va.

ERIK McMILLAN 25 6-2 197 Safety

Headed quickly for superstar status... First Jet since Billy Atkins and Billy Mathis in 1960-61 to go to Pro Bowl in first two seasons... Pro Bowl starter last year after going as backup as rookie... Led Jets with six interceptions after recording eight in '88... Has incredible knack for big plays... Tied NFL season record with two fumble recoveries for TDs... Also returned an interception 92 yards for TD... Third on club in tackles with 95... During Jets' 13-quarter offensive slump, McMillan produced three TDs... As a rookie, had back-to-back games with TD returns and intercepted Dan Marino three times in a game... Third-round draft pick in '88 out of Missouri... Son of former St. Louis All-Pro tackle Ernie McMillan... Born May 3, 1965, in St. Louis.

JAMES HASTY 25 6-0 197   Cornerback

Another stellar soph defensive back... Had five interceptions for second time... Led all Jets with 21 passes defensed... Cocky player who works well with McMillan... Selected to UPI and *Pro Football Weekly* all-rookie teams in '88... Third-round draft pick out of Washington, where he played safety as a junior and cornerback as senior... Played wide receiver for two years at Central Washington before switching schools... Has degree in communications and has begun work on master's... Born May 23, 1965, in Seattle.

JEFF LAGEMAN 23 6-5 250   Linebacker

New York fans nearly fell over in shock when Jets drafted this raw, unheralded player out of Virginia in first round... Steadily won fans' favor, however, starting 15 games at outside linebacker... Finished second in sacks (4½) and fourth in tackles (72)... NBC-TV's Bobby Beathard named him one of the top five rookies of '89, but he didn't make any all-rookie teams... Stock rose in draft after playing well in all-star games... Started three years at inside linebacker at Virginia... Just the second linebacker to be Jets' top pick. Bob Crable in '82 was the other... Has degree in economics... 1989 salary: $222,500. 1990 salary: $297,500... Born July 18, 1967, in Fairfax, Va.

JoJo TOWNSELL 29 5-9 180   Wide Receiver

Escaped tag as purely a kick-return specialist, leading club in receiving yards (787) and was second to Toon with 45 catches... Led team with five TD receptions and finished third in AFC punt returns (9.1 avg.) and 10th in kick returns (19.2)... Named team MVP, ending Toon's three-year streak... Caught just nine passes the last three seasons after pulling in 12 in '85... Led AFC in punt returns in '88 with an 11.7 average... Signed with Jets in '85 after three seasons with Los Angeles Express of the USFL... Caught 126 passes for 1,992 yards and 16 TDs with Express and set league record with 249 receiving yards in a game... Was drafted by Jets in third round of '83 draft before going to USFL... UCLA's all-time leader in TD receptions (20)... Has degree in sociology... College teammate of Jets' Freeman McNeil... Born Nov. 4, 1960, in Reno, Nev.

KEN O'BRIEN 29 6-4 206   Quarterback

Injuries continue to prevent talent to come through consistently... His 74.3 quarterback rating tied career low set in '84... Bounced back from that year to lead NFL in '85 with 96.4... Completed 60 percent of passes in '89 for 3,346 yards while battling shoulder injury... Yardage was third-most of career, but his 12 TDs and 18 interception stats hurt him... Head must have been spinning under Joe Walton, who benched him for former replacement player Kyle Mackey... The plan didn't work and O'Brien returned... Normally a gutsy player whose bravery was called into question by Miami safety Louis Oliver after goal-line stop... Fifth of six quarterbacks drafted in first round in '83... Division II All-American at Cal-Davis... 1989 salary: $1.45 million... Born Nov. 27, 1960, in Brooklyn, N.Y., but moved to Sacramento, Cal., at age three.

TONY EASON 30 6-4 212   Quarterback

Will provide interesting quarterback derby going against longtime friend Ken O'Brien... Signed late in season after Patriots gave up on him... Threw for 1,016 yards all season, including 255 for Jets... Balked at coming to Jets because of O'Brien's presence, but later agreed... Struggled in '88 because of separated shoulder and knee injury... Once was one of most highly regarded quarterbacks in NFL... Led Pats to Super Bowl in '86, when he threw for 3,328 yards... Fifteenth player taken in '83 draft...... Big Ten passing leader while at Illinois... He and Jim McMahon are only QBs in NCAA history to pass for over 3,000 yards twice... Born Oct. 8, 1959, in Blythe, Cal.

NEW YORK JETS 275

JOHNNY HECTOR 29 5-11 202   Running Back

Became Jets' top back as Freeman McNeil fell into disfavor... Ended McNeil's eight-year reign as leader by gaining 702 yards... Previous high was 164 in 1986... Third on team receiving with 38 for 330 yards... Had just three rushing TDs after recording 21 the past two years... His 11 TDs in '87 tied Charles White of Rams for most by running back... Second-round draft pick out of Texas A&M in '83... Set A&M record in long jump with 26-4 leap... Placed second to Carl Lewis in long jump at Southwestern Conference meet in '82... 1989 salary: $700,000... Born Nov. 26, 1960, in Lafayette, La.

FREEMAN McNEIL 31 5-11 209   Running Back

Troubled season for one of game's top talents... Missed five games with ankle injury and finished with 310 yards on 31 carries... Was coming off 944-yard season... Coaching staff reportedly questioned his desire during season and put him behind Johnny Hector... Rushed for 1,000 yards twice, in 1984 and '85... With long history of injury problems, he has played a 16-game season just once... Named to Pro Bowl in '82... First-round pick in '81 who holds UCLA's single-season (1,396) and career (3,195) rushing marks... 1989 salary: $905,000... Born April 22, 1959, in Jackson, Miss.

MICKEY SHULER 34 6-3 231   Tight End

AFC's top tight end missed nine games with rib and knee injuries... Caught 29 passes for 322 yards after catching 70 for 805 in '88... Has been to two Pro Bowls, in '86 and '88... Had caught 70 passes in '88... Top-paid tight end in NFL in '89 with salary of $900,000... Has 438 receptions in 12-year career... Third-round draft pick in '78... Penn State coach Joe Paterno calls him Nittany Lions' best tight end ever... Has degree in health and physical education and owns Shuler's Local Steel & Supply Corp. and Tight-End Leasing in Mineola, N.Y. ... Born Aug. 21, 1956, in Harrisburg, Pa.

COACH BRUCE COSLET: "We won't be dull," Coslet said as he was announced as the man to replace Joe Walton. No one ever suspected he would be after his success in Cincinnati... Served as Bengals' assistant since '81, the last four years as offensive coordinator... In that time, Bengals ranked No. 1 in NFL twice and led AFC in total offense three times... Said Boomer Esiason: "He's a steal for the Jets. He knows more about how to dissect a defense than anyone I've ever seen. He wasn't only my teacher, but my eyes."... At 40, he's second-youngest NFL head coach... Is 3½ months older than Raiders' Art Shell... Played tight end for Bengals from 1969-76 and was coached for eight seasons by Bill Walsh... Career stats: 64 receptions, 877 yards, nine TDs... Played in '68 in the Canadian Football League... Ran construction business from 1977-79, then joined Walsh's 49ers staff for a year before joining Bengals... Played college ball at Pacific... Has degrees in history and psychology... Born Aug. 5, 1946, in Oakdale, Cal.

LONGEST PASS PLAY

KEN O'BRIEN TO WESLEY WALKER

The Jets' Ken O'Brien and Wesley Walker have hooked up for touchdown passes of 80 or more yards three times, but their 96-yard effort in a 27-7 victory at Buffalo on Dec. 8, 1985, will be tough to top.

On a dreary, cold day, O'Brien was red-hot. His bomb to Walker helped the Jets to a 21-0 halftime lead and to a 10-4 record. O'Brien completed 25 of 40 passes on the day for 370 yards and three touchdowns. His lone interception came after a deflection off Walker's hands. Walker caught four passes for 129 yards in the game.

O'Brien and Walker also have hit for scores of 88 and 83 yards, plays which rank fourth and eighth in the club history. Their 96-yard bomb surprassed a 91-yard (non-scoring) pass from Joe Namath to Richard Caster against Miami on Oct. 7, 1974. Namath also hit Caster on an 89-yard touchdown in that game.

INDIVIDUAL JET RECORDS

Rushing

Most Yards Game:	192	Freeman McNeil, vs Buffalo, 1985
Season:	1,331	Freeman McNeil, 1985
Career:	7,104	Freeman McNeil, 1981-89

Passing

Most TD Passes Game:	6	Joe Namath, vs Baltimore, 1972
Season:	26	Al Dorow, 1960
	26	Joe Namath, 1967
Career:	170	Joe Namath, 1965-76

Receiving

Most TD Passes Game:	4	Wesley Walker, vs Miami, 1986
Season:	14	Art Powell, 1960
	14	Don Maynard, 1965
Career:	88	Don Maynard, 1960-72

Scoring

Most Points Game:	19	Jim Turner, vs Buffalo, 1968
	19	Pat Leahy, vs Cincinnati, 1984
Season:	145	Jim Turner, 1968
Career:	1,261	Pat Leahy, 1974-89
Most TDs Game:	4	Wesley Walker, vs Miami, 1986
Season:	14	Art Powell, 1960
	14	Don Maynard, 1965
	14	Emerson Boozer, 1972
Career:	88	Don Maynard, 1960-72

PITTSBURGH STEELERS

TEAM DIRECTORY: Pres.: Daniel Rooney; VP: John McGinley; VP: Art Rooney Jr.; Dir. Player Personnel: Dick Haley; Dir. Communications: Joe Gordon; Dir. Pub. Rel.: Dan Edwards; Head Coach: Chuck Noll. Home field: Three Rivers Stadium (59,000). Colors: Black and gold.

SCOUTING REPORT

OFFENSE: You get the feeling that quarterback Bubby Brister is going to catch fire any day now. But each time the strong-armed Southerner shows flashes, he falls into a rut. The Steelers (9-7) ranked last among NFL offenses because of a spotty passing game. Brister threw for just nine touchdowns and 10 interceptions in '89.

Part of Brister's problem is a thin receiving corps. Louis Lipps is the only established standout, but the team has hope for second-year player Derek Hill and for rookie Eric Green.

Pittsburgh showed late last season it is putting together an impressive, hard-nosed running game. Tim Worley gained 417 yards in his final five games, and Merril Hoge proved to be an unsung, straight-ahead rusher who is hard to drag down. Worley must break his fumbling habit. The Steelers lost seven of his nine drops in '89.

Brister's line, led by tackle Tunch Ilkin, gained consistency at the end of last season.

It will be interesting to see what effect Joe Walton has as new offensive coordinator.

DEFENSE: The Steelers stepped up their defensive intensity in 1989, but still displayed a glaring lack of pass rush. Pittsburgh totalled 31 sacks, which was up from 19 the previous year but still 13th in the AFC. End Aaron Jones, a former No. 1 pick, has just 3½ sacks the past two years. Rookie end Ken Davidson could make a difference here.

The strength of the Steelers' defense is the young secondary. Cornerback Rod Woodson is a marvelous athlete who fits in well with hard-hitting safeties Thomas Everett and Carnell Lake. Dwayne Woodruff, the other cornerback, is a solid veteran.

Greg Lloyd is the Steelers' best linebacker. The former Fort Valley State star had seven sacks last year, was second with 92 tackles and had three interceptions.

Merril Hoge's postseason play was a highlight.

KICKING GAME: Woodson is dangerous on all returns. He led the NFL with a 27.3-yard average on kicks and was fifth in the AFC with a 7.1-yard punt-return average.

Gary Anderson is a clutch kicker who provides consistency. The Steelers must find a punter because Harry Newsome, who averaged 41.1 yards last year, signed with Minnesota in Plan B.

THE ROOKIES: Green played in anonymity at Liberty but was coached by former NFL coach Sam Rutigliano. He had 62 receptions as a senior after making just 37 his first three years. His strength is blocking. The Steelers drafted the big, strong and fast Davidson despite an inconsistent career at LSU.

STEELERS VETERAN ROSTER

HEAD COACH—Chuck Noll. Assistant Coaches—Ron Blackledge, Dave Brazil, John Fox, Joe Greene, Dick Hoak, Jon Kolb, Tom Moore, Dwain Painter, Rod Rust, George Stewart, Bob Valesente, Joe Walton.

No.	Name	Pos.	Ht.	Wt.	NFL Exp.	College
1	Anderson, Gary	K	5-11	170	9	Syracuse
60	Blankenship, Brian	G-C	6-1	275	4	Nebraska
6	Brister, Bubby	QB	6-3	210	5	NE Louisiana
24	Carter, Rodney	RB	6-0	210	4	Purdue
63	Dawson, Dermontti	C-G	6-2	275	3	Kentucky
27	Everett, Thomas	S	5-9	184	4	Baylor
68	Freeman, Lorenzo	NT	6-5	298	4	Pittsburgh
22	Griffin, Larry	S	6-0	200	5	North Carolina
81	Griggs, Billy	TE	6-3	230	6	Virginia
35	Hall, Delton	CB	6-1	207	4	Clemson
82	Hill, Derek	WR	6-1	193	2	Arizona
53	Hinkle, Bryan	LB	6-2	225	9	Oregon
33	Hoge, Merril	RB	6-2	231	4	Idaho State
41	Holmes, Darryl	CB-S	6-2	190	3	Fort Valley State
62	Ilkin, Tunch	T	6-3	265	11	Indiana State
65	Jackson, John	T	6-6	288	3	Eastern Kentucky
99	Jenkins, A. J.	LB-DE	6-2	237	2	Cal State-Fullerton
44	Johnson, David	CB	6-0	185	2	Kentucky
78	Johnson, Tim	DE-NT	6-3	269	4	Penn State
97	Jones, Aaron	DE	6-5	257	3	Eastern Kentucky
37	Lake, Carnell	S	6-0	205	2	UCLA
51	Lanza, Chuck	C	6-2	260	3	Notre Dame
83	Lipps, Louis	WR	5-10	190	7	Southern Mississippi
50	Little, David	LB	6-1	233	10	Florida
95	Lloyd, Greg	LB	6-2	224	3	Fort Valley State
74	Long, Terry	G	5-11	275	7	East Carolina
84	Mularkey, Mike	TE	6-4	237	8	Florida
54	Nickerson, Hardy	LB	6-2	231	4	California
92	Olsavsky, Jerry	LB	6-1	222	2	Pittsburgh
85	O'Shea, Terry	TE	6-4	236	2	California (Pa.)
28	Owens, Billy	CB	6-2	198	2	Pittsburgh
71	Ricketts, Tom	T	6-5	298	2	Pittsburgh
79	Rienstra, John	G	6-5	264	5	Temple
94	Romer, Rich	LB	6-3	214	3	Union College
47	Roundtree, Ray	WR	6-0	182	2	Penn State
90	Shelton, Richard	CB	5-11	186	2	Liberty
80	Stock, Mark	WR	5-11	177	2	Virginia Military
20	Stone, Dwight	WR-RB	6-0	190	4	Middle Tenn. State
90	Stowe, Tyronne	LB	6-1	236	4	Rutgers
11	Strom, Rick	QB	6-2	210	2	Georgia Tech
87	Thompson, Weegie	WR	6-6	215	7	Florida State
23	Tyrrell, Tim	RB	6-2	215	7	Northern Illinois
43	Wallace, Ray	RB	6-0	233	4	Purdue
98	Williams, Gerald	NT	6-3	279	5	Auburn
57	Williams, Jerrol	LB	6-5	242	2	Purdue
42	Williams, Warren	RB	6-0	204	3	Miami
93	Willis, Keith	DE	6-1	263	8	Northeastern
49	Woodruff, Dwayne	CB	6-0	198	11	Louisville
26	Woodson, Rod	CB-KR	6-0	202	4	Purdue
38	Worley, Tim	RB	6-2	216	2	Georgia
9	Wright, Randy	QB	6-2	203	6	Wisconsin

TOP DRAFT CHOICES

Rd.	Name	Sel. No.	Pos.	Ht.	Wt.	College
1	Green, Eric	21	TE	6-4	274	Liberty
2	Davidson, Lenny	43	DE	6-5	274	LSU
3	O'Donnell, Neil	70	QB	6-2	217	Maryland
3	Veasey, Craig	81	DT	6-1	270	Houston
4	Calloway, Chris	97	WR	5-10	176	Michigan

PITTSBURGH STEELERS 281

OUTLOOK: The Steelers' late run in '89 was inspiring and indicated where the team is headed. The future is bright in Pittsburgh, but the Steelers are not yet ready to be a regular in the playoffs.

STEELER PROFILES

BUBBY BRISTER 28 6-3 210　　　　　　　　Quarterback

Emotional leader of Steelers who shows flashes of stardom... Was fourth-rated passer in AFC after six games, then went six consecutive games without a TD pass... Threw for 2,365 yards to move from ninth to sixth on club's passing list... QB rating of 73.1 ranked 11th in NFL but was up from 65.3 in '88... Threw for nine TDs and 10 interceptions... Fiery competitor who has ability to get teammates working hard... Third-round draft pick out of Northeast Louisiana in '86... Didn't get to start there until he was a senior... First signed with Alabama, then chose to pursue baseball... Hit .180 as Appalachian League shortstop, quit and enrolled in Tulane... Left Tulane after two games... Minor-league manager was Jim Leyland, now manager of Pirates... Born Aug. 15, 1962, in Alexandria, La.... Full name is Walter Andrew Brister III.

TIM WORLEY 23 6-2 216　　　　　　　　Running Back

Excessive fumbles marred impressive rookie season... Gained 770 yards and five touchdowns, but fumbled nine times, losing seven... Started slowly because of lengthy holdout, but rushed for 417 yards on 87 carries in final five games... Slippery hands carried over into playoffs, as he lost two fumbles... First Steeler to lead team in rushing as a rookie since Franco Harris in '72... Finished eighth in AFC rushing... Averaged 3.9 yards per carry... Seventh player picked in draft... Rushed for 1,216 yards as senior at Georgia... Barry Sanders was only running back drafted ahead of Worley... Just fourth running back ever drafted in first round by Chuck Noll... 1989 salary: $250,000. 1990 salary: $400,000... Born Sept. 24, 1966, in Lumberton, N.C.

MERRIL HOGE 25 6-2 231　　　　　　　　　Running Back

Tim Worley got all the attention, but Hoge was the team's workhorse... Used his plowing style to gain 621 yards and score eight touchdowns... Fantastic playoff performance delivered Hoge from anonymity... First Steeler ever to have consecutive 100-yard games in the postseason... Was superb in playoffs vs. Denver, rushing for 120 yards and catching eight passes for 60 yards... His 6.7-yard postseason rushing average is a club record... Led team in rushing in '88 with 705 yards and was first Steeler to lead team in both rushing and receiving since 1982, when Franco Harris did so... Tenth-round draft choice out of Idaho State in '87... Played primarily on special teams as rookie... Bulled his way to 2,713 yards and 44 TDs in college ... 1989 salary: $87,000... Born Jan. 26, 1965, in Pocatello, Idaho.

TUNCH ILKIN 32 6-3 265　　　　　　　　　　　　Tackle

Now a regular on all-star ballots... Selected to second consecutive Pro Bowl... First Steeler tackle since Charley Bradshaw in 1964-65 to be named to two Pro Bowls... First Steeler tackle to go to Pro Bowl since Larry Brown in '83... Did not allow a sack in '87 ... Sixth-round draft pick in '80, but was cut in training camp... Brought back because of injuries... Started three seasons at Indiana State... Has degree in broadcasting... Born Sept. 23, 1957, in Istanbul, Turkey... Family moved to Highland Park, Ill., when he was two... Mother was Miss Turkey in 1950... 1989 salary: $258,000.

ROD WOODSON 25 6-0 202　　　　　　　　　Cornerback

On verge of stardom... Named All-Pro and went to first Pro Bowl, as kick-returner, after leading NFL with 27.3 average... Ranked fifth in AFC punt returns with 7.1 average... Tied for second on Steelers with three interceptions and forced a team-high four fumbles... One of top athletes in NFL... Developed quickly after missing first half of '87 rookie season...

Team co-MVP with David Little in '88 after making four interceptions and turning in a 23-yard kick-return average... Tenth player selection in '87 draft after superb career at Purdue... Set Boilermaker record for interceptions (11) and started 44 consecutive games, playing cornerback, safety, running back, wide receiver, punt-returner and kick-returner... Qualified for Olympic trials in 100-meter high hurdles in '84... Has degree in criminal justice... 1989 salary: $325,000... Born March 10, 1965, in Fort Wayne, Ind.

LOUIS LIPPS 28 5-10 190   Wide Receiver

Consistency has returned to Steelers' gamebreaker... Caught 50 passes for second consecutive season and was named team MVP for second time... Fell 56 yards short of second 1,000-yard season... Also was team's No. 3 rusher with career-high 180 yards and a TD on 13 carries... Only Cleveland's Webster Slaughter (19.0) topped Lipps' 18.9 receiving average in AFC... Missed 14 games in '86 and '87 because of injuries... Scored 13 TDs in '85... Hasn't topped six since... NFL Rookie of Year in '84 when he scored 11 TDs and went to Pro Bowl... Twenty-third player selected in '84 draft... Starred at Southern Mississippi... Born Aug. 9, 1962, in New Orleans.

GARY ANDERSON 31 5-11 170   Kicker

Became Steelers' all-time leading scorer, breaking 11-year-old record of 731 points held by Roy Gerela... His 818 points make him seventh among active NFL players... Was a big part of Steelers' late run, going 7-for-7 in playoffs... His 48- and 50-yard kicks at Houston were longest ever by a Steeler in postseason ... Made 21 of 30 tries in regular season... Was 5-for-8 from 30-39 yards and 9-for-15 from 40-49... Has played in two Pro Bowls... Seventh-round pick by Buffalo in '82 but was cut in camp. Steelers signed him and he made all-rookie ... Set NCAA record with 87.4 percent accuracy at Syracuse... Also played rugby and soccer in college... 1989 salary: $400,000 ... Born July 16, 1959, in Parys, South Africa, and moved to Downington, Pa., after high school.

CARNELL LAKE 23 6-0 205 — Safety

Rookie safety hits like a linebacker, the position he played at UCLA... Started 15 games and led team with five fumble recoveries... Led team in playoffs with 15 tackles... Sixth with 70 tackles... Runs 40-yard dash in 4.42 seconds... Second-round draft choice... Had 24½ sacks in college, including 13 as a junior... In high school, rushed for 956 yards and 12 TDs in first five games of senior year, then suffered injury... Born July 15, 1967, in Salt Lake City, Utah.

DWAYNE WOODRUFF 33 6-0 198 — Cornerback

Dean of Steelers' defense led club with four interceptions... Has 34 pickoffs in 10 years to rank fifth in team history... Third on club with 81 tackles... Only remaining player from Steelers' last Super Bowl champions... Was only player in Steeler secondary with more than three years of NFL experience entering '89... Started last nine seasons... Has had at least four interceptions each of the past five years... Has led club last four... Sixth-round draft pick out of Louisville in 1979... Beat out Tony Dungy for roster spot... Played receiver and running back first two years of college... Graduated from Duquesne Law School in '88... Born Feb. 18, 1957, in Bowling Green, Ky.

GREG LLOYD 25 6-2 224 — Linebacker

Came out of nowhere to lead team with seven sacks... Also finished second in tackles (92), fumble recoveries (3) and interceptions (3)... Had just 33 tackles and a half-sack entering '89... Missed first 1½ seasons with severe knee injuries... Sixth-round pick out of Fort Valley State in '87... Won Steelers' 1988 Ed Block Courage Award... Graduated 28th in high-school class of 250... Born May 26, 1965, in Miami.

COACH CHUCK NOLL: Fans wanted him run out of town a year ago, suggesting he was over the hill ... He responded by announcing he would return, then taking a no-name team to the playoffs ... In 21st season with Steelers, he won AFC Coach of Year, presented by pro football writers ... Showed his experience and poise by not panicking after being outscored, 92-10, in first two games ... Players were impressed by way he never changed his demeanor ... Only NFL coach to win four Super Bowls ... One of just four men to have coached same team for 21 consecutive seasons ... Went 1-13 in first season as head coach, then slowly built a dynasty ... Was an assistant under Sid Gillman with Chargers and Don Shula with Colts ... Was team captain at Dayton ... Twenty-first-round draft choice by Cleveland in '53 ... Played guard and linebacker for seven NFL seasons, including two NFL titles ... In 37 years of pro football, he has been in post-season 23 times ... Has 177-132-1 regular-season record ... Born Jan. 5, 1932, in Cleveland.

LONGEST PASS PLAY

TERRY BRADSHAW TO MARK MALONE

Mark Malone's lone NFL reception occurred in grand fashion. The Steelers' backup quarterback pulled in a 90-yard touchdown pass from Terry Bradshaw in a 24-21 loss to Seattle on Nov. 8, 1981.

It was no trick play. Malone came up with a sore elbow in the 1981 training camp, so coach Chuck Noll had the Arizona State product run pass routes. However, Malone suffered a knee injury in camp and missed the first eight games of the season. He returned late in the year for the game at Seattle and made his lone career start as a receiver before returning to quarterback as the starter for the final two contests.

Current Steeler stars Bubby Brister and Louis Lipps connected for the club's second-longest pass play, an 89-yard touchdown against Philadelphia in 1988.

INDIVIDUAL STEELER RECORDS

Rushing

Most Yards Game:	218	John Fuqua, vs Philadelphia, 1970
Season:	1,246	Franco Harris, 1975
Career:	11,950	Franco Harris, 1972-83

Passing

Most TD Passes Game:	5	Terry Bradshaw, vs Atlanta, 1981
	5	Mark Malone, vs Indianapolis, 1985
Season:	28	Terry Bradshaw, 1978
Career:	210	Terry Bradshaw, 1970-82

Receiving

Most TD Passes Game:	4	Roy Jefferson, vs Atlanta, 1968
Season:	12	Buddy Dial, 1961
	12	Louis Lipps, 1985
Career:	63	John Stallworth, 1974-87

Scoring

Most Points Game:	24	Ray Mathews, vs Cleveland, 1954
	24	Roy Jefferson, vs Atlanta, 1968
Season:	139	Gary Anderson, 1985
Career:	818	Gary Anderson, 1982-89
Most TDs Game:	4	Ray Mathews, vs Cleveland, 1954
	4	Roy Jefferson, vs Atlanta, 1968
Season:	14	Franco Harris, 1976
Career:	100	Franco Harris, 1972-83

SAN DIEGO CHARGERS

TEAM DIRECTORY: Chairman/Pres.: Alex G. Spanos; Vice Chairman: Dean Spanos; Dir. Administration: Jack Teele; GM: Bobby Beathard; Dir. Pub. Rel.: Bill Johnston; Head Coach: Dan Henning. Home field: San Diego Jack Murphy Stadium (60,750). Colors: Navy, white and gold.

SCOUTING REPORT

OFFENSE: The Jim McMahon experiment didn't work and he was released. The brash former Chicago Bear was 4-7 as a starter before giving way to strong-armed rookie Billy Joe Tolliver, who appears to be the team's leader of the future. Tolliver threw for more than 300 yards in two of his five starts.

The Chargers (6-10) were forced to look for new stars in '89

Pro Bowler Anthony Miller was Chargers' MVP.

because of the year-long holdout of running back Gary Anderson. One of those who emerged was the surprising Marion Butts, a seventh-round pick who was targeted for special teams. Butts led the club with 683 yards rushing and nine rushing touchdowns.

The Chargers gained quality depth at running back in Plan B, signing Ronnie Harmon from Buffalo, Thomas Sanders from Chicago and Joe Mickles from Washington.

San Diego has the ingredients for an exciting passing game, with Pro Bowler Anthony Miller and Quinn Early catching Tolliver's passes.

The Chargers need help on the offensive line to go along with center Courtney Hall, a standout as a rookie.

DEFENSE: A defensive resurgence took place in San Diego last year, and the unit figures to remain tough to beat, especially with the drafting of outside linebacker Junior Seau. The Chargers held opponents to 20 points or less in 13 of their final 14 games.

The ferocious pass rush makes it all work, with Lee Williams (AFC-leading 14 sacks), Leslie O'Neal (12½) and Burt Grossman (10) coming from all directions. The Chargers' 48 sacks topped the AFC.

The quarterback-hounding has made a good secondary better. Opponents scored just 15 passing touchdowns in '89, thanks to sticky coverage by cornerback Gil Byrd. After going without an interception in '87, Byrd has seven in each of the past two seasons. Overall, the Chargers ranked No. 4 in the NFL against the pass.

O'Neal is listed as a linebacker, but plays end as well. The rest of the linebackers are overshadowed by the line and the DBs, but Gary Plummer has led the club in tackles four years in a row.

KICKING GAME: The Chargers signed punter John Kidd away from the Bills in Plan B. Kidd (39.4 avg.) should be even better away from the snow and ice of Buffalo. Chris Bahr, who hit on 17-of-25 field-goal attempts last year, is adequate.

Miller is a game-breaker on kickoff returns. He ranked fourth in the league last year with a 25.4 average.

THE ROOKIES: The AFC's top pass rush got better with the addition of USC's Seau, the fifth player taken in the draft. Seau started just one season at USC and was used almost solely as a pass-rusher. Linebacker Jeff Mills is fast but didn't stand out at Nebraska. Sixth-round quarterback John Friesz threw for nearly 3,000 yards in each of his three seasons as an Idaho starter.

CHARGERS VETERAN ROSTER

HEAD COACH—Dan Henning. Assistant Coaches—Gunther Cunningham, Alex Gibbs, Mike Haluchak, Bobby Jackson, Charlie Joiner, Ron Lynn, LeCharls McDaniel, Jim Mora, Larry Pasquale, Jack Reilly, Ted Tollner, Ed White.

No.	Name	Pos.	Ht.	Wt.	NFL Exp.	College
15	Archer, David	QB	6-2	208	7	Iowa State
44	Bayless, Martin	S	6-2	212	7	Bowling Green
82	Bernstine, Rod	RB	6-3	238	4	Texas A&M
58	Brandon, David	LB	6-4	230	4	Memphis State
35	Butts, Marion	RB	6-1	248	2	Florida State
22	Byrd, Gill	CB	5-11	198	8	San Jose State
46	Caravello, Joe	RB	6-3	270	4	Tulane
	Carney, John	K	5-11	160	2	Notre Dame
88	Cox, Arthur	TE	6-2	277	8	Texas Southern
87	Early, Quinn	WR	6-0	190	3	Iowa
51	Figaro, Cedric	LB	6-2	250	3	Notre Dame
25	Glenn, Vencie	S	6-0	192	5	Indiana State
92	Grossman, Burt	DE	6-6	270	2	Pittsburgh
53	Hall, Courtney	C	6-1	269	2	Rice
	Harmon, Ronnie	RB	5-11	200	5	Iowa
	Hill, Nate	DE	6-4	275	2	Auburn
97	Hinkle, George	DE	6-5	269	3	Arizona
86	Holland, Jamie	WR	6-1	195	4	Ohio State
79	Howard, Joey	T	6-5	305	2	Tennessee
	Kidd, John	P	6-3	208	7	Northwestern
24	Lyles, Lester	S	6-3	200	6	Virginia
31	McEwen, Craig	RB	6-1	220	4	Utah
60	McKnight, Dennis	C-G	6-3	280	8	Drake
	Mickles, Joe	RB	5-10	221	2	Mississippi
83	Miller, Anthony	WR	5-11	185	3	Tennessee
69	Miller, Les	NT	6-7	293	4	Fort Hayes State
20	Nelson, Darrin	RB	5-9	185	9	Stanford
91	O'Neal, Leslie	LB	6-4	259	4	Oklahoma State
85	Parker, Andy	TE	6-5	245	7	Utah
78	Patten, Joel	T	6-7	307	6	Duke
75	Phillips, Joe	NT	6-5	275	4	Southern Methodist
	Plummer, Bruce	S	6-1	203	4	Mississippi State
50	Plummer, Gary	LB	6-2	240	5	California
7	Reveiz, Fuad	K	5-11	216	4	Tennessee
65	Richards, David	G-T	6-4	310	3	UCLA
98	Robinson, Gerald	DE	6-3	262	3	Auburn
	Rodenhauser, Mark	C	6-5	263	3	Illinois State
	Rolling, Henry	LB	6-2	225	3	Nevada-Reno
	Sanders, Thomas	RB	5-11	203	6	Texas A&M
30	Seale, Sam	CB	5-9	185	7	Western State (Colo.)
	Simmons, Mike	G	6-4	285	2	Indiana State
54	Smith, Billy Ray	LB	6-3	236	8	Arkansas
43	Spencer, Tim	RB	6-1	223	6	Ohio State
76	Thompson, Broderick	G-T	6-4	295	5	Kansas
11	Tolliver, Billy Joe	QB	6-1	218	2	Texas Tech
	Toth, Tom	G	6-5	282	5	Western Michigan
13	Vlasic, Mark	QB	6-3	206	3	Iowa
80	Walker, Wayne	WR	5-8	162	2	Texas Tech
67	Williams, Larry	G	6-5	290	4	Notre Dame
99	Williams, Lee	DE	6-5	271	7	Bethune-Cookman
59	Woodard, Ken	LB	6-1	220	9	Tuskegee Institute
80	Yarber, Eric	WR	5-8	152	2	Idaho

TOP DRAFT CHOICES

Rd.	Name	Sel. No.	Pos.	Ht.	Wt.	College
1	Seau, Junior	5	LB	6-3	243	USC
3	Mills, Jeff	57	LB	6-3	227	Nebraska
3	Goeas, Leo	60	G	6-3	285	Hawaii
3	Wilson, Walter	67	WR	5-10	180	East Carolina
6	Friesz, John	138	QB	6-4	209	Idaho

290 THE COMPLETE HANDBOOK OF PRO FOOTBALL

OUTLOOK: The future is bright for the Chargers. They won their final two games of '89, against Kansas City and Denver, with five rookie starters, then hired personnel whiz Bobby Beathard. This won't be a playoff year, but it will be another step in that direction.

CHARGER PROFILES

LESLIE O'NEAL 26 6-4 259   Linebacker

Completed courageous comeback from knee injury that kept him out almost two years... Led all AFC linebackers with 12½ sacks, third overall, after switch from defensive end... Selected as Pro Bowl reserve... Second on team with 96 tackles... Had 6½ sacks from Weeks 8-10, including 3½ on Eagles' Randall Cunningham... Tackled Eric Dickerson for losses five times in Week 12... Had 12½ sacks as rookie before injury on Nov. 30, 1986... Missed final three games, but still named NFL Defensive Rookie of Year... In all, injury kept him out 23 months... Returned to limited action in '88, getting four sacks in five-week span... As rookie, had five sacks in a game vs. Dallas... Eighth player chosen in '86 draft... All-American at Oklahoma State, where he was runnerup for Lombardi Award as senior... Had 31 sacks in final three college seasons... Born May 7, 1964, in Little Rock, Ark.

LEE WILLIAMS 27 6-5½ 271   Defensive End

Quickly closing in on club sack record... Has 57½ in six seasons and trails Gary Johnson's 67... Led AFC with 14 sacks and was named Pro Bowl starter for second straight season... Has 56½ sacks over last five seasons, second in AFC to Bruce Smith's 57½... Played often as defensive tackle in 4-3 alignment... Fifth player selected in 1984 supplemental draft after playing a season with Los Angeles Express of USFL... Had 27 sacks in final two years at Bethune-Cookman... Has degree in business administration... Born Oct. 15, 1962, in Fort Lauderdale, Fla.

SAN DIEGO CHARGERS 291

GILL BYRD 29 5-11 198 — Cornerback

Has seven interceptions in each of past two seasons after being shut out in '87... Has 25 in seven-year career to tie Kenny Graham for second on team's all-time list... His 14 interceptions over last two seasons tie Jets' Erik McMillan and Browns' Felix Wright for most in NFL... Shunned again in Pro Bowl voting... Voted team's Most Inspirational Player by teammates for second consecutive year... Twenty-third player taken in '83 draft, he won starting job in first mini-camp... Walk-on at San Jose State who started four years, finishing with 12 interceptions... Has degree in finance... One of NFL's most active in charity efforts... Uncle Mac Byrd played for Rams and Vikings... Born Feb. 20, 1961, in San Francisco.

ANTHONY MILLER 25 5-11 185 — Wide Receiver

Fifth in AFC with career-high 75 receptions and second with 1,252 yards... Rewarded with trip to Pro Bowl and selection as team MVP... His 11 TDs are most for Chargers since Chuck Muncie's 13 in '83... His 10 receiving TDs were most since Wes Chandler had 10 in '85... Caught 49 more passes than any other Charger... Had five 100-yard games in '89... Had 91-yard kickoff return for TD vs. Raiders... Third in AFC with 25.4 kick-return average... Caught 36 passes and scored three receiving TDs as rookie and returned a kickoff 93 yards for a TD... Finished second to Redskin Darrell Green in NFL Fastest Man Competition... Fifteenth player and fourth receiver taken in '88 draft... Went to San Diego State on track scholarship, switched to Pasadena City College, then to Tennessee... Has run 100 meters in 10.3 seconds... Born April 15, 1965, in Pasadena, Cal.

BILLY JOE TOLLIVER 24 6-1 218 — Quarterback

Rookie showed he can be Chargers' quarterback of the future, and probably the present, especially with the release of Jim McMahon... Started final four games of '89, winning final two... In all, started five games with two 300-yard games... Final stats: 89-for-185 for 1,097 yards, five TDs and eight interceptions... Only QB to throw for over 300 yards vs. Broncos in '89... His 350 yards vs. Washington is third-highest total ever in NFL for rookie... Missed first six weeks of season after breaking collarbone in preseason finale... Had thrown for 439 yards and four TDs in five quarters... Second-round draft pick out of Texas Tech... Chargers traded third-, fourth- and seventh-round picks to move into position to pick him... Holds school records for yards (6,756), attempts (1,007), completions (493) and TD passes (38)... Four-year starter who threw for conference-record 422 yards as freshman... Used 92 mph fastball to throw 14 no-hitters in high school... Born Feb. 7, 1966, in Dallas.

MARION BUTTS 24 6-1 248   **Running Back**

People around NFL were asking Marion Who? as this seventh-round pick racked up the points... Drafted to play special teams, he led club with 639 yards and nine TDs despite starting just five games... Ranked fourth in rushing among NFL rookies... Had a club-record 39 carries in Week 15 for 176 yards... Accounted for 10 of 12 first downs in that game... Gained just 137 yards as senior at Florida State... Played two seasons at Northeast Oklahoma JC... Was told to never play football again after breaking leg in high school... Born Aug. 1, 1966, in Worth County, Ga.

VENCIE GLENN 25 6-0 192   **Safety**

Dependable four-year veteran has played in 52 consecutive games at free safety... Tied career-high with four interceptions... Returned a fumble 81 yards for a TD... Holds club record for longest return of interception, 103 yards... Has blocked two punts. Both were returned for TD... Club's 1987 Outstanding Defensive Player... Drafted by Patriots in second round of '86 draft, but Chargers traded fifth-round pick for him after four games of '86 season... Set Indiana State record with 17 interceptions... Has degree in business management... Father George coached at Grambling under Eddie Robinson from 1960-73... Born Oct. 26, 1964, in Grambling, La.

SAN DIEGO CHARGERS 293

COURTNEY HALL 22 6-1½ 269   Center

Youngest player in '89 draft started every game as rookie... Only other rookie in NFL to start every game was Atlanta receiver Shawn Miller... Beat out 14-year veteran Don Macek for starting job... Was first offensive lineman to be named Rice's MVP in 20 years... Benched 430 and squatted 650 in college... Led all players at rookie combine with 36 reps at 225 pounds... Always has played with older kids. Attended nursery school at age two, kindergarten at four, high school at 12 and college at 16... Is seven course hours from graduation with dual major in economics and business... Plans to earn master's degree in business... Born Aug. 26, 1968, in Los Angeles.

COACH DAN HENNING: Former Charger backup quarterback has raised hopes in San Diego after just one season... Hired after two seasons as Redskins' offensive coordinator... Was his second stint with Redskins... Between stops in Washington, which included two Super Bowl victories, he served four years as head coach of Atlanta Falcons, for whom he once was an assistant... Also worked as assistant for Oilers, Jets, Dolphins, Florida State and Virginia Tech... Ranked 14th in passing nationally as senior at William & Mary... Was briefly a backup quarterback for Chargers in the AFL, but did not attempt a pass... Played two years in Continental Football League... Is 28-51-1 as NFL head coach... Born June 21, 1952, in the Bronx, N.Y.

LONGEST PASS PLAY

JACK KEMP TO KEITH LINCOLN

Halfback Keith Lincoln began an impressive Chargers' career in 1961 as San Diego went 12-2 and reached the AFL championship game. One of the Chargers' toughest games that season

294 THE COMPLETE HANDBOOK OF PRO FOOTBALL

came at Denver on Nov. 12, when Lincoln's 91-yard reception from Jack Kemp helped put the Broncos away, 19-16.

Lincoln, a second-round draft pick out of Washington State, played for the Chargers from 1961-66 and again in 1968. He is fourth on the club's all-time rushing list with 2,698 yards.

Kemp had a splendid season and appeared to have a home in San Diego. But the Chargers lost him in 1962 when they tried to slip him through waivers with a broken hand. Buffalo picked up Kemp, and the Chargers' 1962 season was a 4-10 mess.

Leslie O'Neal came back to lead AFC linebackers in sacks.

INDIVIDUAL CHARGER RECORDS

Rushing

Most Yards Game:	206	Keith Lincoln, vs Boston, 1964
Season:	1,179	Earnest Jackson, 1984
Career:	4,963	Paul Lowe, 1960-67

Passing

Most TD Passes Game:	6	Dan Fouts, vs Oakland, 1981
Season:	33	Dan Fouts, 1981
Career:	254	Dan Fouts, 1973-87

Receiving

Most TD Passes Game:	5	Kellen Winslow, vs Oakland, 1981
Season:	14	Lance Alworth, 1965
Career:	81	Lance Alworth, 1962-70

Scoring

Most Points Game:	30	Kellen Winslow, vs Oakland, 1981
Season:	118	Rolf Benirschke, 1980
Career:	766	Rolf Benirschke, 1977-86
Most TDs Game:	5	Kellen Winslow, vs Oakland, 1981
Season:	19	Chuck Muncie, 1981
Career:	83	Lance Alworth, 1962-70

SEATTLE SEAHAWKS

TEAM DIRECTORY: Pres./GM: Tom Flores; VP/Asst. GM: Chuck Allen; Dir. Player Personnel: Mike Allman; VP/Dir. Pub. Rel.: Gary Wright; Head Coach: Chuck Knox. Home field: Kingdome (64,757). Colors; Blue, green and silver.

SCOUTING REPORT

OFFENSE: The post-Warner era begins in Seattle. Curt Warner, the team's star running back for the past six years, fled to the Rams through free agency. The departure was expected, but the problem is that the Seahawks (7-9) have little to take his place. John L. Williams is an outstanding player, but while he is a versatile fullback, there is doubt he can make it as a halfback. With Warner, the club ranked 25th running the ball.

Williams has become the Seahawks' workhorse. He gained 499 rushing yards—second to Warner's 631—and caught 76 passes, tops in the NFL for a running back.

Steve Largent's stay in Seattle also has ended. While the standout wide receiver awaits his trip to the Hall of Fame, Brian Blades becomes the club's only true pass-catching threat.

And while we're ending eras, how about Dave Krieg's? Krieg lingered in the middle of the pack of AFC quarterbacks in '89. This might be the year untested Kelly Stouffer takes over.

The Seattle offensive line is suitable, but all the blocking in the world won't help when your team fumbles the ball 43 times, including 18 by Krieg.

DEFENSE: Rufus Porter, a pass-rushing specialist, was a surprise last year with 10½ sacks. After him, though, the Seahawk defense was less than thrilling. The hope is that their first two draft picks—tackle Cortez Kennedy and linebacker Terry Wooden—will produce a turnaround.

Nose tackle Joe Nash had a good 1989, but the line is old and slipping.

Forget The Boz. Brian Bosworth isn't expected to return from his years of shoulder injuries. Inside linebackers David Wyman and Darren Comeaux are steady.

Nesby Glasgow is a dependable strong safety, but he's 33. Free safety Eugene Robinson led the team with 102 tackles and five interceptions.

Tireless Dave Krieg keeps adding to Seahawk marks.

KICKING GAME: Seattle re-signed Bobby Joe Edmonds in Plan B. They lost the kick-return specialist to Detroit a year ago.

Norm Johnson struggled in '89, hitting just 15-of-25 field-goal attempts, including 1-of-5 from 50 yards and out and 4-of-8 from 40-49 yards. He is expected to bounce back. Punter Ruben Rodriguez's net average dropped from 36.8 to 32.9, and the club signed former Falcon Rick Donnelly to challenge.

Porter has been voted into the Pro Bowl the past two years because of his special-teams excellence.

THE ROOKIES: The Seahawks traded up to grab Miami's Kennedy as the No. 3 overall pick. The 295-pound Kennedy plays at a frantic pace and will be outstanding in Seattle's new 4-3 defense if he controls his weight. Syracuse's Wooden will upgrade the pass rush with his quick blitzing ability. Baylor safety Robert Blackmon has great instincts and shouldn't take long to strengthen a soft secondary.

OUTLOOK: The aging Seahawks are slipping while the rest of the AFC West is on the rise. Finding a productive halfback is a necessity. Otherwise, last place appears likely.

SEAHAWKS VETERAN ROSTER

HEAD COACH—Chuck Knox. Assistant Coaches—John Becker, Tom Catlin, George Dyer, Chick Harris, Ken Meyer, Rod Perry, Russ Purnell, Frank Raines, Kent Stephenson, Rusty Tillman, Joe Vitt.

No.	Name	Pos.	Ht.	Wt.	NFL Exp.	College
50	Ahrens, Dave	LB	6-4	245	10	Wisconsin
65	Bailey, Edwin	G	6-4	273	10	South Carolina State
89	Blades, Brian	WR	5-11	184	3	Miami
55	Bosworth, Brian	LB	6-2	236	3	Oklahoma
8	Bouyer, Willie	WR	6-3	200	2	Michigan State
64	Britz, Darrick	G	6-3	270	4	Oregon State
77	Bryant, Jeff	DE	6-5	277	9	Clemson
59	Cain, Joe	LB	6-1	228	2	Oregon Tech
88	Chadwick, Jeff	WR	6-3	190	8	Grand Valley State
84	Clark, Louis	WR	6-0	199	4	Mississippi State
53	Comeaux, Darren	LB	6-1	239	9	Arizona State
3	Donnelly, Rick	P	6-0	190	6	Wyoming
31	Edmonds, Bobby Joe	RB	5-11	186	5	Arkansas
54	Feasel, Grant	C	6-7	279	6	Abilene Christian
44	Fenner, Derrick	RB	6-3	229	2	North Carolina
90	Franklin, Jethro	DE	6-1	258	2	Fresno State
22	Glasgow, Nesby	S	5-10	187	12	Washington
79	Green, Jacob	DE	6-3	254	11	Texas A&M
29	Harper, Dwayne	CB	5-11	174	3	South Carolina State
33	Harris, Elroy	RB	5-9	218	2	Eastern Kentucky
63	Hart, Roy	NT	6-1	279	2	South Carolina
66	Heck, Andy	T	6-6	291	2	Notre Dame
85	Heller, Ron	TE	6-3	236	4	Oregon State
23	Hunter, Patrick	CB	5-11	186	5	Nevada-Reno
26	Jefferson, James	CB	6-1	199	2	Texas A&I
24	Jenkins, Melvin	CB	5-10	182	4	Cincinnati
9	Johnson, Norm	K	6-2	197	9	UCLA
30	Jones, James	RB	6-2	229	8	Florida
81	Kane, Tommy	WR	5-11	176	3	Syracuse
15	Kemp, Jeff	QB	6-0	201	10	Dartmouth
58	Kimmel, Jamie	LB	6-3	235	3	Syracuse
17	Krieg, Dave	QB	6-1	192	11	Milton
70	Mattes, Ron	T	6-6	302	5	Virginia
40	McLemore, Chris	RB	6-1	230	3	Arizona
86	McNeal, Travis	TE	6-3	248	2	Tenn.-Chattanooga
71	Millard, Bryan	G	6-5	281	7	Texas
91	Miller, Darrin	LB	6-1	236	3	Tennessee
72	Nash, Joe	NT	6-2	269	9	Boston College
97	Porter, Rufus	LB	6-1	221	3	Southern University
96	Ridgle, Elston	DE	6-5	270	2	Nevada-Reno
41	Robinson, Eugene	S	6-0	186	6	Colgate
5	Rodriguez, Ruben	P	6-2	217	4	Arizona
82	Skansi, Paul	WR	5-11	186	8	Washington
11	Stouffer, Kelly	QB	6-3	207	3	Colorado State
56	Tofflemire, Joe	C	6-2	274	2	Arizona
87	Tyler, Robert	TE	6-5	257	2	South Carolina State
32	Williams, John L.	RB	5-11	228	5	Florida
57	Woods, Tony	LB	6-4	259	4	Pittsburgh
92	Wyman, David	LB	6-2	242	4	Stanford

TOP DRAFT CHOICES

Rd.	Name	Sel. No.	Pos.	Ht.	Wt.	College
1	Kennedy, Cortez	3	DT	6-3	293	Miami
2	Wooden, Terry	29	LB	6-2	232	Syracuse
2	Blackmon, Robert	34	DB	5-11	198	Baylor
4	Warren, Chris	89	RB	6-1	225	Ferrum
5	Hayes, Eric	119	DT	6-3	290	Florida State

SEAHAWK PROFILES

DAVE KRIEG 31 6-1 192　　　　　　　　　　Quarterback

Continues to break Jim Zorn's Seahawk passing records... Had most prolific season since '85, throwing for 3,309 yards... Threw 21 TD passes and 21 interceptions... Started in Pro Bowl in place of John Elway, who was named to replace Boomer Esiason... Was third Pro Bowl appearance... Broke team records for season competitions (286) and career completions (1,644)... Also set career yardage mark with 20,858... Had NFL-record 18 fumbles, including eight involving exchanges with center Grant Feasel... Had third 3,000-yard season of career... Set Seattle records of 3,671 yards and 32 TDs in '84... Was signed in '80 as unknown free agent out of now-defunct Milton College, where he threw for 1,818 yards as a senior... 1989 salary: $850,000... Born Oct. 20, 1958, in Iola, Wis.

BRIAN BLADES 25 5-11 184　　　　　　　Wide Receiver

As one star receiver (Steve Largent) exits, up rises another... Was lesser-known of Blades brothers in college, but has outplayed brother Bennie, a Lion safety... Named to Pro Bowl as reserve... Joined Largent as only Seahawk receivers ever to top 1,000 yards in a season... Caught 77 passes, second in AFC, including five TDs... Fell two shy of Largent's club record of 79 catches, set in '85... Had five 100-yard games... Led NFL rookie receivers in '88 with eight TDs... Second-round pick out of Miami, where he was overshadowed by flamboyant Michael Irvin, now with the Cowboys... Second on Miami's all-time TD reception list with 15. Irvin leads with 26... Born July 24, 1965, in Fort Lauderdale, Fla.

JOHN L. WILLIAMS 25 5-11 228　　　　　　　　Fullback

Not your typical NFL fullback, Williams continues to be dual rushing-receiving threat... Had club records for running back in receptions (76) and receiving yards (657), breaking own records of 58 and 651, set in '88... Made 12 receptions for 129 yards on Dec. 17 vs. Raiders... He and Blades became first pair in team history to catch over 70 passes in same season

...Team's No. 2 rusher with 499 yards...Scored six receiving TDs but just one rushing...First-round pick out of Florida in '86 ...Has been a starter since arrival...Gators' No. 3 all-time rusher with 2,409 yards...Born Nov. 23, 1964, in Palatka, Fla.

DAVID WYMAN 26 6-2 242   Linebacker

Steady, instinctive player on the inside who has teamed with Darren Comeaux to fill void left by injured Brian Bosworth...Ranked second behind Eugene Robinson on Seahawks' tackle chart for second straight season...Recorded 98 stops, one more than in '88...Second-round pick out of Stanford in '87 who played in just four games as a rookie...Was an All-American as a senior...Gained notice by making 27 tackles in a game vs. Southern Cal...1989 salary: $255,000...Born March 31, 1964, in San Diego.

RUFUS PORTER 24 6-1 221   Linebacker

Efficiency at its best...Nobody expected this kind of production from a special-teams whiz ...Played only on passing downs but managed 10½ sacks, ranking fifth in AFC...Also forced team-high four fumbles...Selected to Pro Bowl in each of his two NFL seasons as special-teams player...Led club with 13 special-teams tackles and four tackles inside the 20...Had three sacks and two forced fumbles on Oct. 1 vs. San Diego...Was signed as undrafted free agent out of Southern in '88...Had 18 sacks in college career and was second-team all-Southwestern Athletic Conference twice...Born May 18, 1966, in Amite, La.

JACOB GREEN 33 6-3 254   Defensive End

Seahawks' all-time sack leader is finally slipping in his pursuit of quarterbacks...Tied career-low with three sacks in '89, a drop from nine the year before...Has 97½ sacks in 10 seasons, including 16 in '83...Has 79 sacks since '82, when NFL began keeping the stat ...That ranks third behind Lawrence Taylor (104) and Dexter Manley (91)...Left end was eighth on club with 47 tackles...Holds team record with

14 fumble recoveries... Made Pro Bowl in 1986 and '87... First-round pick out of Texas A&M in '80... Had 38 sacks with Aggies, including 20 as senior... 1989 salary: $800,000... Born Jan. 21, 1957, in Pasadena, Tex.

NORM JOHNSON 30 6-2 197 — Kicker

Seahawks' all-time leading scorer turned in lowest point total (72) since '82, when he played just nine games as a rookie... Was 15-for-25 on field goals, but was asked to try five from beyond 50 yards. He made one... Has 708 points in eight seasons, including team-record 110 in '84... Made all 27 PATs in '89 and hasn't missed in a regular-season game since '85, a string of 156... He missed a PAT in an '88 playoff game... Made five-of-seven from 50-plus yards in '86... Went to Pro Bowl in '84... Signed as undrafted free agent out of UCLA in '82... Played tight end in high school... 1989 salary: $315,000... Born May 31, 1960, in Inglewood, Cal.

EUGENE ROBINSON 27 6-0 186 — Safety

Defensive co-captain led club with 102 tackles... Second straight year he has been the tackle leader... Also led club with career-high five interceptions... Steady free safety who made club as free agent in '85 and has started since '86... Unheralded at Colgate, where he earned degree in computer science... Had three interceptions in '86 and '87 but dipped to one in '88... Born May 28, 1963, in Hartford, Conn.

JOE NASH 29 6-2 269 — Nose Tackle

Veteran plugger in middle had best year of career... Made 92 tackles, topping career-high of 87 in '85... Only one other Seattle defensive lineman has ever had more tackles in a season... Had 12 tackles, 2½ sacks and two forced fumbles at Cincinnati on Dec. 10... Blocked team-record three field goals in '89, giving him seven for career.... Didn't miss a game because of injury until '88... Selected to Pro Bowl in '84 and '85... Had nine sacks in '85... Signed as free agent out of Boston College in '82... Works for real estate company in off-season... Born Oct. 11, 1960, in Boston.

ANDY HECK 23 6-6 291　　　　　　　　　　　　　　　　Tackle

Talented athlete who will be Seahawks' left tackle for years to come... Played in all 16 games as a rookie, with nine starts—six at left tackle and one at tight end... No. 15 in draft after playing at Notre Dame... Played tight end for Irish for three years, then switched to line prior to senior season... Started every game at tight end as a junior, catching five passes for 59 yards and a TD... Had 16 receptions and two TDs in college career... Has degree in American Studies... 1989 salary: $225,000, plus $1-million signing bonus. 1990 salary: $275,000... Born Jan. 1, 1967, in Fargo, N.D.

COACH CHUCK KNOX: Faces somewhat of a rebuilding job, but adjusting hasn't been a problem for Knox... In 17 seasons, has won 155 games... Only Don Shula (269) and Chuck Noll (177) have won more among active coaches... Regular-season winning percentage of 61.0 ranks only behind Shula's 69.0... Only NFL coach to win divisional titles with three different teams... Won with the Rams from 1973-77, Bills in '80 and Seahawks in '88... Eleven of his 17 teams have reached postseason, including four of his seven Seattle clubs... Is 65-45 with Seahawks and 155-98-1 overall... Was an NFL assistant for 10 seasons, with Jets and Lions... Coached at Wake Forest and Kentucky prior to moving to the pros... Played tackle at Juniata College in Huntington, Pa.... Has two years left on a $1 million-per-year contract... Born April 27, 1932, in Sewickley, Pa.

LONGEST PASS PLAY

JIM ZORN TO DAVID SIMS

Jim Zorn and David Sims provided the only bright spots for the Seahawks in a 42-20 loss to the Bengals at Seattle on Sept. 25, 1977. Sims, a running back who played for Seattle from 1977-79, gained 137 total yards, including a team-record 82-yard touchdown reception from Zorn. He also scored on a touchdown run.

Zorn was the Seahawk quarterback from 1974-84. He started

100 games and held the club all-time records in yards (20,122) and completions (1,593) until Dave Krieg passed him in 1989.

Sims, a seventh-round draft pick out of Georgia Tech, led the team in scoring in '78 with an NFL-leading 15 touchdowns.

INDIVIDUAL SEAHAWK RECORDS

Rushing

Most Yards Game:	207	Curt Warner, vs Kansas City, 1983
Season:	1,481	Curt Warner, 1986
Career:	6,705	Curt Warner, 1983-89

Passing

Most TD Passes Game:	5	Dave Krieg, vs Detroit, 1984
	5	Dave Krieg, vs San Diego, 1985
	5	Dave Krieg, vs LA Raiders, 1988
Season:	32	Dave Krieg, 1984
Career:	169	Dave Krieg, 1980-89

Receiving

Most TD Passes Game:	4	Daryl Turner, vs San Diego, 1985
Season:	13	Daryl Turner, 1985
Career:	100	Steve Largent, 1976-89

Scoring

Most Points Game:	24	Daryl Turner, vs San Diego, 1985
	24	Curt Warner, vs Denver, 1988
Season:	110	Norm Johnson, 1984
Career:	708	Norm Johnson, 1982-89
Most TDs Game:	4	Daryl Turner, vs San Diego, 1985
	4	Curt Warner, vs Denver, 1988
Season:	15	David Sims, 1978
	15	Sherman Smith, 1979
Career:	101	Steve Largent, 1976-89

OFFICIAL 1989 NFL STATISTICS

(Compiled by Elias Sports Bureau)

RUSHING

TOP TEN RUSHERS

	Att	Yards	Avg	Long	TD
Okoye, Christian, K.C.	370	1480	4.0	59	12
Sanders, Barry, Det.	280	1470	5.3	34	14
Dickerson, Eric, Ind.	314	1311	4.2	t21	7
Anderson, Neal, Chi.	274	1275	4.7	73	11
Hilliard, Dalton, N.O.	344	1262	3.7	40	13
Thomas, Thurman, Buff.	298	1244	4.2	38	6
Brooks, James, Cin.	221	1239	5.6	t65	7
Humphrey, Bobby, Den.	294	1151	3.9	40	7
Bell, Greg, Rams	272	1137	4.2	47	15
Craig, Roger, S.F.	271	1054	3.9	27	6

NFC – INDIVIDUAL RUSHERS

	Att	Yards	Avg	Long	TD
Sanders, Barry, Det.	280	1470	5.3	34	14
Anderson, Neal, Chi.	274	1275	4.7	73	11
Hilliard, Dalton, N.O.	344	1262	3.7	40	13
Bell, Greg, Rams	272	1137	4.2	47	15
Craig, Roger, S.F.	271	1054	3.9	27	6
Anderson, Ottis, Giants	325	1023	3.1	t36	14
Walker, Herschel, Dall.-Minn.	250	915	3.7	47	7
Riggs, Gerald, Wash.	201	834	4.1	58	4
Fullwood, Brent, G.B.	204	821	4.0	38	5
Settle, John, Atl.	179	689	3.8	20	3
Cunningham, Randall, Phil.	104	621	6.0	51	4
Tate, Lars, T.B.	167	589	3.5	48	8
Fenney, Rick, Minn.	151	588	3.9	25	4
Toney, Anthony, Phil.	172	582	3.4	44	3
Byner, Earnest, Wash.	134	580	4.3	24	7
Ferrell, Earl, Phoe.	149	502	3.4	t44	6

t = Touchdown
Leader based on yards gained

NFL STATISTICS 305

	Att	Yards	Avg	Long	TD
Byars, Keith, Phil.	133	452	3.4	t16	5
Palmer, Paul, Dall.	112	446	4.0	t63	2
Delpino, Robert, Rams	78	368	4.7	t32	1
Majkowski, Don, G.B.	75	358	4.8	20	5
Howard, William, T.B.	108	357	3.3	15	1
Morris, Jamie, Wash.	124	336	2.7	t12	2
Muster, Brad, Chi.	82	327	4.0	20	5
Rathman, Tom, S.F.	79	305	3.9	13	1
Aikman, Troy, Dall.	38	302	7.9	25	0
Tillman, Lewis, Giants	79	290	3.7	19	0
Harbaugh, Jim, Chi.	45	276	6.1	t26	3
Woodside, Keith, G.B.	46	273	5.9	t68	1
Wilder, James, T.B.	70	244	3.5	14	0
Montana, Joe, S.F.	49	227	4.6	19	3
Johnston, Daryl, Dall.	67	212	3.2	13	0
Jordan, Tony, Phoe.	83	211	2.5	15	2
Dozier, D.J., Minn.	46	207	4.5	38	0
Jones, Keith, Atl.	52	202	3.9	19	6
Gagliano, Bob, Det.	41	192	4.7	19	4
Anderson, Alfred, Minn.	52	189	3.6	14	2
Higgs, Mark, Phil.	49	184	3.8	13	0
Heyward, Craig, N.O.	49	183	3.7	15	1
Jordan, Buford, N.O.	38	179	4.7	32	3
Sherman, Heath, Phil.	40	177	4.4	37	2
Lang, Gene, Atl.	47	176	3.7	22	1
Mitchell, Stump, Phoe.	43	165	3.8	14	0
Gary, Cleveland, Rams	37	163	4.4	18	1
Carthon, Maurice, Giants	57	153	2.7	18	0
Peete, Rodney, Det.	33	148	4.5	t14	4
Sikahema, Vai, Phoe.	38	145	3.8	27	0
Simms, Phil, Giants	32	141	4.4	15	1
Stamps, Sylvester, T.B.	29	141	4.9	t21	1
Testaverde, Vinny, T.B.	25	139	5.6	16	0
Haddix, Michael, G.B.	44	135	3.1	10	0
Wilson, Wade, Minn.	32	132	4.1	23	1
Flagler, Terrence, S.F.	33	129	3.9	t29	1
Drummond, Robert, Phil.	32	127	4.0	16	0
Sanders, Thomas, Chi.	41	127	3.1	19	0
Young, Steve, S.F.	38	126	3.3	22	2
Meggett, Dave, Giants	28	117	4.2	18	0
Frazier, Paul, N.O.	25	112	4.5	21	1
Dupard, Reggie, N.E.-Wash.	37	111	3.0	19	1
Gentry, Dennis, Chi.	17	106	6.2	29	0
Paige, Tony, Det.	30	105	3.5	16	0
Clark, Jessie, Phoe.-Minn.	20	99	5.0	14	0
McGee, Buford, Rams	21	99	4.7	15	1

THE COMPLETE HANDBOOK OF PRO FOOTBALL

	Att	Yards	Avg	Long	TD
Fourcade, John, N.O.	14	91	6.5	14	1
Hogeboom, Gary, Phoe.	27	89	3.3	15	1
Hebert, Bobby, N.O.	25	87	3.5	11	0
Sargent, Broderick, Dall.	20	87	4.4	43	1
Tupa, Tom, Phoe.	15	75	5.0	13	0
Green, Gaston, Rams	26	73	2.8	9	0
Hostetler, Jeff, Giants	11	71	6.5	t19	2
Tomczak, Mike, Chi.	24	71	3.0	18	1
Fontenot, Herman, G.B.	17	69	4.1	19	1
Painter, Carl, Det.	15	64	4.3	9	0
Rypien, Mark, Wash.	26	56	2.2	15	1
Sydney, Harry, S.F.	9	56	6.2	18	0
Rouson, Lee, Giants	11	51	4.6	9	0
Suhey, Matt, Chi.	20	51	2.6	8	1
Green, Mark, Chi.	5	46	9.2	t37	1
Kemp, Perry, G.B.	5	43	8.6	14	0
Morse, Bobby, N.O.	2	43	21.5	39	0
Clack, Darryl, Dall.	14	40	2.9	17	2
Johnson, Richard, Det.	12	38	3.2	14	0
Jones, Hassan, Minn.	1	37	37.0	37	0
Smith, Don, T.B.	7	37	5.3	17	0
Wolfley, Ron, Phoe.	13	36	2.8	t5	1
Haynes, Michael, Atl.	4	35	8.8	21	0
Rice, Jerry, S.F.	5	33	6.6	17	0
Paterra, Greg, Atl.	9	32	3.6	8	0
Baker, Tony, Phoe.	20	31	1.6	6	0
Everett, Jim, Rams	25	31	1.2	t13	1
Dixon, James, Dall.	3	30	10.0	13	0
Henderson, Keith, S.F.	7	30	4.3	t11	1
Reichenbach, Mike, Phil.	1	30	30.0	30	0
Adams, George, Giants	9	29	3.2	8	0
Brown, Ron, Rams	6	27	4.5	12	0
Rosenbach, Timm, Phoe.	6	26	4.3	8	0
Rice, Allen, Minn.	6	25	4.2	10	0
Sharpe, Sterling, G.B.	2	25	12.5	26	0
Flowers, Kenny, Atl.	13	24	1.8	4	1
Teltschik, John, Phil.	1	23	23.0	23	0
Gray, Mel, Det.	3	22	7.3	14	0
Smith, J.T., Phoe.	2	21	10.5	11	0
Miller, Chris, Atl.	10	20	2.0	7	0
Clark, Gary, Wash.	2	19	9.5	11	0
Sanders, Ricky, Wash.	4	19	4.8	13	0
Carter, Anthony, Minn.	3	18	6.0	17	0
Jones, Ernie, Phoe.	1	18	18.0	18	0
Carter, Cris, Phil.	2	16	8.0	11	0
Walsh, Steve, Dall.	6	16	2.7	14	0

NFL STATISTICS

	Att	Yards	Avg	Long	TD
Tautalatasi, Junior, Dall. ...	6	15	2.5	6	0
Shepard, Derrick, Dall.	3	12	4.0	12	0
Hipple, Eric, Det.	2	11	5.5	10	1
Lewis, Leo, Minn.	1	11	11.0	11	0
Turner, Odessa, Giants	2	11	5.5	14	0
Ellard, Henry, Rams	2	10	5.0	6	0
Humphries, Stan, Wash.	5	10	2.0	9	0
Kramer, Tommy, Minn.	12	9	0.8	5	0
Monk, Art, Wash.	3	8	2.7	14	0
Turner, Floyd, N.O.	2	8	4.0	6	0
Workman, Vince, G.B.	4	8	2.0	3	1
Taylor, Brian, Chi.	2	7	3.5	7	0
Buford, Maury, Chi.	1	6	6.0	6	0
Ferguson, Joe, T.B.	4	6	1.5	7	0
Irvin, Michael, Dall.	1	6	6.0	6	0
Taylor, John, S.F.	1	6	6.0	6	0
McKinnon, Dennis, Chi.	3	5	1.7	3	0
Runager, Max, Phil.	2	5	2.5	5	0
Thornton, James, Chi.	1	4	4.0	4	0
Brown, Lomas, Det.	1	3	3.0	3	0
Holohan, Pete, Rams	1	3	3.0	3	0
Johnson, Ron, Phil.	1	3	3.0	3	0
Long, Chuck, Det.	3	2	0.7	6	0
Reasons, Gary, Giants	1	2	2.0	2	0
Ingram, Mark, Giants	1	1	1.0	1	0
Saxon, Mike, Dall.	1	1	1.0	1	0
Bates, Bill, Dall.	1	0	0.0	0	0
Fulhage, Scott, Atl.	1	0	0.0	0	0
Hatcher, Dale, Rams	1	0	0.0	0	0
Helton, Barry, S.F.	1	0	0.0	0	0
Millen, Hugh, Atl.	1	0	0.0	0	0
Winslow, George, N.O.	1	0	0.0	0	0
Anderson, Willie, Rams	1	-1	-1.0	-1	0
Coleman, Monte, Wash.	1	-1	-1.0	-1	0
Herrmann, Mark, Rams	2	-1	-0.5	0	0
Reaves, Willard, Wash.	1	-1	-1.0	-1	0
McDonald, Keith, Det.	1	-2	-2.0	-2	0
Cavanaugh, Matt, Phil.	2	-3	-1.5	0	0
Scott, Kevin, Dall.	2	-4	-2.0	-1	0
Williams, Doug, Wash.	1	-4	-4.0	-4	0
Peebles, Danny, T.B.	2	-6	-3.0	1	0
Hill, Lonzell, N.O.	1	-7	-7.0	-7	0
Carson, Carlos, Phil.	1	-9	-9.0	-9	0
Perriman, Brett, N.O.	1	-10	-10.0	-10	0
Morris, Ron, Chi.	1	-14	-14.0	-14	0
Dixon, Floyd, Atl.	2	-23	-11.5	0	0

AFC – INDIVIDUAL RUSHERS

	Att	Yards	Avg	Long	TD
Okoye, Christian, K.C.	370	1480	4.0	59	12
Dickerson, Eric, Ind.	314	1311	4.2	t21	7
Thomas, Thurman, Buff.	298	1244	4.2	38	6
Brooks, James, Cin.	221	1239	5.6	t65	7
Humphrey, Bobby, Den.	294	1151	3.9	40	7
Jackson, Bo, Raiders	173	950	5.5	t92	4
Stephens, John, N.E.	244	833	3.4	t35	7
Worley, Tim, Pitt.	195	770	3.9	38	5
Hector, Johnny, Jets	177	702	4.0	24	3
Butts, Marion, S.D.	170	683	4.0	t50	9
Smith, Sammie, Mia.	200	659	3.3	25	6
Metcalf, Eric, Clev.	187	633	3.4	t43	6
Warner, Curt, Sea.	194	631	3.3	34	3
Hoge, Merril, Pitt.	186	621	3.3	31	8
Perryman, Bob, N.E.	150	562	3.7	18	2
Kinnebrew, Larry, Buff.	131	533	4.1	25	6
Highsmith, Alonzo, Hou.	128	531	4.1	25	4
Spencer, Tim, S.D.	134	521	3.9	15	3
Williams, John L., Sea.	146	499	3.4	21	1
Smith, Steve, Raiders	117	471	4.0	21	1
Pinkett, Allen, Hou.	94	449	4.8	60	1
Vick, Roger, Jets	112	434	3.9	t39	5
Ball, Eric, Cin.	98	391	4.0	27	3
McNeil, Freeman, Jets	80	352	4.4	t19	2
Winder, Sammy, Den.	110	351	3.2	16	2
White, Lorenzo, Hou.	104	349	3.4	33	5
Nelson, Darrin, Minn.-S.D.	67	321	4.8	28	0
Rozier, Mike, Hou.	88	301	3.4	17	2
Bentley, Albert, Ind.	75	299	4.0	22	1
Allen, Marcus, Raiders	69	293	4.2	15	2
Jennings, Stanford, Cin.	83	293	3.5	17	2
Manoa, Tim, Clev.	87	289	3.3	22	3
Esiason, Boomer, Cin.	47	278	5.9	24	0
Moon, Warren, Hou.	70	268	3.8	19	4
Elway, John, Den.	48	244	5.1	31	3
Stradford, Troy, Mia.	66	240	3.6	13	1
Saxon, James, K.C.	58	233	4.0	19	3
Heard, Herman, K.C.	63	216	3.4	28	0
Logan, Marc, Mia.	57	201	3.5	14	0
Lipps, Louis, Pitt.	13	180	13.8	t58	1
Redden, Barry, Clev.	40	180	4.5	t38	1
Mueller, Vance, Raiders	48	161	3.4	19	2
Jones, Keith, Clev.	43	160	3.7	15	1
Krieg, Dave, Sea.	40	160	4.0	18	0

NFL STATISTICS 309

	Att	Yards	Avg	Long	TD
Davis, Kenneth, Buff.	29	149	5.1	21	1
Alexander, Jeff, Den.	45	146	3.2	11	2
Pelluer, Steve, K.C.	17	143	8.4	27	2
McMahon, Jim, S.D.	29	141	4.9	15	0
Bernstine, Rod, S.D.	15	137	9.1	t32	1
Kelly, Jim, Buff.	29	137	4.7	19	2
Williams, Warren, Pitt.	37	131	3.5	13	1
Mack, Kevin, Clev.	37	130	3.5	12	1
McNair, Todd, K.C.	23	121	5.3	25	0
Taylor, Craig, Cin.	30	111	3.7	16	3
Bratton, Mel, Den.	30	108	3.6	9	1
Harmon, Ronnie, Buff.	17	99	5.8	24	0
Oliphant, Mike, Clev.	15	97	6.5	t21	1
Woods, Ickey, Cin.	29	94	3.2	12	2
Trudeau, Jack, Ind.	35	91	2.6	17	2
Flutie, Doug, N.E.	16	87	5.4	22	0
Kosar, Bernie, Clev.	30	70	2.3	23	1
Brinson, Dana, S.D.	17	64	3.8	9	0
Brown, Anthony, Jets	12	63	5.3	17	0
Chandler, Chris, Ind.	7	57	8.1	23	1
Davenport, Ron, Mia.	14	56	4.0	9	1
Porter, Kerry, Raiders	13	54	4.2	23	0
Stone, Dwight, Pitt.	10	53	5.3	32	0
Allen, Marvin, N.E.	11	51	4.6	18	1
Jensen, Jim, Mia.	8	50	6.3	14	0
Hampton, Lorenzo, Mia.	17	47	2.8	9	0
Hunter, Ivy Joe, Ind.	13	47	3.6	11	0
Holland, Jamie, S.D.	6	46	7.7	24	0
Mueller, Jamie, Buff.	16	44	2.8	9	0
Sewell, Steve, Den.	7	44	6.3	10	0
Wilson, Marc, N.E.	7	42	6.0	11	0
Fenner, Derrick, Sea.	11	41	3.7	9	1
Beuerlein, Steve, Raiders	16	39	2.4	10	0
Secules, Scott, Mia.	4	39	9.8	17	0
Verdin, Clarence, Ind.	4	39	9.8	26	0
Schroeder, Jay, Raiders	15	38	2.5	19	0
Tatupu, Mosi, N.E.	11	38	3.5	20	0
McGee, Tim, Cin.	2	36	18.0	25	0
Kubiak, Gary, Den.	15	35	2.3	10	0
McNeil, Gerald, Clev.	2	32	16.0	18	0
Reed, Andre, Buff.	2	31	15.5	23	0
Reich, Frank, Buff.	9	30	3.3	9	0
Wilhelm, Erik, Cin.	6	30	5.0	14	0
Brown, Tom, Mia.	13	26	2.0	6	0
Brister, Bubby, Pitt.	27	25	0.9	15	0
Gamble, Kenny, K.C.	6	24	4.0	20	1

THE COMPLETE HANDBOOK OF PRO FOOTBALL

	Att	Yards	Avg	Long	TD
Harmon, Kevin, Sea.	1	24	24.0	24	0
Harris, Elroy, Sea.	8	23	2.9	8	0
Miller, Anthony, S.D.	4	21	5.3	24	0
Blackledge, Todd, Pitt.	9	20	2.2	11	0
Egu, Patrick, N.E.	3	20	6.7	t15	1
Holifield, John, Cin.	11	20	1.8	11	0
Martin, Sammy, N.E.	2	20	10.0	13	0
Early, Quinn, S.D.	1	19	19.0	19	0
Grogan, Steve, N.E.	9	19	2.1	7	0
Langhorne, Reggie, Clev.	5	19	3.8	18	0
O'Brien, Ken, Jets	9	18	2.0	5	0
Rison, Andre, Ind.	3	18	6.0	18	0
Montgomery, Greg, Hou.	3	17	5.7	11	0
Prokop, Joe, Jets	1	17	17.0	t17	1
Carter, Rodney, Pitt.	11	16	1.5	7	1
Evans, Vince, Raiders	1	16	16.0	16	0
Fernandez, Mervyn, Raiders	2	16	8.0	12	0
Johnson, Tracy, Hou.	4	16	4.0	8	0
Floyd, Victor, S.D.	8	15	1.9	5	0
Fryar, Irving, N.E.	2	15	7.5	11	0
Archer, David, S.D.	2	14	7.0	14	0
Epps, Phillip, Jets	1	14	14.0	14	0
Jackson, Mark, Den.	5	13	2.6	8	0
Stouffer, Kelly, Sea.	2	11	5.5	9	0
Faaola, Nuu, Mia.	2	10	5.0	5	0
Wallace, Ray, Pitt.	5	10	2.0	5	1
Clayton, Mark, Mia.	3	9	3.0	11	0
Harry, Emile, K.C.	1	9	9.0	9	0
Walker, Wayne, S.D.	1	9	9.0	9	0
Plummer, Gary, S.D.	1	6	6.0	6	0
Jaworski, Ron, K.C.	4	5	1.3	4	0
Ramsey, Tom, Ind.	4	5	1.3	3	0
Agee, Tommie, K.C.	1	3	3.0	3	0
Blades, Brian, Sea.	1	3	3.0	3	0
Harper, Michael, Jets	1	3	3.0	3	0
Jones, Cedric, N.E.	1	3	3.0	3	0
Mackey, Kyle, Jets	2	3	1.5	5	0
Tyrrell, Tim, Pitt.	1	3	3.0	3	0
Mandley, Pete, K.C.	2	1	0.5	8	0
Caravello, Joe, S.D.	1	0	0.0	0	0
Duncan, Curtis, Hou.	1	0	0.0	0	0
Kemp, Jeff, Sea.	1	0	0.0	0	0
Malone, Mark, Jets	1	0	0.0	0	0
Roby, Reggie, Mia.	2	0	0.0	0	0
Rodriguez, Ruben, Sea.	1	0	0.0	0	0
Tolliver, Billy Joe, S.D.	7	0	0.0	3	0

NFL STATISTICS

	Att	Yards	Avg	Long	TD
Pagel, Mike, Clev.	2	-1	-0.5	4	0
Ryan, Pat, Jets	1	-1	-1.0	-1	0
Eason, Tony, N.E.-Jets	3	-2	-0.7	0	0
Hillary, Ira, Cin.	1	-2	-2.0	-2	0
Wonsley, George, N.E.	2	-2	-1.0	0	0
Brooks, Bill, Ind.	2	-3	-1.5	0	0
Carlson, Cody, Hou.	3	-3	-1.0	0	0
Gelbaugh, Stan, Buff.	1	-3	-3.0	-3	0
Strom, Rick, Pitt.	4	-3	-0.8	0	0
Burkett, Chris, Jets	1	-4	-4.0	-4	0
Lageman, Jeff, Jets	1	-5	-5.0	-5	0
Johnson, Lee, Cin.	1	-7	-7.0	-7	0
Marino, Dan, Mia.	14	-7	-0.5	2	2
DeBerg, Steve, K.C.	14	-8	-0.6	15	0
Newsome, Harry, Pitt.	2	-8	-4.0	0	0
Stark, Rohn, Ind.	1	-11	-11.0	-11	0

Ram (now Raider) Greg Bell led the NFL in rushing TDs (15).

PASSING

TOP TEN PASSERS

	Att	Comp	Pct Comp	Yds
Montana, Joe, S.F.	386	271	70.2	3521
Esiason, Boomer, Cin.	455	258	56.7	3525
Everett, Jim, Rams	518	304	58.7	4310
Moon, Warren, Hou.	464	280	60.3	3631
Rypien, Mark, Wash.	476	280	58.8	3768
Kelly, Jim, Buff.	391	228	58.3	3130
Hebert, Bobby, N.O.	353	222	62.9	2686
Majkowski, Don, G.B.	599	353	58.9	4318
Kosar, Bernie, Clev.	513	303	59.1	3533
Simms, Phil, Giants	405	228	56.3	3061

NFC — INDIVIDUAL PASSERS

	Att	Comp	Pct Comp	Yds
Montana, Joe, S.F.	386	271	70.2	3521
Everett, Jim, Rams	518	304	58.7	4310
Rypien, Mark, Wash.	476	280	58.8	3768
Hebert, Bobby, N.O.	353	222	62.9	2686
Majkowski, Don, G.B.	599	353	58.9	4318
Simms, Phil, Giants	405	228	56.3	3061
Miller, Chris, Atl.	526	280	53.2	3459
Cunningham, Randall, Phil.	532	290	54.5	3400
Wilson, Wade, Minn.	362	194	53.6	2543
Hogeboom, Gary, Phoe.	364	204	56.0	2591
Testaverde, Vinny, T.B.	480	258	53.8	3133
Tomczak, Mike, Chi.	306	156	51.0	2058
Gagliano, Bob, Det.	232	117	50.4	1671
Aikman, Troy, Dall.	293	155	52.9	1749

(Nonqualifiers)

	Att	Comp	Pct Comp	Yds
Young, Steve, S.F.	92	64	69.6	1001
Fourcade, John, N.O.	107	61	57.0	930
Hostetler, Jeff, Giants	39	20	51.3	294
Millen, Hugh, Atl.	50	31	62.0	432
Humphries, Stan, Wash.	10	5	50.0	91

t = Touchdown
Leader based on rating points, minimum 224 attempts

NFL STATISTICS

Avg Gain	TD	Pct TD	Long	Int	Pct Int	Sack	Yds Lost	Rating Points
9.12	26	6.7	t95	8	2.1	33	198	112.4
7.75	28	6.2	t74	11	2.4	36	288	92.1
8.32	29	5.6	t78	17	3.3	29	214	90.6
7.83	23	5.0	55	14	3.0	35	267	88.9
7.92	22	4.6	t80	13	2.7	16	108	88.1
8.01	25	6.4	t78	18	4.6	30	216	86.2
7.61	15	4.2	t54	15	4.2	22	171	82.7
7.21	27	4.5	t79	20	3.3	47	268	82.3
6.89	18	3.5	t97	14	2.7	34	192	80.3
7.56	14	3.5	t62	14	3.5	40	244	77.6

Avg Gain	TD	Pct TD	Long	Int	Pct Int	Sack	Yds Lost	Rating Points
9.12	26	6.7	t95	8	2.1	33	198	112.4
8.32	29	5.6	t78	17	3.3	29	214	90.6
7.92	22	4.6	t80	13	2.7	16	108	88.1
7.61	15	4.2	t54	15	4.2	22	171	82.7
7.21	27	4.5	t79	20	3.3	47	268	82.3
7.56	14	3.5	t62	14	3.5	40	244	77.6
6.58	16	3.0	t72	10	1.9	41	318	76.1
6.39	21	3.9	t66	15	2.8	45	343	75.5
7.02	9	2.5	50	12	3.3	27	194	70.5
7.12	14	3.8	t59	19	5.2	40	266	69.5
6.53	20	4.2	t78	22	4.6	38	294	68.9
6.73	16	5.2	t79	16	5.2	10	68	68.2
7.20	6	2.6	t75	12	5.2	25	153	61.2
5.97	9	3.1	t75	18	6.1	19	155	55.7

Avg Gain	TD	Pct TD	Long	Int	Pct Int	Sack	Yds Lost	Rating Points
10.88	8	8.7	t50	3	3.3	12	84	120.8
8.69	7	6.5	t54	4	3.7	13	96	92.0
7.54	3	7.7	t35	2	5.1	6	37	80.5
8.64	1	2.0	47	2	4.0	10	71	79.8
9.10	1	10.0	39	1	10.0	3	9	75.4

314 THE COMPLETE HANDBOOK OF PRO FOOTBALL

	Att	Comp	Pct Comp	Yds
Kramer, Tommy, Minn.	136	77	56.6	906
Harbaugh, Jim, Chi.	178	111	62.4	1204
Peete, Rodney, Det.	195	103	52.8	1479
Williams, Doug, Wash.	93	51	54.8	585
Walsh, Steve, Dall.	219	110	50.2	1371
Tupa, Tom, Phoe.	134	65	48.5	973
Ferguson, Joe, T.B.	90	44	48.9	533
Rosenbach, Timm, Phoe.	22	9	40.9	95
Hipple, Eric, Det.	18	7	38.9	90
(Fewer than 10 attempts)				
Awalt, Robert, Phoe.	1	0	0.0	0
Bono, Steve, S.F.	5	4	80.0	62
Byner, Earnest, Wash.	1	0	0.0	0
Camarillo, Rich, Phoe.	1	1	100.0	0
Cavanaugh, Matt, Phil.	5	3	60.0	33
Dilweg, Anthony, G.B.	1	1	100.0	7
Dozier, D.J., Minn.	1	1	100.0	19
Fontenot, Herman, G.B.	0	0	---	0
Fulhage, Scott, Atl.	1	1	100.0	12
Herrmann, Mark, Rams	5	4	80.0	59
Hill, Lonzell, N.O.	0	0	---	0
Hilliard, Dalton, N.O.	1	1	100.0	35
Jones, Keith, Atl.	1	0	0.0	0
Long, Chuck, Det.	5	2	40.0	42
Rice, Allen, Minn.	0	0	---	0
Ruzek, Roger, Phil.	1	1	100.0	22
Sanders, Ricky, Wash.	1	1	100.0	32
Saxon, Mike, Dall.	1	1	100.0	4
Sikahema, Vai, Phoe.	1	0	0.0	0

AFC - INDIVIDUAL PASSERS

	Att	Comp	Pct Comp	Yds
Esiason, Boomer, Cin.	455	258	56.7	3525
Moon, Warren, Hou.	464	280	60.3	3631
Kelly, Jim, Buff.	391	228	58.3	3130
Kosar, Bernie, Clev.	513	303	59.1	3533
Marino, Dan, Mia.	550	308	56.0	3997
DeBerg, Steve, K.C.	324	196	60.5	2529
Krieg, Dave, Sea.	499	286	57.3	3309
O'Brien, Ken, Jets	477	288	60.4	3346
Elway, John, Den.	416	223	53.6	3051
McMahon, Jim, S.D.	318	176	55.3	2132
Brister, Bubby, Pitt.	342	187	54.7	2365

NFL STATISTICS 315

Avg Gain	TD	Pct TD	Long	Int	Pct Int	Sack	Yds Lost	Rating Points
6.66	7	5.1	39	7	5.1	12	75	72.7
6.76	5	2.8	t49	9	5.1	18	106	70.5
7.58	5	2.6	69	9	4.6	27	164	67.0
6.29	1	1.1	46	3	3.2	2	10	64.1
6.26	5	2.3	46	9	4.1	11	84	60.5
7.26	3	2.2	t77	9	6.7	14	94	52.2
5.92	3	3.3	t69	6	6.7	5	37	50.8
4.32	0	0.0	24	1	4.5	2	19	35.2
5.00	0	0.0	30	3	16.7	5	26	15.7
0.00	0	0.0	0	1	100.0	0	0	0.0
12.40	1	20.0	t45	0	0.0	0	0	157.9
0.00	0	0.0	0	0	0.0	0	0	39.6
0.00	0	0.0	0	0	0.0	0	0	79.2
6.60	1	20.0	t13	1	20.0	0	0	79.6
7.00	0	0.0	7	0	0.0	0	0	95.8
19.00	1	100.0	t19	0	0.0	0	0	158.3
----	0	---	0	0	---	1	9	0.0
12.00	0	0.0	12	0	0.0	0	0	116.7
11.80	0	0.0	23	1	20.0	3	22	76.3
----	0	---	0	0	---	1	4	0.0
35.00	1	100.0	t35	0	0.0	0	0	158.3
0.00	0	0.0	0	0	0.0	0	0	39.6
8.40	0	0.0	37	0	0.0	0	0	70.4
----	0	---	0	0	---	1	10	0.0
22.00	1	100.0	t22	0	0.0	0	0	158.3
32.00	0	0.0	32	0	0.0	0	0	118.8
4.00	0	0.0	4	0	0.0	0	0	83.3
0.00	0	0.0	0	0	0.0	0	0	39.6

7.75	28	6.2	t74	11	2.4	36	288	92.1
7.83	23	5.0	55	14	3.0	35	267	88.9
8.01	25	6.4	t78	18	4.6	30	216	86.2
6.89	18	3.5	t97	14	2.7	34	192	80.3
7.27	24	4.4	t78	22	4.0	10	86	76.9
7.81	11	3.4	50	16	4.9	14	111	75.8
6.63	21	4.2	t60	20	4.0	37	289	74.8
7.01	12	2.5	57	18	3.8	50	391	74.3
7.33	18	4.3	69	18	4.3	35	298	73.7
6.70	10	3.1	t69	10	3.1	28	167	73.5
6.92	9	2.6	t79	10	2.9	45	452	73.1

	Att	Comp	Pct Comp	Yds
Trudeau, Jack, Ind.	362	190	52.5	2317
Grogan, Steve, N.E.	261	133	51.0	1697
(Nonqualifiers)				
Reich, Frank, Buff.	87	53	60.9	701
Wilhelm, Erik, Cin.	56	30	53.6	425
Pelluer, Steve, K.C.	47	26	55.3	301
Beuerlein, Steve, Raiders	217	108	49.8	1677
Eason, Tony, N.E.-Jets	141	79	56.0	1016
Kubiak, Gary, Den.	55	32	58.2	284
Wilson, Marc, N.E.	150	75	50.0	1006
Ramsey, Tom, Ind.	50	24	48.0	280
Chandler, Chris, Ind.	80	39	48.8	537
Schroeder, Jay, Raiders	194	91	46.9	1550
Tolliver, Billy Joe, S.D.	185	89	48.1	1097
Jaworski, Ron, K.C.	61	36	59.0	385
Carlson, Cody, Hou.	31	15	48.4	155
Flutie, Doug, N.E.	91	36	39.6	493
Secules, Scott, Mia.	50	22	44.0	286
Pagel, Mike, Clev.	14	5	35.7	60
Mackey, Kyle, Jets	25	11	44.0	125
Stouffer, Kelly, Sea.	59	29	49.2	270
Blackledge, Todd, Pitt.	60	22	36.7	282
Ryan, Pat, Jets	30	15	50.0	153
Archer, David, S.D.	12	5	41.7	62
(Fewer than 10 attempts)				
Bentley, Albert, Ind.	1	0	0.0	0
Carter, Rodney, Pitt.	1	1	100.0	15
Dickerson, Eric, Ind.	0	0	---	0
Elkins, Mike, K.C.	2	1	50.0	5
Evans, Vince, Raiders	2	2	100.0	50
Feagles, Jeff, N.E.	2	0	0.0	0
Gossett, Jeff, Raiders	1	0	0.0	0
Humphrey, Bobby, Den.	2	1	50.0	17
Jensen, Jim, Mia.	1	1	100.0	19
Johnson, Flip, Buff.	0	0	---	0
Johnson, Vance, Den.	1	0	0.0	0
Malone, Mark, Jets	2	2	100.0	13
Metcalf, Eric, Clev.	2	1	50.0	32
Rodriguez, Ruben, Sea.	1	1	100.0	4
Saxon, James, K.C.	1	0	0.0	0
Schonert, Turk, Cin.	2	0	0.0	0
Strom, Rick, Pitt.	1	0	0.0	0
Tatupu, Mosi, N.E.	1	1	100.0	15
Zendejas, Tony, Hou.	1	0	0.0	0

NFL STATISTICS 317

Avg Gain	TD	Pct TD	Long	Int	Pct Int	Sack	Yds Lost	Rating Points
6.40	15	4.1	71	13	3.6	20	125	71.3
6.50	9	3.4	t55	14	5.4	8	64	60.8
8.06	7	8.0	t63	2	2.3	4	24	103.7
7.59	4	7.1	t46	2	3.6	3	17	87.3
6.40	1	2.1	24	0	0.0	8	61	82.0
7.73	13	6.0	t67	9	4.1	22	175	78.4
7.21	4	2.8	t63	6	4.3	17	120	70.5
5.16	2	3.6	22	2	3.6	8	53	69.1
6.71	3	2.0	t65	5	3.3	10	71	64.5
5.60	1	2.0	47	1	2.0	4	26	63.8
6.71	2	2.5	t82	3	3.8	3	17	63.4
7.99	8	4.1	t84	13	6.7	20	132	60.3
5.93	5	2.7	49	8	4.3	9	75	57.9
6.31	2	3.3	32	5	8.2	1	10	54.3
5.00	0	0.0	23	1	3.2	2	20	49.8
5.42	2	2.2	36	4	4.4	6	52	46.6
5.72	1	2.0	t44	3	6.0	0	0	44.3
4.29	1	7.1	18	1	7.1	0	0	43.8
5.00	0	0.0	22	1	4.0	3	18	42.9
4.58	0	0.0	29	3	5.1	9	90	40.9
4.70	1	1.7	30	3	5.0	4	25	36.9
5.10	1	3.3	25	3	10.0	2	26	36.5
5.17	0	0.0	17	1	8.3	2	12	23.6
0.00	0	0.0	0	0	0.0	0	0	39.6
15.00	0	0.0	15	0	0.0	2	7	118.8
----	0	---	0	0	---	1	6	0.0
2.50	0	0.0	5	1	50.0	0	0	16.7
25.00	0	0.0	40	0	0.0	2	19	118.8
0.00	0	0.0	0	0	0.0	0	0	39.6
0.00	0	0.0	0	0	0.0	0	0	39.6
8.50	1	50.0	t17	0	0.0	0	0	118.8
19.00	1	100.0	t19	0	0.0	0	0	158.3
----	0	---	0	0	---	1	2	0.0
0.00	0	0.0	0	0	0.0	0	0	39.6
6.50	0	0.0	11	0	0.0	0	0	93.8
16.00	1	50.0	t32	0	0.0	0	0	135.4
4.00	0	0.0	4	0	0.0	0	0	83.3
0.00	0	0.0	0	1	100.0	0	0	0.0
0.00	0	0.0	0	0	0.0	2	27	39.6
0.00	0	0.0	0	0	0.0	0	0	39.6
15.00	0	0.0	15	0	0.0	0	0	118.8
0.00	0	0.0	0	1	100.0	0	0	0.0

318 THE COMPLETE HANDBOOK OF PRO FOOTBALL

Steeler Rod Woodson's 27.3 avg. led kickoff returners.

NFL STATISTICS 319

NFL sacks champ with 21 was Minnesota's Chris Doleman.

TOP TEN PASS RECEIVERS

	No	Yards	Avg	Long	TD
Sharpe, Sterling, G.B.	90	1423	15.8	t79	12
Reed, Andre, Buff.	88	1312	14.9	t78	9
Carrier, Mark, T.B.	86	1422	16.5	t78	9
Monk, Art, Wash.	86	1186	13.8	t60	8
Rice, Jerry, S.F.	82	1483	18.1	t68	17
Sanders, Ricky, Wash.	80	1138	14.2	68	4
Clark, Gary, Wash.	79	1229	15.6	t80	9
Blades, Brian, Sea.	77	1063	13.8	t60	5
Johnson, Vance, Den.	76	1095	14.4	69	7
Williams, John L., Sea.	76	657	8.6	t51	6

TOP TEN RECEIVERS BY YARDS

	Yards	No	Avg	Long	TD
Rice, Jerry, S.F.	1483	82	18.1	t68	17
Sharpe, Sterling, G.B.	1423	90	15.8	t79	12
Carrier, Mark, T.B.	1422	86	16.5	t78	9
Ellard, Henry, Rams	1382	70	19.7	53	8
Reed, Andre, Buff.	1312	88	14.9	t78	9
Miller, Anthony, S.D.	1252	75	16.7	t69	10
Slaughter, Webster, Clev.	1236	65	19.0	t97	6
Clark, Gary, Wash.	1229	79	15.6	t80	9
McGee, Tim, Cin.	1211	65	18.6	t74	8
Monk, Art, Wash.	1186	86	13.8	t60	8

TOP TEN INTERCEPTORS

	No	Yards	Avg	Long	TD
Wright, Felix, Clev.	9	91	10.1	t27	1
Fulcher, David, Cin.	8	87	10.9	22	0
Allen, Eric, Phil.	8	38	4.8	18	0
Taylor, Keith, Ind.	7	225	32.1	t80	1
McDonald, Tim, Phoe.	7	170	24.3	t53	1
Byrd, Gill, S.D.	7	38	5.4	22	0
McMillan, Erik, Jets	6	180	30.0	t92	1
Braxton, Tyrone, Den.	6	103	17.2	t34	1
Kelso, Mark, Buff.	6	101	16.8	43	0
Prior, Mike, Ind.	6	88	14.7	t58	1
Holmes, Jerry, Det.	6	77	12.8	36	1
Hamilton, Harry, T.B.	6	70	11.7	30	0
Waymer, Dave, N.O.	6	66	11.0	42	0
Gray, Jerry, Rams	6	48	8.0	t27	1
Robinson, Mark, T.B.	6	44	7.3	16	0
Brown, Dave, G.B.	6	12	2.0	12	0

NFL STATISTICS

TOP TEN KICKOFF RETURNERS

	No	Yards	Avg	Long	TD
Woodson, Rod, Pitt.	36	982	27.3	t84	1
Gray, Mel, Det.	24	640	26.7	57	0
Logan, Marc, Mia.	24	613	25.5	t97	1
Miller, Anthony, S.D.	21	533	25.4	t91	1
Dixon, James, Dall.	47	1181	25.1	t97	1
Howard, Joe, Wash.	21	522	24.9	t99	1
Martin, Sammy, N.E.	24	584	24.3	38	0
Gentry, Dennis, Chi.	28	667	23.8	63	0
Jefferson, James, Sea.	22	511	23.2	t97	1
Metcalf, Eric, Clev.	31	718	23.2	49	0

TOP TEN PUNT RETURNERS

	No	FC	Yards	Avg	Long	TD
Stanley, Walter, Det.	36	5	496	13.8	74	0
Verdin, Clarence, Ind.	23	5	296	12.9	t49	1
Meggett, Dave, Giants	46	14	582	12.7	t76	1
Sikahema, Vai, Phoe.	37	13	433	11.7	53	0
Taylor, John, S.F.	36	20	417	11.6	37	0
Drewrey, Willie, T.B.	20	2	220	11.0	55	0
Sanders, Deion, Atl.	28	7	307	11.0	t68	1
Lewis, Leo, Minn.	44	27	446	10.1	65	0
McNeil, Gerald, Clev.	49	15	496	10.1	49	0
Howard, Joe, Wash.	21	18	200	9.5	38	0

TOP TEN LEADERS - SACKS

Doleman, Chris, Minn.	21.0
Harris, Tim, G.B.	19.5
Millard, Keith, Minn.	18.0
Greene, Kevin, Rams	16.5
Swilling, Pat, N.O.	16.5
Simmons, Clyde, Phil.	15.5
Taylor, Lawrence, Giants	15.0
Williams, Lee, S.D.	14.0
Smith, Bruce, Buff.	13.0
O'Neal, Leslie, S.D.	12.5

TOP TEN PUNTERS

	No	Yards	Long	Avg
Camarillo, Rich, Phoe.	76	3298	58	43.4
Montgomery, Greg, Hou.	56	2422	63	43.3
Arnold, Jim, Det.	82	3538	64	43.1
Landeta, Sean, Giants	70	3019	71	43.1
Mojsiejenko, Ralf, Wash.	62	2663	74	43.0
Stark, Rohn, Ind.	79	3392	64	42.9
Roby, Reggie, Mia.	58	2458	58	42.4
Fulhage, Scott, Atl.	84	3472	65	41.3
Newsome, Harry, Pitt.	82	3368	57	41.1
Saxon, Mike, Dall.	79	3233	56	40.9

TOP TEN SCORERS – KICKERS

	XP	XPA	FG	FGA	PTS
Cofer, Mike, S.F.	49	51	29	36	136
Lohmiller, Chip, Wash.	41	41	29	40	128
Karlis, Rich, Minn.	27	28	31	39	120
Lansford, Mike, Rams	51	51	23	30	120
Treadwell, David, Den.	39	40	27	33	120
Norwood, Scott, Buff.	46	47	23	30	115
Zendejas, Tony, Hou.	40	40	25	37	115
Jacke, Chris, G.B.	42	42	22	28	108
Lowery, Nick, K.C.	34	35	24	33	106
Andersen, Morten, N.O.	44	45	20	29	104

Total Punts	TB	Blk	Opp Ret	Ret Yds	In 20	Net Avg
76	6	0	42	330	21	37.5
58	7	2	24	191	15	36.1
83	9	1	46	373	14	36.0
70	7	0	29	236	19	37.8
63	9	1	34	383	21	33.3
80	10	1	51	558	14	32.9
59	6	1	26	256	18	35.3
85	9	1	43	460	24	33.3
83	9	1	45	361	15	34.1
81	6	2	37	334	19	34.3

TOP TEN SCORERS — NONKICKERS

	TD	TDR	TDP	TDM	PTS
Hilliard, Dalton, N.O.	18	13	5	0	108
Rice, Jerry, S.F.	17	0	17	0	102
Anderson, Neal, Chi.	15	11	4	0	90
Bell, Greg, Rams	15	15	0	0	90
Anderson, Ottis, Giants	14	14	0	0	84
Sanders, Barry, Det.	14	14	0	0	84
Sharpe, Sterling, G.B.	13	0	12	1	78
Okoye, Christian, K.C.	12	12	0	0	72
Thomas, Thurman, Buff.	12	6	6	0	72
Carter, Cris, Phil.	11	0	11	0	66
Miller, Anthony, S.D.	11	0	10	1	66

NFL STANDINGS 1921-1989

1921

	W	L	T	Pct.
Chicago Staleys	10	1	1	.909
Buffalo All-Americans	9	1	2	.900
Akron, Ohio, Pros	7	2	1	.778
Green Bay Packers	6	2	2	.750
Canton, Ohio, Bulldogs	4	3	3	.571
Dayton Triangles	4	3	1	.571
Rock Island Independents	5	4	1	.556
Chicago Cardinals	2	3	2	.400
Cleveland Indians	2	6	0	.250
Rochester Jeffersons	2	6	0	.250
Detroit Heralds	1	7	1	.125
Columbus Panhandles	0	6	0	.000
Cincinnati Celts	0	8	0	.000

1922

	W	L	T	Pct.
Canton, Ohio, Bulldogs	10	0	2	1.000
Chicago Bears	9	3	0	.750
Chicago Cardinals	8	3	0	.727
Toledo Maroons	5	2	2	.714
Rock Island Independents	4	2	1	.667
Dayton Triangles	4	3	1	.571
Green Bay Packers	4	3	3	.571
Racine, Wis., Legion	5	4	1	.556
Akron, Ohio, Pros	3	4	2	.429
Buffalo All-Americans	3	4	1	.429
Milwaukee Badgers	2	4	3	.333
Marion, O., Oorang Indians	2	6	0	.250
Minneapolis Marines	1	3	0	.250
Evansville Crimson Giants	0	2	0	.000
Louisville Brecks	0	3	0	.000
Rochester Jeffersons	0	3	1	.000
Hammond, Ind., Pros	0	4	1	.000
Columbus Panhandles	0	7	0	.000

1923

	W	L	T	Pct.
Canton, Ohio, Bulldogs	11	0	1	1.000
Chicago Bears	9	2	1	.818
Green Bay Packers	7	2	1	.778
Milwaukee Badgers	7	2	3	.778
Cleveland Indians	3	1	3	.750
Chicago Cardinals	8	4	0	.667
Duluth Kelleys	4	3	0	.571
Buffalo All-Americans	5	4	3	.556
Columbus Tigers	5	4	1	.556
Racine, Wis., Legion	4	4	2	.500
Toledo Maroons	2	3	2	.400
Rock Island Independents	2	3	3	.400
Minneapolis Marines	2	5	2	.286
St. Louis All-Stars	1	4	2	.200
Hammond, Ind., Pros	1	5	1	.167
Dayton Triangles	1	6	1	.143
Akron, Ohio, Indians	1	6	0	.143
Marion, O., Oorang Indians	1	10	0	.091
Rochester Jeffersons	0	2	0	.000
Louisville Brecks	0	3	0	.000

1924

	W	L	T	Pct.
Cleveland Bulldogs	7	1	1	.875
Chicago Bears	6	1	4	.857
Frankford Yellowjackets	11	2	1	.846
Duluth Kelleys	5	1	0	.833
Rock Island Independents	6	2	2	.750
Green Bay Packers	8	4	0	.667
Buffalo Bisons	6	4	0	.600
Racine, Wis., Legion	4	3	3	.571
Chicago Cardinals	5	4	1	.556
Columbus Tigers	4	4	0	.500
Hammond, Ind., Pros	2	2	1	.500
Milwaukee Badgers	5	8	0	.385
Dayton Triangles	2	7	0	.222
Kansas City Cowboys	2	7	0	.222
Akron, Ohio, Indians	1	6	0	.143
Kenosha, Wis., Maroons	0	5	1	.000
Minneapolis Marines	0	6	0	.000
Rochester Jeffersons	0	7	0	.000

1925

	W	L	T	Pct.
Chicago Cardinals	11	2	1	.846
Pottsville, Pa., Maroons	10	2	0	.833
Detroit Panthers	8	2	2	.800
New York Giants	8	4	0	.667
Akron, Ohio, Indians	4	2	2	.667
Frankford Yellowjackets	13	7	0	.650
Chicago Bears	9	5	3	.643
Rock Island Independents	5	3	3	.625
Green Bay Packers	8	5	0	.615
Providence Steamroller	6	5	1	.545
Canton, Ohio, Bulldogs	4	4	0	.500
Cleveland Bulldogs	5	8	1	.385
Kansas City Cowboys	2	5	1	.286
Hammond, Ind., Pros	1	3	0	.250
Buffalo Bisons	1	6	2	.143
Duluth Kelleys	0	3	0	.000
Rochester Jeffersons	0	6	1	.000
Milwaukee Badgers	0	6	0	.000
Dayton Triangles	0	7	1	.000
Columbus Tigers	0	9	0	.000

ALL-TIME NFL STANDINGS

1926

	W	L	T	Pct.
Frankford Yellowjackets	14	1	1	.933
Chicago Bears	12	1	3	.923
Pottsville, Pa., Maroons	10	2	1	.833
Kansas City Cowboys	8	3	1	.727
Green Bay Packers	7	3	3	.700
Los Angeles Buccaneers	6	3	1	.667
New York Giants	8	4	1	.667
Duluth Eskimos	6	5	2	.545
Buffalo Rangers	4	4	2	.500
Chicago Cardinals	5	6	1	.455
Providence Steamroller	5	7	0	.417
Detroit Panthers	4	6	2	.400
Hartford Blues	3	7	0	.300
Brooklyn Lions	3	8	0	.273
Milwaukee Badgers	2	7	0	.222
Akron, Ohio, Indians	1	4	3	.200
Dayton Triangles	1	4	1	.200
Racine, Wis., Legion	1	4	0	.200
Columbus Tigers	1	6	0	.143
Canton, Ohio, Bulldogs	1	9	3	.100
Hammond, Ind., Pros	0	4	0	.000
Louisville Colonels	0	4	0	.000

1927

	W	L	T	Pct.
New York Giants	11	1	1	.917
Green Bay Packers	7	2	1	.778
Chicago Bears	9	3	2	.750
Cleveland Bulldogs	8	4	1	.667
Providence Steamroller	8	5	1	.615
New York Yankees	7	8	1	.467
Frankford Yellowjackets	6	9	3	.400
Pottsville, Pa., Maroons	5	8	0	.385
Chicago Cardinals	3	7	1	.300
Dayton Triangles	1	6	1	.143
Duluth Eskimos	1	8	0	.111
Buffalo Bisons	0	5	0	.000

1928

	W	L	T	Pct.
Providence Steamroller	8	1	2	.889
Frankford Yellowjackets	11	3	2	.786
Detroit Wolverines	7	2	1	.778
Green Bay Packers	6	4	3	.600
Chicago Bears	7	5	1	.583
New York Giants	4	7	2	.364
New York Yankees	4	8	1	.333
Pottsville, Pa., Maroons	2	8	0	.200
Chicago Cardinals	1	5	0	.167
Dayton Triangles	0	7	0	.000

1929

	W	L	T	Pct.
Green Bay Packers	12	0	1	1.000
New York Giants	13	1	1	.929
Frankford Yellowjackets	9	4	5	.692
Chicago Cardinals	6	6	1	.500
Boston Bulldogs	4	4	0	.500
Orange, N.J., Tornadoes	3	4	4	.429
Stapleton Stapes	3	4	3	.429
Providence Steamroller	4	6	2	.400
Chicago Bears	4	9	2	.308
Buffalo Bisons	1	7	1	.125
Minneapolis Red Jackets	1	9	0	.100
Dayton Triangles	0	6	0	.000

1930

	W	L	T	Pct.
Green Bay Packers	10	3	1	.769
New York Giants	13	4	0	.765
Chicago Bears	9	4	1	.692
Brooklyn Dodgers	7	4	1	.636
Providence Steamroller	6	4	1	.600
Stapleton Stapes	5	5	2	.500
Chicago Cardinals	5	6	2	.455
Portsmouth, O., Spartans	5	6	3	.455
Frankford Yellowjackets	4	14	1	.222
Minneapolis Red Jackets	1	7	1	.125
Newark Tornadoes	1	10	1	.091

1931

	W	L	T	Pct.
Green Bay Packers	12	2	0	.857
Portsmouth, O., Spartans	11	3	0	.786
Chicago Bears	8	5	0	.615
Chicago Cardinals	5	4	0	.556
New York Giants	7	6	1	.538
Providence Steamroller	4	4	3	.500
Stapleton Stapes	4	6	1	.400
Cleveland Indians	2	8	0	.200
Brooklyn Dodgers	2	12	0	.143
Frankford Yellowjackets	1	6	1	.143

1932

	W	L	T	Pct.
Chicago Bears	7	1	6	.875
Green Bay Packers	10	3	1	.769
Portsmouth, O., Spartans	6	2	4	.750
Boston Braves	4	4	2	.500
New York Giants	4	6	2	.400
Brooklyn Dodgers	3	9	0	.250
Chicago Cardinals	2	6	2	.250
Stapleton Stapes	2	7	3	.222

1933

EASTERN DIVISION

	W	L	T	Pct.	Pts.	OP
N.Y. Giants	11	3	0	.786	244	101
Brooklyn	5	4	1	.556	93	54
Boston	5	5	2	.500	103	97
Philadelphia	3	5	1	.375	77	158
Pittsburgh	3	6	2	.333	67	208

WESTERN DIVISION

	W	L	T	Pct.	Pts.	OP
Chi. Bears	10	2	1	.833	133	82
Portsmouth	6	5	0	.545	128	87
Green Bay	5	7	1	.417	170	107
Cincinnati	3	6	1	.333	38	110
Chi. Cardinals	1	9	1	.100	52	101

NFL Championship: Chicago Bears 23, N.Y. Giants 21

1934

EASTERN DIVISION

	W	L	T	Pct.	Pts.	OP
N.Y. Giants	8	5	0	.615	147	107
Boston	6	6	0	.500	107	94
Brooklyn	4	7	0	.364	61	153
Philadelphia	4	7	0	.364	127	85
Pittsburgh	2	10	0	.167	51	206

WESTERN DIVISION

	W	L	T	Pct.	Pts.	OP
Chi. Bears	13	0	0	1.000	286	86
Detroit	10	3	0	.769	238	59
Green Bay	7	6	0	.538	156	112
Chi. Cardinals	5	6	0	.455	80	84
St. Louis	1	2	0	.333	27	61
Cincinnati	0	8	0	.000	10	243

NFL Championship: N.Y. Giants 30, Chicago Bears 13

1935

EASTERN DIVISION

	W	L	T	Pct.	Pts.	OP
N.Y. Giants	9	3	0	.750	180	96
Brooklyn	5	6	1	.455	90	141
Pittsburgh	4	8	0	.333	100	209
Boston	2	8	1	.200	65	123
Philadelphia	2	9	0	.182	60	179

WESTERN DIVISION

	W	L	T	Pct.	Pts.	OP
Detroit	7	3	2	.700	191	111
Green Bay	8	4	0	.667	181	96
Chi. Bears	6	4	2	.600	192	106
Chi. Cardinals	6	4	2	.600	99	97

NFL Championship: Detroit 26, N.Y. Giants 7
One game between Boston and Philadelphia was canceled.

1936

EASTERN DIVISION

	W	L	T	Pct.	Pts.	OP
Boston	7	5	0	.583	149	110
Pittsburgh	6	6	0	.500	98	187
N.Y. Giants	5	6	1	.455	115	163
Brooklyn	3	8	1	.273	92	161
Philadelphia	1	11	0	.083	51	206

WESTERN DIVISION

	W	L	T	Pct.	Pts.	OP
Green Bay	10	1	1	.909	248	118
Chi. Bears	9	3	0	.750	222	94
Detroit	8	4	0	.667	235	102
Chi. Cardinals	3	8	1	.273	74	143

NFL Championship: Green Bay 21, Boston 6

1937

EASTERN DIVISION

	W	L	T	Pct.	Pts.	OP
Washington	8	3	0	.727	195	120
N.Y. Giants	6	3	2	.667	128	109
Pittsburgh	4	7	0	.364	122	145
Brooklyn	3	7	1	.300	82	174
Philadelphia	2	8	1	.200	86	177

WESTERN DIVISION

	W	L	T	Pct.	Pts.	OP
Chi. Bears	9	1	1	.900	201	100
Green Bay	7	4	0	.636	220	122
Detroit	7	4	0	.636	180	105
Chi. Cardinals	5	5	1	.500	135	165
Cleveland	1	10	0	.091	75	207

NFL Championship: Washington 28, Chicago Bears 21

1938

EASTERN DIVISION

	W	L	T	Pct.	Pts.	OP
N.Y Giants	8	2	1	.800	194	79
Washington	6	3	2	.667	148	154
Brooklyn	4	4	3	.500	131	161
Philadelphia	5	6	0	.455	154	164
Pittsburgh	2	9	0	.182	79	169

WESTERN DIVISION

	W	L	T	Pct.	Pts.	OP
Green Bay	8	3	0	.727	223	118
Detroit	7	4	0	.636	119	108
Chi. Bears	6	5	0	.545	194	148
Cleveland	4	7	0	.364	131	215
Chi. Cardinals	2	9	0	.182	111	168

NFL Championship: N.Y. Giants 23, Green Bay 17

1939

EASTERN DIVISION

	W	L	T	Pct.	Pts.	OP
N.Y. Giants	9	1	1	.900	168	85
Washington	8	2	1	.800	242	94
Brooklyn	4	6	1	.400	108	219
Philadelphia	1	9	1	.100	105	200
Pittsburgh	1	9	1	.100	114	216

WESTERN DIVISION

	W	L	T	Pct.	Pts.	OP
Green Bay	9	2	0	.818	233	153
Chi. Bears	8	3	0	.727	298	157
Detroit	6	5	0	.545	145	150
Cleveland	5	5	1	.500	195	164
Chi. Cardinals	1	10	0	.091	84	254

NFL Championship: Green Bay 27, N.Y. Giants 0

ALL-TIME NFL STANDINGS

1940

EASTERN DIVISION

	W	L	T	Pct.	Pts.	OP
Washington	9	2	0	.818	245	142
Brooklyn	8	3	0	.727	186	120
N.Y. Giants	6	4	1	.600	131	133
Pittsburgh	2	7	2	.222	60	178
Philadelphia	1	10	0	.091	111	211

WESTERN DIVISION

	W	L	T	Pct.	Pts.	OP
Chi. Bears	8	3	0	.727	238	152
Green Bay	6	4	1	.600	238	155
Detroit	5	5	0	.500	138	153
Cleveland	4	6	1	.400	171	191
Chi. Cardinals	2	7	2	.222	139	222

NFL Championship: Chicago Bears 73, Washington 0

1941

EASTERN DIVISION

	W	L	T	Pct.	Pts.	OP
N.Y. Giants	8	3	0	.727	238	114
Brooklyn	7	4	0	.636	158	127
Washington	6	5	0	.545	176	174
Philadelphia	2	8	1	.200	119	218
Pittsburgh	1	9	1	.100	103	276

WESTERN DIVISION

	W	L	T	Pct.	Pts.	OP
Chi. Bears	10	1	0	.909	396	147
Green Bay	10	1	0	.909	258	120
Detroit	4	6	1	.400	121	195
Chi. Cardinals	3	7	1	.300	127	197
Cleveland	2	9	0	.182	116	244

Western Division playoff: Chicago Bears 33, Green Bay 14
NFL Championship: Chicago Bears 37, N.Y. Giants 9

1942

EASTERN DIVISION

	W	L	T	Pct.	Pts.	OP
Washington	10	1	0	.909	227	102
Pittsburgh	7	4	0	.636	167	119
N.Y. Giants	5	5	1	.500	155	139
Brooklyn	3	8	0	.273	100	168
Philadelphia	2	9	0	.182	134	239

WESTERN DIVISION

	W	L	T	Pct.	Pts.	OP
Chi. Bears	11	0	0	1.000	376	84
Green Bay	8	2	1	.800	300	215
Cleveland	5	6	0	.455	150	207
Chi. Cardinals	3	8	0	.273	98	209
Detroit	0	11	0	.000	38	263

NFL Championship: Washington 14, Chicago Bears 6

1943

EASTERN DIVISION

	W	L	T	Pct.	Pts.	OP
Washington	6	3	1	.667	229	137
N.Y. Giants	6	3	1	.667	197	170
Phil-Pitt	5	4	1	.556	225	230
Brooklyn	2	8	0	.200	65	234

WESTERN DIVISION

	W	L	T	Pct.	Pts.	OP
Chi. Bears	8	1	1	.889	303	157
Green Bay	7	2	1	.778	264	172
Detroit	3	6	1	.333	178	218
Chi. Cardinals	0	10	0	.000	95	238

Eastern Division playoff: Washington 28, N.Y. Giants 0
NFL Championship: Chicago Bears 41, Washington 21

1944

EASTERN DIVISION

	W	L	T	Pct.	Pts.	OP
N.Y. Giants	8	1	1	.889	206	75
Philadelphia	7	1	2	.875	267	131
Washington	6	3	1	.667	169	180
Boston	2	8	0	.200	82	233
Brooklyn	0	10	0	.000	69	166

WESTERN DIVISION

	W	L	T	Pct.	Pts.	OP
Green Bay	8	2	0	.800	238	141
Chi. Bears	6	3	1	.667	258	172
Detroit	6	3	1	.667	216	151
Cleveland	4	6	0	.400	188	224
Card-Pitt	0	10	0	.000	108	328

NFL Championship: Green Bay 14, N.Y. Giants 7

1945

EASTERN DIVISION

	W	L	T	Pct.	Pts.	OP
Washington	8	2	0	.800	209	121
Philadelphia	7	3	0	.700	272	133
N.Y. Giants	3	6	1	.333	179	198
Boston	3	6	1	.333	123	211
Pittsburgh	2	8	0	.200	79	220

WESTERN DIVISION

	W	L	T	Pct.	Pts.	OP
Cleveland	9	1	0	.900	244	136
Detroit	7	3	0	.700	195	194
Green Bay	6	4	0	.600	258	173
Chi. Bears	3	7	0	.300	192	235
Chi. Cardinals	1	9	0	.100	98	228

NFL Championship: Cleveland 15, Washington 14

1946

EASTERN DIVISION
	W	L	T	Pct.	Pts.	OP
N.Y. Giants	7	3	1	.700	236	162
Philadelphia	6	5	0	.545	231	220
Washington	5	5	1	.500	171	191
Pittsburgh	5	5	1	.500	136	117
Boston	2	8	1	.200	189	273

WESTERN DIVISION
	W	L	T	Pct.	Pts.	OP
Chi. Bears	8	2	1	.800	289	193
Los Angeles	6	4	1	.600	277	257
Green Bay	6	5	0	.545	148	158
Chi. Cardinals	6	5	0	.545	260	198
Detroit	1	10	0	.091	142	310

NFL Championship: Chicago Bears 24, N.Y. Giants 14

1947

EASTERN DIVISION
	W	L	T	Pct.	Pts.	OP
Philadelphia	8	4	0	.667	308	242
Pittsburgh	8	4	0	.667	240	259
Boston	4	7	1	.364	168	256
Washington	4	8	0	.333	295	367
N.Y. Giants	2	8	2	.200	190	309

WESTERN DIVISION
	W	L	T	Pct.	Pts.	OP
Chi. Cardinals	9	3	0	.750	306	231
Chi. Bears	8	4	0	.667	363	241
Green Bay	6	5	1	.545	274	210
Los Angeles	6	6	0	.500	259	214
Detroit	3	9	0	.250	231	305

Eastern Division playoff: Philadelphia 21, Pittsburgh 0
NFL Championship: Chicago Cardinals 28, Philadelphia 21

1948

EASTERN DIVISION
	W	L	T	Pct.	Pts.	OP
Philadelphia	9	2	1	.818	376	156
Washington	7	5	0	.583	291	287
N.Y. Giants	4	8	0	.333	297	388
Pittsburgh	4	8	0	.333	200	243
Boston	3	9	0	.250	174	372

WESTERN DIVISION
	W	L	T	Pct.	Pts.	OP
Chi. Cardinals	11	1	0	.917	395	226
Chi. Bears	10	2	0	.833	375	151
Los Angeles	6	5	1	.545	327	269
Green Bay	3	9	0	.250	154	290
Detroit	2	10	0	.167	200	407

NFL Championship: Philadelphia 7, Chicago Cardinals 0

1949

EASTERN DIVISION
	W	L	T	Pct.	Pts.	OP
Philadelphia	11	1	0	.917	364	134
Pittsburgh	6	5	1	.545	224	214
N.Y. Giants	6	6	0	.500	287	298
Washington	4	7	1	.364	268	339
N.Y. Bulldogs	1	10	1	.091	153	368

WESTERN DIVISION
	W	L	T	Pct.	Pts.	OP
Los Angeles	8	2	2	.800	360	239
Chi. Bears	9	3	0	.750	332	218
Chi. Cardinals	6	5	1	.545	360	301
Detroit	4	8	0	.333	237	259
Green Bay	2	10	0	.167	114	329

NFL Championship: Philadelphia 14, Los Angeles 0

1950

AMERICAN CONFERENCE
	W	L	T	Pct.	Pts.	OP
Cleveland	10	2	0	.833	310	144
N.Y. Giants	10	2	0	.833	268	150
Philadelphia	6	6	0	.500	254	141
Pittsburgh	6	6	0	.500	180	195
Chi. Cardinals	5	7	0	.417	233	287
Washington	3	9	0	.250	232	326

NATIONAL CONFERENCE
	W	L	T	Pct.	Pts.	OP
Los Angeles	9	3	0	.750	466	309
Chi. Bears	9	3	0	.750	279	207
N.Y. Yanks	7	5	0	.583	366	367
Detroit	6	6	0	.500	321	285
Green Bay	3	9	0	.250	244	406
San Francisco	3	9	0	.250	213	300
Baltimore	1	11	0	.083	213	462

American Conference playoff: Cleveland 8, N.Y. Giants 3
National Conference playoff: Los Angeles 24, Chicago Bears 14
NFL Championship: Cleveland 30, Los Angeles 28

1951

AMERICAN CONFERENCE
	W	L	T	Pct.	Pts.	OP
Cleveland	11	1	0	.917	331	152
N.Y. Giants	9	2	1	.818	254	161
Washington	5	7	0	.417	183	296
Pittsburgh	4	7	1	.364	183	235
Philadelphia	4	8	0	.333	234	264
Chi. Cardinals	3	9	0	.250	210	287

NATIONAL CONFERENCE
	W	L	T	Pct.	Pts.	OP
Los Angeles	8	4	0	.667	392	261
Detroit	7	4	1	.636	336	259
San Francisco	7	4	1	.636	255	205
Chi. Bears	7	5	0	.583	286	282
Green Bay	3	9	0	.250	254	375
N.Y. Yanks	1	9	2	.100	241	382

NFL Championship: Los Angeles 24, Cleveland 17

ALL-TIME NFL STANDINGS

1952

AMERICAN CONFERENCE
	W	L	T	Pct.	Pts.	OP
Cleveland	8	4	0	.667	310	213
N.Y. Giants	7	5	0	.583	234	231
Philadelphia	7	5	0	.583	252	271
Pittsburgh	5	7	0	.417	300	273
Chi. Cardinals	4	8	0	.333	172	221
Washington	4	8	0	.333	240	287

NATIONAL CONFERENCE
	W	L	T	Pct.	Pts.	OP
Detroit	9	3	0	.750	344	192
Los Angeles	9	3	0	.750	349	234
San Francisco	7	5	0	.583	285	221
Green Bay	6	6	0	.500	295	312
Chi. Bears	5	7	0	.417	245	326
Dallas	1	11	0	.083	182	427

National Conference playoff: Detroit 31, Los Angeles 21
NFL Championship: Detroit 17, Cleveland 7

1953

EASTERN CONFERENCE
	W	L	T	Pct.	Pts.	OP
Cleveland	11	1	0	.917	348	162
Philadelphia	7	4	1	.636	352	215
Washington	6	5	1	.545	208	215
Pittsburgh	6	6	0	.500	211	263
N.Y. Giants	3	9	0	.250	179	277
Chi. Cardinals	1	10	1	.091	190	337

WESTERN CONFERENCE
	W	L	T	Pct.	Pts.	OP
Detroit	10	2	0	.833	271	205
San Francisco	9	3	0	.750	372	237
Los Angeles	8	3	1	.727	366	236
Chi. Bears	3	8	1	.273	218	262
Baltimore	3	9	0	.250	182	350
Green Bay	2	9	1	.182	200	338

NFL Championship: Detroit 17, Cleveland 16

1954

EASTERN CONFERENCE
	W	L	T	Pct.	Pts.	OP
Cleveland	9	3	0	.750	336	162
Philadelphia	7	4	1	.636	284	230
N.Y. Giants	7	5	0	.583	293	184
Pittsburgh	5	7	0	.417	219	263
Washington	3	9	0	.250	207	432
Chi. Cardinals	2	10	0	.167	183	347

WESTERN CONFERENCE
	W	L	T	Pct.	Pts.	OP
Detroit	9	2	1	.818	337	189
Chi. Bears	8	4	0	.667	301	279
San Francisco	7	4	1	.636	313	251
Los Angeles	6	5	1	.545	314	285
Green Bay	4	8	0	.333	234	251
Baltimore	3	9	0	.250	131	279

NFL Championship: Cleveland 56, Detroit 10

1955

EASTERN CONFERENCE
	W	L	T	Pct.	Pts.	OP
Cleveland	9	2	1	.818	349	218
Washington	8	4	0	.667	246	222
N.Y. Giants	6	5	1	.545	267	223
Chi. Cardinals	4	7	1	.364	224	252
Philadelphia	4	7	1	.364	248	231
Pittsburgh	4	8	0	.333	195	285

WESTERN CONFERENCE
	W	L	T	Pct.	Pts.	OP
Los Angeles	8	3	1	.727	260	231
Chi. Bears	8	4	0	.667	294	251
Green Bay	6	6	0	.500	258	276
Baltimore	5	6	1	.455	214	239
San Francisco	4	8	0	.333	216	298
Detroit	3	9	0	.250	230	275

NFL Championship: Cleveland 38, Los Angeles 14

1956

EASTERN CONFERENCE
	W	L	T	Pct.	Pts.	OP
N.Y. Giants	8	3	1	.727	264	197
Chi. Cardinals	7	5	0	.583	240	182
Washington	6	6	0	.500	183	225
Cleveland	5	7	0	.417	167	177
Pittsburgh	5	7	0	.417	217	250
Philadelphia	3	8	1	.273	143	215

WESTERN CONFERENCE
	W	L	T	Pct.	Pts.	OP
Chi. Bears	9	2	1	.818	363	246
Detroit	9	3	0	.750	300	188
San Francisco	5	6	1	.455	233	284
Baltimore	5	7	0	.417	270	322
Green Bay	4	8	0	.333	264	342
Los Angeles	4	8	0	.333	291	307

NFL Championship: N.Y. Giants 47, Chicago Bears 7

1957

EASTERN CONFERENCE
	W	L	T	Pct.	Pts.	OP
Cleveland	9	2	1	.818	269	172
N.Y. Giants	7	5	0	.583	254	211
Pittsburgh	6	6	0	.500	161	178
Washington	5	6	1	.455	251	230
Philadelphia	4	8	0	.333	173	230
Chi. Cardinals	3	9	0	.250	200	299

WESTERN CONFERENCE
	W	L	T	Pct.	Pts.	OP
Detroit	8	4	0	.667	251	231
San Francisco	8	4	0	.667	260	264
Baltimore	7	5	0	.583	303	235
Los Angeles	6	6	0	.500	307	278
Chi. Bears	5	7	0	.417	203	211
Green Bay	3	9	0	.250	218	311

Western Conference playoff: Detroit 31, San Francisco 27
NFL Championship: Detroit 59, Cleveland 14

1958

EASTERN CONFERENCE
	W	L	T	Pct.	Pts.	OP
N.Y. Giants	9	3	0	.750	246	183
Cleveland	9	3	0	.750	302	217
Pittsburgh	7	4	1	.636	261	230
Washington	4	7	1	.364	214	268
Chi. Cardinals	2	9	1	.182	261	356
Philadelphia	2	9	1	.182	235	306

WESTERN CONFERENCE
	W	L	T	Pct.	Pts.	OP
Baltimore	9	3	0	.750	381	203
Chi. Bears	8	4	0	.667	298	230
Los Angeles	8	4	0	.667	344	278
San Francisco	6	6	0	.500	257	324
Detroit	4	7	1	.364	261	276
Green Bay	1	10	1	.091	193	382

Eastern Conference playoff: N.Y. Giants 10, Cleveland 0
NFL Championship: Baltimore 23, N.Y. Giants 17, sudden-death overtime

1959

EASTERN CONFERENCE
	W	L	T	Pct.	Pts.	OP
N.Y. Giants	10	2	0	.833	284	170
Cleveland	7	5	0	.583	270	214
Philadelphia	7	5	0	.583	268	278
Pittsburgh	6	5	1	.545	257	216
Washington	3	9	0	.250	185	350
Chi. Cardinals	2	10	0	.167	234	324

WESTERN CONFERENCE
	W	L	T	Pct.	Pts.	OP
Baltimore	9	3	0	.750	374	251
Chi. Bears	8	4	0	.667	252	196
Green Bay	7	5	0	.583	248	246
San Francisco	7	5	0	.583	255	237
Detroit	3	8	1	.273	203	275
Los Angeles	2	10	0	.167	242	315

NFL Championship: Baltimore 31, N.Y. Giants 16

1960 AFL

EASTERN DIVISION
	W	L	T	Pct.	Pts.	OP
Houston	10	4	0	.714	379	285
N.Y. Titans	7	7	0	.500	382	399
Buffalo	5	8	1	.385	296	303
Boston	5	9	0	.357	286	349

WESTERN DIVISION
	W	L	T	Pct.	Pts.	OP
L.A. Chargers	10	4	0	.714	373	336
Dall. Texans	8	6	0	.571	362	253
Oakland	6	8	0	.429	319	388
Denver	4	9	1	.308	309	393

AFL Championship: Houston 24, L.A. Chargers 16

1960 NFL

EASTERN CONFERENCE
	W	L	T	Pct.	Pts.	OP
Philadelphia	10	2	0	.833	321	246
Cleveland	8	3	1	.727	362	217
N.Y. Giants	6	4	2	.600	271	261
St. Louis	6	5	1	.545	288	230
Pittsburgh	5	6	1	.455	240	275
Washington	1	9	2	.100	178	309

WESTERN CONFERENCE
	W	L	T	Pct.	Pts.	OP
Green Bay	8	4	0	.667	332	209
Detroit	7	5	0	.583	239	212
San Francisco	7	5	0	.583	208	205
Baltimore	6	6	0	.500	288	234
Chicago	5	6	1	.455	194	299
L.A. Rams	4	7	1	.364	265	297
Dall. Cowboys	0	11	1	.000	177	369

NFL Championship: Philadelphia 17, Green Bay 13

ALL-TIME NFL STANDINGS 331

1961 AFL

EASTERN DIVISION
	W	L	T	Pct.	Pts.	OP
Houston	10	3	1	.769	513	242
Boston	9	4	1	.692	413	313
N.Y. Titans	7	7	0	.500	301	390
Buffalo	6	8	0	.429	294	342

WESTERN DIVISION
	W	L	T	Pct.	Pts.	OP
San Diego	12	2	0	.857	396	219
Dall. Texans	6	8	0	.429	334	343
Denver	3	11	0	.214	251	432
Oakland	2	12	0	.143	237	458

AFL Championship: Houston 10, San Diego 3

1961 NFL

EASTERN CONFERENCE
	W	L	T	Pct.	Pts.	OP
N.Y. Giants	10	3	1	.769	368	220
Philadelphia	10	4	0	.714	361	297
Cleveland	8	5	1	.615	319	270
St. Louis	7	7	0	.500	279	267
Pittsburgh	6	8	0	.429	295	287
Dall. Cowboys	4	9	1	.308	236	380
Washington	1	12	1	.077	174	392

WESTERN CONFERENCE
	W	L	T	Pct.	Pts.	OP
Green Bay	11	3	0	.786	391	223
Detroit	8	5	1	.615	270	258
Baltimore	8	6	0	.571	302	307
Chicago	8	6	0	.571	326	302
San Francisco	7	6	1	.538	346	272
Los Angeles	4	10	0	.286	263	333
Minnesota	3	11	0	.214	285	407

NFL Championship: Green Bay 37, N.Y. Giants 0

1962 AFL

EASTERN DIVISION
	W	L	T	Pct.	Pts.	OP
Houston	11	3	0	.786	387	270
Boston	9	4	1	.692	346	295
Buffalo	7	6	1	.538	309	272
N.Y. Titans	5	9	0	.357	278	423

WESTERN DIVISION
	W	L	T	Pct.	Pts.	OP
Dall. Texans	11	3	0	.786	389	233
Denver	7	7	0	.500	353	334
San Diego	4	10	0	.286	314	392
Oakland	1	13	0	.071	213	370

AFL Championship: Dallas Texans 20, Houston 17, sudden-death overtime

1962 NFL

EASTERN CONFERENCE
	W	L	T	Pct.	Pts.	OP
N.Y. Giants	12	2	0	.857	398	283
Pittsburgh	9	5	0	.643	312	363
Cleveland	7	6	1	.538	291	257
Washington	5	7	2	.417	305	376
Dall. Cowboys	5	8	1	.385	398	402
St. Louis	4	9	1	.308	287	361
Philadelphia	3	10	1	.231	282	356

WESTERN CONFERENCE
	W	L	T	Pct.	Pts.	OP
Green Bay	13	1	0	.929	415	148
Detroit	11	3	0	.786	315	177
Chicago	9	5	0	.643	321	287
Baltimore	7	7	0	.500	293	288
San Francisco	6	8	0	.429	282	331
Minnesota	2	11	1	.154	254	410
Los Angeles	1	12	1	.077	220	334

NFL Championship: Green Bay 16, N.Y. Giants 7

1963 AFL

EASTERN DIVISION
	W	L	T	Pct.	Pts.	OP
Boston	7	6	1	.538	317	257
Buffalo	7	6	1	.538	304	291
Houston	6	8	0	.429	302	372
N.Y. Jets	5	8	1	.385	249	399

WESTERN DIVISION
	W	L	T	Pct.	Pts.	OP
San Diego	11	3	0	.786	399	255
Oakland	10	4	0	.714	363	282
Kansas City	5	7	2	.417	347	263
Denver	2	11	1	.154	301	473

Eastern Division playoff: Boston 26, Buffalo 8
AFL Championship: San Diego 51, Boston 10

1963 NFL

EASTERN CONFERENCE
	W	L	T	Pct.	Pts.	OP
N.Y. Giants	11	3	0	.786	448	280
Cleveland	10	4	0	.714	343	262
St. Louis	9	5	0	.643	341	283
Pittsburgh	7	4	3	.636	321	295
Dallas	4	10	0	.286	305	378
Washington	3	11	0	.214	279	398
Philadelphia	2	10	2	.167	242	381

WESTERN CONFERENCE
	W	L	T	Pct.	Pts.	OP
Chicago	11	1	2	.917	301	144
Green Bay	11	2	1	.846	369	206
Baltimore	8	6	0	.571	316	285
Detroit	5	8	1	.385	326	265
Minnesota	5	8	1	.385	309	390
Los Angeles	5	9	0	.357	210	350
San Francisco	2	12	0	.143	198	391

NFL Championship: Chicago 14, N.Y. Giants 10

1964 AFL

EASTERN DIVISION
	W	L	T	Pct.	Pts.	OP
Buffalo	12	2	0	.857	400	242
Boston	10	3	1	.769	365	297
N.Y. Jets	5	8	1	.385	278	315
Houston	4	10	0	.286	310	355

WESTERN DIVISION
	W	L	T	Pct.	Pts.	OP
San Diego	8	5	1	.615	341	300
Kansas City	7	7	0	.500	366	306
Oakland	5	7	2	.417	303	350
Denver	2	11	1	.154	240	438

AFL Championship: Buffalo 20, San Diego 7

1964 NFL

EASTERN CONFERENCE
	W	L	T	Pct.	Pts.	OP
Cleveland	10	3	1	.769	415	293
St. Louis	9	3	2	.750	357	331
Philadelphia	6	8	0	.429	312	313
Washington	6	8	0	.429	307	305
Dallas	5	8	1	.385	250	289
Pittsburgh	5	9	0	.357	253	315
N.Y. Giants	2	10	2	.167	241	399

WESTERN CONFERENCE
	W	L	T	Pct.	Pts.	OP
Baltimore	12	2	0	.857	428	225
Green Bay	8	5	1	.615	342	245
Minnesota	8	5	1	.615	355	296
Detroit	7	5	2	.583	280	260
Los Angeles	5	7	2	.417	283	339
Chicago	5	9	0	.357	260	379
San Francisco	4	10	0	.286	236	330

NFL Championship: Cleveland 27, Baltimore 0

1965 AFL

EASTERN DIVISION
	W	L	T	Pct.	Pts.	OP
Buffalo	10	3	1	.769	313	226
N.Y. Jets	5	8	1	.385	285	303
Boston	4	8	2	.333	244	302
Houston	4	10	0	.286	298	429

WESTERN DIVISION
	W	L	T	Pct.	Pts.	OP
San Diego	9	2	3	.818	340	227
Oakland	8	5	1	.615	298	239
Kansas City	7	5	2	.583	322	285
Denver	4	10	0	.286	303	392

AFL Championship: Buffalo 23, San Diego 0

1965 NFL

EASTERN CONFERENCE
	W	L	T	Pct.	Pts.	OP
Cleveland	11	3	0	.786	363	325
Dallas	7	7	0	.500	325	280
N.Y. Giants	7	7	0	.500	270	338
Washington	6	8	0	.429	257	301
Philadelphia	5	9	0	.357	363	359
St. Louis	5	9	0	.357	296	309
Pittsburgh	2	12	0	.143	202	397

WESTERN CONFERENCE
	W	L	T	Pct.	Pts.	OP
Green Bay	10	3	1	.769	316	224
Baltimore	10	3	1	.769	389	284
Chicago	9	5	0	.643	409	275
San Francisco	7	6	1	.538	421	402
Minnesota	7	7	0	.500	383	403
Detroit	6	7	1	.462	257	295
Los Angeles	4	10	0	.286	269	328

Western Conference playoff: Green Bay 13, Baltimore 10, sudden-death overtime
NFL Championship: Green Bay 23, Cleveland 12

1966 AFL

EASTERN DIVISION
	W	L	T	Pct.	Pts.	OP
Buffalo	9	4	1	.692	358	255
Boston	8	4	2	.667	315	283
N.Y. Jets	6	6	2	.500	322	312
Houston	3	11	0	.214	335	396
Miami	3	11	0	.214	213	362

WESTERN DIVISION
	W	L	T	Pct.	Pts.	OP
Kansas City	11	2	1	.846	448	276
Oakland	8	5	1	.615	315	288
San Diego	7	6	1	.538	335	284
Denver	4	10	0	.286	196	381

AFL Championship: Kansas City 31, Buffalo 7

1966 NFL

EASTERN CONFERENCE
	W	L	T	Pct.	Pts.	OP
Dallas	10	3	1	.769	445	239
Cleveland	9	5	0	.643	403	259
Philadelphia	9	5	0	.643	326	340
St. Louis	8	5	1	.615	264	265
Washington	7	7	0	.500	351	355
Pittsburgh	5	8	1	.385	316	347
Atlanta	3	11	0	.214	204	437
N.Y. Giants	1	12	1	.077	263	501

WESTERN CONFERENCE
	W	L	T	Pct.	Pts.	OP
Green Bay	12	2	0	.857	335	163
Baltimore	9	5	0	.643	314	226
Los Angeles	8	6	0	.571	289	212
San Francisco	6	6	2	.500	320	325
Chicago	5	7	2	.417	234	272
Detroit	4	9	1	.308	206	317
Minnesota	4	9	1	.308	292	304

NFL Championship: Green Bay 34, Dallas 27
Super Bowl I: Green Bay (NFL) 35, Kansas City (AFL) 10

ALL-TIME NFL STANDINGS 333

Crushed here, Packers' Bart Starr was Super Bowl I MVP.

1967 AFL

EASTERN DIVISION
	W	L	T	Pct.	Pts.	OP
Houston	9	4	1	.692	258	199
N.Y. Jets	8	5	1	.615	371	329
Buffalo	4	10	0	.286	237	285
Miami	4	10	0	.286	219	407
Boston	3	10	1	.231	280	389

WESTERN DIVISION
	W	L	T	Pct.	Pts.	OP
Oakland	13	1	0	.929	468	238
Kansas City	9	5	0	.643	408	254
San Diego	8	5	1	.615	360	352
Denver	3	11	0	.214	256	409

AFL Championship: Oakland 40, Houston 7

1967 NFL

EASTERN CONFERENCE
Capitol Division
	W	L	T	Pct.	Pts.	OP
Dallas	9	5	0	.643	342	268
Philadelphia	6	7	1	.462	351	409
Washington	5	6	3	.455	347	353
New Orleans	3	11	0	.214	233	379

WESTERN CONFERENCE
Coastal Division
	W	L	T	Pct.	Pts.	OP
Los Angeles	11	1	2	.917	398	196
Baltimore	11	1	2	.917	394	198
San Francisco	7	7	0	.500	273	337
Atlanta	1	12	1	.077	175	422

Century Division
	W	L	T	Pct.	Pts.	OP
Cleveland	9	5	0	.643	334	297
N.Y. Giants	7	7	0	.500	369	379
St. Louis	6	7	1	.462	333	356
Pittsburgh	4	9	1	.308	281	320

Central Division
	W	L	T	Pct.	Pts.	OP
Green Bay	9	4	1	.692	332	209
Chicago	7	6	1	.538	239	218
Detroit	5	7	2	.417	260	259
Minnesota	3	8	3	.273	233	294

Conference Championships: Dallas 52, Cleveland 14; Green Bay 28, Los Angeles 7
NFL Championship: Green Bay 21, Dallas 17
Super Bowl II: Green Bay (NFL) 33, Oakland (AFL) 14

1968 AFL

EASTERN DIVISION
	W	L	T	Pct.	Pts.	OP
N.Y. Jets	11	3	0	.786	419	280
Houston	7	7	0	.500	303	248
Miami	5	8	1	.385	276	355
Boston	4	10	0	.286	229	406
Buffalo	1	12	1	.077	199	367

WESTERN DIVISION
	W	L	T	Pct.	Pts.	OP
Oakland	12	2	0	.857	453	233
Kansas City	12	2	0	.857	371	170
San Diego	9	5	0	.643	382	310
Denver	5	9	0	.357	255	404
Cincinnati	3	11	0	.214	215	329

Western Division playoff: Oakland 41, Kansas City 6
AFL Championship: N.Y. Jets 27, Oakland 23

1968 NFL

EASTERN CONFERENCE
Capitol Division
	W	L	T	Pct.	Pts.	OP
Dallas	12	2	0	.857	431	186
N.Y. Giants	7	7	0	.500	294	325
Washington	5	9	0	.357	249	358
Philadelphia	2	12	0	.143	202	351

WESTERN CONFERENCE
Coastal Division
	W	L	T	Pct.	Pts.	OP
Baltimore	13	1	0	.929	402	144
Los Angeles	10	3	1	.769	312	200
San Francisco	7	6	1	.538	303	310
Atlanta	2	12	0	.143	170	389

Century Division
	W	L	T	Pct.	Pts.	OP
Cleveland	10	4	0	.714	394	273
St. Louis	9	4	1	.692	325	289
New Orleans	4	9	1	.308	246	327
Pittsburgh	2	11	1	.154	244	397

Central Division
	W	L	T	Pct.	Pts.	OP
Minnesota	8	6	0	.571	282	242
Chicago	7	7	0	.500	250	333
Green Bay	6	7	1	.462	281	227
Detroit	4	8	2	.333	207	241

Conference Championships: Cleveland 31, Dallas 20; Baltimore 24, Minnesota 14
NFL Championship: Baltimore 34, Cleveland 0
Super Bowl III: N.Y. Jets (AFL) 16, Baltimore (NFL) 7

ALL-TIME NFL STANDINGS

1969 AFL

EASTERN DIVISION
	W	L	T	Pct.	Pts.	OP
N.Y. Jets	10	4	0	.714	353	269
Houston	6	6	2	.500	278	279
Boston	4	10	0	.286	266	316
Buffalo	4	10	0	.286	230	359
Miami	3	10	1	.231	233	332

WESTERN DIVISION
	W	L	T	Pct.	Pts.	OP
Oakland	12	1	1	.923	377	242
Kansas City	11	3	0	.786	359	177
San Diego	8	6	0	.571	288	276
Denver	5	8	1	.385	297	344
Cincinnati	4	9	1	.308	280	367

Divisional playoffs: Kansas City 13, N.Y. Jets 6; Oakland 56, Houston 7
AFL Championship: Kansas City 17, Oakland 7

1969 NFL

EASTERN CONFERENCE
Capitol Division
	W	L	T	Pct.	Pts.	OP
Dallas	11	2	1	.846	369	223
Washington	7	5	2	.583	307	319
New Orleans	5	9	0	.357	311	393
Philadelphia	4	9	1	.308	279	377

WESTERN CONFERENCE
Coastal Division
	W	L	T	Pct.	Pts.	OP
Los Angeles	11	3	0	.786	320	243
Baltimore	8	5	1	.615	279	268
Atlanta	6	8	0	.429	276	268
San Francisco	4	8	2	.333	277	319

Century Division
	W	L	T	Pct.	Pts.	OP
Cleveland	10	3	1	.769	351	300
N.Y. Giants	6	8	0	.429	264	298
St. Louis	4	9	1	.308	314	389
Pittsburgh	1	13	0	.071	218	404

Central Division
	W	L	T	Pct.	Pts.	OP
Minnesota	12	2	0	.857	379	133
Detroit	9	4	1	.692	259	188
Green Bay	8	6	0	.571	269	221
Chicago	1	13	0	.071	210	339

Conference Championships: Cleveland 38, Dallas 14; Minnesota 23, Los Angeles 20
NFL Championship: Minnesota 27, Cleveland 7
Super Bowl IV: Kansas City (AFL) 23, Minnesota (NFL) 7

1970

AMERICAN CONFERENCE
Eastern Division
	W	L	T	Pct.	Pts.	OP
Baltimore	11	2	1	.846	321	234
Miami*	10	4	0	.714	297	228
N.Y. Jets	4	10	0	.286	255	286
Buffalo	3	10	1	.231	204	337
Boston	2	12	0	.143	149	361

NATIONAL CONFERENCE
Eastern Division
	W	L	T	Pct.	Pts.	OP
Dallas	10	4	0	.714	299	221
N.Y. Giants	9	5	0	.643	301	270
St. Louis	8	5	1	.615	325	228
Washington	6	8	0	.429	297	314
Philadelphia	3	10	1	.231	241	332

Central Division
	W	L	T	Pct.	Pts.	OP
Cincinnati	8	6	0	.571	312	255
Cleveland	7	7	0	.500	286	265
Pittsburgh	5	9	0	.357	210	272
Houston	3	10	1	.231	217	352

Central Division
	W	L	T	Pct.	Pts.	OP
Minnesota	12	2	0	.857	335	143
Detroit*	10	4	0	.714	347	202
Chicago	6	8	0	.429	256	261
Green Bay	6	8	0	.429	196	293

Western Division
	W	L	T	Pct.	Pts.	OP
Oakland	8	4	2	.667	300	293
Kansas City	7	5	2	.583	272	244
San Diego	5	6	3	.455	282	278
Denver	5	8	1	.385	253	264

Western Division
	W	L	T	Pct.	Pts.	OP
San Francisco	10	3	1	.769	352	267
Los Angeles	9	4	1	.692	325	202
Atlanta	4	8	2	.333	206	261
New Orleans	2	11	1	.154	172	347

Wild Card qualifier for playoffs
Divisional playoffs: Baltimore 17, Cincinnati 0; Oakland 21, Miami 14
AFC Championship: Baltimore 27, Oakland 17
Divisional playoffs: Dallas 5, Detroit 0; San Francisco 17, Minnesota 14
NFC Championship: Dallas 17, San Francisco 10
Super Bowl V: Baltimore (AFC) 16, Dallas (NFC) 13

336　THE COMPLETE HANDBOOK OF PRO FOOTBALL

1971

AMERICAN CONFERENCE
Eastern Division
	W	L	T	Pct.	Pts.	OP
Miami	10	3	1	.769	315	174
Baltimore*	10	4	0	.714	313	140
New England	6	8	0	.429	238	325
N.Y. Jets	6	8	0	.429	212	299
Buffalo	1	13	0	.071	184	394

Central Division
	W	L	T	Pct.	Pts.	OP
Cleveland	9	5	0	.643	285	273
Pittsburgh	6	8	0	.429	246	292
Houston	4	9	1	.308	251	330
Cincinnati	4	10	0	.286	284	265

Western Division
	W	L	T	Pct.	Pts.	OP
Kansas City	10	3	1	.769	302	208
Oakland	8	4	2	.667	344	278
San Diego	6	8	0	.429	311	341
Denver	4	9	1	.308	203	275

NATIONAL CONFERENCE
Eastern Division
	W	L	T	Pct.	Pts.	OP
Dallas	11	3	0	.786	406	222
Washington*	9	4	1	.692	276	190
Philadelphia	6	7	1	.462	221	302
St. Louis	4	9	1	.308	231	279
N.Y. Giants	4	10	0	.286	228	362

Central Division
	W	L	T	Pct.	Pts.	OP
Minnesota	11	3	0	.786	245	139
Detroit	7	6	1	.538	341	286
Chicago	6	8	0	.429	185	276
Green Bay	4	8	2	.333	274	298

Western Division
	W	L	T	Pct.	Pts.	OP
San Francisco	9	5	0	.643	300	216
Los Angeles	8	5	1	.615	313	260
Atlanta	7	6	1	.538	274	277
New Orleans	4	8	2	.333	266	347

*Wild Card qualifier for playoffs
Divisional playoffs: Miami 27, Kansas City 24, sudden-death overtime; Baltimore 20, Cleveland 3
AFC Championship: Miami 21, Baltimore 0
Divisional playoffs: Dallas 20, Minnesota 12; San Francisco 24, Washington 20
NFC Championship: Dallas 14, San Francisco 3
Super Bowl VI: Dallas (NFC) 24, Miami (AFC) 3

1972

AMERICAN CONFERENCE
Eastern Division
	W	L	T	Pct.	Pts.	OP
Miami	14	0	0	1.000	385	171
N.Y. Jets	7	7	0	.500	367	324
Baltimore	5	9	0	.357	235	252
Buffalo	4	9	1	.321	257	377
New England	3	11	0	.214	192	446

Central Division
	W	L	T	Pct.	Pts.	OP
Pittsburgh	11	3	0	.786	343	175
Cleveland*	10	4	0	.714	268	249
Cincinnati	8	6	0	.571	299	229
Houston	1	13	0	.071	164	380

Western Division
	W	L	T	Pct.	Pts.	OP
Oakland	10	3	1	.750	365	248
Kansas City	8	6	0	.571	287	254
Denver	5	9	0	.357	325	350
San Diego	4	9	1	.321	264	344

NATIONAL CONFERENCE
Eastern Division
	W	L	T	Pct.	Pts.	OP
Washington	11	3	0	.786	336	218
Dallas*	10	4	0	.714	319	240
N.Y. Giants	8	6	0	.571	331	247
St. Louis	4	9	1	.321	193	303
Philadelphia	2	11	1	.179	145	352

Central Division
	W	L	T	Pct.	Pts.	OP
Green Bay	10	4	0	.714	304	226
Detroit	8	5	1	.607	339	290
Minnesota	7	7	0	.500	301	252
Chicago	4	9	1	.321	225	275

Western Division
	W	L	T	Pct.	Pts.	OP
San Francisco	8	5	1	.607	353	249
Atlanta	7	7	0	.500	269	274
Los Angeles	6	7	1	.464	291	286
New Orleans	2	11	1	.179	215	361

*Wild Card qualifier for playoffs
Divisional playoffs: Pittsburgh 13, Oakland 7; Miami 20, Cleveland 14
AFC Championship: Miami 21, Pittsburgh 17
Divisional playoffs: Dallas 30, San Francisco 28; Washington 16, Green Bay 3
NFC Championship: Washington 26, Dallas 3
Super Bowl VII: Miami (AFC) 14, Washington (NFC) 7

ALL-TIME NFL STANDINGS 337

1973

AMERICAN CONFERENCE
Eastern Division

	W	L	T	Pct.	Pts.	OP
Miami	12	2	0	.857	343	150
Buffalo	9	5	0	.643	259	230
New England	5	9	0	.357	258	300
Baltimore	4	10	0	.286	226	341
N.Y. Jets	4	10	0	.286	240	306

Central Division

	W	L	T	Pct.	Pts.	OP
Cincinnati	10	4	0	.714	286	231
Pittsburgh*	10	4	0	.714	347	210
Cleveland	7	5	2	.571	234	255
Houston	1	13	0	.071	199	447

Western Division

	W	L	T	Pct.	Pts.	OP
Oakland	9	4	1	.679	292	175
Denver	7	5	2	.571	354	296
Kansas City	7	5	2	.571	231	192
San Diego	2	11	1	.179	188	386

NATIONAL CONFERENCE
Eastern Division

	W	L	T	Pct.	Pts.	OP
Dallas	10	4	0	.714	382	203
Washington*	10	4	0	.714	325	198
Philadelphia	5	8	1	.393	310	393
St. Louis	4	9	1	.321	286	365
N.Y. Giants	2	11	1	.179	226	362

Central Division

	W	L	T	Pct.	Pts.	OP
Minnesota	12	2	0	.857	296	168
Detroit	6	7	1	.464	271	247
Green Bay	5	7	2	.429	202	259
Chicago	3	11	0	.214	195	334

Western Division

	W	L	T	Pct.	Pts.	OP
Los Angeles	12	2	0	.857	388	178
Atlanta	9	5	0	.643	318	224
New Orleans	5	9	0	.357	163	312
San Francisco	5	9	0	.357	262	319

Wild Card qualifier for playoffs
Divisional playoffs: Oakland 33, Pittsburgh 14; Miami 34, Cincinnati 16
AFC Championship: Miami 27, Oakland 10
Divisional playoffs: Minnesota 27, Washington 20; Dallas 27, Los Angeles 16
NFC Championship: Minnesota 27, Dallas 10
Super Bowl VIII: Miami (AFC) 24, Minnesota (NFC) 7

1974

AMERICAN CONFERENCE
Eastern Division

	W	L	T	Pct.	Pts.	OP
Miami	11	3	0	.786	327	216
Buffalo*	9	5	0	.643	264	244
New England	7	7	0	.500	348	289
N.Y. Jets	7	7	0	.500	279	300
Baltimore	2	12	0	.143	190	329

Central Division

	W	L	T	Pct.	Pts.	OP
Pittsburgh	10	3	1	.750	305	189
Cincinnati	7	7	0	.500	283	259
Houston	7	7	0	.500	236	282
Cleveland	4	10	0	.286	251	344

Western Division

	W	L	T	Pct.	Pts.	OP
Oakland	12	2	0	.857	355	228
Denver	7	6	1	.536	302	294
Kansas City	5	9	0	.357	233	293
San Diego	5	9	0	.357	212	285

NATIONAL CONFERENCE
Eastern Division

	W	L	T	Pct.	Pts.	OP
St. Louis	10	4	0	.714	285	218
Washington*	10	4	0	.714	320	196
Dallas	8	6	0	.571	297	235
Philadelphia	7	7	0	.500	242	217
N.Y. Giants	2	12	0	.143	195	299

Central Division

	W	L	T	Pct.	Pts.	OP
Minnesota	10	4	0	.714	310	195
Detroit	7	7	0	.500	256	270
Green Bay	6	8	0	.429	210	206
Chicago	4	10	0	.286	152	279

Western Division

	W	L	T	Pct.	Pts.	OP
Los Angeles	10	4	0	.714	263	181
San Francisco	6	8	0	.429	226	236
New Orleans	5	9	0	.357	166	263
Atlanta	3	11	0	.214	111	271

Wild Card qualifier for playoffs
Divisional playoffs: Oakland 28, Miami 26; Pittsburgh 32, Buffalo 14
AFC Championship: Pittsburgh 24, Oakland 13
Divisional playoffs: Minnesota 30, St. Louis 14; Los Angeles 19, Washington 10
NFC Championship: Minnesota 14, Los Angeles 10
Super Bowl IX: Pittsburgh (AFC) 16, Minnesota (NFC) 6

1975

AMERICAN CONFERENCE
Eastern Division

	W	L	T	Pct.	Pts.	OP
Baltimore	10	4	0	.714	395	269
Miami	10	4	0	.714	357	222
Buffalo	8	6	0	.571	420	355
New England	3	11	0	.214	258	358
N.Y. Jets	3	11	0	.214	258	433

Central Division

	W	L	T	Pct.	Pts.	OP
Pittsburgh	12	2	0	.857	373	162
Cincinnati*	11	3	0	.786	340	246
Houston	10	4	0	.714	293	226
Cleveland	3	11	0	.214	218	372

Western Division

	W	L	T	Pct.	Pts.	OP
Oakland	11	3	0	.786	375	255
Denver	6	8	0	.429	254	307
Kansas City	5	9	0	.357	282	341
San Diego	2	12	0	.143	189	345

NATIONAL CONFERENCE
Eastern Division

	W	L	T	Pct.	Pts.	OP
St. Louis	11	3	0	.786	356	276
Dallas*	10	4	0	.714	350	268
Washington	8	6	0	.571	325	276
N.Y. Giants	5	9	0	.357	216	306
Philadelphia	4	10	0	.286	225	302

Central Division

	W	L	T	Pct.	Pts.	OP
Minnesota	12	2	0	.857	377	180
Detroit	7	7	0	.500	245	262
Chicago	4	10	0	.286	191	379
Green Bay	4	10	0	.286	226	285

Western Division

	W	L	T	Pct.	Pts.	OP
Los Angeles	12	2	0	.857	312	135
San Francisco	5	9	0	.357	255	286
Atlanta	4	10	0	.286	240	289
New Orleans	2	12	0	.143	165	360

Wild Card qualifier for playoffs
Divisional playoffs: Pittsburgh 28, Baltimore 10; Oakland 31, Cincinnati 28
AFC Championship: Pittsburgh 16, Oakland 10
Divisional playoffs: Los Angeles 35, St. Louis 23; Dallas 17, Minnesota 14
NFC Championship: Dallas 37, Los Angeles 7
Super Bowl X: Pittsburgh (AFC) 21, Dallas (NFC) 17

1976

AMERICAN CONFERENCE
Eastern Division

	W	L	T	Pct.	Pts.	OP
Baltimore	11	3	0	.786	417	246
New England*	11	3	0	.786	376	236
Miami	6	8	0	.429	263	264
N.Y. Jets	3	11	0	.214	169	383
Buffalo	2	12	0	.143	245	363

Central Division

	W	L	T	Pct.	Pts.	OP
Pittsburgh	10	4	0	.714	342	138
Cincinnati	10	4	0	.714	335	210
Cleveland	9	5	0	.643	267	287
Houston	5	9	0	.357	222	273

Western Division

	W	L	T	Pct.	Pts.	OP
Oakland	13	1	0	.929	350	237
Denver	9	5	0	.643	315	206
San Diego	6	8	0	.429	248	285
Kansas City	5	9	0	.357	290	376
Tampa Bay	0	14	0	.000	125	412

NATIONAL CONFERENCE
Eastern Division

	W	L	T	Pct.	Pts.	OP
Dallas	11	3	0	.786	296	194
Washington*	10	4	0	.714	291	217
St. Louis	10	4	0	.714	309	267
Philadelphia	4	10	0	.286	165	286
N.Y. Giants	3	11	0	.214	170	250

Central Division

	W	L	T	Pct.	Pts.	OP
Minnesota	11	2	1	.821	305	176
Chicago	7	7	0	.500	253	216
Detroit	6	8	0	.429	262	220
Green Bay	5	9	0	.357	218	299

Western Division

	W	L	T	Pct.	Pts.	OP
Los Angeles	10	3	1	.750	351	190
San Francisco	8	6	0	.571	270	190
Atlanta	4	10	0	.286	172	312
New Orleans	4	10	0	.286	253	346
Seattle	2	12	0	.143	229	429

Wild Card qualifier for playoffs
Divisional playoffs: Oakland 24, New England 21; Pittsburgh 40, Baltimore 14
AFC Championship: Oakland 24, Pittsburgh 7
Divisional playoffs: Minnesota 35, Washington 20; Los Angeles 14, Dallas 12
NFC Championship: Minnesota 24, Los Angeles 13
Super Bowl XI: Oakland (AFC) 32, Minnesota (NFC) 14

ALL-TIME NFL STANDINGS

1977

AMERICAN CONFERENCE
Eastern Division
	W	L	T	Pct.	Pts.	OP
Baltimore	10	4	0	.714	295	221
Miami	10	4	0	.714	313	197
New England	9	5	0	.643	278	217
N.Y. Jets	3	11	0	.214	191	300
Buffalo	3	11	0	.214	160	313

Central Division
	W	L	T	Pct.	Pts.	OP
Pittsburgh	9	5	0	.643	283	243
Houston	8	6	0	.571	299	230
Cincinnati	8	6	0	.571	238	235
Cleveland	6	8	0	.429	269	267

Western Division
	W	L	T	Pct.	Pts.	OP
Denver	12	2	0	.857	274	148
Oakland*	11	3	0	.786	351	230
San Diego	7	7	0	.500	222	205
Seattle	5	9	0	.357	282	373
Kansas City	2	12	0	.143	225	349

NATIONAL CONFERENCE
Eastern Division
	W	L	T	Pct.	Pts.	OP
Dallas	12	2	0	.857	345	212
Washington	9	5	0	.643	196	189
St. Louis	7	7	0	.500	272	287
Philadelphia	5	9	0	.357	220	207
N.Y. Giants	5	9	0	.357	181	265

Central Division
	W	L	T	Pct.	Pts.	OP
Minnesota	9	5	0	.643	231	227
Chicago*	9	5	0	.643	255	253
Detroit	6	8	0	.429	183	252
Green Bay	4	10	0	.286	134	219
Tampa Bay	2	12	0	.143	103	223

Western Division
	W	L	T	Pct.	Pts.	OP
Los Angeles	10	4	0	.714	302	146
Atlanta	7	7	0	.500	179	129
San Francisco	5	9	0	.357	220	260
New Orleans	3	11	0	.214	232	336

*Wild Card qualifier for playoffs

Divisional playoffs: Denver 34, Pittsburgh 21; Oakland 37, Baltimore 31, sudden-death overtime
AFC Championship: Denver 20, Oakland 17
Divisional playoffs: Dallas 37, Chicago 7; Minnesota 14, Los Angeles 7
NFC Championship: Dallas 23, Minnesota 6
Super Bowl XII: Dallas (NFC) 27, Denver (AFC) 10

1978

AMERICAN CONFERENCE
Eastern Division
	W	L	T	Pct.	Pts.	OP
New England	11	5	0	.688	358	286
Miami*	11	5	0	.688	372	254
N.Y. Jets	8	8	0	.500	359	364
Buffalo	5	11	0	.313	302	354
Baltimore	5	11	0	.313	239	421

Central Division
	W	L	T	Pct.	Pts.	OP
Pittsburgh	14	2	0	.875	356	195
Houston*	10	6	0	.625	283	298
Cleveland	8	8	0	.500	334	356
Cincinnati	4	12	0	.250	252	284

Western Division
	W	L	T	Pct.	Pts.	OP
Denver	10	6	0	.625	282	198
Oakland	9	7	0	.563	311	283
Seattle	9	7	0	.563	345	358
San Diego	9	7	0	.563	355	309
Kansas City	4	12	0	.250	243	327

NATIONAL CONFERENCE
Eastern Division
	W	L	T	Pct.	Pts.	OP
Dallas	12	4	0	.750	384	208
Philadelphia*	9	7	0	.563	270	250
Washington	8	8	0	.500	273	283
St. Louis	6	10	0	.375	248	296
N.Y. Giants	6	10	0	.375	264	298

Central Division
	W	L	T	Pct.	Pts.	OP
Minnesota	8	7	1	.531	294	306
Green Bay	8	7	1	.531	249	269
Detroit	7	9	0	.438	290	300
Chicago	7	9	0	.438	253	274
Tampa Bay	5	11	0	.313	241	259

Western Division
	W	L	T	Pct.	Pts.	OP
Los Angeles	12	4	0	.750	316	245
Atlanta*	9	7	0	.563	240	290
New Orleans	7	9	0	.438	281	298
San Francisco	2	14	0	.125	219	350

*Wild Card qualifier for playoffs

First-round playoff: Houston 17, Miami 9
Divisional playoffs: Houston 31, New England 14; Pittsburgh 33, Denver 10
AFC Championship: Pittsburgh 34, Houston 5
First-round playoff: Atlanta 14, Philadelphia 13
Divisional playoffs: Dallas 27, Atlanta 20; Los Angeles 34, Minnesota 10
NFC Championship: Dallas 28, Los Angeles 0
Super Bowl XIII: Pittsburgh (AFC) 35, Dallas (NFC) 31

340 THE COMPLETE HANDBOOK OF PRO FOOTBALL

1979

AMERICAN CONFERENCE

Eastern Division

	W	L	T	Pct.	Pts.	OP
Miami	10	6	0	.625	341	257
New England	9	7	0	.563	411	326
N.Y. Jets	8	8	0	.500	337	383
Buffalo	7	9	0	.438	268	279
Baltimore	5	11	0	.313	271	351

Central Division

	W	L	T	Pct.	Pts.	OP
Pittsburgh	12	4	0	.750	416	262
Houston*	11	5	0	.688	362	331
Cleveland	9	7	0	.563	359	352
Cincinnati	4	12	0	.250	337	421

Western Division

	W	L	T	Pct.	Pts.	OP
San Diego	12	4	0	.750	411	246
Denver*	10	6	0	.625	289	262
Seattle	9	7	0	.563	378	372
Oakland	9	7	0	.563	365	337
Kansas City	7	9	0	.438	238	262

NATIONAL CONFERENCE

Eastern Division

	W	L	T	Pct.	Pts.	OP
Dallas	11	5	0	.688	371	313
Philadelphia*	11	5	0	.688	339	282
Washington	10	6	0	.625	348	295
N.Y. Giants	6	10	0	.375	237	323
St. Louis	5	11	0	.313	307	358

Central Division

	W	L	T	Pct.	Pts.	OP
Tampa Bay	10	6	0	.625	273	237
Chicago*	10	6	0	.625	306	249
Minnesota	7	9	0	.438	259	337
Green Bay	5	11	0	.313	246	316
Detroit	2	14	0	.125	219	365

Western Division

	W	L	T	Pct.	Pts.	OP
Los Angeles	9	7	0	.563	323	309
New Orleans	8	8	0	.500	370	360
Atlanta	6	10	0	.375	300	388
San Francisco	2	14	0	.125	308	416

*Wild Card qualifier for playoffs
First-round playoff: Houston 13, Denver 7
Divisional playoffs: Houston 17, San Diego 14; Pittsburgh 34, Miami 14
AFC Championship: Pittsburgh 27, Houston 13
First-round playoff: Philadelphia 27, Chicago 17
Divisional playoffs: Tampa Bay 24, Philadelphia 17; Los Angeles 21, Dallas 19
NFC Championship: Los Angeles 9, Tampa Bay 0
Super Bowl XIV: Pittsburgh (AFC) 31, Los Angeles (NFC) 19

1980

AMERICAN CONFERENCE

Eastern Division

	W	L	T	Pct.	Pts.	OP
Buffalo	11	5	0	.688	320	260
New England	10	6	0	.625	441	325
Miami	8	8	0	.500	266	305
Baltimore	7	9	0	.438	355	387
N.Y. Jets	4	12	0	.250	302	395

Central Division

	W	L	T	Pct.	Pts.	OP
Cleveland	11	5	0	.688	357	310
Houston*	11	5	0	.688	295	251
Pittsburgh	9	7	0	.563	352	313
Cincinnati	6	10	0	.375	244	312

Western Division

	W	L	T	Pct.	Pts.	OP
San Diego	11	5	0	.688	418	327
Oakland*	11	5	0	.688	364	306
Kansas City	8	8	0	.500	319	336
Denver	8	8	0	.500	310	323
Seattle	4	12	0	.250	291	408

NATIONAL CONFERENCE

Eastern Division

	W	L	T	Pct.	Pts.	OP
Philadelphia	12	4	0	.750	384	222
Dallas*	12	4	0	.750	454	311
Washington	6	10	0	.375	261	293
St. Louis	5	11	0	.313	299	350
N.Y. Giants	4	12	0	.250	249	425

Central Division

	W	L	T	Pct.	Pts.	OP
Minnesota	9	7	0	.563	317	308
Detroit	9	7	0	.563	334	272
Chicago	7	9	0	.437	304	264
Tampa Bay	5	10	1	.343	271	341
Green Bay	5	10	1	.343	231	371

Western Division

	W	L	T	Pct.	Pts.	OP
Atlanta	12	4	0	.750	405	272
Los Angeles*	11	5	0	.688	424	289
San Francisco	6	10	0	.375	320	415
New Orleans	1	15	0	.063	291	487

*Wild Card qualifier for playoffs
First-round playoff: Oakland 27, Houston 7
Divisional playoffs: San Diego 20, Buffalo 14; Oakland 14, Cleveland 12
AFC Championship: Oakland 34, San Diego 27
First-round playoff: Dallas 34, Los Angeles 13
Divisional playoffs: Philadelphia 31, Minnesota 16; Dallas 30, Atlanta 27
NFC Championship: Philadelphia 20, Dallas 7
Super Bowl XV: Oakland (AFC) 27, Philadelphia (NFC) 10

ALL-TIME NFL STANDINGS

1981

AMERICAN CONFERENCE
Eastern Division

	W	L	T	Pct.	Pts.	OP
Miami	11	4	1	.719	345	275
N.Y. Jets*	10	5	1	.656	355	287
Buffalo*	10	6	0	.625	311	276
Baltimore	2	14	0	.125	259	533
New England	2	14	0	.125	322	370

Central Division

	W	L	T	Pct.	Pts.	OP
Cincinnati	12	4	0	.750	421	304
Pittsburgh	8	8	0	.500	356	297
Houston	7	9	0	.438	281	355
Cleveland	5	11	0	.313	276	375

Western Division

	W	L	T	Pct.	Pts.	OP
San Diego	10	6	0	.625	478	390
Denver	10	6	0	.625	321	289
Kansas City	9	7	0	.563	343	290
Oakland	7	9	0	.438	273	343
Seattle	6	10	0	.375	322	388

NATIONAL CONFERENCE
Eastern Division

	W	L	T	Pct.	Pts.	OP
Dallas	12	4	0	.750	367	277
Philadelphia*	10	6	0	.625	368	221
N.Y. Giants*	9	7	0	.563	295	257
Washington	8	8	0	.500	347	349
St. Louis	7	9	0	.438	315	408

Central Division

	W	L	T	Pct.	Pts.	OP
Tampa Bay	9	7	0	.563	315	268
Detroit	8	8	0	.500	397	322
Green Bay	8	8	0	.500	324	361
Minnesota	7	9	0	.438	325	369
Chicago	6	10	0	.375	253	324

Western Division

	W	L	T	Pct.	Pts.	OP
San Francisco	13	3	0	.813	357	250
Atlanta	7	9	0	.438	426	355
Los Angeles	6	10	0	.375	303	351
New Orleans	4	12	0	.250	207	378

Wild card qualifier for playoffs

First-round playoff: Buffalo 31, N.Y. Jets 27
Divisional playoffs: San Diego 41, Miami 38 (OT); Cincinnati 28, Buffalo 21
AFC Championship: Cincinnati 27, San Diego 7
First-round playoff: N.Y. Giants 27, Philadelphia 21
Divisional playoffs: Dallas 38, Tampa Bay 0; San Francisco 38, N.Y. Giants 24
NFC Championship: San Francisco 28, Dallas 27
Super Bowl XVI: San Francisco (NFC) 26, Cincinnati (AFC) 21

*1982

AMERICAN CONFERENCE

	W	L	T	Pct.	Pts.	OP
L.A. Raiders	8	1	0	.889	260	200
Miami	7	2	0	.778	198	131
Cincinnati	7	2	0	.778	232	177
Pittsburgh	6	3	0	.667	204	146
San Diego	6	3	0	.667	288	221
N.Y. Jets	6	3	0	.667	245	166
New England	5	4	0	.556	143	157
Cleveland	4	5	0	.444	140	182
Buffalo	4	5	0	.444	150	154
Seattle	4	5	0	.444	127	147
Kansas City	3	6	0	.333	176	184
Denver	2	7	0	.222	148	226
Houston	1	8	0	.111	136	245
Baltimore	0	8	1	.063	113	236

NATIONAL CONFERENCE

	W	L	T	Pct.	Pts.	OP
Washington	8	1	0	.889	190	128
Dallas	6	3	0	.667	226	145
Green Bay	5	3	1	.611	226	169
Minnesota	5	4	0	.556	187	198
Atlanta	5	4	0	.556	183	199
St. Louis	5	4	0	.556	135	170
Tampa Bay	5	4	0	.556	158	178
Detroit	4	5	0	.444	181	176
New Orleans	4	5	0	.444	129	160
N.Y. Giants	4	5	0	.444	164	160
San Francisco	3	6	0	.333	209	206
Chicago	3	6	0	.333	141	174
Philadelphia	3	6	0	.333	191	195
L.A. Rams	2	7	0	.222	200	250

Top eight teams in each Conference qualified for playoffs under format necessitated by strike-shortened season

First-round playoffs: Miami 28, New England 13; L.A. Raiders 27, Cleveland 10; N.Y. Jets 44, Cincinnati 17; San Diego 31, Pittsburgh 28
Second-round playoffs: N.Y. Jets 17, L.A. Raiders 14; Miami 34, San Diego 13
AFC Championship: Miami 14, N.Y. Jets 0
First-round playoffs: Green Bay 41, St. Louis 16; Washington 31, Detroit 7; Minnesota 30, Atlanta 24; Dallas 30, Tampa Bay 17
Second-round playoffs: Washington 21, Minnesota 7; Dallas 37, Green Bay 26
NFC Championship: Washington 31, Dallas 17
Super Bowl XVII: Washington 27, Miami 17

1983

AMERICAN CONFERENCE

Eastern Division

	W	L	T	Pct.	Pts.	OP
Miami	12	4	0	.750	389	250
New England	8	8	0	.500	274	289
Buffalo	8	8	0	.500	283	351
Baltimore	7	9	0	.438	264	354
N.Y. Jets	7	9	0	.438	313	331

Central Division

	W	L	T	Pct.	Pts.	OP
Pittsburgh	10	6	0	.625	355	303
Cleveland	9	7	0	.562	356	342
Cincinnati	7	9	0	.438	346	302
Houston	2	14	0	.125	288	460

Western Division

	W	L	T	Pct.	Pts.	OP
L.A. Raiders	12	4	0	.750	442	338
Seattle*	9	7	0	.562	403	397
Denver*	9	7	0	.562	302	327
San Diego	6	10	0	.375	358	462
Kansas City	6	10	0	.375	386	367

NATIONAL CONFERENCE

Eastern Division

	W	L	T	Pct.	Pts.	OP
Washington	14	2	0	.875	541	332
Dallas*	12	4	0	.750	479	360
St. Louis	8	7	1	.531	374	428
Philadelphia	5	11	0	.313	233	322
N.Y. Giants	3	12	1	.219	267	347

Central Division

	W	L	T	Pct.	Pts.	OP
Detroit	9	7	0	.562	347	286
Green Bay	8	8	0	.500	429	439
Chicago	8	8	0	.500	311	301
Minnesota	8	8	0	.500	316	348
Tampa Bay	2	14	0	.125	241	380

Western Division

	W	L	T	Pct.	Pts.	OP
San Francisco	10	6	0	.625	432	293
L.A. Rams*	9	7	0	.562	361	344
New Orleans	8	8	0	.500	319	337
Atlanta	7	9	0	.438	370	389

*Wild card qualifier for playoffs
First-round playoff: Seattle 31, Denver 7
Divisional playoffs: Seattle 27, Miami 20; L.A. Raiders 38, Pittsburgh 10
AFC Championship: L.A. Raiders 30, Seattle 14
First-round playoff: L.A. Rams 24, Dallas 17
Divisional playoffs: San Francisco 24, Detroit 23; Washington 51, L.A. Rams 7
NFC Championship: Washington 24, San Francisco 21
Super Bowl XVIII: L.A. Raiders 38, Washington 9

1984

NATIONAL CONFERENCE

Eastern Division

	W	L	T	Pct.	Pts.	OP
Washington	11	5	0	.688	426	310
N.Y. Giants*	9	7	0	.563	299	301
St. Louis	9	7	0	.563	423	345
Dallas	9	7	0	.563	308	308
Philadelphia	6	9	1	.406	278	320

Central Division

	W	L	T	Pct.	Pts.	OP
Chicago	10	6	0	.625	325	248
Green Bay	8	8	0	.500	390	309
Tampa Bay	6	10	0	.375	335	380
Detroit	4	11	1	.281	283	408
Minnesota	3	13	0	.188	276	484

Western Division

	W	L	T	Pct.	Pts.	OP
San Francisco	15	1	0	.939	475	227
L.A. Rams*	10	6	0	.625	346	316
New Orleans	7	9	0	.438	298	361
Atlanta	4	12	0	.250	281	382

AMERICAN CONFERENCE

Eastern Division

	W	L	T	Pct.	Pts.	OP
Miami	14	2	0	.875	513	298
New England	9	7	0	.563	362	352
N.Y. Jets	7	9	0	.438	332	364
Indianapolis	4	12	0	.250	239	414
Buffalo	2	14	0	.125	250	454

Central Division

	W	L	T	Pct.	Pts.	OP
Pittsburgh	9	7	0	.563	387	310
Cincinnati	8	8	0	.500	339	339
Cleveland	5	11	0	.313	250	297
Houston	3	13	0	.188	240	437

Western Division

	W	L	T	Pct.	Pts.	OP
Denver	13	3	0	.813	353	241
Seattle*	12	4	0	.750	418	282
L.A. Raiders*	11	5	0	.688	368	278
Kansas City	8	8	0	.500	314	324
San Diego	7	9	0	.438	394	413

*Wild card qualifier for playoffs
Wild Card Game: N.Y. Giants 16, L.A. Rams 13
NFC Divisional playoffs: San Francisco 21, N.Y. Giants 10; Chicago 23, Washington 19
NFC Championship: San Francisco 23, Chicago 0
Wild Card Game: Seattle 13, L.A. Raiders 7
AFC Divisional playoffs: Miami 31, Seattle 10; Pittsburgh 24, Denver 17
AFC Championship: Miami 45, Pittsburgh 28
Super Bowl XIX: San Francisco 38, Miami 16

ALL-TIME NFL STANDINGS 343

1985

AMERICAN CONFERENCE
Eastern Division

	W	L	T	Pct.	Pts.	OP
Miami	12	4	0	.750	428	320
N.Y. Jets	11	5	0	.688	393	264
New England	11	5	0	.688	362	290
Indianapolis	5	11	0	.313	320	386
Buffalo	2	14	0	.125	200	381

CENTRAL DIVISION

	W	L	T	Pct.	Pts.	OP
Cleveland	8	8	0	.500	287	294
Cincinnati	7	9	0	.438	441	437
Pittsburgh	7	9	0	.438	379	355
Houston	5	11	0	.313	284	412

WESTERN DIVISION

	W	L	T	Pct.	Pts.	OP
L.A. Raiders	12	4	0	.750	354	308
Denver	11	5	0	.688	380	329
Seattle	8	8	0	.500	349	303
San Diego	8	8	0	.500	467	435
Kansas City	6	10	0	.375	327	360

NATIONAL CONFERENCE
Eastern Division

	W	L	T	Pct.	Pts.	OP
Dallas	10	6	0	.625	357	333
N.Y. Giants	10	6	0	.625	399	283
Washington	10	6	0	.625	298	313
Philadelphia	7	9	0	.438	286	310
St. Louis	5	11	0	.313	279	415

CENTRAL DIVISION

	W	L	T	Pct.	Pts.	OP
Chicago	15	1	0	.938	456	198
Green Bay	8	8	0	.500	337	355
Minnesota	7	9	0	.438	346	359
Detroit	7	9	0	.438	307	366
Tampa Bay	2	14	0	.125	294	448

WESTERN DIVISION

	W	L	T	Pct.	Pts.	OP
L.A. Rams	11	5	0	.688	340	287
San Francisco	10	6	0	.625	411	263
New Orleans	5	11	0	.313	294	401
Atlanta	4	12	0	.250	282	452

Wild Card Game: New England 26, N.Y. Jets 14
AFC Divisional playoffs: Miami 24, Cleveland 21; New England 27, L.A. Raiders 20
AFC Championship: New England 31, Miami 14
Wild Card Game: N.Y. Giants 17, San Francisco 3
NFC Divisional playoffs: L.A. Rams 20, Dallas 0; Chicago 21, N.Y. Giants 0
NFC Championship: Chicago 24, L.A. Rams 0
Super Bowl XX: Chicago 46, New England 10

1986

AMERICAN CONFERENCE
Eastern Division

	W	L	T	Pct.	Pts.	OP
N.Y. Giants	14	2	0	.875	371	236
Washington	12	4	0	.750	368	296
Dallas	7	9	0	.438	346	337
Philadelphia	5	10	1	.344	256	312
St. Louis	4	11	1	.281	218	351

Central Division

	W	L	T	Pct.	Pts.	OP
Chicago	14	2	0	.875	352	187
Minnesota	9	7	0	.563	398	273
Detroit	5	11	0	.313	277	326
Green Bay	4	12	0	.250	254	418
Tampa Bay	2	14	0	.125	239	473

Western Division

	W	L	T	Pct.	Pts.	OP
San Francisco	10	5	1	.656	374	247
L.A. Rams	10	6	0	.625	309	267
Atlanta	7	8	1	.469	280	280
New Orleans	7	9	0	.438	288	287

NATIONAL CONFERENCE
Eastern Division

	W	L	T	Pct.	Pts.	OP
New England	11	5	0	.688	412	307
N.Y. Jets	10	6	0	.625	364	386
Miami	8	8	0	.500	430	405
Buffalo	4	12	0	.250	287	348
Indianapolis	3	13	0	.188	229	400

Central Division

	W	L	T	Pct.	Pts.	OP
Cleveland	12	4	0	.750	391	310
Cincinnati	10	6	0	.625	409	394
Pittsburgh	6	10	0	.375	307	336
Houston	5	11	0	.313	274	329

Western Division

	W	L	T	Pct.	Pts.	OP
Denver	11	5	0	.688	378	327
Kansas City	10	6	0	.625	358	326
Seattle	10	6	0	.625	366	293
L.A. Raiders	8	8	0	.500	323	346
San Diego	4	12	0	.250	335	396

NFC Wild Card Game: Washington 19, L.A. Rams 7
NFC Divisional playoffs: Washington 27, Chicago 13; N.Y. Giants 49, San Francisco 3
NFC Championship: N.Y. Giants 17, Washington 0
AFC Wild Card Game: N.Y. Jets 35, Kansas City 15
AFC Divisional playoffs: Cleveland 23, N.Y. Jets 20 (2 OT); Denver 22, New England 17
AFC Championship: Denver 23, Cleveland 20 (OT)
Super Bowl XXI: N.Y. Giants 39, Denver 20

1987

NATIONAL CONFERENCE
Eastern Division
	W	L	T	Pct.	Pts.	OP
Washington	11	4	0	.733	379	285
St. Louis	7	8	0	.467	362	368
Dallas	7	8	0	.467	340	348
Philadelphia	7	8	0	.467	337	380
N.Y. Giants	6	9	0	.400	280	312

Central Division
	W	L	T	Pct.	Pts.	OP
Chicago	11	4	0	.733	356	282
Minnesota	8	7	0	.533	336	335
Green Bay	5	9	1	.367	255	300
Tampa Bay	4	11	0	.267	286	360
Detroit	4	11	0	.267	269	384

Western Division
	W	L	T	Pct.	Pts.	OP
San Francisco	13	2	0	.867	459	253
New Orleans	12	3	0	.800	422	283
L.A. Rams	6	9	0	.400	317	361
Atlanta	3	12	0	.200	205	436

AMERICAN CONFERENCE
Eastern Division
	W	L	T	Pct.	Pts.	OP
Indianapolis	9	6	0	.600	300	238
New England	8	7	0	.533	320	293
Miami	8	7	0	.533	362	335
Buffalo	7	8	0	.467	270	305
N.Y. Jets	6	9	0	.400	334	360

Central Division
	W	L	T	Pct.	Pts.	OP
Cleveland	10	5	0	.667	390	239
Houston	9	6	0	.600	345	349
Pittsburgh	8	7	0	.533	285	299
Cincinnati	4	11	0	.267	285	370

Western Division
	W	L	T	Pct.	Pts.	OP
Denver	10	4	1	.700	379	288
Seattle	9	6	0	.600	371	314
San Diego	8	7	0	.533	253	317
L.A. Raiders	5	10	0	.333	301	289
Kansas City	4	11	0	.267	273	388

NFC Wild Card Game: Minnesota 44, New Orleans 10
NFC Divisional playoffs: Minnesota 36, San Francisco 24; Wash. 21, Chicago 17
NFC Championship: Washington 17, Minnesota 10
AFC Wild Card Game: Houston 23, Seattle 20 (OT)
AFC Divisional playoffs: Cleveland 38, Indianapolis 21; Denver 34, Houston 10
AFC Championship: Denver 38, Cleveland 33
Super Bowl XXII: Washington 42, Denver 10

1988

AMERICAN CONFERENCE
Eastern Division
	W	L	T	Pct.	Pts.	OP
Buffalo	12	4	0	.750	329	237
Indianapolis	9	7	0	.563	354	315
New England	9	7	0	.563	250	284
N.Y. Jets	8	7	1	.531	372	354
Miami	6	10	0	.375	319	380

Central Division
	W	L	T	Pct.	Pts.	OP
Cincinnati	12	4	0	.750	448	329
Cleveland	10	6	0	.625	304	288
Houston	10	6	0	.625	424	365
Pittsburgh	5	11	0	.313	336	421

Western Division
	W	L	T	Pct.	Pts.	OP
Seattle	9	7	0	.563	339	329
Denver	8	8	0	.500	327	352
L.A. Raiders	7	9	0	.438	325	369
San Diego	6	10	0	.375	231	332
Kansas City	4	11	1	.281	254	320

NATIONAL CONFERENCE
Eastern Division
	W	L	T	Pct.	Pts.	OP
Philadelphia	10	6	0	.625	379	319
N.Y. Giants	10	6	0	.625	359	304
Washington	7	9	0	.438	345	387
Phoenix	7	9	0	.438	344	398
Dallas	3	13	0	.188	265	381

Central Division
	W	L	T	Pct.	Pts.	OP
Chicago	12	4	0	.750	312	215
Minnesota	11	5	0	.688	406	233
Tampa Bay	5	11	0	.313	261	350
Detroit	4	12	0	.250	220	313
Green Bay	4	12	0	.250	240	315

Western Division
	W	L	T	Pct.	Pts.	OP
San Francisco	10	6	0	.625	369	294
L.A. Rams	10	6	0	.625	407	293
New Orleans	10	6	0	.625	312	283
Atlanta	5	11	0	.313	244	315

AFC Wild Card Game: Houston 24, Cleveland 23
AFC Divisional playoffs: Cincinnati 21, Seattle 13; Buffalo 17, Houston 10
AFC Championship: Cincinnati 21, Buffalo 10
NFC Wild Card Game: Minnesota 28, L.A. Rams 17
NFC Divisional playoffs: Chicago 20, Philadelphia 12; San Francisco 34, Minnesota 9
NFC Championship: San Francisco 28, Chicago 3
Super Bowl XXIII: San Francisco 20, Cincinnati 16

ALL-TIME NFL STANDINGS

1989

AMERICAN CONFERENCE

Eastern Division

	W	L	T	Pct.	Pts.	OP
Buffalo	9	7	0	.563	409	317
Indianapolis	8	8	0	.500	298	301
Miami	8	8	0	.500	331	379
New England	5	11	0	.313	297	391
N.Y. Jets	4	12	0	.250	253	411

Central Division

	W	L	T	Pct.	Pts.	OP
Cleveland	9	6	1	.594	334	254
Houston	9	7	0	.563	365	412
Pittsburgh	9	7	0	.563	265	326
Cincinnati	8	8	0	.500	404	285

Western Division

	W	L	T	Pct.	Pts.	OP
Denver	11	5	0	.688	362	226
Kansas City	8	7	1	.531	318	286
L.A. Raiders	8	8	0	.500	315	297
Seattle	7	9	0	.438	241	327
San Diego	6	10	0	.375	266	290

NATIONAL CONFERENCE

Eastern Division

	W	L	T	Pct.	Pts.	OP
N.Y. Giants	12	4	0	.750	348	252
Philadelphia	11	5	0	.688	342	274
Washington	10	6	0	.625	386	308
Phoenix	5	11	0	.313	258	377
Dallas	1	15	0	.063	204	393

Central Division

	W	L	T	Pct.	Pts.	OP
Minnesota	10	6	0	.625	351	275
Green Bay	10	6	0	.625	362	356
Detroit	7	9	0	.438	312	364
Chicago	6	10	0	.375	358	377
Tampa Bay	5	11	0	.313	320	419

Western Division

	W	L	T	Pct.	Pts.	OP
San Francisco	14	2	0	.875	442	253
L.A. Rams	11	5	0	.688	426	344
New Orleans	9	7	0	.563	386	301
Atlanta	3	13	0	.188	279	437

AFC Wild Card Game: Pittsburgh 26, Houston 23 (OT)
AFC Divisional playoffs: Cleveland 34, Buffalo 30; Denver 24, Pittsburgh 23
AFC Championship: Denver 37, Cleveland 21
NFC Wild Card Game: L.A. Rams 21, Philadelphia 7
NFC Divisional playoffs: L.A. Rams 19, N.Y. Giants 13 (OT); San Francisco 41, Minnesota 13
NFC Championship: San Francisco 30, L.A. Rams 3
Super Bowl XXIV: San Francisco 55, Denver 10

1990 NFL DRAFT

Player	Order No.	Pos.	College	Club	Round
Adams, Orlando	273	DT	Jacksonville State	Philadelphia	10
Agnew, Ray	10	DE	North Carolina State	New England	1
Allen, Terry	241	RB	Clemson	Minnesota	9
Alm, Jeff	41	DT	Notre Dame	Houston	2
Anderson, Bill	176	C	Iowa	Chicago	7
Anderson, Jesse	87	TE	Mississippi State	Tampa Bay	4
Anthony, Terry	281	WR	Florida State	Tampa Bay	11
Arbuckle, Charles	125	TE	UCLA	New Orleans	5
Archambeau, Lester	186	DE	Stanford	Green Bay	7
Bailey, Johnny	228	RB	Texas A&I	Chicago	9
Banes, Joey	295	T	Houston	Houston	11
Barnett, Fred	77	WR	Arkansas State	Philadelphia	3
Barnett, Harlon	101	DB	Michigan State	Cleveland	4
Barnett, Oliver	55	DE	Kentucky	Atlanta	3
Bates, Steve	272	DE	James Madison	Los Angeles Rams	10
Baumgartner, Kirk	242	QB	Stevens Point (Wis.)	Green Bay	9
Bavaro, David	225	LB	Syracuse	Phoenix	9
Beckles, Ian	114	G	Indiana	Tampa Bay	5
Bell, Richard	319	RB	Nebraska	Pittsburgh	12
Bellamy, Mike	50	WR	Illinois	Philadelphia	2
Benhart, Gene	311	QB	Western Illinois	Indianapolis	12
Bennett, Tony	18	LB	Mississippi	Green Bay	1
Berry, Kenny	256	DB	Miami	San Diego	10
Berry, Latin	78	RB	Oregon	Los Angeles Rams	3
Blackmon, Robert	34	DB	Baylor	Seattle	2
Bolcar, Ned	146	LB	Notre Dame	Seattle	6
Bouwens, Shawn	226	G	Nebraska Wesleyan	New England	9
Brennan, Mike	91	T	Notre Dame	Cincinnati	4
Brockman, Lonnie	236	LB	West Virginia	New Orleans	9
Brostek, Bern	23	C	Washington	Los Angeles Rams	1
Broussard, Steve	20	RB	Washington State	Atlanta	1
Brown, Dean	316	G	Notre Dame	Indianapolis	12
Brown, Dennis	47	DT	Washington	San Francisco	2
Brown, Roger	215	DB	Virginia Tech	Green Bay	8
Buck, Mike	156	QB	Maine	New Orleans	6
Buck, Vince	44	DB	Central State (Ohio)	New Orleans	2
Burnett, Rob	129	DE	Syracuse	Cleveland	5
Burnett, Webbie	287	NT	Western Kentucky	New Orleans	11
Busch, Mike	254	TE	Iowa State	Tampa Bay	10
Butler, Le Roy	48	DB	Florida State	Green Bay	2
Caliguire, Dean	92	C	Pittsburgh	San Francisco	4
Calloway, Chris	97	WR	Michigan	Pittsburgh	4
Campbell, Jeff	118	WR	Colorado	Detroit	5
Carr, Derrick	210	DE	Bowling Green	New Orleans	8
Carrier, Mark	6	DB	Southern California	Chicago	1
Carter, Dexter	25	RB	Florida State	San Francisco	1
Centers, Larry	115	RB	Steven F. Austin	Phoenix	5
Chaffey, Pat	117	RB	Oregon State	Chicago	5
Claiborne, Robert	313	WR	San Diego State	Detroit	12
Clark, Bernard	65	LB	Miami	Cincinnati	3

NFL DRAFT 347

Penn State RB Blair Thomas ran to the Jets.

Player	Order No.	Pos.	College	Club	Round
Clark, Ken	206	RB	Nebraska	Indiana	8
Cobb, Reggie	30	RB	Tennessee	Tampa Bay	2
Coleman, Pat	237	WR	Mississippi	Houston	9
Collins, Andre	46	LB	Penn State	Washington	2
Collins, Brent	170	LB	Carson-Newman	Buffalo	7
Collins, Keith	193	DB	Appalachian State	San Diego	7
Conklin, Cary	86	QB	Washington	Washington	4
Conner, Darion	27	LB	Jackson State	Atlanta	2
Cook, Terry	224	DE	Fresno State	Tampa Bay	9
Cooney, Anthony	310	DB	Arkansas	Chicago	12
Cooper, Gary	260	WR	Clemson	New Orleans	10
Cornish, Frank	143	C	UCLA	San Diego	6
Cox, Ron	33	LB	Fresno State	Chicago	2
Crawford, Elbert	216	C	Arkansas	Los Angeles	8
Crigler, Eric	261	T	Murray State	Cincinnati	10
Cunningham, Pat	106	T	Texas A&M	Indianapolis	4
Davidson, Jeff	111	G	Ohio State	Denver	5
Davidson, Kenny	43	DE	Louisiana State	Pittsburgh	2

348 THE COMPLETE HANDBOOK OF PRO FOOTBALL

Player	Order No.	Pos.	College	Club	Round
Davis, Darrell	306	LB	Texas Christian	New York Jets	12
Davis, Demetrius	331	TE	Nevada-Reno	Los Angeles Raiders	12
Davis, Eric	53	DB	Jacksonville State	San Francisco	2
Davis, Travis	85	DT	Michigan State	Phoenix	4
Dawkins, Dale	223	WR	Miami	New York Jets	9
De Riggi, Fred	181	NT	Syracuse	Buffalo	7
Donelson, Ventson	309	DB	Michigan State	New England	12
Dorn, Torin	95	DB	North Carolina	Los Angeles Raiders	4
Douglas, Derrick	141	RB	Louisiana Tech	Tampa Bay	6
Downing, Tim	302	DE	Washington State	New York Giants	11
Duffy, Roger	196	C	Penn State	New York Jets	8
Dunbar, Karl	209	DT	Louisiana State	Pittsburgh	8
Dykes, Curt	217	T	Oregon	Philadelphia	8
Edwards, Al	292	WR	N.W. Louisiana	Buffalo	11
Elewonibi, Mohammed	76	G	Brigham Young	Washington	3
Elle, Dave	252	TE	South Dakota	Phoenix	10
Ellis, Todd	247	QB	South Carolina	Denver	9
Ellison, Chris	278	DB	Houston	Atlanta	11
Elmore, Kent	190	P	Tennessee	Los Angeles Rams	7
Emanuel, Aaron	191	RB	Southern California	New York Giants	7
Epps, Tory	195	NT	Memphis State	Atlanta	8
Flannigan, J.J.	201	RB	Colorado	San Diego	8
Fortin, Roman	203	G	San Diego State	Detroit	8
Foster, Barry	128	RB	Arkansas	Pittsburgh	5
Fox, Mike	51	DT	West Virginia	New York Giants	2
Francis, James	12	LB	Baylor	Cincinnati	1
Francisco, D'Juan	262	DB	Notre Dame	Washington	10
Friesz, John	138	QB	Idaho	San Diego	6
Fuller, Eddie	100	RB	Louisiana State	Buffalo	4
Galbraith, Scott	178	TE	Southern California	Cleveland	7
Gant, Kenneth	221	DB	Albany State (Ga.)	Dallas	9
Gardner, Carwell	42	RB	Louisville	Buffalo	2
Gardner, Donnie	171	DE	Kentucky	Tampa Bay	7
Garrett, Judd	327	RB	Princeton	Philadelphia	12
Gdowski, Gerry	207	QB	Nebraska	New Orleans	8
George, Jeff	1	QB	Illinois	Indianapolis	1
Goeas, Leo	60	G	Hawaii	San Diego	3
Goetz, Chris	227	G	Pittsburgh	San Diego	9
Goetz, Ron	324	LB	Minnesota	Minnesota	12
Goldberg, Bill	301	DT	Georgia	Los Angeles Rams	11
Gordon, Clemente	296	QB	Grambling	Cleveland	11
Graham, Derrick	124	T	Appalachian State	Kansas City	5
Grant, Alan	103	DB	Stanford	Indianapolis	4
Graves, Broderick	233	RB	Winston-Salem	New Orleans	9
Gray, Cecil	244	DT	North Carolina	Philadelphia	9
Gray, James	120	RB	Texas Tech	New England	5
Grayson, Dan	182	LB	Washington State	Pittsburgh	7
Green, Eric	21	TE	Liberty	Pittsburgh	1
Green, Harold	38	RB	South Carolina	Cincinnati	2
Green, Willie	194	WR	Mississippi	Detroit	8
Griffith, Brent	166	G	Minnesota-Duluth	Buffalo	7
Gromos, John	312	QB	Vanderbilt	Seattle	12
Grunhard, Tim	40	C	Notre Dame	Kansas City	2
Hackemack, Ken	127	T	Texas	Kansas City	5
Haggins, Odell	248	DT	Florida State	San Francisco	9

NFL DRAFT 349

USC's Junior Seau, a junior LB, got Charger call.

350 THE COMPLETE HANDBOOK OF PRO FOOTBALL

USC junior safety Mark Carrier landed in Chicago.

NFL DRAFT 351

Houston junior QB Andre Ware won Heisman and Lion nod.

Patriots made Arizona LB Chris Singleton No. 8.

NFL DRAFT 353

Player	Order No.	Pos.	College	Club	Round
Haliburton, Ronnie	164	TE	Louisiana State	Denver	6
Hammel, Todd	307	QB	Stephen F. Austin	Tampa Bay	12
Hampton, Alonzo	104	DB	Pittsburgh	Minnesota	4
Hampton, Rodney	24	RB	Georgia	New York Giants	1
Harden, Bobby	315	DB	Miami	Miami	12
Harper, Dave	277	LB	Humboldt State	Dallas	11
Harris, Jackie	102	TE	N.E. Louisiana	Green Bay	4
Harris, Major	317	QB	West Virginia	Los Angeles Raiders	12
Harrison, Martin	276	DE	Washington	San Francisco	10
Hayes, Eric	119	DT	Florida State	Seattle	5
Hayworth, Tracy	174	LB	Tennessee	Detroit	7
Heard, Ronald	155	WR	Bowling Green	Pittsburgh	6
Henry, Maurice	147	LB	Kansas State	Detroit	6
Hilliard, Randy	157	DB	N.W. Louisiana	Cleveland	6
Hinckley, Rob	90	LB	Stanford	Detroit	4
Hines, Clarkston	238	WR	Duke	Buffalo	9
Hitchcock, Bill	202	T	Purdue	Seattle	8
Hoard, Leroy	45	RB	Michigan	Cleveland	2
Hobby, Marion	74	DE	Tennessee	Minnesota	3
Hodson, Tommy	59	QB	Louisiana State	New England	3
Holt, Leroy	137	RB	Southern California	Miami	5
Hough, Scott	183	G	Maine	New Orleans	7
Houston, Bobby	75	LB	North Carolina State	Green Bay	3
Hudson, Craig	263	TE	Wisconsin	Kansas City	10
Hudson, John	294	C	Auburn	Philadelphia	11
Huffman, Darvell	232	WR	Boston U.	Indianapolis	9
Jackson, Harry	299	RB	St. Cloud (Minn.)	Green Bay	11
James, Clint	246	DE	Louisiana State	New York Giants	9
James, Lynn	122	WR	Arizona State	Cincinnati	5
Jeffery, Tony	318	WR	San Jose State	Kansas City	12
Jimerson, Arthur	197	LB	Norfolk State	Los Angeles Raiders	8
Johnson, Anthony	36	RB	Notre Dame	Indianapolis	2
Johnson, Johnny	169	RB	San Jose State	Phoenix	7
Jones, Fred	96	WR	Grambling	Kansas City	4
Jones, Gary	239	DB	Texas A&M	Pittsburgh	9
Jones, Jimmie	64	DT	Miami	Dallas	3
Jones, Jock	212	LB	Virginia Tech	Cleveland	8
Jones, Mike	54	TE	Texas A&M	Minnesota	3
Jones, Myron	304	RB	Fresno State	Los Angeles Raiders	11
Jones, Tony	153	WR	Texas	Houston	6
Jordan, Darrell	222	LB	Northern Arizona	Atlanta	9
Kelson, Derrick	279	DB	Purdue	New York Jets	11
Kennedy, Cortez	3	DT	Miami	Seattle	1
Kula, Bob	175	T	Michigan State	Seattle	7
Kupp, Craig	135	QB	Pacific Lutheran	New York Giants	5
Labbe, Rico	109	DB	Boston College	Washington	4
Landry, Anthony	253	RB	Stephen F. Austin	New England	10
Lang, David	328	RB	Northern Arizona	Los Angeles Rams	12
Lang, Le-Lo	136	DB	Washington	Denver	5
Lathon, Lamar	15	LB	Houston	Houston	1
Leggett, Brad	219	C	Southern California	Denver	8
Levelis, John	188	LB	C.W. Post	Minnesota	7
Leverenz, Jon	297	LB	Minnesota	Washington	11
Lewis, Garry	173	DB	Alcorn State	Los Angeles Raiders	7
Lewis, Nate	187	WR	Oregon Tech	San Diego	7
Lewis, Ron	68	WR	Florida State	San Francisco	3

Florida junior RB Emmitt Smith is a Cowboy.

Giants' No. 1 was Georgia RB Rodney Hampton.

356   THE COMPLETE HANDBOOK OF PRO FOOTBALL

Chiefs went for Michigan State LB Percy Snow.

NFL DRAFT

Player	Order No.	Pos.	College	Club	Round
Lewis, Ron	303	WR	Jackson State	Los Angeles Raiders	11
Linn, Jack	229	T	West Virginia	Detroit	9
Lodish, Mike	265	DT	UCLA	Buffalo	10
Lomack, Tony	245	WR	Florida	Los Angeles	9
Maggio, Kirk	325	P	UCLA	Green Bay	12
Mangum, John	144	DB	Alabama	Chicago	6
Mark, Greg	79	DE	Miami	New York Giants	3
Martin, Jerome	269	DB	Western Kentucky	Green Bay	10
Mathis, Terance	140	WR	New Mexico	New York Jets	6
Matusz, Roman	298	T	Pittsburgh	Chicago	11
Mayberry, Tony	108	C	Wake Forest	Tampa Bay	4
McCants, Keith	4	LB	Alabama	Tampa Bay	1
McCarthy, Shawn	305	P	Purdue	Atlanta	12
McMichel, Ken	330	LB	Oklahoma	Phoenix	12
McMurtry, Greg	80	WR	Michigan	New England	3
McWright, Robert	134	DB	Texas Christian	New York Jets	5
Melander, Jon	113	T	Minnesota	New England	5
Miles, Eddie	266	LB	Minnesota	Pittsburgh	10
Miller, Bill	258	WR	Illinois State	Detroit	10
Mills, Jeff	57	LB	Nebraska	San Diego	3
Mitchell, Brian	130	RB	S.W. Louisiana	Washington	5
Mitchell, Scott	93	QB	Utah	Miami	4
Montgomery, Alton	52	DB	Houston	Denver	2
Moore, Otis	274	DT	Clemson	New York Giants	10
Morris, Robert	257	DE	Valdosta State	Seattle	10
Moss, Tony	88	WR	Louisiana State	Chicago	4
Moxley, Tim	243	G	Ohio State	Washington	9
Murray, Andy	184	RB	Kentucky	Houston	7
Newbill, Richard	126	LB	Miami	Houston	5
Newman, Pat	249	WR	Utah State	Minnesota	10
Nies, John	154	P	Arizona	Buffalo	6
Norman, Dempsey	282	WR	St. Francis (Ill.)	Phoenix	11
Novak, Jeff	172	G	S.W. Texas State	San Diego	7
O'Connor, Tim	288	T	Virginia	Cincinnati	11
O'Donnell, Neil	70	QB	Maryland	Pittsburgh	3
Odegard, Don	150	DB	Nevada-Las Vegas	Cincinnati	6
Oglesby, Alfred	66	DT	Houston	Miami	3
Ogletree, Craig	177	LB	Auburn	Cincinnati	7
Oldham, Chris	105	DB	Oregon	Detroit	4
Owens, Dan	35	DE	Southern California	Detroit	2
Owens, Michael	235	RB	Syracuse	Kansas City	9
Parker, Glenn	69	T	Arizona	Buffalo	3
Patton, Marvcus	208	LB	UCLA	Buffalo	8
Paup, Bryce	159	LB	Northern Iowa	Green Bay	6
Peguese, Willis	72	DE	Miami	Houston	3
Perry, Leon	230	RB	Oklahoma	Los Angeles Raiders	9
Pickens, Dwight	220	WR	Fresno State	San Francisco	8
Pleasant, Anthony	73	DE	Tennessee State	Cleveland	3
Pollack, Frank	165	T	Northern Arizona	San Francisco	6
Pool, David	145	DB	Carson-Newman	San Diego	6
Port, Chris	320	G	Duke	New Orleans	12
Price, Mitchell	234	DB	Tulane	Cincinnati	9
Price, Terry	255	DT	Texas A&M	Chicago	10
Pringle, Mike	139	RB	Cal State-Fullerton	Atlanta	6
Proctor, Basil	168	LB	West Virginia	New York Jets	7

358 THE COMPLETE HANDBOOK OF PRO FOOTBALL

Cortez Kennedy, Miami DT Seahawks (No. 3)

Darrell Thompson, Minn. RB Packers (No. 19)

Player	Order No.	Pos.	College	Club	Round
Proehl, Ricky	58	WR	Wake Forest	Phoenix	3
Quast, Brad	251	LB	Iowa	New York Jets	10
Rayam, Thomas	270	DT	Alabama	Washington	10
Redding, Reggie	121	TE	Cal State-Fullerton	Atlanta	5
Reed, Daryl	286	DB	Oregon	Seattle	11
Rembert, Reggie	28	WR	West Virginia	New York Jets	2
Riley, Andre	314	WR	Washington	Cincinnati	12
Riley, Donnie	308	RB	Central Michigan	Phoenix	12
Robinson, Jeroy	82	LB	Texas A&M	Denver	4
Robinson, Junior	110	DB	East Carolina	New England	5
Rose, Blaine	322	G	Maryland	New England	12
Ross, Phil	231	TE	Oregon State	Miami	9
Rouse, James	200	RB	Arkansas	Chicago	8
Rowell, Eugene	240	WR	So. Mississippi	Cleveland	9
Ryan, Tim	61	DT	Southern California	Chicago	3
Salum, Donnie	250	LB	Arizona	Atlanta	10
Savage, Ray	198	LB	Virginia	Los Angeles Rams	8
Savage, Tony	112	DT	Washington State	New York Jets	5
Schlichting, Craig	214	DE	Wyoming	Minnesota	8
Schultz, Bill	94	G	Southern California	Indianapolis	4
Searcy, Elliott	326	WR	Southern U.	San Diego	12
Seau, Junior	5	LB	Southern California	San Diego	1
Sharpe, Shannon	192	WR	Savannah State	Denver	7
Shavers, Tyrone	142	WR	Lamar	Phoenix	6
Shelton, Anthony	289	DB	Tennessee State	San Francisco	11
Simien, Kerry	323	WR	Texas A&I	Cleveland	12
Simmons, Stacey	83	WR	Florida	Indianapolis	4
Sims, Keith	39	G	Iowa State	Miami	2
Sims, Tom	152	DT	Pittsburgh	Kansas City	6

BYU guard Mohammed Elewonibi went to Washington.

Player	Order No.	Pos.	College	Club	Round
Singletary, James	179	LB	East Carolina	Indianapolis	7
Singleton, Chris	8	LB	Arizona	New England	1
Slack, Reggie	321	QB	Auburn	Houston	12
Smagala, Stan	123	DB	Notre Dame	Los Angeles Raiders	5
Smeenge, Joel	71	DE	Western Michigan	New Orleans	3
Smith, Anthony	11	DE	Arizona	Los Angeles Raiders	1
Smith, Ben	22	DB	Georgia	Philadelphia	1
Smith, Carnel	290	DE	Pittsburgh	Indianapolis	11
Smith, Cedric	131	RB	Florida	Minnesota	5
Smith, Donald	271	DB	Liberty	Minnesota	10
Smith, Emmitt	17	RB	Florida	Dallas	1
Smith, Sean	280	DE	Georgia Tech	New England	11
Snow, Percy	13	LB	Michigan State	Kansas City	1
Spears, Ernest	267	DB	Southern California	New Orleans	10
Spindler, Marc	62	DE	Pittsburgh	Detroit	3
Stallworth, Tim	161	WR	Washington State	Los Angeles Rams	6
Stargell, Tony	56	DB	Tennessee State	New York Jets	3
Staysniak, Joe	185	T	Ohio State	San Diego	7

360 THE COMPLETE HANDBOOK OF PRO FOOTBALL

Seahawks look for blitz from Syracuse LB Terry Wooden.

Player	Order No.	Pos.	College	Club	Round
Still, Eric	99	G	Tennessee	Houston	4
Stover, Matt	329	K	Louisiana Tech	New York Giants	12
Stowers, Tommie	283	TE	Missouri	San Diego	11
Strouf, Terry	189	T	La Crosse, Wis.	Philadelphia	7
Strzelczyk, Justin	283	T	Maine	Pittsburgh	11
Szott, Dave	180	G	Penn State	Kansas City	7
Szymanski, James	258	DE	Michigan State	Denver	10
Taylor, Troy	84	QB	California	New York Jets	4
Terrell, Pat	49	DB	Notre Dame	Los Angeles Rams	2
Thomas, Blair	2	RB	Penn State	New York Jets	1
Thomas, Dee	264	DB	Nicholls State	Houston	10
Thompson, Anthony	275	DB	East Carolina	Denver	10
Thompson, Anthony	31	RB	Indiana	Phoenix	2
Thompson, Darrell	19	RB	Minnesota	Green Bay	1
Thompson, Ernest	291	RB	Georgia Southern	Kansas City	11
Thompson, Kevin	162	DB	Oklahoma	Philadelphia	6
Thornton, Reggie	116	WR	Bowling Green	Minnesota	5
Tucker, Brett	211	LB	Northern Illinois	Houston	8
Turnbull, Renaldo	14	DE	West Virginia	New Orleans	1
Vanhorse, Sean	151	DB	Howard	Miami	6
Veasey, Craig	81	DT	Houston	Pittsburgh	3
Voorhees, Barry	218	T	Cal State-Northridge	New York Giants	8
Walker, Derrick	163	TE	Michigan	San Diego	6
Walker, Tony	148	LB	S.E. Missouri	Indianapolis	6

NFL DRAFT

West Virginia WR Reggie Rembert will fly as a Jet.

Player	Order No.	Pos.	College	Club	Round
Wallace, Aaron	37	LB	Texas A&M	Los Angeles Raiders	2
Wallace, Michael	268	DB	Jackson State	Cleveland	10
Ware, Andre	7	QB	Houston	Detroit	1
Warnsley, Reginald	285	RB	So. Mississippi	Detroit	11
Warren, Chris	89	RB	Ferrum, Va.	Seattle	4
Washington, Fred	32	DT	Texas Christian	Chicago	2
Washington, Mickey	199	DB	Texas A&M	Phoenix	8
Watson, Tyrone	300	WR	Tennessee State	Philadelphia	11
Webb, Richmond	9	T	Texas A&M	Miami	1
Wells, Kent	160	DT	Nebraska	Washington	6
Wellsandt, Doug	204	TE	Washington State	Cincinnati	8
White, Brent	284	DE	Michigan	Chicago	11
White, Dwayne	167	G	Alcorn State	New York Jets	7
Whitmore, David	107	DB	Stephen F. Austin	New York Giants	4
Williams, Calvin	133	WR	Purdue	Philadelphia	5
Williams, James	158	LB	Mississippi State	New Orleans	6
Williams, James	16	DB	Fresno State	Buffalo	1
Willis, Peter Tom	63	QB	Florida State	Chicago	3
Wilson, Charles	132	WR	Memphis State	Green Bay	5
Wilson, Harvey	213	DB	Southern U.	Indianapolis	8
Wilson, Marcus	149	RB	Virginia	Los Angeles Raiders	6
Wilson, Walter	67	WR	East Carolina	San Diego	3
Winston, DeMond	98	LB	Vanderbilt	New Orleans	4
Wooden, Terry	29	LB	Syracuse	Seattle	2
Woods, Thomas	205	WR	Tennessee	Miami	8
Wright, Alexander	26	WR	Auburn	Dallas	2

1990 NFL SCHEDULE

*NIGHT GAME

SUNDAY, SEPT. 9
Denver at Los Angeles Raiders
Houston at Atlanta
Indianapolis at Buffalo
New York Jets at Cincinnati
Miami at New England
Minnesota at Kansas City
Phoenix at Washington
Pittsburgh at Cleveland
Los Angeles Rams at Green Bay
San Diego at Dallas
Seattle at Chicago
Tampa Bay at Detroit
*Philadelphia at New York Giants

MONDAY, SEPT. 10
*San Francisco at New Orleans

SUNDAY, SEPT. 16
Atlanta at Detroit
Buffalo at Miami
Chicago at Green Bay
Cincinnati at San Diego
Cleveland at New York Jets
New England at Indianapolis
New Orleans at Minnesota
New York Giants at Dallas
Los Angeles Raiders at Seattle
Los Angeles Rams at Tampa Bay
Phoenix at Philadelphia
Washington at San Francisco
*Houston at Pittsburgh

MONDAY, SEPT. 17
*Kansas City at Denver

SUNDAY, SEPT. 23
Atlanta at San Francisco
Dallas at Washington
Indianapolis at Houston
Kansas City at Green Bay
Miami at New York Giants
Minnesota at Chicago
New England at Cincinnati
Philadelphia at Los Angeles Rams
Phoenix at New Orleans
Pittsburgh at Los Angeles Raiders
San Diego at Cleveland
Seattle at Denver
*Detroit at Tampa Bay

MONDAY, SEPT. 24
*Buffalo at New York Jets

SUNDAY, SEPT. 30
Chicago at Los Angeles Raiders
Cleveland at Kansas City
Dallas at New York Giants
Denver at Buffalo
Green Bay at Detroit
Houston at San Diego
Indianapolis at Philadelphia
Miami at Pittsburgh
New York Jets at New England
Tampa Bay at Minnesota
*Washington at Phoenix

MONDAY, OCT. 1
*Cincinnati at Seattle

SUNDAY, OCT. 7
Cincinnati at Los Angeles Rams
Detroit at Minnesota
Green Bay at Chicago
Kansas City at Indianapolis
New Orleans at Atlanta

Cowboys' Troy Aikman has arm, needs receivers.

New York Jets at Miami
San Diego at Pittsburgh
San Francisco at Houston
Seattle at New England
Tampa Bay at Dallas
*Los Angeles Raiders at Buffalo

MONDAY, OCT. 8
*Cleveland at Denver

SUNDAY, OCT. 14
Cleveland at New Orleans
Dallas at Phoenix
Detroit at Kansas City

Green Bay at Tampa Bay
Houston at Cincinnati
New York Giants at Washington
Pittsburgh at Denver
San Diego at New York Jets
San Francisco at Atlanta
Seattle at Los Angeles Raiders
*Los Angeles Rams at Chicago

MONDAY, OCT. 15
*Minnesota at Philadelphia

THURSDAY, OCT. 18
*New England at Miami

364 THE COMPLETE HANDBOOK OF PRO FOOTBALL

SUNDAY, OCT. 21
Atlanta at Los Angeles Rams
Dallas at Tampa Bay
Denver at Indianapolis
Kansas City at Seattle
New Orleans at Houston
New York Jets at Buffalo
Philadelphia at Washington
Phoenix at New York Giants
Pittsburgh at San Francisco
Los Angeles Raiders at San Diego

MONDAY, OCT. 22
*Cincinnati at Cleveland

SUNDAY, OCT. 28
Buffalo at New England
Chicago at Phoenix
Cleveland at San Francisco
Detroit at New Orleans
Miami at Indianapolis
Minnesota vs. Green Bay
  at Milwaukee
New York Jets at Houston
Philadelphia at Dallas
Tampa Bay at San Diego
Washington at New York Giants
*Cincinnati at Atlanta

MONDAY, OCT. 29
*Los Angeles Rams at Pittsburgh

SUNDAY, NOV. 4
Atlanta at Pittsburgh
Buffalo at Cleveland
Chicago at Tampa Bay
Dallas at New York Jets
Houston at Los Angeles Rams
New England at Philadelphia
New Orleans at Cincinnati
Phoenix at Miami
Los Angeles Raiders at Kansas City
San Diego at Seattle
San Francisco at Green Bay
Washington at Detroit
*Denver at Minnesota

MONDAY, NOV. 5
*New York Giants at Indianapolis

SUNDAY, NOV. 11
Atlanta at Chicago
Denver at San Diego
Green Bay at Los Angeles Raiders
Indianapolis at New England
Miami at New York Jets
Minnesota at Detroit
New York Giants at Los Angeles Rams
Phoenix at Buffalo
Seattle at Kansas City
Tampa Bay at New Orleans
*San Francisco at Dallas

MONDAY, NOV. 12
*Washington at Philadelphia

SUNDAY, NOV. 18
Chicago at Denver
Dallas at Los Angeles Rams
Detroit at New York Giants
Green Bay at Phoenix
Houston at Cleveland
Minnesota at Seattle
New England at Buffalo
New Orleans at Washington
New York Jets at Indianapolis
Philadelphia at Atlanta
San Diego at Kansas City
Tampa Bay at San Francisco
*Pittsburgh at Cincinnati

MONDAY, NOV. 19
*Los Angeles Raiders at Miami

THURSDAY, NOV. 22
Denver at Detroit
Washington at Dallas

SUNDAY, NOV. 25
Atlanta at New Orleans
Chicago at Minnesota
Indianapolis at Cincinnati
Kansas City at Los Angeles Raiders
Los Angeles Rams at San Francisco
Miami at Cleveland
New England at Phoenix
New York Giants at Philadelphia
Pittsburgh at New York Jets

NFL SCHEDULE

Tampa Bay vs. Green Bay
  at Milwaukee
*Seattle at San Diego

MONDAY, NOV. 26
*Buffalo at Houston

SUNDAY, DEC. 2
Atlanta at Tampa Bay
Cincinnati at Pittsburgh
Detroit at Chicago
Houston at Seattle
Indianapolis at Phoenix
Kansas City at New England
Los Angeles Raiders at Denver
Los Angeles Rams at Cleveland
Miami at Washington
New Orleans at Dallas
New York Jets at San Diego
Philadelphia at Buffalo
*Green Bay at Minnesota

MONDAY, DEC. 3
*New York Giants at San Francisco

SUNDAY DEC. 9
Buffalo at Indianapolis
Chicago at Washington
Cleveland at Houston
Denver at Kansas City
Minnesota at New York Giants
New Orleans at Los Angeles Rams
New England at Pittsburgh
Phoenix at Atlanta
San Francisco at Cincinnati
Seattle vs. Green Bay
  at Milwaukee
*Philadelphia at Miami

MONDAY, DEC. 10
*Los Angeles Raiders at Detroit

SATURDAY, DEC. 15
Buffalo at New York Giants
Washington at New England

SUNDAY, DEC. 16
Atlanta at Cleveland
Cincinnati at Los Angeles Raiders
Green Bay at Philadelphia
Houston at Kansas City
Indianapolis at New York Jets
Minnesota at Tampa Bay
Phoenix at Dallas
Pittsburgh at New Orleans
San Diego at Denver
Seattle at Miami
*Chicago at Detroit

MONDAY, DEC. 17
*San Francisco at Los Angeles Rams

SATURDAY, DEC. 22
Detroit at Green Bay
Los Angeles Raiders at Minnesota
*Washington at Indianapolis

SUNDAY, DEC. 23
Cincinnati at Houston
Cleveland at Pittsburgh
Dallas at Philadelphia
Kansas City at San Diego
Miami at Buffalo
New England at New York Jets
New Orleans at San Francisco
New York Giants at Phoenix
Los Angeles Rams at Atlanta
Tampa Bay at Chicago
*Denver at Seattle

SATURDAY, DEC. 29
Kansas City at Chicago
Philadelphia at Phoenix

SUNDAY, DEC. 30
Buffalo at Washington
Cleveland at Cincinnati
Dallas at Atlanta
Detroit at Seattle
Green Bay at Denver
Indianapolis at Miami
New York Giants at New England
New York Jets at Tampa Bay
San Diego at Los Angeles Raiders
San Francisco at Minnesota
*Pittsburgh at Houston

MONDAY, DEC. 31
*Los Angeles Rams at New Orleans

Nationally Televised Games

(All games carried on CBS Radio Network)

REGULAR SEASON

Sunday, Sept. 9-Denver at Los Angeles Raiders (day, NBC)
Philadelphia at New York Giants (night, TNT)
Monday, Sept. 10-San Francisco at New Orleans (night, ABC)
Sunday, Sept. 16-Washington at San Francisco (day, CBS)
Houston at Pittsburgh (night, TNT)
Monday, Sept. 17-Kansas City at Denver (night, ABC)
Sunday, Sept. 23-Philadelphia at Los Angeles Rams (day, CBS)
Detroit at Tampa Bay (night, TNT)
Monday, Sept. 24-Buffalo at New York Jets (night, ABC)
Sunday, Sept. 30-Cleveland at Kansas City (day, NBC)
Washington at Phoenix (night, TNT)
Monday, Oct. 1-Cincinnati at Seattle (night, ABC)
Sunday, Oct. 7-Cincinnati at Los Angeles Rams (day, NBC)
Los Angeles Raiders at Buffalo (night, TNT)
Monday, Oct. 8-Cleveland at Denver (night, ABC)
Sunday, Oct. 14-New York Giants at Washington (day, CBS)
Los Angeles Rams at Chicago (night, TNT)
Monday, Oct. 15-Minnesota at Philadelphia (night, ABC)
Thursday, Oct. 18-New England at Miami (night, TNT)
Sunday, Oct. 21-Pittsburgh at San Francisco (day, NBC)
Monday, Oct. 22-Cincinnati at Cleveland (night, ABC)
Sunday, Oct. 28-Washington at New York Giants (day, CBS)
Cincinnati at Atlanta (night, TNT)
Monday, Oct. 29-Los Angeles Rams at Pittsburgh (night, ABC)
Sunday, Nov. 4-Houston at Los Angeles Rams (day, NBC)
Denver at Minnesota (night, TNT)
Monday, Nov. 5-New York Giants at Indianapolis (night, ABC)
Sunday, Nov. 11-New York Giants at Los Angeles Rams (day, CBS)
San Francisco at Dallas (night, ESPN)
Monday, Nov. 12-Washington at Philadelphia (night, ABC)
Sunday, Nov. 18-Chicago at Denver (day, NBC)
Pittsburgh at Cincinnati (night, ESPN)
Monday, Nov. 19-Los Angeles Raiders at Miami (night, ABC)
Thursday, Nov. 22-Denver at Detroit (day, NBC)
Washington at Dallas (day, CBS)
Sunday, Nov. 25-Kansas City at Los Angeles Raiders (day, NBC)
Seattle at San Diego (night, ESPN)
Monday, Nov. 26-Buffalo at Houston (night, ABC)
Sunday, Dec. 2-Los Angeles Raiders at Denver (day, NBC)
Green Bay at Minnesota (night, ESPN)
Monday, Dec. 3-New York Giants at San Francisco (night, ABC)
Sunday, Dec. 9-New Orleans at Los Angeles Rams (day, CBS)
Philadelphia at Miami (night, ESPN)
Monday, Dec. 10-Los Angeles Raiders at Detroit (night, ABC)
Saturday, Dec. 15-Buffalo at New York Giants (day, ABC)
Washington at New England (day, CBS)
Sunday, Dec. 16-Cincinnati at Los Angeles Raiders (day, NBC)
Chicago at Detroit (night, ESPN)

Eagles' Keith Jackson has made two straight Pro Bowls.

Monday, Dec. 17-San Francisco at Los Angeles Rams (night, ABC)
Saturday, Dec. 22-Detroit at Green Bay (day, CBS)
　　　　　　　　Los Angeles Raiders at Minnesota (day, NBC)
　　　　　　　　Washington at Indianapolis (night, ABC)
Sunday, Dec. 23-New Orleans at San Francisco (day, CBS)
　　　　　　　Denver at Seattle (night, ESPN)
Saturday, Dec. 29-Kansas City at Chicago (day, NBC)
　　　　　　　　Philadelphia at Phoenix (day, CBS)
Sunday, Dec. 30-Green Bay at Denver (day, CBS)
　　　　　　　Pittsburgh at Houston (night, ESPN)
Monday, Dec. 31-Los Angeles Rams at New Orleans (night, ABC)

POSTSEASON

Saturday, Jan. 5-AFC and NFC First-Round Playoffs (ABC)
Sunday, Jan. 6-AFC and NFC First-Round Playoffs (NBC and CBS)
Saturday, Jan. 12-AFC and NFC Second-Round Playoffs (NBC and CBS)
Sunday, Jan. 13-AFC and NFC Second-Round Playoffs (NBC and CBS)
Sunday, Jan. 20-AFC and NFC Championship Games (NBC and CBS)
Sunday, Jan. 27-Super Bowl XXV, Tampa Stadium, Tampa (ABC)
Sunday, Feb. 3-AFC-NFC Pro Bowl, Honolulu (ESPN)

Revised and updated with over 75 all new sports records and photographs!

THE ILLUSTRATED SPORTS RECORD BOOK
Zander Hollander and David Schulz

Here, in a single book, are more than 350 all-time sports records with stories and photos so vivid it's like "being there." All the sports classics are here: Babe Ruth, Wilt Chamberlain, Muhammad Ali ... plus the stories of such active stars as Dwight Gooden and Wayne Gretzky. This is the authoritative book on what the great records are, and who set them—an engrossing, fun-filled reference guide filled with anecdotes of hundreds of renowned athletes whose remarkable records remain as fresh as when they were set.

Buy it at your local bookstore or use this convenient coupon for ordering.

NEW AMERICAN LIBRARY
P.O. Box 999, Bergenfield, New Jersey 07621

Please send me _____ paperback copies of THE ILLUSTRATED SPORTS RECORD BOOK 0-451-15743-5 at $3.95/$4.95 Can. each. (Please enclose $1.00 per order to cover postage and handling). I enclose ☐ check or ☐ money order.

Name_____

Address_____

City _____ State _____ Zip Code _____

Allow a minimum of 4-6 weeks for delivery.
This offer, prices and numbers are subject to change without notice.